Parliament and Democratic Consolidation in Southern Europe:
Greece, Italy, Portugal, Spain and Turkey

Edited by
Ulrike Liebert and Maurizio Cotta

Pinter Publishers, London and New York

© Ulrike Liebert and Maurizio Cotta 1990

First published in Great Britain in 1990 by
Pinter Publishers Limited
25 Floral Street, London WC2E 9DS

British Library Cataloguing in Publication Data

A CIP catalogue record for this book is available from the
British Library
ISBN 0-86187-819-1

Library of Congress Cataloging in Publication Data

Parliament and democratic consolidation in southern Europe : Greece,
Italy, Portugal, Spain, and Turkey / edited by Ulrike Liebert and
Maurizio Cotta.
    p.   cm.
    Rev. papers originally presented at two conferences held in 1986
and 1987.
    ISBN 0-86187-819-1
    1. Legislative bodies—Europe, Southern.   2. Europe, Southern—
Politics and government.   I. Liebert, Ulrike.   II. Cotta.
Muarizio, 1947–
JN94.A71P37   1990
328'.094—dc20   89-28677
                                              CIP

Typeset by Florencetype, Kewstoke, Avon
Printed and bound in Great Britain by Biddles Ltd.

For Tilmann,
Benedetta and Giulia

Contents

Notes on contributors

Nicos Alivizatos: Associate Professor of Constitutional Law, University of Athens. Major books: *Les institutions àpolitiques de la Grèce à travers les crises 1922–1974* (1970); *The Constitutional Status of the Armed Forces, the Principle of Civiliam Supremacy* (1987).

Manuel Braga da Cruz: Professor, the Institute of Social Sciences, University of Lisbon, Portugal. Books: *As origens da democracia crista nu Salazarismo, U partido i o estado no Salazarismo*.

Jordi Capo Giol: Associate Professor of Political Science, Law Department of the Central University of Barcelona. Books: *La formaciòn de las Cortes Generales en la legislatura 1977–1979* (Phd Thesis, 1981); *La institucionalizaciòn de las Cortes Generales*, (1983).

Ramón García Cotarelo: Professor of Political Science, Department of Political Science and Sociology, University Complutense of Madrid. Books: *Teoria del estado* (1988); *La izouierda: desenoaño, resionacíon y utopia* (1989); with J.F. Tezanos and A. De Blas: *La Transicion democratica en España* (1989).

Maurizio Cotta: Professor of Political Science, Law Department, University of Siena and member of the editorial board of the Rivista Italiana de Scienza Politica. Books: *Classe politica e parlamento in Italia (1946–1976)* (1979); co-author of *Manuale della Scienza Politica* (1986).

Giuseppe Di Palma: Professor of Political Science at University of California, Berkeley. Books: *Surviving without Governing: The Italian Parties in Parliament* (1977); co-editor of *The Central America Impasse* (1986).

Ersin Kalaycioğlu: Professor, Ataturk Institute, Bogazici University, Istanbul. Books: co-author of *State and Society in Turkey: The Transition to Democracy in the 1980s* (forthcoming) and author of numerous studies on the Turkish legislature.

Ulrike Liebert: Assistant Professor, Department of Political Science, University of Heidelberg. Books: *Neue Autonomiebewegung und Dezentralisierung in Spanien* (1986); *Parlament und Interessengruppen in Italien und Spanien* (forthcoming).

Miguel Lobo Antunes: Legal Counsellor to the Constitutional Court of Portugal. Has written studies on the role of Portuguese Constitutional Court in the political system.

Diego Lopez Garrido: *Letrado* (legal councillor) of the Spanish Parliament and Professor of Constitutional Law at the Autonomous University, Madrid.

Geoffrey Pridham: Director of the Centre for Mediterranean Studies, University of Bristol. Books: Editor, *The New Mediterranean Democracies* (1984); *Coalition Behavior in Theory and Practice* (1986); Editor, *Securing Democracy: Political Parties and Regime Consolidation in Southern Europe* (1989).

Joan Subirats: Associate Professor of Political Science, Department of Political Science and Public Law, Autonomous University, Barcelona. Books: co-editor of *El Parlamento Europeo* (1984); co-author of *The Politics of Economic Crisis: Lessons from Western Europe* (1989) and author of *Administracion y Politicas Publicas* (forthcoming).

Acknowledgements

This book assembles case studies on parliamentary practice—the renewal and evolution of parliaments during democratic transition and consolidation in Italy, Spain, Portugal, Greece and Turkey and links them through theoretical and comparative perspectives. These studies are the fruit of an international and interdisciplinary working party made up of Greek, Italian, Portuguese, Spanish, Turkish, American, British and German political scientists and lawyers who specialize in parliamentary research. The book gathers together completely reworked contributions previously presented at two occasions: at the conference on 'The Formation of Parliaments in Southern Europe' at the European University Institute (Florence, May 1986), sponsored by the EUI, and supported especially by Philippe Schmitter in connection with his research project on 'Organized Interests and Democratic Consolidation in Southern Europe'; and at the conference on 'Parliaments and Democratic Consolidation' (Bofill Foundation, Barcelona, October 1987), sponsored by the German Volkswagen Foundation and the Jaume Bofill Foundation under the tutorship of Klaus von Beyme.

We owe therefore an enormous debt in particular to Klaus von Beyme and Philippe C. Schmitter, whose research over the past two decades has provided an invaluable foundation upon which our investigations have been based. Both were also most generous with advice and comments in many stages of the project.

We also want to thank Andrea Manzella and Gianni Long, both high functionaires of the Italian Parliament with a broad knowledge of the institutional mechanisms of both the Italian and the Spanish Chambers from which our project benefited in many ways. Nikolaus Wenturis (Universität Tübingen) and Rainer Eisfeld (Universität Osnabrück) as well as Uwe Thaysen (Universität Lüneburg) contributed stimulating and valuable comments concerning various portions of our collective work.

Generous financial assistance and support for the organization of both conferences as well as for the editing of this book was granted by the European University Institute and the German Volkswagen Foundation. Thanks are particularly directed to the President of the EUI until 1988, Werner Maihofer, as well as to those responsible for the programme area 'Southward Enlargement of the EEC' of the SVW, Alfred Schmidt.

Complementary funds and infrastructural support for the organization of the second conference and the editing were provided by the Jaume Bofill Foundation, Barcelona, and the University of Siena. Our thanks therefore also go to the director of the Bofill Foundation, Jordi Porta, as well as to the Publications Committee officer of the EUI, Brigitte Schwab.

Part I Theoretical perspectives

1 Parliament as a central site in democratic consolidation: a preliminary exploration

Ulrike Liebert

Introduction

The aim of this volume is to analyse the ways in which parliaments have developed and performed in the last decades in southern Europe, specifically in the new democracies of Italy, Portugal, Greece, Spain and Turkey. The available evidence suggests a new trend particularly during the last decade and half, towards reinforcement and strengthening of parliaments in this area. But may we not speak of a veritable 'rise' of parliaments in southern Europe, and not merely a 'return' after more or less prolonged authoritarian intervals? Considering the European Mediterranean countries as 'a cluster of societies distinct from other European societies' (Linz, 1985), is there perhaps a 'mediterranean model of parliamentarism' emerging? Assuming a generalized 'centrality' of parliaments in southern Europe would certainly clash with the 'decline of parliament' thesis suggested for many other contemporary Western, more established democracies,[1] and be at variance even more with available data for instance on the mass perceptions of the power position of southern European legislatures (CIS, 1985).

But one should indicate more precisely the normative references for parliamentary 'centrality', or, on the contrary, of 'decline', and distinguish more thoroughly between the symbolic and the instrumental aspects of parliamentary activities.

Parliaments in southern Europe in their constitutional design as well as in their practical development vary substantially along several dimensions. We find a potential key for understanding the differential evolution of parliaments in these countries in the debate on the particular role and functions which parliaments are expected to assume and to perform during the processes of democratic consolidation.[2] Contrary to those who conceive parliament as 'a central site' in the instauration and consolidation of a new democratic regime (Schmitter, 1988), at least potentially (Morlino 1986a, b), there are others who maintain that processes of democratic transition and restoration are generally directed by other actors and arenas while legislatures begin to play some role only after consolidation is concluded.

This controversy to a large part deals with questions of an empirical nature. Only comparative parliamentary research can determine the effective position and role of the different types of southern European legislatures and can detect the reasons why some parliaments assume the role of a protagonist relatively early (for instance in Italy and in Spain), while others become more salient only at a later stage (for example in Portugal and Greece) while still others have yet to enter this phase (Turkey or, referring to extra-European experiences, for instance in Argentina; cf. De Riz, 1988).

By comparing the new parliaments—in particular those of Greece, Portugal and Spain—with the older Italian legislature during the processes of democratic consolidation, we hope to shed some more light on the conditions for parliamentary centrality and marginality. The Italian case may be referrred to in two ways: either conceiving the four decades from 1946 to 1986 as a process of 'protracted consolidation' (as Maurizio Cotta does in Chapter 3 in this volume), or considering this period as subdivided into two cycles which can be fairly well distinguished: first a period of transition to restoration and consolidation of the new democratic regime, from 1943–1958 (approximately), culminating in a profound crisis at the end of the sixties, followed by a second period of institutional reform in 1970–1 with a process of reconsolidation between 1972 and 1983 (Morlino, 1984).

Although not having yet entered into the stage of consolidation, the case of Turkey shall also be included. The Turkish 'limited democracy' of the eighties shows certain similarities with the first phase of transition in Portugal (1974–82), for instance with regard to the role of the military as 'guardians'– 'decision-makers' (Harris, 1988), and the corresponding limitations on parliamentary sovereignty. However, with respect to the liberalization of political parties, especially those on the Left, and its peculiar electoral system, Turkey still represents the 'most different case' within our southern European setting.

By analysing these five cases in the framework of normative and empirical theories on parliament and theories on democratic transition and consolidation we shall try to contribute to the systematic understanding of politics in this region.[3] We also hope to provide some interdisciplinary—juridical-institutional and political science—insights into the working of the parliamentary institution which could be relevant to processes of democratization underway in other areas, namely Latin America, east and south-east Asia or eastern Europe.

This introductory chapter develops a theoretical framework and some hypotheses which underlie our comparative project. In the first section, we describe some of the manifestations which sustain the 'rise of parliaments' thesis in southern Europe and confront it with some of the arguments of the 'crisis of parliament' diagnoses. Both types of argumentation require a critical assessment. A part of the 'parliamentary crises' thesis obviously derives from antiquated normative models and expectations from the nineteenth century, when organized and disciplined parliamentary party groups did yet not exist (Nohlen, 1988: 375). The next section focuses on critical statements, which detect problems of adaptation in parliamentary institutions which have inherited too much of past parliamentary and political traditions in order to perform effectively the functions which they should play in contemporary democracy. If there was recently a 'rise' and reinforcement of legislatures this was due to the role and functions parliaments assumed during the instauration and consolidation of the new democratic regimes (the next section). In which sense, why and with which consequences parliament may be a 'central site' in these processes is the subject of the concluding sections.

Rise and decline of southern European legislatures

At some time during the seventies and part of the eighties, parliaments in southern Europe have emerged as important platforms in the political life of their countries. They became if not actors, then major arenas in the dramas of the newly restored democratic systems. With differing emphasis they attracted popular attention and growing support, strengthened their institutional resources and infrastructures and political position, in either more symbolic or instrumental terms:

— In Italy, the Chamber of Deputies' position and powers were reinforced to a great extent after the end of the fifth legislature (1968–72). The Chamber assumed, for instance, not only control but also direct management competences (institutionalization of the parliamentary committee on television), began to programme its proper legislative activities, developed parliamentary information activities and relations with external organs and social and economic interest groups and granted important guarantees to the minorities and opposition (Cheli, 1981).
— In the case of Spain, the *Cortes* became—during the constituent period (1977–8), as well as during the first legislature (1979–82)—the major arena for negotiations and decision-making on the new Constitution and all major reform issues among the top political elites (see Chapter 4), a role which declined after 1982 under the absolute majority of the Socialist government.
— In Portugal, Parliament during the first legislatures was constrained to a subordinate role in comparison with the Military Council and national executives, many of which were appointed by the president. During the eighties, however, the Assembly gradually increased its public prestige and decision-making influence, assuming among others a number of powers which had previously been in the hands of the Council of the Revolution, strengthened its role in the budgetary process and established exclusive legislative powers in certain areas. The Assembly subsequently became a 'protagonist of the most important scenes in the drama' (see Chapter 6).
— The Greek Assembly, though limited in powers by the strong prerogatives

of the State President and the dominating position of the majority governments during its first decade, has become the major arena of Greek political life where bi-polarized conflict between left and right becomes public and the ideological battles between both are staged (see Chapter 5).
— Only in Turkey, where transition to democracy began again in 1982, has the 'Grand National Assembly' remained in a subordinate position, following a complete reorganization after the military coup of 1980 (see Chapter 7).

Except for this latter case, at one time or another during the seventies and eighties, parliaments in southern Europe with an apparent parallelism have become major public arenas of partisan dispute, of encounters with social subjects, of negotiations and important decision-making among political elites. This phenomenon of parliamentary reinforcement contradicts not only the more outspoken anti-liberal and anti-parliamentary traditions which have persisted in the new democracies in southern Europe. It confounds in particular liberal and 'progressive' intellectuals and scholars in these countries who had just adapted the 'decline of parliament in contemporary democracy' thesis to their domestic environments (Guerra, 1982; Cotarelo, Chapter 4).

This thesis, which gives rise to varying formulations and different explanations regarding many Western democracies, in southern Europe certainly encounters elements of corroboration. Numerous critical assessments of parliamentary practice in these cases support this impression. They suggest that parliamentary practice in southern Europe has not achieved the normative standards of the classical model of a sovereign parliamentary and legislative assembly.

The ambitious project to develop the Italian chambers as the 'central' organ of the political system in terms of interest representation, legitimation as well as of decision-making and control, has in practice remained much behind the normative conceptions (Baldassarre, 1985). Although Parliament was occasionally able to assert its centrality in the definition of the objectives of national policies (for instance by reformulating the government programme in July 1977), or by instituting the parliamentary committee of television control, it remained isolated and was contradicted by opposed trends towards oligarchic leadership bargaining among the parties of the majority, the newly emerging trade unions and new international protagonists (Ingrao, 1985: 50ff.). The extreme institutional weakness and penetrability of the chambers was also a result of *partitocrazia*—'party government Italian style' (Pasquino, 1987a, 1987b, Di Palma 1977), as it facilitated the emergence of 'government by the lobbies' (Pasquino 1988). What determines the 'crisis of parliament' in the Italian case are not only the specific internal problems of institutionalization from which the Italian Parliament suffers (Cotta, 1979, Chapter V), or the profound and qualitative changes which have undermined parliamentary normative competences from outside by the emergence of new sources of law such as the EC institutions, the regions, the Constitutional Court as well as by the increased use government makes of 'urgent decretation' (Bonifacio, 1985). Above all, it is the 'incapable government and a backward administration', the persisting 'incapacity, poverty and ignorance in the public administration and inclusively in the area of government' for which Parliament, however strong and qualified it might be, may not compensate (Labriola, 1982: 43).

In Spain, the mass media have made the *Cortes Generales* one of their most frequent objects of criticism, especially after 1982. Their different ideological and political diagnoses agree on the 'immense loss of parliamentary prestige', the 'agony of parliamentary activities' and the 'loss of its credibility' (Montero, 1981). The inequalities in political representation due to the political reform law with its various benefits for certain political formations and the corresponding electoral system have been much lamented (Aguilo Lucia, 1981; Martinez Sospedra, 1981). The lack of transparancy of parliamentary proceedings and the deficient flow of information towards the citizenry have been criticized (Molas and Pitarch, 1987). The inadequacy of the Senate as an organ of territorial representation has provoked an ongoing constitutional debate (Capo Giol, 1980). Especially with the existence of an absolute majority in both houses—as has been the case since 1982—it has been argued that the Cortes has been converted increasingly into a simple 'organ of ratification and juridical legitimation' of decisions taken outside of it (Sole Tura and Aparicio Perez, 1984; Chapter 4 of this volume).

In Greece, the 'authoritarian structure' of the post-dictatorial 'executive democracy' (Wenturis, 1987) is criticized because of the 'potentially dangerous lack of balance in the powers which the new constitution assigned the executive and the legislative branches', leading to a 'dominance of the executive over the legislature' and to a parliament which is 'used as the formal setting where decisions already taken at the level of the government are given legal validity' (Diamandouros, 1987). The new regime is criticized as leaving too little space in decision-making for the opposition compared to the majority (Wenturis, 1987); and as favouring the largest traditional political formations at the cost of small parties with new ideological orientations (Alivizatos, 1986; Papadopoulos forthcoming).

In the case of Portugal, it has been pointed out that the National Assembly has emerged as a 'parliament without prestige' and 'Portugal's least understood political institution' (Bruneau and Macleod, 1986). A decade after its creation, the Assembly had not experienced institutionalization, but rather de-institutionalization, decay, and breakdown to the extent that it appeared 'completely incapable of transforming the broader political conflict into workable public policy' (Opello, 1986).

Liberal public opinion especially strongly suspected that the heritage of the authoritarian past—oligarchic rule, strong executives, a wide gap between political class and popular forces—could be perpetuated in the guise of a parliamentary or semi-parliamentary system (Giner and Sevilla, 1979; Wenturis, 1987). And foreign observers tended to measure the performance of the newly emerging parliamentary institutions by applying the standards of evolved ones.

Trying to assess parliamentary practice in southern Europe we find ourselves puzzled by contradicting and incompatible trends. Both the evidence of an apparent rise of parliaments as well as the statements of a crisis of parliaments very similar to that in other Western democracies demand some explanation. We propose two lines of explanation:

(1) Parliament is the most prominent among the new institutions in southern
     European new democracies on which conflicting expectations and contro-
     versial assessments deriving from past parliamentary experiences and
     domestic as well as foreign parliamentarism doctrines are focused. The
     particularly long and tormented history of parliament in southern Europe
     certainly accounts for these controversies in part. But not all 'negative
     judgements and perceptions of a general decline of the quality and political
     importance of the representative assemblies' can be reduced to 'nothing
     more than the result of applying the standards of a previous stage of
     institutional development to the parliamentary behavior of the moment'
     (Loewenberg, 1971: 15f.). We should learn to disentangle the type of
     criticism linked to past and outdated standards of parliamentary doctrine
     from that type of critique which points to problematic aspects of present
     parliamentary practice.
(2) The 'rise' of parliaments in southern Europe cannot be explained by
     normative parliamentary theory, for instance by models like 'parliamentary
     supremacy', or the 'centrality of parliament', not even in the case of Italy
     where this model played an important role in the political discussion. If
     there was a 'reinforcement' of southern European parliaments, this was
     primarily of a symbolic nature and related to the role which parliament
     plays with respect to the consolidation of a new democratic system—or
     respectively the reconsolidation of a democratic regime in crisis.

Parliamentary traditions and doctrines and the 'crisis' of parliament in southern Europe

Some of the present controversy about the role of parliament in modern mass
democracy is—implicitly or explicitly—committed to past traditions and parameters of Western normative political thought. This is not only true for
established Western democracies, but especially for the new southern
European ones. Liberal constitutionalism and parliamentary traditions in the
post-World War II period were certainly not created *ex novo* in this area. At
that time they already could look back at more or less long-lasting and, in all
cases, rather tormented experiences. Parliamentary systems were introduced
throughout southern Europe as early as in the first half of the nineteenth
century, thus in a context of liberal constitutionalism and oligarchic rule. Only in
Turkey did parliamentarism start a century later, when it had to cope
immediately with universal suffrage.

In Spain, a series of experiments with liberal and progressive constitutions
(in 1812, in 1837, during the First and the Second Republic) remained
unsuccessful and were replaced after extremely short time-spans by rather
long-lived conservative or authoritarian regimes (von Beyme, 1970; Nohlen,
1970).

In Portugal, the parliamentary system emerged in 1822, and fluctuated
throughout the nineteenth century between repeated affirmations of popular
sovereignty and the power of the Crown, until the arrival of military dictatorship in 1926, and the following Salazar regime (Caetano, 1971: Chapter 6).

Parliamentarism in Greece began in 1843 and ended only with the advent of dictatorships, the first in 1936 and the second in 1967 (Alivizatos, 1979 and in this volume).

The most comparatively long-lived and consolidated parliamentary system of a liberal type emerged in southern Europe in Italy, under the statute of Piedmont since 1848, and within the Italian kingdom since 1861. The advent of mass parties and universal suffrage put an end to this system practically on the eve of World War I, and formally with the take-over by the Fascists during 1922–25 (von Beyme, 1970).

Parliamentarism on the basis of multiparty politics was introduced last in Turkey—after 1946. Here too it was tormented by periodic breakdowns and transitions, suspensions by military intervention and reorganizations—three times since the end of World War II (Heper, 1985; Chapter 7).

Also the length of the interruptions of these parliamentary traditions, hence the duration of the various 'authoritarian interplays' has an impact on the facility with which a certain parliamentary tradition can be revitalized during the instauration of a new democratic regime. Most long lived were the Portuguese Salazar regime with over fifty years (1922–74), and the Spanish Franco regime (1939–75), both of which constituted a profound rupture with respect to the preceding parliamentary models: in Spain with the assembly government of the Second Republic (1931–9); in the case of Portugal with the system of parliamentary supremacy which had been enacted by the 1910 republican revolution. Italy (where Fascism had lasted scarcely twenty years) and above all, Greece (with only seven years of junta rule), had the least difficulties in re-establishing the continuity of their parliamentary traditions: a liberal parliamentary system with nineteenth-century 'ultra-garantist' norms in favour of the opposition and minorities in the Italian case (Manzella, 1986); an executive-dominated regime in the Greek one, an executive-dominated assembly in the latter case. Only Turkey provides an exception to this rule: although the last military regime after less than three years convoked parliamentary elections, at the same time it managed to produce a fundamental rupture with the preceding system of proportional parliamentary representation and strong polarization in and outside the legislature.

Parliamentary theory in the contexts of post-World War II democratization in southern Europe, however, signified, only in part revitalization of parliamentary traditions from the past. Instead, comparative constitutional doctrine, and, above all, the reception or rejection of significant foreign 'models' became of major importance in the constituent processes.

Italy is the only case where the re-establishment of a republican parliamentary government in 1946–7 gave a privileged position to the ideas of popular sovereignty and proportional parliamentary representation, subordinating the requirements of stable and strong government. In all other cases in southern Europe, the constituents of the seventies and eighties adopted governmental stability and strength as a priority *vis-à-vis* that of parliamentary representation. But while Spain opted for a monarchical state form with parliamentary government, Greece, Portugal and Turkey adopted varieties of presidential or semi-presidential government.

In theory, a system of parliamentary government promises a balance of powers among the executive and the legislatures such that none may win supremacy over the other—a vain expectation since 1789 (Loewenstein, 1938: 680ff.). To the weaknesses of parliamentary government belongs the problem of executive instability, especially in multiparty systems without cohesive majorities. Endemic cabinet instability characterized for instance the French Third and Fourth Republics and the Republic of Weimar. Although the assumption of this model—the separation of powers—has proven vain with the arrival of organized mass parties as the major political actors, this model continues to be in force at least as a normative reference of the 'parliament in crisis' hypotheses. Presidential or semi-presidential systems, on the other hand, solve the problem of executive stability by making the president independent from the legislature, but they create potentially serious deadlocks between both (Lijphart, 1984: 74f.).

The Italian constituents in 1946–7 repudiated both the Weimar model which—with its high cabinet instability—excessively favoured the power of the head of the state, and the British majoritarian version of parliamentary government, where cabinet formation lies in the hands of the prime minister and not the parties; both were regarded as being impossible to apply to the Italian situation. At the same time they were aware of the lack of guaranties for stable government in the French Third and Fourth Republic models of parliamentary government which gave parliament supremacy (Armaroli, 1986: 17–29). The Republican Constitution therefore tried to design a 'rationalized parliamentary government', based on a strong government with constitutional autonomy, but left enough space for the subsequent adoption of the 'ultra-garantist' House Rules of the period 1900–22 which created the conditions if not for an 'assembly government' as favoured by the Communist party, then at least for the 'weakest government in parliament in Europe' (Manzella, 1986). One of the significant keys for understanding the development of the Italian political system afer World War II is the idea of the 'centrality of parliament' which to both its advocators and opponents meant 'assembly parliamentarism with strengthened proportionality and scarce unity and authority of the executive' (Long, 1986). This concept permeated the whole republican experience with alternating success, but became more precise only at the end of the sixties with the passage from the 5th to the 6th legislature, the strong social dynamism and the corresponding strong tensions in the functioning of the political institutions and the reform of the parliamentary standing orders in 1971 (Cheli, 1981: 343–4). According to this model the Italian Chambers were no longer conceived as simple 'arenas of intermediation' between secondary political interests, but as the 'geometrical site of the social and institutional pluralism', as the 'arena of encounter of all political forces', and the 'site of compensation between majority and opposition' (ibid.: 344f.). Parliament is expected to perform as the natural place for the elaboration of the guidelines of national policies, and of direction and control of the whole action of the public administration (ibid.). The gap between this conception of parliament and parliamentary performance in practice soon became evident, and has kept on growing at least since the end of the seventies (Ingrao, 1985: Baldassarre, 1985).

The dominant concern of the Spanish constituents of 1977–8 was, on the contrary, nearly exclusively strong government. The numerous crises and 20 anticipated dissolutions of parliament under the Spanish Constitution of 1876; the break-down of the Second Spanish Republic with its system of assembly parliamentarism; the Third French Republic with its 96 governments in 59 years; the Fourth French Republic where the average duration of a minister was less than eight months and not least the Italian experiences certainly motivated the strong fear of a possible chronic instablity of government. This made the Spanish constituents opt for a clear-cut model of rationalized parliamentary government in which executive–legislature relations were unbalanced without reserve in favour of a strongly reinforced executive. Among these mechanisms were: an electoral system with significant correctives in favour of the largest parties; no parliamentary vote of confidence for a new cabinet, but a demand for a vote of investiture put forward by the candidate which the king proposes as prime minister and for which a simple majority may be sufficient, the ministers being nominated subsequently by the prime minister; only a constructive vote of censure, inspired by the Fundamental Law of the Federal Republic of Germany; a simple majority being sufficient for government to win a question of confidence; the power of the executive to govern by decrete-laws 'in case of urgent necessity' (Alzaga Villaamil, 1988). The provisional parliamentary standing orders of 1977 and the final ones of 1982 contained provisions which are the 'most pro-governmental ones of Europe', defending government against the distinct minorities (ibid.): they assured on one side the submission of deputies to their respective parliamentary groups; on the other they granted an important weight to the Chamber's speaker (who always belonged to the governing party) in the elaboration of the parliamentary agenda; required for the creation of an investigation committee the favourable vote of the majority of the plenary (ibid.). This model was originally designed with the expectation that one-party governments with an absolute majority would not exist, so that weak and frequently changing governments needed to be protected against the opposition. Thus the constitutional design not only of this type of 'prime minister regime', but also of regional decentralization and of the Constitutional Court made parliamentary sovereignty a myth from the beginning (Manzella, 1980). After 1982, the permanent majority of the Socialist party with its high level of discipline and cohesion, and the concentration of party and parliamentary group leadership in the hands of the prime minister has put most of the provisions of this model out of order and has increased the gap between Constitution and a reality in which the opposition 'survives badly' (ibid.). Parliament in a system of 'rationalized parliamentary government' under these conditions of an absolute and extremely disciplined majority appears a mere 'formality' (see Chapter 4), and has declined into an organ of 'ratification of decisions which are taken at other sites' (Alzaga, 1988).

The Greek Constitution of a 'republican–parliamentary democracy' in 1975 was even more concerned with a strong executive. The conservative leader of the Greek transition, Karamanlis, followed closely the French Gaullist model of the Fifth Republic with a strong presidency and a cabinet dependent from the legislature (Diamandouros, 1987). Despite the influence of this model, the new Greek political system was never genuinely presidential, given that the president is elected by Parliament and not by the electorate, and hence lacks

direct democratic legitimation. The originally strong presidential prerogatives
—which rarely were used by President Karamanlis—were nearly completely
abolished by the constitutional amendments of 1986. With this constitutional
reform the Socialist government concentrated still more powers in the hands of
the prime minister and increased the imbalance of executive–legislature
relations further to the advantage of the former. The opposition largely
abstained from the constituent process and the issue of executive–legislature
imbalance did not even provoke any important constitutional debate during the
instauration of the new regime (Alivizatos, 1986). Only after the Socialist
government's constitutional revision did the opposition from the Right and Left
embark on a large debate on the reform of the parliamentary standing orders,
concentrating on the issue of the powers of the opposition and minorities
(ibid.).

Portugal's 1976 Constitution was an attempt to overcome the shortcomings
not only of parliamentary supremacy during the First Republic, but also of
executive dominance during the dictatorship (Opello, 1985: 147f.). The
Constitution thus chose for the Portuguese 'pluralist socialist regime' (Eisfeld,
1984) the quite original and hybrid form of a 'semi-presidential' system of
government (Duverger, 1983), with a president elected directly and with
considerable executive power, but ultimately less powerful than for instance
the presidents of the Fifth Republic, Finland or the United States. This system,
which the armed forces imposed on the newly emerging political parties with
two pacts in 1974–6, established a double responsibility of government
with respect to the president (who until 1986 was a military figure) as well as
vis-à-vis parliament, and hence produced numerous deadlocks. The Military
Council and the Assembly were conceived as two parallel circuits with
independent legitimation. In practice, the former and the presidency detracted
much from the parliamentary role—at least until the 1982 constitutional
revision. Given that this reform reduced the powers of the president, which
furthermore since 1986 has not been a military office, it appears reasonable to
classify the Portuguese regime as having returned to the parliamentary system
(Lijphart et al., 1988: 228).

Hence, the models which have guided constitution-building in southern
Europe—'rationalized parliamentary government' in Spain, 'presidentialist,
executive democracy' in Greece and 'semi-presidentialism' in Portugal—
contradict expressively the traditional models of 'parliament–government
balance', 'parliamentary supremacy', or 'assembly government' which guided
experiences of democratic government in some of these countries in the past.
These constitutional models which the southern European constituents adopted
in the seventies do not at all provide for parliamentary reinforcement, but,
rather on the contrary, the elements of 'rationalization' largely prevail
and subordinate parliamentary prerogatives to the requirements of stable
government. This is also one of the factors underlying the perception of a
generalized parliamentary crisis in southern Europe. Only the case of Italy,
where the debate on 'parliamentary centrality' led to the attempt to implement
this model institutionally, represented at least until the end of the seventies an
exception to this rule. Historical memories of parliamentary supremacy (for
instance in the cases of Portugal and Spain) and persisting liberal democratic

traditions prevent public opinion from accepting the new unity of the 'parliament –government subsystem', organized and dominated by political party leadership.

But many of the nineteenth-century constitutional models appear antiquated from the practice-orientated political scientist point of view and particularly with respect to post-World War II parliaments in the context of universal suffrage and mass parties. This is true not only for the anglo-saxon 'separation of powers' doctrine (Cotta, 1987), or the French Fourth Republic's concept of 'parliamentary supremacy' (Birnbaum, 1980) but also the Italian model of 'parliamentary centrality' (Ingrao, 1985). Even if political parties are weak in terms of membership or suffer from a legitimation crisis, and party leadership appears insufficiently accountable to its proper party basis, the concentration of parliamentary power in the hands of a small party elite does not necessarily indicate the 'decline' of parliament.

Not despite, but because of the presence of organized political parties and the need for strong government, parliaments fulfil a number of functions, especially in new democracies, which make them play a 'central' role during certain stages of political development.

The role of parliament in democratic consolidation

Hypotheses which explain the 'rise' of parliaments during the first stages of democratization as a result of the specific functions which parliament assumes during the consolidation of a new democratic regime have been advanced within comparative parliamentary research as well as by theoretical studies on democratic consolidation.

The functions of parliament in parliamentary research

A concern with the role of parliament in new or unstable democracies is not new in empirical and comparative parliamentary research, but this topic has been dealt with under different labels and in varying theoretical perspectives.[4] One of the most significant findings which comparative parliamentary research provides with respect to our question is that parliaments do not perform a fixed set of functions, as the functionalist doctrine proposed, among them the functions of *government formation, legislation, education, interest articulation and intermediation, publication.*[5] Parliaments possess an intriguing 'all-purpose flexibility' at different times and in different circumstances they do many different things; they become involved in a variety of environmental settings; resist external changes or adapt their internal structures in response to them (Polsby, 1975). The importance, but to a certain degree also the substance of the catalogue of functions has changed considerably in the last 120 years, as a result—among other factors—of the introduction of popular sovereignty and universal suffrage, and the rise of mass political parties representing class, religious, ethnic and other identities and cleavages. One example is the 'mediation function', which evolved for instance in the case of the Italian

Parliament as early as the fifties as an important parliamentary activity, involving generally a small number of deputies in the legislative bargaining which transforms the law 'from an expression of the will of the majority into the production of mediation between majority and opposition' (Sartori, 1963; Cheli, 1981).

The theories of democratic consolidation which have been formulated in recent years with respect to the experiences of redemocratization in southern Europe and Latin America[6] have pointed out further functions of parliament. The different approaches provide contradictory hypotheses about the importance of parliament in these processes. Some suggest that parliaments, along with interest associations, are the 'central site' in building legitimacy for the new regime, and hence, are crucial for democratic consolidation (Schmitter, 1988). Others consider parliament as only one possible—and relatively rare— path to democratic consolidation, which in the normal case is reached primarily via parties or via charismatic leaders, under the condition that parliament is able to gain decision-making capacity with respect to pressing policy problems, neutralize the military and reform the inherited juridical order (Morlino, 1986a). A third, minimalist approach retains parliament as nearly superfluous in the setting up of the original consensus on the rules of the new game among the main political actors, and only relevant for the subsequent stage of institutionalization and the 'reproduction of the democratic consent' (Di Palma, Chapter 2 of this volume).

Drawing on these theories and studies we will develop our argument about the role of parliament in the processes of transition, installation and consolidation of a new democratic regime.

Parliament in democratic transition

Parliament may occupy a central position during transition, and in particular in the establishment of a new democratic regime, but this is not necessarily the case, and empirically even improbable. Government, a charismatic leader, the military or party leadership may play the crucial role during the setting up of the rules of the new game without much reference to a representative body like parliament. The rules of the new game may also be worked out by technical or governmental bodies without any important checks and controls by elected organs. Incentives and motivations to play the new game can be provided to the participants of the 'founding coalition' mainly by governmental and not parliamentary resources. Crucial reform decisions can be taken at the governmental level or other sites of the regime. Parliament can be relatively marginal in the establishment of most of the new regime institutions, the reform of the inherited juridical order etc., without impeding the democratic process in proceeding from transition to consolidation. It is an empirical question whether the parliamentary arena occupies a more or less central position during this stage of regime establishment, not only in the design of the new order but for the bargaining processes among the political elites, in the mass media and for public opinion in general. If parliament does play an important role for instance with respect to constitution-building or the reform of the inherited order, this may be explained by the particular features of the transition process. And it may be expected to have an important impact on the type of system being established and the opportunities of democracy to consolidate.

Parliament as a 'central site' in democratic consolidation

As the process of regime change, however, moves from transition to consolidation, the unpredictable behaviour of actors trying to overwhelm or eliminate each other becomes gradually settled, their positions defined by mutual perceptions of interests and their conflict increasingly regulated by known rules and techniques (Schmitter, 1988: 9).

In this new stage the parliamentary rules and procedures and the parliamentary elites necessarily assume a more important role. Due to the mobilization of the electorate in election campaigns, the organization by parties of their mass followings, civil society is being resurrected (O'Donnell *et al.*, 1986, Chapter IV/5.). This new variable can have a decisive impact on the political game, making new actors appear on the stage, and changing existing interrelations of forces profoundly. At that stage it is precisely the parliamentary game which helps to channel and regulate social movements and mobilization (Liebert, 1986: 259ff.). During this stage there are three aspects of the contributions of parliament to the consolidation of a new democratic regime:

1. The integration of the political and social forces of the country—those of the ancient regime as well as the newly emerging ones, and, in particular, the (potential or actual) anti-system oppositions.
2. The stabilization of peaceful conflict regulation among the main political actors as a condition of decision-making capacity and governability of the new regime.
3. The building of support among mass publics.

We will explain these three functions in more detail and try to give some indicators for measuring them in parliamentary practice.

Parliament is able to contribute to the integration of the forces of the extreme left or right, in particular of *anti-system oppositions*[7] during the stage of democratic consolidation. This may be particularly important, for instance with respect to collective actors who have been excluded from the 'founding coalition' although possessing important resources for vetoing the new game.

One of the crucial challenges which new democratic regimes have to resolve is this integration of the political forces of the extreme left and right, as well as of the economic power groups—organized interests from both sides of the labour market. These political and socio-economic collective actors are important especially in societies—as the southern European ones—where left–right polarization and class cleavage are still intense. The antagonistic interests of workers and capitalists are only compatible under specific conditions—among which the existence of democratic institutions which allow workers to articulate their demands for the improvement of their material conditions and which at the same time are accepted by the capitalists—play a crucial role (Przeworski and Wallerstein 1982: 215). The economic interest groups which belong to the elites of a country deal continuously, either directly or mediated by party-leadership, with legislatures and hence will develop clearly articulated expectations regarding how this institution should conform to their interests. All 'elites are likely to have powerful sanctions at their disposal to encourage the conformance of legislative behavior to their expectations' (Mezey, 1979: 34).

In this perspective, parliament has to incorporate in one way or another a factual compromise between the preferences of left and right, of workers and capitalists and other economic power groups if the democratic system is to survive and stabilize. Parliament does so by providing opportunities for instrumental or at least symbolic participation, infrastructural and material resources and public prestige to all political parties with parliamentary representation and indirectly to those socio-economic groups which these parties organize (Morisi, 1988). Those forces especially which are excluded temporarily or permanently from government may thus find some compensation. By this means, parliament may motivate certain extreme groups to moderate too radical claims.

In structural terms integration of political and social groups means that parliament establishes 'partial regimes' (Schmitter, 1988): with respect to the politically relevant parties the 'electoral regime', and with regard to the relevant socio-economic groups the 'pressure regime'.[8] Hence, the analysis of existing networks of interaction—by elite interviews and document study—and the examination of the norms which regulate them allow us to assess to what extent and in which way different groups have become integrated into the working of the parliamentary institution.

Parliament allows for peaceful conflict regulation within the parliamentary arena mainly by structuring itself, establishing, implementing and stabilizing the 'house rules', the parliamentary standing orders. By doing so it assumes a 'central role in the reproduction of democratic consent' (see Chapter 2). The parliamentary elite by consensus and deliberate decisions establishes the set of parliamentary rules and procedures to regulate their interactions and accommodate their conflicts within and outside parliament. The range of possible rules is wide, and there is no single set which would work equally well under all conditions. In all cases the level of rule-abiding behaviour may serve as an indicator to assess to what extent the rules are 'beyond dispute and fully accepted by all relevant political actors' (Morlino, 1986a), hence to measure how successful parliamentary conflict management is.

Parliament builds support among mass publics if it is able to produce 'a set of attitudes that look to the legislature as a valued and popular political institution' (Mezey, 1979: 27f.) by virtue of its electoral and representative links with the citizenry. As indicators we can choose (a) the level of participation in legislative elections; (b) events such as attacks upon the existence or integrity of the legislature; (c) public statements of significant political actors, for instance verbal attacks launched against the legislature; (d) expressions of popular trust or distrust with respect to the legislature, charges of corruption and/or incompetency; (e) analysis of attitudes towards the legislature among mass publics, the identification of supportive or nonsupportive latent attitudes

(Mezey, 1979: 34).[9] The higher the level of public support, the better the chances that parliamentary conflict regulation 'spreads over' into civil society, operating an integrating and socializing—and not, as in the negative case, a polarizing—effect on society.

The extension of parliamentary support is considered as contributing to regime legitimation by 'rooting' the emerging regime within the citizenry and organized social forces (Schmitter, 1988). It certainly enhances the chances for a constitutionalization of the armed forces, the political neutralization of the military and the enforcement of the 'principle of civilian supremacy' (cf. Alivizatos, 1987).

It is not the third, the legitimation function, which makes parliament a 'central' site in the process of democratic consolidation, but primarily the first two of these functions—the integration of the extreme left and right and, indirectly or directly, of the economic power groups, and the accommodation of political and social conflict among them. By exercising both parliament contributes to regime consolidation.

The majoritarian and the consociational variant

There are two principally different forms which the 'parliamentary compromise' may adopt; a 'majoritarian' or a 'consociational' one.[10] The adoption of a particular electoral system and the constitutional design of parliament–executive relations, including the provisions of the parliamentary standing orders, determine as much as political events the outcome in favour of one or the other of both models.

The first majoritarian hypothesis makes parliament offer channels of public interest articulation to those forces which are excluded from government, and at the same time allows for strong and stable government. The majoritarian model of parliament functions as a 'sounding board' for popular interests in the improvement of the material conditions of life, and at the same time is 'cooperative', 'subordinate' or even 'submissive' to centre or centre–right government.

In the second case, a 'consociational' parliament offers opportunities for effective legislative mediation in the daily legislative workings to all major political and social forces with parliamentary representation. The costs are a weak government, and a lack of openness and transparency of parliamentary activities, many of which take place at the committee level, and hence do not bring discussions and battles between principle rival groups to the attention of mass publics.

The institutional mechanisms which enhance this integrative function consist in the majoritarian model in a combination of channels for the public articulation of interests with safeguards for cohesive and stable parliamentary majorities which in some cases require provisions of parliamentary group discipline and control of the MP; in others there are facilities for the factions (*correnti*) within the majority to express themselves (by secret vote, for instance).

In the 'consociational' model the parliamentary 'compromise' is based on mechanisms for legislative mediation and powers of co-decision in agenda-setting, legislative work and control of government for the opposition and minorities, and a significant role of subcommittees in the legislative process. The high level of 'openness' of parliamentary procedures towards the public with manifold access points, formal instruments and informal occasions for citizen and group participation enhances the parliamentary 'integration function' of this model especially with regard to interest groups (Pasquino, 1988).[11]

Both varieties of the parliamentary game possess certain advantages and costs for the various political actors. Participation in consensual decision-making on major political issues may imply high costs in terms of threatening the identity of some of the more ideologized political parties. A subordinate parliament with respect to decision-making powers and control by a strong and cohesive governing majority can be more efficient and less costly for 'reluctant' players because it allows for the articulation of symbolic opposition without imposing the obligation to pay the costs of participation in governmental responsibility.

Parliamentary resources and democratic consolidation

With respect to these functions of integration and conflict resolution, parliament may not easily be replaced by other institutions, especially if party organizations are weak, party systems not yet consolidated and polarized, and charismatic leadership is lacking. Parliament appears not just as one possible 'path to democratic consolidation' and not at all as 'superfluous' in the stage of democratic consolidation because it possesses—perhaps more than any other organ, be it an elected president, a hegemonic party, or a representative government cabinet—properties which allow it to provide for the integration of political and socio-economic groups and peaceful conflict regulation among them largely independently from its decision-making competences.

Parliament controls important symbolic resources, namely 'popular representation' which—from the normative point of view—serves as a major principle of democratic legitimation. But the content of this principle has changed substantially with the course of democratic evolution. Thomas Hobbes, for instance, conceived representation formalistically as symbolic 'authorization' of one person to act on behalf of others, and linked it to the 'accountability' of the representative. According to the descriptive concept of representation, formulated by Walter Bagehot or John Stuart Mill, the legislature is a mirror image of the population. This model has been replaced by Hannah Pitkin's concept of representation focusing on 'policy-responsiveness'.[12] However, other scholars have objected that most citizens do not have clear policy demands or positions on public issues and that relatively few communicate with their representatives or take any interest in the policy-making process (Wahlke, 1971: 273). Modern representation especially involves the 'highly complex problems' of 'choices forced on a representative by multiple demands and the various forms of linkages between representatives and constituents' (Jewell, 1985: 123). Parliamentary representation may therefore serve as a source of public prestige and legitimation for newly emerging or discredited political parties.

Parliament produces a variety of material resources and has capacities which can benefit and consequently motivate political actors—mainly parties with their need to organize their party apparatuses and mobilize mass followings —but also interest groups and other social organizations. For instance, parliamentary elections enable, first of all, the measurement of the relative force of each party in terms of seats; parliament provides financial resources via parliamentary group financing and other infrastrutural facilities and offers sources of political and technical information (Morisi, 1988).

Parliament possesses a peculiar advantage which allows the 'parliament-arization' of the strategies of very different types of political actors. The parties of thc cxtrcmc lcft, of the moderate left, the centre and the moderate or extreme right come from ideological traditions which are not only different but may in some cases be incompatible with respect to the basic principles of the social, economic and political order they propose. To give an example, the concepts of representation may vary extremely along the political spectrum: while some may conceive the role of the deputy as a representative of the national interest, others interpret it as a 'mandate' of specific sectors of society, namely the working class, while in a third perspective the role of the MP is seen as the 'parochial' representative of local interests.[13] These divergencies—and hence party political identities—can be maintained and made compatible within a certain margin thanks to the peculiar 'ambiguity' of the parliamentary institution, of its rules and procedures which allow for different and even contradictory interpretations of representational roles.

Thanks to the persuasiveness of these symbolic and material resources, the parliamentary game may become important and motivate some of the actors even in the transition stage to develop from 'anti-system' parties to parties which fully integrate into the system. Thus it contributes to that process of 'growing and reciprocal acknowledgement of all parties as parts of the whole', a process of depolarization which may represent the 'surrogate of a lacking or non perfect process of nation- and state-building'. According to the classical analysis of Paolo Farneti and Leopoldo Elia this took place in post-war Italy (Baldassarre, 1985: 339), and especially in the case of the Italian Communist Party (Sassoon, 1989; Baldassarre, op. cit.). A comparable process of depolarization can be observed in the majority of the Spanish regional-nationalist parties after 1977 (Liebert, 1989).

Determinants of parliament as the 'central site in democratic consolidation'

A thorough review of the institutional and political variables with a possible impact on the performance of parliament in democratic consolidation has to move within the broad field of empirical and comparative parliamentary research (Liebert, 1988). In the following we will select only a few of the potentially relevant factors.

Parliamentary decision-making powers

The notion of parliament as a 'central site' in the integration of social and political forces and peaceful conflict accommodation is very different from the concept of 'centrality of parliament' in the Italian debate, or the French model of 'parliamentary supremacy', both of which focus on a type of 'predominance' of parliament in decision-making terms *vis-à-vis* the executive. At least from the point of view of government and regime stability, the 'centrality' of parliament in this sense of predominance and high levels of decision-making powers represents a permanent threat rather than a desideratum (Colliard, 1978; Montero, 1985).

Parliament as a 'central site' in democratic consolidation has quite a distinct meaning. In this perspective, the main focus is not on the relationship between parliament and government, but rather on the interactions of parliament with the intermediary organizations (parties, interest groups etc.) In this view, parliamentary centrality is not measured by its role in constitution-building nor in directing and controlling national policies and the executive action, even though these powers may represent important incentives for some of the political actors. Post-World War II limitations to assembly parliamentarism and the 'deprivation' of some of the prerogatives of parliament to the advantage of the executive, of the parties or other organs, in the name of 'rationalized parliamentary government' must not necessarily jeopardize the parliamentary capacity to contribute to regime integration.

Parliament may achieve the collaboration or at least acquiescence of social and political forces not primarily by exercising an effective influence in decision-making on important issues of national policies, but insofar as it deals at least symbolically and in public with these topics, thus requiring the participation of the major political forces in the parliamentary game. Hence, not the level and extent of effective parliamentary influence in decision-making, but the importance of the matters with which parliament deals appears a decisive determinant for parliamentary 'centrality' in democratic consolidation. Hence those legislatures which Jean Blondel classifies as 'nascent' or 'truncated' in this respect appear marginal because they deal only with detailed matters and do not concern themselves with some of the most important aspects of the life of the country, whether on foreign affairs or on broad social and economic matters', whereas the 'inhibited' as well as the 'real' legislatures are 'involved in general questions as well as intermediate matters', the second possessing various means of intervention (Blondel, 1973: 133ff.).

The characteristics of the parliamentary groups

The nature of the parliamentary majority and party groups—their level of stabilization and discipline—are other important criteria for the classification of legislatures, and a determinant of the integrative and conflict-regulating capacity of parliament in the course of democratic consolidation. Thus the 'coordinate' and 'subordinate' type of legislature appear to succeed better than the 'indeterminate', 'competitive-dominant' or 'submissive' ones in stabilizing patterns of conflict management (Weinbaum, 1975: 35ff.). Another variable is given by the different models of the 'government–parliament subsystem' according to the characteristic type of party organization of the legislature. The impact of the 'polycentric' versus the 'party-government' and the 'grand coalitional' arrangements for the integration of extremist parties, for depolarization and stable conflict regulation in a process of democratic consolidation should be assessed empirically (Cotta, 1987; Castles and Wildenmann, 1986). The role of parliament in democratic consolidation is certainly reinforced the more parliamentary groups become structured and stabilized ('structured and stabilized parliamentarism'; Colliard, 1978), not only those of the majority but opposition groups as well.

Relations between groups and parties

If most contemporary parliaments are 'arena-type' and not 'transformative legislatures' (Polsby, 1975), and hence dependent on outside forces, legislatures may differ with respect to the strength of parliamentary groups in relation to the external parties. Parliamentary groups are in general enhanced or diminished by a variety of institutional factors (von Beyme, 1983). But, while many studies on party–legislature relations, including southern Europe, have underlined the capacity of strong parties to reduce the autonomy of the legislature, empirical studies on Third World legislatures in the seventies have pointed out that legislatures are far more vulnerable to extraconstitutional attacks against their prerogatives in systems where political parties are weak; stronger parties help the legislature to generate the support it needs from mass publics to withstand challenges from bureaucratic elites (Jewell, 1973). They maintain parliament as a functioning entity, although within certain parameters generally defined by the governing party (Mezey, 1985).

Electoral system

The composition of parliaments differs with respect to electoral proportionality. The parliamentary integration function appears reinforced by electoral systems of proportional representation and formula which translate votes into seats without major distortions and low thresholds of access to parliamentary representation, although all electoral systems have to some extent a redistributive effect in favour of a few big parties at the costs of many small ones (Nohlen, 1978; Rae, 1967). Where political cleavages are multidimensional and societies heterogeneous and plural, an artificially reduced number of parties gaining parliamentary representation could prove incapable of political integration and conflict resolution. In homogeneous societies with only one or two political cleavages the fragmentation of parliamentary forces can lead to deadlocks.

'Talk' versus 'work-legislatures'

'Talk legislatures' which aspire to be an 'arena of public opinion' and an 'official platform of all important debates which involve the nation' appear to be able to integrate extreme parties of the left or right more easily than 'work legislatures' where sessions take place behind closed doors and presuppose a certain level of cooperative behaviour (Steffani, 1965).

Conclusion: the limits of the parliamentary game

The problem-solving capacity of parliament — especially with respect to pressing social and economic redistributive issues — has of course certain limits. Conditions of economic growth and social homogeneity obviously facilitate the opportunities of any democratic regime to consolidate. Whether parliament is overwhelmed where societal cleavages are severe and resources are limited (cf. Mishler and Hildreth, 1984: 25) or whether it is capable of survival certainly depends on whether the parliamentary institution has been able to integrate the major political actors and social power groups and to regulate — although not resolve — conflict among them.

In this preliminary exploration we have pointed out major differences reflecting the controversies between those who glorify parliament in the tradition of liberal parliamentary theory as the symbol of popular sovereignty and representation, and those who see its role presently as having been reduced to a 'mere formality' within the new mass- and party-democracies. Due to the lack of systematic, empirical and comparative analysis, the image of the new parliamentary bodies in southern European public opinion is still ambiguous and a frequent object of partisan polemics.

In order to understand which are the important achievements which southern European parliaments and parliamentarians in the last 10–15 years have to their credit — not all of which are obvious to public opinion — we developed a number of hypotheses on parliament as a central site in processes of democratic consolidation. In particular, we pointed out that the manifestations of a recent 'rise', reinforcement and strengthening of legislatures in southern Europe during the seventies and partly during the eighties can be explained by the functions these parliaments performed with respect to the integration of the major political and economic forces and to conflict regulation among them. In this perspective the 'rise' of parliament can be of two different types:

(1) In some cases — under conditions of a majoritarian model of parliamentary government — the reinforcement of parliament is of a predominantly symbolic nature and involves the parliamentary function as a 'sounding board' for the articulation of social demands and as an 'arena' for the discussion of the major political themes of the country.

(2) In the case of the consociational variant of parliamentary government parliament assumes the function of an arena for instrumental mediation and decision-making among the major political and social forces of the country.

Southern European legislatures in the course of their evolution have not always fitted into one of these pure types, but in some cases have also switched between them. We require a substantial body of systematic empirical information in order to identify the patterns of integration and conflict management in each case, and to assess their underlying political and institutional conditions and consequences for the consolidation of the new democratic regimes.

Notes

1. In France it was the transition from the Fourth to the Fifth Republic which deprived the National Assembly of a large part of its prerogatives with respect to the executive and the president (Birnbaum *et al.*, 1978, 1980). In the United States, since the last century complaints about the weakening of the role of the Congress *vis-à-vis* the president have surfaced periodically. In Great Britain, as early as in the middle of the nineteenth century parliament was seen as just the façade of British political life, which was conceived instead as essentially shaped by the council of ministers (Bagehot, 1867). In the seventies of this century, the laments were that the executive controlled the legislature rather than the other way round (Walkland and Ryle, 1977; Lukes 1982). In the Federal Republic of Germany, the neo-Marxist parliamentary critique since the end of the sixties complains about the lack of transparence and of citizen participation in parliamentary activities (Abendroth, 1967; Agnoli and Brückner, 1967). The trend towards neo-corporatist interest intermediation which has been observed and analysed since the seventies in several Western polities (Schmitter and Lehmbruch, 1982; Berger, 1981; Schmitter, 1974) provides further arguments to the thesis which holds that contemporary parliamentary decision-making processes were progressively undermined or by-passed by competitive, or even alternative circuits.
2. 'Democratic consolidation' has been defined in different formulations, but in substance quite similarly as a process of 'freezing-adaptation of modes of peaceful conflict-resolution, and especially the widening of the legitimacy of the regime with regard to civil society' which follows a preceding stage of transition and establish-ment (Morlino, 1986a); or respectively as 'a process synonymous to 'structuration', 'routinization', 'stabilization', and 'institutionalization' which transforms the 'ad hoc patterns' characteristic of the period of transition into stable structures in such a way that the ensuing forms/channels of access, inclusion/exclusion of actors, resources/strategies for action and rules about decision-making conform to the basic principle of citizenship and a 'procedural minimum' (Schmitter, 1988: 12).
3. Despite the existence of a considerable body of classical and recent studies dealing with cultural, social, historical, political and economic topics related to the individual countries in southern Europe, most of them are monographs, as the collectively written 'Bibliographical Essay on Southern Europe and its Recent Transition to Political Democracy' demonstrates (cf. Diamandouros *et al.*, 1986). Among the few genuinely comparative southern European political science studies which have to be mentioned above all are those on regime change and transition to democracy (Kohler, 1981; Santamaria, 1982; Pridham, 1984; O'Donnell *et al.*, 1986). A second 'wave' of studies deals with aspects related to 'democratic consolidation', for instance on parties and democratic consolidation (cf. Pridham, 1989); on interest groups and democratic consolidation (cf. Schmitter, forthcoming; Morlino, forthcoming).

4. In the United States, Samuel Huntington has treated the problem of democratic consolidation as one of political institutionalization (1968). Gerhard Loewenberg and Samuel Patterson (1979), as well as Michael Mezey (1979), have focused on the performance of parliaments in a world-wide comparative perspective. Mishler and Hildreth inquired into the relationship between legislatures, environment and political stability (1984). Research in the Western European tradition of historical and institutional analyses of parliamentary government has also focused on related aspects. Major examples are Klaus von Beyme's comparative account of the genesis and functioning of parliamentary systems of government in Europe, with its emphasis on parliamentary crises and techniques of crisis management (1970). Maurice Duverger focused rather on the problem of stable parliamentary majorities (1974). Jean-Claude Colliard analysed the structuration and stabilization of parliamentary groups as conditions for government stability (Colliard, 1978).

5. The functionalist tradition in parliamentary theory has found one of its classical formulations in Walter Bagehot. In the middle of the last century, the English constitutionalist expected that in order

that a House of Commons may work well it must perform . . . five functions well: it must elect a Ministry well, legislate well, teach the nation well, express the nation's will well, bring matters to the nation's attention well. [Bagehot, 1867].

6. The processes of liberalization and democratization which occurred in the decade between the mid-seventies and the mid-eighties in different areas of the world, above all in southern Europe, Latin and Central America, have stimulated the effort of a number of political scientists—namely Geoffrey Pridham (1984), Leonardo Morlino (1986a, b), Philippe Schmitter (1985, 1988), Giuseppe Di Palma (1989)— to fill the gap in democratic theory with respect to the forms, conditions and requirements of the consolidation of these new regimes. At the time being, no single 'theory of democratic consolidation' (DC) has evolved. Instead, there are different conceptualizations and hypotheses in discussion.

7. Major types of opposition are Otto Kirchheimer's 'classical opposition' (developed in England during the eighteenth century), the 'principled opposition' (typical of the socialist parties at the end of the nineteenth century, and of the communist parties after World War II); finally the 'sporadic opposition' (in cases in which government reaches various forms of agreement with opposition forces within the parliamentary institution) (Kirchheimer, 1957: 127). Giovanni Sartori distinguishes between the 'constitutional opposition' and the 'tout court opposition' in systems where a minimum consensus on fundamental principles is lacking (Sartori, 1966: 151). We use the concept of 'anti-system opposition' in this sense of 'principled' or 'tout court oppositions'.

8. Schmitter defines 'partial regimes' as 'networks of power among interdependent or hierarchically ordered institutions' which emerge in the course of regime building. To these belong the 'electoral regime', the 'pressure regime', the 'concertation regime', the 'clientelist regime' and the 'representation regime' (Schmitter, 1988).

9. The analysis of mass survey data has not only enormous problems in generating appropriate cross-national data, but it can also be misleading in new nations which did not have the time to develop a reservoir of diffuse support so that people 'in the abstract world of survey research' may state supportive attitudes which when put to the test, may yield easily (Mezey, 1979: 34).
   Loewenberg and Chong Lim Kim measured responsiveness by three types of data: how members of parliaments conceptualize their constituencies; the extent of their communication with their constituents; their receptivity to their constituents' views (Loewenberg and Chong Lim Kim 1978: 27–49).

10. These two models of the majoritarian 'Westminster model' and the 'consensus model' of democracy have been conceptualized by Arend Lijphart. The majoritarian model is characterized by elements (the concentration of executive power (one-party and bare-majority cabinets); fusion of executive and legislative power and cabinet dominance; 'near unicameralism' or asymmetric bicameralism; a two-party system; a one-dimensional political cleavage; a plurality electoral system; centralized government; parliament (and practically the parliamentary majority) as the ultimate sovereign authority; exclusively representative democracy (without elements of direct democracy and popular sovereignty) which concentrate, fuse and centralize power (Lijphart, 1984: 4–9). The 'consensus model' is characterized by a number of elements (executive power-sharing by grand coalitions; formal and informal separation of powers; balanced bicameralism and minority representation; a multiparty system with multidimensional cleavages; proportional representation; federalism and decentralization; minority vetoes as a 'concurrent majority principle' which restrain majority rule by encouraging the sharing, dispersal, delegation and limitation of power (Lijphart, 1984: 21–30).

11. The openness of parliamentary procedures regards the degree to which external 'private' subjects, be they individuals or organized interest groups, may gain access to parliamentary activity. The most prominent instrument which allows direct contact between parliament and organized groups, experts and individuals are the so-called 'hearings', originating in Anglo-saxon parliamentary law. These inquiries, which normally take place at the committee stage, allow for the direct acquisition of news and information necessary for parliamentary activity, not only with respect to the state of problems of particular interest, but also with regard to the needs of the various groups making up the social context.

12. Representation according to Pitkin

    means acting in the interest of the represented, in a manner responsive to them. The representative must act independently; his action must involve discretion and judgement; he must be the one who acts . . . And, despite the resulting potential for conflict between representative and represented about what is to be done, that conflict must not normally take place. The representative must act in such a way that there is no conflict, or if it occurs an explanation is called for [Pitkin, 1967: 209–10].

13. Loewenberg and Chong Lim Kim (1978: 27ff.) detected in their four-nations study on Turkey, Korea, Switzerland and Italy four different types of representativeness: participatory, elitist, parochial and limited representativeness, Italy coming closest to the participatory, and Turkey to the parochial categories. The Loewenberg/ Chong Lim Kim typology demonstrates that in cases of weak policy-responsiveness of legislatures, other links with the citizenry may be more important: for example open communication with constituents, personal service and allocation responsiveness in the sense of advantages, benefits and legislative allocations of public projects which the representative is able to obtain for particular constituents or for the district as a whole; or 'symbolic responsiveness' as a relationship 'built on trust and confidence expressed in the support that the represented give to the representative and to which he responds by symbolic, significant gestures, in order to, in turn, generate and maintain continuing support' (Eulau and Karps, 1977: 242ff.).

References

Abendroth, W. (1967), *Antagonistische Gesellschaft und politische Demokratie*, Neuwied und Berlin, Luchterhand.

Agnoli, J. and Brückner, P. (1967), *Die Transformation der Demokratie*, Frankfurt, Europaische Verlagsanstalt.

Aguilo Lucia, L. (1981), 'La ley para la reforma politica como precedente de la actual desigualdad en la representacion politica' in M. Aparicio Perez (ed.), *Parlamento y sociedad civil*, University of Barcelona, 173–86.

Alivizatos, N. (1979), *Les institutions politiques de la Grèce a travers les crises 1922–1974*, Paris, Bibliotheque Constitutionnelle et de Science Politique.

Alivizatos, N. (1986), *Le Parlement Hellenique. Actualisation récente d'un débat manqué*. Paper delivered at conference on 'The Formation of Parliaments in Southern Europe', European University Institute, Florence, May.

Alzaga Villaamil, O. (1988), *Relaçiones Gobierno-Cortes Generales*. Conference paper given on occasion of the 'The Tenth Anniversary of the Spanish Constitution', University of Siena, Centre for Constitutional Studies, Pontignano, 4–5 November.

Aparicio Perez, M.A. (1980), *Parlamento y sociedad civil*, Barcelona, University of Barcelona.

Armaroli, P. (1986), *L'introvabile governability. Le strategie istituzionali dei partiti dalla costituente alla commissione Bozzi*, padova, Cedam.

Bagehot, W. (1867), *The English Constitution*, Glasgow, William Collins (17th edition, 1983).

Baldassarre, A. (1985): 'Le "performances" del Parlamento italiano nell'ultimo quindicennio' in *Il sistema politico italiano*, G. Pasquino (ed.), Roma-Bari, Laterza, 304–44.

Berger, S. (1981) (ed.): Organizing Interests in Western Europe: Pluralism, corporatism and the transformation of politics; Cambridge, Cambridge University Press.

von Beyme, K. (1970), *Die parliamentarischen Regierungssysteme in Europa*, vols I–II, Munich, Piper.

von Beyme, K. (1983), 'Governments, Parliaments and the Structure of Power in Political Parties', in Daalder and Mair (eds), *Western European Party Systems, Continuity and Change*, Sage, London: 341–367.

Bianchi, R. (1986), 'Interest Group Politics in the Third World', *Third World Quarterly*, **2**.

Birnbaum, P. (1980), 'Les nouvelles fonctions du parlement dans la France contemporaine' in M.A. Aparicio (ed.), *Parlamento y Sociedad Civil*, University of Barcelona.

—, F. Hamon, and M. Troper (1978), *Réinventer le parlement*, Paris, Flammarion.

Blondel, J. (1973), *Comparative Legislatures*, Englewood Cliffs, Prentice-Hall.

Bonifacio, F.P. (1985), 'Le leggi del parlamento e la pluralita dei soggetti legittimati a porre comandi normativi' in *Il Parlamento tra crisi e riforma*, A. Barbera, P. Barcellona, F.P. Bonifacio, G. Ferrara, A. Manzella (eds), Milan, Franco Angeli.

Bruneau, T.C., and A. Macleod (eds) (1986), *Politics in Contemporary Portugal: Parties and the Consolidation of Democracy*, Boulder, Lynne Rienner.

Caetano, M. (1971), *Historia Breve das Constituicoes Portuguesas*, Lisboa, Verbo (3rd edition).

Capo Giol, J. (1980), 'El debate sobre el bicameralismo: la camara denominada de representacion territorial' in *Parlamento y sociedad civil*, M. Aparicio Perez (ed.), University of Barcelona, 283–90.

— (1981), *La formación de las Cortes Generales en la legislatura 1977–1979*, Phd thesis, University of Barcelona, Faculty of Law, Barcelona.

— (1983), *La institucionalización de las Cortes Generales*, Ediçions de la Universitat de Barcelona, Barcelona.

Castles, F.G., and R. Wildenmann (eds) (1986), *Visions and Realities of Party Government*, Berlin and New York, de Gruyter.

Cazorla Prieto, L.M. (1985), *Las Cortes Generales: Parlamento contemporaneo?* Madrid, Cuadernos Civitas.

Cheli, E. (1981), 'La "centralita" parlamentare: sviluppo e decadenza di un modello', *Quaderni costituzionali*, **2**, 343–51. Centro de Investigaciones Sociologicas (CIS) (1985), *Partidos y Cultura Politica en la Europa del Sur*. (Four-nations mass survey in Italy, Spain, Greece, and Portugal, directed by J. Santamaria *et al.*).

Colliard, J.-C. (1978), *Les régimes parlamentaires contemporains*, Presses de la Fondation Nationale des Sciences Politiques, Paris.

Cotta, M. (1979), *Classe politica e parlamento in Italia*, Bologna, Il Mulino.

—(1987), 'Il sotto-sistema governo-parlamento', *Rivista Italiana di Scienza Politica* **2**.

De Riz, L. (1988): *Alfonsin's Argentina: Renewal of Parties and Congress* (manuscript), Buenos Aires, Cedes.

Diamandouros, N. (1987), *The Politics of Constitution-making in Postauthoritarian Greece in Historical Perspective*, paper delivered at the Annual Meeting of the American Political Science Association, The Palmer House, 3–6 September.

—, P. Rivilla, J. Lopez Novo, H. Tursan, P.C. Schmitter (1986), *A Bibliographical Essay on Southern Europe and its Recent Transition to Political Democracy*, EUI Working Paper No. 86/208, Florence.

Di Palma, G. (1977), *Surviving without Governing: The Italian Parties in Parliament*, Berkeley, University of California Press.

— (1986), 'Party Government and Democratic Reproducibility: The Dilemma of New Democracies' in *Visions and Realities of Party Government*, F.G Castles and R. Wildenmann (eds), de Gruyter, Berlin and New York.

Duverger, M. (1974), *La monarchie republicaine*, Laffont, Paris.

— (1983), 'La nozione di regime "semi-presidenziale" e l'esperienza francese', in *Quaderni costituzionali*, **2**, 259–75.

Eisfeld, R. (1984), *Sozialistischer Pluralismus in Europa, Ansätze und Scheitern am Beispiel Portugal*, Verlag Wissenschaft und Politik, Köln.

— (1987), 'The Portuguese "Assembleia", Comment'. Paper given at Conference on Parliaments and Democratic Consolidation in Southern Europe, Volkswagen Foundation, Fundaçion Bofill, Barcelona, 29–31 October.

Eulau, H. and P.D. Karps (1977), 'The Puzzle of Representation: Specifying Components of Responsiveness', in *Legislative Studies Quarterly*, **2**, 233–54.

Garcia Cotarelo, R. (1987), 'Parliament and democratic legitimacy: the Spanish case', Conference on Parliaments and Democratic Consolidation in Southern Europe, Volkswagen Foundation and Fundaçion Bofill, Barcelona, 29–31 October.

Giner, S. and Sevilla, E. (1980), 'From Despotism to Parliamentarianism: Class Domination and Political Order in the Spanish State' in *The State in Western Europe*, R. Scase (ed.), London, Croom Helm.

Guerra, A. (1982): 'El Parlamento, instrumento fundamental para la construcción de una sociedad librè e igualitaria' in *Parlamento y Democracia, problemas y perspectivas en los años 80*, Fundaçion Pablo Iglesias (ed.), Madrid.

Harris, G. (1988), 'The Role of the Military in Turkey: Guardians or Decision-Makers?' in M. Heper and A. Evin (eds) *State, Democracy and the Military: Turkey in the 1980s*, Berlin and New York, de Gruyter.

Heper, M. (1985), *The State Tradition in Turkey*, Walkington, England, Eothen Press.

Huntington, S. (1968), *Political Order in Changing Societies*, Yale University Press, New Haven.

Ingrao, P. (1985), 'Crisi e riforma del parlamento', *Democrazia e diritto*, **2**, 35–66.

Jewell, M.E. (1973), 'Linkages Between Legislative Parties and External Parties', in Kornberg (ed.), *Legislatures in Comparative Perspective*, David McKay, New York: 203–234.

— (1985), 'Legislators and Constituents in the Representative Process', *Handbook of Legislative Research*, Harvard University Press, Cambridge (Mass).

Kirchheimer, O. (1957), 'The Waning of Opposition in Parliamentary Regimes', in *Social Research*, XXIV.

Kohler, B. (1981): *Politischer Umbruch in Südeuropa. Portugal, Griechenland, Spanien auf dem Weg zur Demokratie*. Bonn, Europa Union Verlag.

Labriola, S. (1982), 'La crisis del parlamento desde la optica italiana' in *Parlamento y democracia, problemas y perspectivas en los años 80*, op. cit., 23–34.

Lehmbruch, G. (1979), 'Liberal Corporatism and Party Government' in *Trends Towards Corporatist Intermediation*, P.C. Schmitter and G. Lehmbruch (eds), Beverly Hills, Sage, 147–84.

— (1983), 'Neokorporatismus in Westeuropa: Hauptprobleme im internationalen Vergleich', *Journal für Sozialforschung*, **4**, 407–20.

Liebert, U. (1986), *Neue Autonomiebewegung und Dezentralisierung in Spanien: Der Fall Andalusien*, Frankfurt and New York, Campus.

— (1988), 'Parlamento y consolidacion de la democracia en la Europa del Sur', *Revista Espanola de Investigaciones Sociologicas*, **42**, 93–136.

— (1989), 'From Polarization to Pluralism: Regional-Nationalist Parties in the Process of Democratic Consolidation in Post-Franco Spain' in G. Pridham (ed.), *Securing Democracy: Political Parties and Regime Consolidation in Southern Europe*, London, Routledge.

Lijphart, A. (1984), *Democracies, Patterns of Majoritarian and Consensus Government in Twenty-One Countries*, New Haven and London, Yale University Press.

—, T.C. Bruneau, P.N. Diamandouros, and R. Gunther (1988): A Mediterranean Model of Democracy? The Southern European Democracies in Comparative Perspective, *Western European Politics*, **1**.

Linz, J. (1985), 'Notes toward a Memorandum or Paper on the Mediterranean as an Area for Comparative Social Research', Seminar on *Democracy in Southern Europe*, Florence, European University Institute, November.

Loewenberg, G. (1971), *Modern Parliaments: Change or Decline?* Chicago and New York, Aldine.

— and Patterson, S.C. (1979): Comparing Legislatures, Little Brown, Boston.

—, S.C. Patterson and M.E. Jewell (eds) (1985), *Handbook of Legislative Research*, Cambridge, Mass., Harvard University Press.

Loewenstein, L. (1938), 'The Balance between Legislative and Executive Power: A Study in Comparative Constitutional Law', in *University of Chicago Law Review*, V.

Long, G. (1987), 'Parliamentary Rules of Procedure in Southern Europe: Italy, Spain, Greece and Portugal in Comparison', paper presented at the Conference on Parliaments and Democratic Consolidation in Southern Europe, James Bofill Foundation, Barcelona, 29–31 October.

Lukes, S. (1982), 'El debate sobre el "declive" del Parlamento britanico' in *Parlamento y democracia*, op. cit., 23–34.

Manzella, A. (1975), 'Le funzioni del parlamento in Italia' in *I Parlamenti della Communita Europea*, Camera dei Deputati, Rome.

— (1980), 'Las Cortes en el sistema constitucional español', in Garcia de Enterria and Predieri (eds), *La Constitucion española*, Civitas, Madrid.

— (1986), *La formazione del Parlamento italiano*, conference-paper, European University Institute, Florence.

Martinez Sospedra, M. (1980), 'Desigualdad y representacion en la Constitucion española de 1978' in *Parlamento y sociedad civil*, M. Aparicio Perez (ed.), University of Barcelona, 187–214.

Mezey, M. (1979), *Comparative Legislatures*, Durham, Duke University Press.

— (1985), 'The Functions of Legislatures in the Third World', in Loewenberg, Patterson and Jewell (eds), 733–72.

Mishler, W. and A. Hildreth, (1984), 'Legislatures and Political Stability: An Exploratory Analysis', in *The Journal of Politics*, vol. 46: 25–59.

Molas, I. (1982), 'Democracia, representacion y partidos politicos' in *Parlamento y democracia*, op. cit., 70–7.
—, and I.E. Pitarch (1987), *Las Cortes Generales en el sistema parlamentario de Gobierno*, Madrid, Tecnos.
Montero, J.R. (1989), Parlamento y opinion publica: Las percepciones y los niveles de apoyo de las Cortes Generales Centro de Estudios Constitucionales, Madrid.
Morisi, M. (1988), 'Il parlamento in Italia. Vecchie e nuove ipotesi di ricerca', in *Rivista Italiana di Scienza Politica*, **2**, 191–222.
Morlino, L. (1984): 'The Changing Relationship between Parties and Society in Italy' in S. Bartolini and P. Mair (eds), *Party Politics in Contemporary Western Europe*, London, Frank Cass.
— (1986a), 'Consolidamento democratico: definizione e modelli', *Rivista Italiana di Scienza Politica*, **2**.
— (1986b), 'Consolidamento democratico: alcune ipotesi explicative', *Rivista Italian de Scienza Politica*, **3**.
— (ed.) (forthcoming), 'Interessi, Gruppi, e consolidamento democratico in Italia'.
Nohlen, D. (1978), *Wahlsysteme der Welt*, Piper, Munich.
— (1988), 'Parliamentarismus in Spanien in verfassungssystematischer Perspektive', in *Zeitschrift für Parlamentsfragen*, **3**, 366–76.
O'Donnell, G., P.C. Schmitter, and L. Whitehead (1986), *Transitions from Authoritarian Rule: Prospects for Democracy*, Baltimore and London, Johns Hopkins University Press.
Opello, W.C. (1985), *Portugal's Political Development, A Comparative Approach*, Westview Press, Boulder and London.
— (1986), 'Portugal's Parliament: An Organizational Analysis of Legislative Performance', *Legislative Studies Quarterly*, **XI**, 291–319.
Özbudun, E. (1988), 'The Status of the President of the Republic under the Turkish Constitution of 1982: Presidentialism or Parliamentarism?' in *State, Democracy and the Military*, op. cit., 37–45.
Papadopoulos, I. (forthcoming), 'The Greek Party System from Transition to Consolidation? The Decline of Small Parties and the Emergence of Two-Partyism' in G. Pridham and F. Müller-Rommel (eds), *Small Parties in Western Europe in National and Comparative Perspective*, London, Sage.
Pasquino, G. (1987a), 'Regolatori sregolati: partiti e governo dei partiti' in P. Lange and M. Regini (eds), *Stato e regolazione sociale: Nuove prospettive sul caso italiano*, Bologna, il Mulino.
— (1987b), 'Rappresentanza degli interessi, attivita di lobby e processi decisionali: il caso italiano di istituzioni permeabili', *Stato e Mercato*, **21**, 403–29.
— (1988), *Istituzioni, partiti, lobbies*, Roma-Bari, Laterza.
Pitkin, H.F. (1967), *The Concept of Representation*, University of California Press, Berkeley.
Polsby, N.B. (1975), 'Legislatures', in Greenstein and Polsby (eds), *Handbook of Political Science*, vol. 5, Addison-Wesley, Reading, (Mass).
Pridham, G. (ed.) (1984), *The New Mediterranean Democracies: Regime Transition in Spain, Greece and Portugal*, London, Frank Cass (and Special Issue of *West European Politics*, **2**).
— (ed.) (1989): *Securing Democracy*, London, Routledge.
Przeworksi, A., and M. Wallerstein (1982), 'The Structure of Class Conflict in Democratic Capitalist Societies', *American Political Science Review*, **2**, 215–38.
Rustow, D.A. (1970), 'Transitions to Democracy, Toward a Dynamic Model', *Comparative Politics*, **3**.
Santamaria, J. (ed.) (1982), *Transicion a la democracia en el sur de europa y America Latina*, Madrid, Centro de Investigaciones Sociologicas.

Sartori, G. (1963), 'Dove va il parlamento?', in Somogyi, Lotti and Sartori, *Il Parlamento italiano, 1946–1963*, Esi, Naples.
— (1966), 'European Political Parties: The Case of Polarized Pluralism', in La Palombara and Weiner (eds), *Political Parties and Political Development*, Princeton University Press, 137–76.
Sassoon, D. (1989), 'The Role of the Italian Communist Party in the consolidation of Parliamentary democracy in Italy' in G. Pridham (ed.), *Securing Democracy: Political Parties and Regime Consolidation in Southern Europe*, London, Routledge.
Schmitter, P.C. (1974), 'Still the Century of Corporatism?' *Review of Politics*, **36**, 85–131.
— (1977), 'Modes of Interest Intermediation and Models of Societal Change in Western Europe', *Comparative Political Studies*, **1**.
— (1982), 'Reflections on Where the Theory of Neo-Corporatism has Gone and Where the Praxis of Neo-Corporatism May Be Going' in *Patterns of Corporatist Policy-making*, G. Lehmbruch and P.C. Schmitter (eds), London and Beverly Hills, Sage.
— (1988), *The Consolidation of Political Democracy in Southern Europe*, Stanford University and Istituto Universitario Europeo (manuscript, third revised introd. version) first version: 1985.
— (ed.) (forthcoming), *Interest Groups and Democratic Consolidation in Southern Europe*.
Solé Tura, J. (1982), 'Democracia y eficacia en las Cortes españolas de la transicion', *Parlamento y democracia*, op. cit., 93–108.
—, and M.A. Aparicio Perez (1984), *Las Cortes Generales en el sistema constitucional*, Madrid, Tecnos.
Steffani, W. (1965), 'Amerikanischer Kongress und Deutscher Bundestag—ein Vergleich', in *Aus Politik und Zeitgeschichte*, **43**, 12–24.
Walkland, S.A., and M. Ryle (eds) (1977), *The Commons in the 70s*, London, Fontana.
Weinbaum, M.G. (1975), 'Classification and Change in Legislative Systems: With Particular Application to Iran, Turkey, and Afghanistan', in Boynton and Kim (eds), *Legislative Systems in Developing Countries*, Duke University Press, Durham (N.C.), 31–68.
Wenturis, N. (1987), 'Parliamentarism in Greece', Conference on Parliaments and Democratic Consolidation in Southern Europe, Volkswagen Foundation and Fundaçion Bofill, Barcelona, 29–31 October.

2 Parliaments, consolidation, institutionalization: a minimalist view*

Giuseppe Di Palma

What does it take to consolidate a new democracy—one that replaces a dictatorship of sorts? Most analysts, I feel, would counter the question with another: what do we mean by consolidation? And there, I am afraid, lies a danger. To counter an empirical/theoretical question with a semantic/definitional one, that is, to rephrase a concern with explaining something as a concern with the nature of what is to be explained, is a common defensive impulse. There is a tendency to react like this when we confront concepts that contain implicit, poorly articulated, conventionally held theories. Classical political concepts like modernization and development are good examples. Yet the issue, as the history of those concepts shows, remains theoretical. Thus, when it comes to consolidation, we should try to avoid the impulse to take refuge behind questions of definition—which would be poorly driven by the implicit theories. The task, on the contrary, is to focus on the theories, their inherent problems and inconsistencies, in order to arrive at a definition. In a way, if what it takes to consolidate democracy depends on what we mean by consolidation, the meaning of consolidation depends on what it takes to achieve it.

This seems, of course, a rather embarrassingly vicious circle; precisely the circle which the discussion on the nature of consolidation is largely and unwittingly caught in. We can break out of the circle if we reflect on some of the motives for the recent scholarly interest in democratic consolidation. In so doing, I intend to put forward a minimalist or simple view of consolidation: a view (dare I say a definition?) drawn from the theoretical argument that it takes

*This chapter has been published previously be *Revista Española de Investigaciones Sociologicas*, n. 42, April–June 1988.

less to 'consolidate' a democracy than we conventionally used to think. I will corroborate my argument by reference to the role of parliaments in consolidation, taking account of recent transitions to democracy.

On consolidation

One striking feature of the resurgence of interest in consolidation is that it closely follows from or anticipates the advent of democratic governments in a number of countries ranging over three continents: southern Europe, Latin America, and more recently south-east and east Asia.[1] What these countries have in common is that in view of their previous political records and the standards of classical literature on democratization they should be difficult democracies. Plainly speaking, then, to study democratic consolidation with reference to these countries is another way of addressing the old problems of success, failure, endurance, stability in these and, by extension, other ostensibly difficult democracies of the past. After all, although the exercise would have methodological merits, we do not question in retrospect the consolidation of success stories like West Germany or Japan. Whatever we may mean by consolidation, we 'know' it was not at issue in those countries. The problem arises when we look at Spain, or Brazil, or the Philippines, or retrospectively the Weimar Republic.

Is the new focus on consolidation also a better way of addressing these old problems? It is at least potentially. In the first place, it involves an explicit decision to concentrate systematically on the phenomenology of democratic formation *per se*, in a wide range of cases. The purpose is to identify a common core to democratic formation, from which *minimal* prescriptions for difficult democracies can be derived. In the second place, this requires an equally explicit effort to distinguish consolidation from other analytically or empirically related concepts. Third, and most importantly, this new systematic focus on consolidation is accompanied by a critical reading of most past contributions to democratic formation, and the development of new theoretical orientations that look upon the process more favourably. I have said before that uncertainty about the meaning of a concept reflects the fact that the concept encapsulates poorly articulated theories. In the recent debate on democratic consolidation, the residual flaw is that the new and more positive theoretical orientations are not brought to bear fully on the explication of the concept. Hence the lingering uncertainty.

Let me show both the virtues and the flaw by starting with the previous literature on democratic experiments.[2] The problem with most of this literature (I will mention the very few notable exceptions later on) is not a dearth of hypotheses or hunches, but rather a superabundance of obsolescent ones. Its catalogue of everything that was or could go wrong with a new democracy, and why, was quite large. Indeed, it is not always clear what weaknesses in the democratic record the literature meant to explain: the impression is often of a plethora of factors which have an interchangeable bearing on multiple targets. The reason for this is that the literature was mainly inspired, and therefore captured, by instances of resounding and unquestionable failures: the failures of the inter-war period in Europe. The lesson of those failures has then been extended to the study of new European democracies after World War II, and to the endemically most difficult context of that cultural fragment of Europe which is Latin America. This has resulted in a theoretical orientation that looks at new democracies in the twentieth century as saddled with original problems that are inherently difficult to remove. The problem is one of legitimacy, no less, compounded by one of performance. Since, typically, these new democracies replace dictatorial or traditional oligarchical regimes rather abruptly, and under conditions of crisis, they are born without the support and consent of the losers. And since they are by definition systems of compromise that cannot satisfy those who expect more radical and unilateral socio-political results from the change, they are ultimately beleaguered on both sides. The effects on performance, even overlooking objective structural and socio-economic obstacles, can be quite staggering. Therefore, within this theoretical orientation, the successful redemocratization of—for example—West Germany is seen as an exception largely linked to the exogenous factor of foreign occupation and reconstruction under Allied supervision. The case is still outweighed by the examples—to remain within Europe—of Weimar, inter-war Austria, the Spanish Republic, Italy after both wars and the Fourth French Republic (Di Palma, 1984: 172–73).

It is, however, rather problematic to generalize from the few and very difficult cases of the inter-war period to other contexts. One is reminded, among other things, of Juan Linz's cautionary analysis of the significant role of time in regime changes (Linz, 1986). Also, it should be stressed that the object of immediate investigation of much of the literature on the inter-war period was not so much the onset of democracy, as its demise. The pre-eminent interest in explaining its demise—an event that had already occurred—accounts in turn for the understandable tendency to see the event retrospectively as rooted in the origins of the new democracies. Yet, it is clear that the demise may have neither necessary nor sufficient connection with defects inherent in its birth (assuming that there were any). Even a well-consolidated democracy, however we may choose to define it, is not thereby granted eternity. Birth, consolidation, demise *may* belong to different phases, deserving analysis in their own terms.

A greater attention to these issues and to the open-ended nature of the process of democratic construction is what makes the more recent literature on democratic transitions so valuable. The literature reveals a telling shift of attention towards other problems. To be sure, it remains sensitive to the early cases of difficult democracy. As I have already pointed out, behind this attention to the novel concept of consolidation, there is the instinctive and long-standing concern with democratic success or failure. But it is also a prospectively orientated literature, engaged not so much in explaining past democratic records as in assessing, predicting and prescribing ongoing processes of democratization. It is a literature stimulated by a wave of democratic inaugurations, which have taken place over the last decade in three continents. And it is a literature that takes some comfort from the fact that these new democracies, thought difficult by the objective criteria given salience in the old literature, seem to be doing, at least in some cases (Spain being the most revealing), better than that literature would have led us to believe. This promising record, but perhaps even more the novel attention to what are still prospective processes, help explain why the study of contemporary democratic transitions has given rise to a new theoretical orientation—labelled by David Collier, who borrows the term from Albert Hirshman, as *possibilism* (Collier and Norden, 1986).

Possibilism, explains Collier, stems from two simple methodological considerations. The first (which he calls the objective premise of possibilism) is the fact that in political matters, and in matters of regime change in particular causal relations are only probable, and outcomes uncertain. This is so even without reference to choice and discretion. The second consideration (the subjective premise to possibilism) is that choice and discretion, while constrained, must therefore play a crucial role in bending uncertain outcomes and promoting goals—a role the more deterministic orientations to regime change are slow to recognize.

This strategic choice view of change is, naturally, quite appropriate when dealing with prospective events. To say the least, it is more pliable (and less risky!) when it comes to attempting predictions than a structural-deterministic view. Moreover, it can be extended to reassess just as effectively the difficult record of new democracies from the past. It can look at it as possibly a matter of strategies that went wrong at some point in the life of those democracies. I mentioned that this line of analysis is not entirely new. It owes much to a few selected pioneers, who set themselves apart from the received wisdom by their early attention to the role of strategic choice. I am thinking in particular of Juan Linz, whose extensive work on past and present regimes looks at political survival and breakdown as questions of 'political crafting'; of Albert Hirschman, whose unconventional possibilist view of Latin American development I have just mentioned; of Dankwart Rustow, whose long-overlooked seminal article on democratic transitions takes issue with the view that democracy is the rare product of very special objective conditions and cultural traditions, with which only selected countries are blessed (Linz, 1978; Linz and Stepan, undated; Hirschman, 1965, 1971; Rustow, 1970).

In fact, the work of these pioneers suggests that a strategic choice approach to democratization is not simply possibilistic; more to the point, by stressing choice and discretion it also leads to a minimalist view of democratization. It rediscovers, to follow Rustow, that democracy functions ideally as an open and open-ended game (hence the aptness of the strategic approach to democratiz-ation). And precisely because it is a game designed to seek a fair balance of winning and losing over time and in multiple arenas, without requesting from the players anything more than readiness to play, the democratic bargain (as others have called it) shows itself as potentially attractive to many players, and capable of converting the reluctant ones. This means that '. . . the rules of the democratic game are more a matter of instrumental agreement worked out among competitive leaderships and institutions, *which accept to remain competitive within the new agreement*, than one of pre-existing popular or elite consensus on fundamentals'. It means that ' "genuine" democrats need not pre-exist democracy, and in point of fact they rarely do so in any substantial numbers' (Di Palma, 1984: 173).

All of this has consequences for the analysis of consolidation. A theoretical orientation that stresses possibilism suggests and justifies a systematic focus on the process of democratization. It also guides us towards an appropriate definition of consolidation within the context of democratization. The advantage of freeing theories of democratization from any assumptions about the need for consensus on fundamentals or for any other cultural or structural requisites, or to put it more accurately, the advantage of transforming these requisites into challenges to those who build democracy, is to free consolidation from excessive conceptual baggage and to distinguish between what consolidation is and what it may take. We are required to look at consolidation as merely 'crafting', to use Linz's term. In my opinion crafting, or consolidation, must be given a rather essential minimalist meaning, one dictated by the essence of the prospective democratic game as it relates to its candidate players. Since the democratic game is an open and open-ended one that expects nothing of its players beyond their readiness to play, setting up and consolidating democracy (the two processes, we will see, are not much different) refers to crafting the rules of competition so as to attract players, many of whom may be unconvinced by the game of even opposed to it. More precisely, it refers to crafting those rules so as to remove or render inoperative for the foreseeable future the temptation of essential players, most obviously but not exclusively those who had reservations to begin with, to boycott the game.

I realize that most of what I will say in the remainder of the chapter rests on the persuasiveness of this last statement. Be this as it may, it should be clear that to emphasize the potential virtues of crafting as a device to recruit and hold on to players is not to belittle the difficulties attending the process—quite the contrary. The rules we are talking about (what we may call the procedural core of the democratic game) are the rules regulating competitive access to government. To guarantee access, they must protect the rights of the opposition and its prospects of winning at the same time as they protect the rights of those who govern. For this reason they may be considered as excessively restrictive by some prospective players, and excessively permissive by others. On the other hand, they may inspire the same type of players to comply, or alternatively to turn competition into licence till the game breaks down. That is why fixing the rules and bringing players and rules together must be connected, logically and optimally in time.[3] That is why setting the rules to everybody's satisfaction is no mean feat. And that is why we need to examine closely how the rules are crafted—in the deputized places, such as constitutional assemblies, and anywhere else where rules are hammered out or negotiated.

Once we recognize that defining and fixing the core rules for competition is the essence of the process of consolidation, no further assumptions can and should be made about what it takes to consolidate—especially, as I said, if the assumptions are of the requisite type, which would contaminate and inflate its meaning. Indeed, having agreed that the meaning of consolidation should be extracted from a possibilist and minimalist theoretical orientation toward democratization, nothing else we can say about ways of pursuing consolidation adds anything of significance to its meaning. There is in fact no universally prescribed way of pursuing consolidation, for the simple and largely uncontested

reason that there is no optimal set of rules for competition ie, no single set of
rules capable of attracting essential players under most circumstances.

My claims seem to have unfortunate consequences when it comes to
recognizing and pointing out 'when' a particular democracy is consolidated.
They imply no easy way of determining exactly this point. On the other hand,
most of the conventional ways of recognizing when consolidation comes about
are no more successful. Some of them tend to beg more questions than they
answer; some reify the event; some push it into too remote a future. Problems
arise because those ways either borrow another concept—often, if possibly
unwittingly, from excessively demanding theoretical orientations towards
democratization—or they adopt *ad hoc* criteria and indicators of convenience.
Such shortcomings are found even in the literature on democratization most
sympathetic to a possibilist and minimalist approach. They reveal a residual
hesitation to draw the full implications of the chosen approach to the concept of
consolidation. Guillermo O'Donnell's reflections on consolidation which have
inspired my analysis offer good illustrations of the shortcomings (O'Donnell,
1985).

For example, equating consolidation with achievement of regime legitimacy
—in the sense of principled allegiance—raises a myriad of objections. The most
important one, as O'Donnell and a few other scholars have argued recently, is
unquestionably one of validity (O'Donnell, 1985; Linz (undated); Przeworski,
1986). I have already made the point in previous pages, but let me restate it.
Even if we assume (a daring assumption) that public opinion surveys or other
measuring instruments can capture the relevant sections of public opinion, the
relevant objects of allegiance (regimes, not goverments, nor single institutions),
and the necessary degree of allegiance, there is little doubt that legitimacy is not
required. Therefore, using legitimacy in connection with consolidation—as a
necessary and sufficient criterion or indicator, or as part and parcel of the
definition—is a typical instance of inflating the latter concept.

Obviously, legitimacy, though not necessary, may be sufficient. But here we
shade into another type of shortcoming: the tendency to chose procedural
criteria for consolidation which have the advantage of being unfailingly recogniz-
able has the disadvantage of being too demanding (or else *ad hoc* and make-do).
The criterion event of peaceful rotation of parties in government is a typical
example. Several authors, including myself, have used the event—especially
after the victory of opposition in Spain, Portugal, Greece—as almost fail-safe
evidence of regime legitimation. We could therefore use it with even greater
assurance to recognize consolidation. Similarly, if reliability is our prime concern
in establishing the presence of consolidation, then it would be certainly prudent
to protect ourselves and employ more than one criterion. But this way of
proceeding, which is adopted particularly where there is an absence of a clear
theoretical underpinning to the concept of consolidation, amounts to having the
concept driven by the measuring problem.[4] Thus, the adoption of criteria that
are easy to recognize and sufficient, yet difficult to achieve and not necessary,
ends up by giving an equally demanding definition of consolidation—to the point
where the overburdened concept loses the power to discriminate. An excellent
case in point is contemporary Italy—a country with unique democratic history,
whose significant events would fail to pass most conventional hard tests of

consolidation. Yet labelling Italian democracy 'unconsolidated' would be unenlightening and extravagant. To do so would bring us back to the conventional theories of democratization which the example of Italy has helped to revise.[5] Naturally, absence of rotation in the Italian governments is no accident—but does it having anything to do with consolidation?

Not all procedural tests for consolidation are inherently difficult to meet. Some criteria can be made as easy (or as difficult) as we wish—but the cost is arbitrariness. Usually, these criteria are linked not to a single event, but to repetition and cumulation: a number of free elections, a number of parliaments, a stabilization in electoral results, the development of seniority in parliament, government, or party cadres. The idea is intuitive that the passing of time (hence the routinization and stabilization of events, personnel and institutions) are part of the process of consolidation. But how much time? Without a theoretical guide, the arbitrariness of any time-limit is easy to see. There are cases, which we have already mentioned and to which I will return, in which time (more precisely a number of elections and parliaments or other institutional occurrences) does not help consolidation—on the contrary. Elections and parliaments may themselves be at issue. And there are cases in which time, a repetition of events, are past in consolidation and add nothing *decisive* to it. Let me pursue the latter point at length.

What I am suggesting in this regard is that criteria of repetition and cumulation come uncomfortably close to criteria, called by O'Donnell 'substantive criteria', which emphasize the development and establishment of specific democratic institutions. To be sure, as O'Donnell notes, one problem with these criteria is that they push the definition one step backward: how do we recognize that these institutions have acquired those qualities of institution-alization, cohesiveness, autonomy, authenticity, durability that presumably indicate regime consolidation? To begin with what does each of these concepts refer to? But the problem is not really one of tautology and circularity—one definition sending us back to the other. I wish to argue that the problem is again one of validity, of overburdening and contaminating the concept with concerns about phases, events, and processes of democratic life which, though probably connected with consolidation, may go beyond its requirements and stretch its time parameters.

The notion that democratic consolidation is no more and no less than consolidation of democratic institutions, in their internal structuring and external relations, seems an intuitive and almost unassailable notion. This is so because the consolidation of institutions seems to imply their own and the regime's legitimation. But does consolidation in effect amount to no more and no less than consolidation of specific institutions and their networks? Philippe Schmitter speaks of these networks as partial regimes and sees democratic consolidation as a process that involves the structuration of several partial regimes, each linking different institutions and their respective publics, clients, members or voters (Schmitter, 1987). He sees structuration as transforming what are initially accidental and contingent relationships into relationships that are reliably known, regularly practiced, and habitually accepted. My own impression is that the study of how democratic institutions settle down (to use a neutral term) is a very important aspect of the study of democratization. It is worth pursuing *per se*, especially when it comes to relationships between institutions. Undoubtedly, understanding the genesis and functioning of institutional networks will tell us a lot about the performance of a new democracy, its political style etc. The catalogue of what we can learn is infinite. Among other things, institutional networks reflect the special ways in which democratic consolidation has been engineered, including the residual problems and costs which may have resulted from the process. I will return to this issue and some other intriguing possibilities later.

On institutionalization

Yet, when everything is said and done, the consolidation of a democratic regime remains something logically different from the structuration of its institutions and their networks. Hence, it is more appropriate to talk of structuration, and particularly institutionalization in Samuel Huntington's sense, rather than consolidation when referring to institutions and networks (Huntington, 1965). The logical disjuncture should be particularly clear, and its theoretical implications farreaching, if we remain fully aware that we are starting from a possibilist/minimalist approach to democratization—one that looks at consolidation as crafting the competitive rules so as to prevent essential players from boycotting the game. Crafting is a notion quite different from institutionalization, especially when it involves the straight, urgent and demanding task of keeping players in the game. Crafting is a time-bound process designed to ensure that even unwilling players enter the game, so as to remove the issue from the democratization agenda. The essence of its success is timing and speed, as much as inventiveness. Institutionalization is, almost by definition, a process that takes its time and cannot be cut short— irrespective of how other aspects of the democratization process are going. Institutionalization, according to Huntington, gives institutions value and stability, and is assessed by a number of criteria, of which coherence and autonomy are the most revealing; all point to the role of time, habituation, testing. In sum, crafting (in the sense described above) logically precedes institutionalization. If successful, we may well claim consolidation well before institutionalization is advanced. If unsuccessful, then the longer process of institutionalization is itself stalemated.

For example, a new democracy whose essential players include none who are recalcitrant should define the rules of the game rather swiftly (and without special crafting). Nevertheless, institutionalization will have to take its time. A good case in point could be West Germany. Let us take—as counter example of a case of difficult democratization—El Salvador. The government of Napoleon Duarte has tried to run democratic elections for some years, yet acceptance of the democratic game by reluctant players remains a distant prospect. Thus, even granting that the government is running democratic elections because it intends to build a democratic regime, and for no other ambiguous purpose, we must conclude that El Salvador does not yet have a democratic regime. Crafting, in effect, is failing. As regards institutionalization in El Salvador, the point is not that it is taking its time, but that the recurrence of democratic behaviour (the elections) does not constitute, even in part, institutionalization. Because crafting is failing, it makes no sense to think of institutionalization.

These examples bring us back to the points raised earlier that consolidation benefits from being concluded swiftly (although, witness El Salvador, it may not), and that in any case the process is logically part and parcel of the first phase of democratization. There is an instinctive inclination to think of consolidation as something that follows a phase of democratic transition. But, though the distinction has some immediate convenience, it is largely illusory. The reason we think of democratic transition and consolidation as consecutive phases is that we have difficulties shaking off the assumption that consolidation is closely enmeshed with protracted processes of institutionalization. Once we accept that the relation is far from symbiotic, we can then look at consolidation as the logical conclusion of the transition phase. It stands to reason that the transition phase should not be considered over when the first democratic elections take place, or when a constitutional assembly gathers, but when competition is no longer at issue. And whether democratic elections or, more likely, the gathering of a constituent body have an impact on the closing of that issue is itself a problematic question (see again El Salvador) to which I shall return.

But the more interesting aspect of consolidation and institutionalization is not their sequencing but their causal relation. In fact, my discussion of phases has already suggested a reversal of the argument that places institutionalization at the roots of consolidation; instead, the removal of the breakdown potentials from the competitive issue has now become the necessary and sufficient condition for institutionalization to proceed—especially for those institutions and networks encompassing the competitive game. Once the players have entered into the spirit of the democratic bargain, the drama of a potential breakdown is gone and the routinization of the bargain through institutions and institutional networks can get under way. I should stress, however, that the implications for democratic institutions are less mechanical and straightforward, and possibly more intriguing, than my statement suggests. Institutionalization is not a residual process, and institutions are not inert containers. The way in which consolidation comes about, the strains and sacrifices that accompany it, may tell us much about how institutionalization may proceed, but they do not tell us everything. Further, institutional processes may have their own impact, in some cases a significant one, on how the democratic game is continued. I shall offer two reasons why this should be the case. First, the process of translating the terms of the democratic settlement into institutional roles and routines is a prolonged one and its outcome somewhat open. We are dealing with emerging institutions, whose future performance is still in the realm of the probable and expected. This means that whether the risk of a breakdown stays out of the agenda of a new democracy depends also on how institutions turn out. Thus, on the one hand, as institutions emerge, they should become valued *per se* and should make the chances of players backing out ever more remote. They should at least render inoperative any reservations that players may residually hold. On the other hand, such players' 'socialization' (following, as it were, their recruitment to the game) remains contingent, and consent relies on institutional performance.

This contingency is even more apparent if we bear in mind Rustow's point that the democratic compromise is a second-best choice for practically all competing players. That is to say that the compromise is instrumental and calculated, and must be tested, for this and for the previous reason, against performance (Di Palma, 1986: 184). My assertion is not meant to reintroduce through the backdoor the risk of a breakdown in the phase of institutionalization, with the unwitting result of stretching consolidation into institutionalization. Once the players have entered into democratic bargain, and once its translation into institutions and networks is under way, the drama of a possible breakdown is largely gone. More precisely, the risks of a breakdown must be viewed in a new and more constrained context—the context of the new phase. As new institutions begin to emerge, the way they operate will increasingly constitute the relevant criteria for testing the compromise—even for players who were originally reluctant. In other words, because democracy is essentially an open and open-ended game, testing will progressively occur *on democracy's own democratic terms*. It will emerge, less dramatically, from within the democratic compromise (Di Palma, 1986: 189). But since testing will involve institutions and processes, it may have consequences for institutionalization which were not originally anticipated.

Under some circumstances, testing the democratic compromise against institutional performance is not that demanding. It may be an occasional and implicit process, and accommodate considerable variation around institutional arrangements, considerable uncertainty around expected oucomes and considerable tolerance by competing actors for a string of defeats. This is the case particularly when the original convergence on the rules of the game involves preponderantly players with a largely implicit bias for democracy. In such a case, not only is consolidation achieved early and smoothly, it also opens no particular issues of lingering contention for the emerging institutions. Under other, and in fact more common circumstances, a whole assortment of recalcitrant or uncommitted players may be induced to subscribe to these rules, with sacrifices that are not sustained by an instinctive bias for democracy. This may leave substantial fuzziness concerning the terms of the compromise, and its exact interpretation. Players may pull on those terms and, later, on how they are being implemented institutionally, more than is expected even of players in a competitive context. Here, more interesting vistas open up, as embarking upon institutionalization shows the extent to which the beginning of the democratic game may reflect a constrictive stalemate of contrasting expectations.

One institutional outcome is that contrasting expectations and interpretations disappear more or less of their own accord during the phase of institutionaliz-ation, possibly by informal accommodations and without dogged renegotiations. After all, routinization has its ways of socializing players, clarifying norms, reshaping roles beyond original projections. In such a case, institutionalization serves to perfect and improve upon the original game. One example of this, although not perfect, could be Greece as it moved from conservative to socialist governments. What appeared to be a democratic system slanted in a presidential direction and unappealing to the socialists of PASOK has evolved into a full accepted more genuinely parliamentary system. True, this required constitutional reform at the sufferance of the conservatives; nevertheless, neither the reform nor its aftermath have the makings of a serious constitutional conflict. But things may not always work out this smoothly. Given a constrictive compromise between players to begin with, institutionalization can have its share of problems. Can institutions still respond? Is there a range of responses? In one rather unpromising scenario, best exemplified by the Portuguese transition to democracy, an excessive and constrictive concern with the terms of the democratic agreement may call upon wary and reluctant players to work out early on—in constitutional or pre-constitutional pacts—a rather elaborate and detailed set of competitive rules. These may include, as in Portugal, rules 'monitoring' competition by means of a special institutional guarantor (the army, a joint council or junta of sort). The function of the rules should be to reconcile contrasting expectations between government and opposition, cabinets and presidents, elected institutions and self-appointed guarantors. Reconciliation should be sought in the relations between different institutions (electoral machineries, parties, parliaments, governments, presidents, guarantors), but also inside single institutions. Hence, operational difficulties will surface precisely when those rules must find institutional implementation. The problems caused by the Portuguese unwieldy constitutional pact amply demonstrate this. Though it may be too little or too late to pull out, one solution adopted in Portugal is to alter radically the original agreement, perhaps with the help of a change in the relative popularity of players. Meanwhile, institutional processes fail to acquire value and coherence; though in failing to do so they also help reveal the problems created by the direction that the bargain first took. But in another scenario that concern with the terms of the competitive agreement may lead to exactly the opposite strategy: no painstakingly detailed pacts to begin with, but a broadly couched agreement *a futuro* so as to increase the interest in entering the game. In this case, the most intriguing strategy is to accept fuzziness—if it does not disappear on its own—to agree to disagree and to continue to argue. Trying to clarify and pin down the agreement once and for all, we know, has costs that are not always palatable or necessary. Somebody will be required to make sacrifices which were previously hidden. Or it may not be possible, given an unchanging balance of forces. If properly understood and put to use, fuzziness has, on the other hand, its merits—as readers familiar with my work, especially on Italy, may appreciate. We shall return to this issue when we look at parliaments. In a nutshell however, learning to live with fuzziness means giving the reasons for fuzziness a political dignity of their own. It recognizes the essential roles of all players, even if they entered the compromise from different perspectives. And it calls for a degree of muddling through and accommodation in institutional implementation and performance that makes that recognition operative. All of this is of substantial value precisely because, as I have already stated when introducing the notion that consent must be tested and reproduced, fuzziness invites a more demanding and continuous testing of institutions.[6]

However this leads us to a counterintuitive conclusion, especially those among us who move from a close equation between consolidation, institutionalization and democratization. Poor institutionalization—especially a degree of incoherence in single institutions and in institutional networks that encompass the competitive game—is neither always nor entirely detrimental to democratic stabilization. It can be the inert cost that must be paid in order to bring reluctant players into the game. More than that, poor institutionalization can in fact be turned, with some virtue and fortune, into a means for keeping those players in the game. Strange as it seems poor institutional coherence may give institutions a value of their own in the eyes of contrasting players.

On parliaments

Much of what I am about to say regarding the place of parliaments in democratic consolidation is already contained in, or can be derived directly from, the first part of this chapter: from my minimalist view of consolidation, and from my call for a more guarded distinction between strategies of consolidation and processes of institution building. To restate my case, it is important to distinguish between the role of parliaments as agents of consolidation and their role as agents–subjects of institution-building. It is in regard to the latter role, more than in regard to the former—when parliaments are themselves still *in fieri*—that they reveal more fully their importance as institutions, by the way they weigh on the reproduction of democratic consent.

As regards parliaments as agents of consolidation, what understandly captures the attention of the analyst is the fact that parliaments are elected. As elections are the benchmark of the competitive game, it would stand to reason that the election of a first parliament, especially in a parliamentary system and especially if entrusted with constitution-making power, should bring consolidation closer. Yet, there are limits: in more cases than we realize, parliaments can either be institutionally insufficient, or an unnecessary surplus in removing breakdown games. To be sure, there are good reasons why moving the democratic transition toward 'founding elections' should have consequences for consolidation. As Guillermo O'Donnell and Philippe Schmitter argue convincingly, calling for elections, and by extension putting the first representative body to work, means that political parties should at last emerge as the central political actors; that their attention should shift to the more orderly and constructive business of building diverse national support and defining–implementing the rules of contestation; that even a prospective opposition should have an added incentive to sacrifice the support of more radical groups and reluctant players, in the interest of finally holding elections and securing representation from the very start (O'Donnell *et al.*, 1986: 57–9).

All of this is eminently sensible, but it is based on an obvious and yet insufficiently stressed assumption. The assumption is that, in one way or another, explicitly or implicitly, willy-nilly, the significant parties have already come to an understanding, *before* entering the elections, that the electoral context will offer tolerable chances of representation to all, and that the newly elected body will act to constitutionalize the rules of contestation.[7] If so, it stands to reason that the convening of that body should further strengthen previous commitments to the game. Once the democratic bargain is entered into, this initial success is an incentive to continue; and those who believe in the bargain or can at least rationalize it should be rewarded. None the less, I should stress that, given the previous understanding, the actions of parliament—although necessary to further articulate, possibly renegotiate, and finally constitutionalize the bargain—may be, more often that we think, 'over-determing' (to use a word that, by claiming too much, should nail down my point). The chances of going back have been severely curtailed, and the democratic game looks more and more like the only game in town. On the other hand, if a previous understanding of sorts does not exist, elections and parliaments may lose considerable effectiveness as devices to remove breakdown games. The contrast between the experiences of democratization in Europe and Central America serves to illustrate the difference.

I have argued elsewhere that the democratic transitions of Europe, after World War II and during the seventies, gained considerably from the fact that the new democracies could count on recycling for democracy a host of political and state institutions with a long historical tradition of their own, a tradition which predated dictatorship and was stronger than any alliance of convenience with the latter (Di Palma, 1986). Thus, once the crisis of a European dictatorship was underway, those institutions, each with their coveted spheres of autonomy and social presence to reassert were compelled toward coexistence—the kind of institutional coexistence that is the at heart of democracy. That is why, as I have argued, the founding elections of Europe's new democracies were never really meant to decide upon democracy. As a tool for demcracy, they were a surplus; as a tool against it, they proved to be late and insufficient. Rather, elections and elected institutions were knowingly used to legitimize after the fact, and even with some delay, choices that had already been made through the revival of civil society and of political and state institutions. And it is instructive to notice that in possibly the only case where the legitimizing function of elections and a new parliament were impeached (Portugal in the mid-seventies), the eventual losers were those forces—the military-civilian left—that tried to impeach the process.[8] In other European democracies, the fact that elections and representation were open to all sorts of political forces, including parties whose commitment to democracy may originally have been in question, never seriously endangered the process. If I limit my remarks to southern Europe, it is true that in both post-war Italy and post-Franco Spain interparty negotiations continued after elections and during the constituent periods and acquired legitimacy from this very fact. But was there ever a serious risk that negotiations would break down and democratiz-ations suffer a major setback? In effect, even in the Italian case—a highly contentious one, for reasons that hardly need restatement—the commitment to mutual survival, the realization of its advantages and the costs of acting otherwise, had prepared political parties, even discounting the similar influence of the international context, for the hardfought sacrifices required of constitutional negotiations. In Italy, those negotiations *coincided* with the expulsion of the extreme left from the post-war government coalition and did not collapse because of that. As far as Spain is concerned, the particularly smooth and consensual nature of the constitutional process makes it a very fitting illustration of overdetermination in the European context. Again, this is not to belittle constitutional crafting, but, rather to emphasize that the need for mutually tolerable solutions was already recognized and only awaited constitutional legitimation. But, in different ways, Greece is just as revealing an illustration of overdetermination. Here, the drafting of the constitution showed little cooperation among parties. By and large, the left stayed out, and the process was dominated by Karamanlis's *Nea Demokratia*. It was not as auspicious a beginning. But did this greater partisanship reflect a realization that the left was lost to the democratic process (hence Karamanlis's decision to go it alone)? It seems more convincing to argue the opposite way. Did the left at least reject the particular democratic model embodied in the constitution? It did reject it since presidentialism and the electoral law seemed to stack the cards against the left. However, when winning a majority, it managed to revise the constitution to its liking. As I pointed out in the first part of the chapter, constitutional disagreement never escalated into a full constitutional crisis.[9]

When we move, on the other hand, to Central America, elections — which in Europe seem to be *within* democracy — seem instead to be *about* democracy. They seem to be employed as a strategic tool to settle the context between dissenting political forces during periods of uncertainty and protracted transition. And they seem to be preferred by some factions at the sufferance or against the resistance of other factions. In this and similar cases elections are employed and parliaments convened despite the absence or weakness of those conditions for institutional coexistence more typical of new European democracies. Assuming that good intentions are present, assuming that elections and parliaments are revived, in a *fuite en avant*, to pre-empt the forces that work against institutional coexistence, it is still intuitively the case that even a string of parliaments will find the feat of pre-empting those forces exceeding difficult. Will it find it downright impossible? I would not claim this much. Forcing an electoral and parliamentary solution *is* one way of convincing reluctant players of the need for a democratic compromise. Assuming that committed democratic players manage to run free competitive elections in a stalemated context and to obtain significant electoral support, this *per se* would be a major strategic achievement. Electoral support is an added resource, and discounting a freely elected parliament takes some doing. Nevertheless, attractive as this scenario may be from the perspective of a possibilistic approach to consolidation, it remains extremely difficult to execute it. Political developments in El Salvador since 1984 resemble this scenario very much, but consolidation is not yet in sight, despite the presence of a freely elected parliament (Karl, 1986). On the contrary, a combination of centrifugal pulls within and outside parliament continues to prevent its emergence as *the* institution for processing conflict. Similar considerations apply to the freely elected parliament of the Philippines, after the fall of Marcos.[10]

I shall finally consider parliaments operating in systems where the danger of a breakdown has been removed. My observations concentrate on parliamentary systems, as the post-war democracies of southern Europe basically are. Whatever the role of parliaments in removing breakdown games — whether it is disputed, as in Portugal, or overdetermining, as in Spain, Greece and Italy — parliaments now emerge as subjects/agents in the phase of institution-building. As such, they should assume a central role in the reproduction of democratic consent. Further, as I have suggested in the discussion on institutionalization, this role, just like the ways in which parliaments (and other democratic institutions) turn out, should be somewhat or largely independent of how consolidation has been achieved. For example, even if the removal of breakdown games has been particularly difficult and protracted, ways of shoring up or monitoring and correcting the precarious agreement thus reached can develop in the process of building parliaments. I shall devote the rest of the chapter to further illustrations of these points.

In order to understand how parliaments in particular play their own role in the reproduction of consent, and in order to conduct systematic comparisons, we must start by removing a misconception. To speak of parliaments as agents in the reproduction of consent is to speak elliptically and elusively. This language is the often inadvertent legacy of nineteenth-century constitutionalism, which sees parliaments (and governments) as separate and independent institutional subjects in their own right.[11] It is a legacy still present in post-war constitutional pacts, where rules and prerogatives concerning parliaments and executives occupy a key role but little is said about parties. However, within parliamentary systems, parliaments, like governments, are not so much their own institutional agents, as they are arenas within which, since the demise of nineteenth-century constitutional dualism, political parties act as agents. Because of this unique 'heteronomy' of parliaments, it is to parties that we must turn to understand how the constitutional functions of parliaments come to be implemented and how, as implementation (ie institutionalization) occurs, parliaments come to play a role in the reproduction of consent. As Nelson Polsby pointed out—when drawing his classical distinction between transformative parliaments (the only paradigmatic example of which is the American Congress) and arena-like parliaments (largely coincident with parliamentary systems)—the student of transformative parliaments will tend to focus his attention on the internal structures of those parliaments. On the other hand, the student of arenas will focus instead on party systems, social stratifications, government expectations (Polsby, 1975: 291, 307). Furthermore, because in parliamentary systems the same heteronomy applies to governments, because parties cut across both parliaments and governments, because these constitute the connected arenas within which the competitive game is implemented and the range of its anticipated outcomes is tested, the institutionalization of parliaments does not develop in isolation. What gets institutionalized is not so much parliament as the government–parliament *sottosistema*—ie an interaction network (what Schmitter calls a partial regime) controlled by parties, whose institutions are initially defined externally, and with regard to their role within the *sottosistema*. Compared with a parliament's external roles, its *interna corporis* develop later and as a function of the former: in other words, they lack, especially in the early phases of institutionalization, both internal autonomy and external weight. Once again, in such phases, and whenever institutional changes and adaptations occur, it is to party-controlled interactions within the *sottosistema* that we must turn (Di Palma, 1987).

But what can be said about parties in parliaments/governments that makes systematic sense of how parliaments in particular are formed to reproduce consent? I am inclined to turn to themes and levers that I already employed in previous works and that recur in Cotta's essay cited above.

Given the nature of the two reciprocally connected issues in the reproduction of consent—how the parties will fill the gap between the original compromise and its implementation in the *sottosistema* and how they will verify that implementation against original expectations—three sets of factors seem appropriate and central. They are: the number of parties in government (most decisively, whether the government is coalitional or single party), their internal cohesiveness (especially that of a dominant *formateur* party, if any), the foreseeable chances of credible alternance in government. None of these factors are usually fixed and known at the time of consolidation; hence the gap I just referred to, hence the need to verify it and hence the possibility that parliament's rules of the game be defined or redefined in ways that consolidation could not predict.

Drawing from Cotta's analysis, it can be argued that the smaller the number of parties in government (optimally, the government is by one party), the more cohesive the majority party(ies), and the better *above all*[12] the prospects of credible alternance, the more the set of institutional rules developed by the parties to regulate their interaction within the *sottosistema* and in parliament will approach the model of party government. The model is consensual by definition (otherwise it could hardly operate), and assigns clearly stated and congruent roles to government and opposition, as well as to party and institutional leaderships, in the institutions of the *sottosistema*. In this sense, we may speak of those roles as fully institutionalized roles, in Huntington's sense—even as we recognize the essential heteronomy of the *sottosistema*. One important aspect of the party-government model that speaks to the point of full institutionalization, despite heteronomy, is that its parties act fully and predictably within the institutions they have given themselves. The same cannot be said, as we will see later, when the absence of alternance (as in Italy) rules out party government.

Contemporary Spain, Greece, perhaps Portugal offer reasonably developed approximations of the party-government model. However, if not in Spain, at least in Greece, and certainly in Portugal, it was difficult to imagine such a model at the moment of democratic consolidation, when breakdown games were removed. Not only was the question of alternance still an open one, but another interesting and special aspect of the Greek and particularly of the Portuguese transitions was the fact that the original compromise took a guided and presidentialist form which was not in keeping with a parliamentary system. The problem with this was the duality of authority: a popularly elected president (buttressed in Portugal by a non-democratic institution like the military) and the parties, representing the electorate in parliament and government. If this institutional duality was possible under nineteenth-century constitutionalism, it becomes instead the source of grave conflict (even graver for a new democracy) in an era when parties see themselves as the exclusive propulsive force in the parliament–government *sottosistema*. It is these original institutional choices, made to the detriment of some of the parties (Greece) or practically all of them (Portugal) that put these new democracies on the wrong footing: hence the original reluctance of some of the players, and the later, more or less painful, corrective measures. It would be interesting to document how and to what extent those corrective measures have caused or are causing alterations in the *interna corporis* of the Greek and perhaps more especially the Portuguese parliaments, but this is a matter beyond the scope of this chapter.

The party-government model, however, does not apply easily in a situation in which the prospects of alternance in government are not credible. This is the Italian case, a case in which the parties have been led to adopt what Cotta calls a policentric model, and what I call a *garantista* model. Here too, the model was not quite fixed from the outset, but developed over time. True, the constitutional provisions adopted in Italy, when the question of who could legitimately govern was still open, were designed in *garantista* fashion so as to place a minimum of 'rationalizing' institutional obstacles to free and plural political competition, to the free and effective expression of organized opposition, and from that, to entry into government. By the same token, however, if the prospects of alternance had become credible, nothing in those constitutional provisions—fuzzy and sketchy as they were—would have prevented parties from interpreting and applying them as part of a party-government model. The features of the policentric model, as it finally took hold, are fairly well known. In brief, the model operates by dispersing and diffusing centres of decisional influence between government and opposition, between parliamentary and government leaderships and between these institutional leaderships of the *sottosistema* and party leadership proper. The points which deserve special emphasis are two connected effects of the model. The first is that, by dispersing and diffusing the centres of influence in ill-defined and ill-agreed upon ways within the *sottosistema*, and by allowing party secretariats to overstep the very institutional structures they have created, the model erodes institutional congruence. The second effect permits me to return to a counterintuitive point made at the end of the section on institutionalization. Lack of congruence, the fuzzy institutionalization of parliament in particular, may assist rather than discourage the reproduction of consent. It may do this by opening spaces for the opposition that lack of alternance would otherwise have closed. Clearly, as the last statement implies, reproducing consent under these circumstances requires codes of behaviour quite different, and more taxing, than in cases where party government operates unchallenged. I have indicated how taxing these codes can be in the section on institutionalization. In essence, they are taxing because they require painstaking accommodation of all parties, across and around institutions, blurring the line between majority and opposition; because they are likely to be subject to closer and more frequent scrutiny; because they impose narrower and more exacting margins on the reproduction of consent.

However, my main concern in the conclusion of this chapter is not to elaborate these points of difference,[13] but to stress again the counterintuitive point regarding consent. I shall restate this concern in my brief summary.

Conclusion

This last section on the role of parliaments in consolidation and in the subsequent reproduction of consent, was meant to give flesh to the two main themes that have structured my exploratory analysis. Both themes are derived from Hirschman's methodological possibilism in the study of regime changes, and from Linz's view of democratization as an exercise in timely and efficient political crafting. The first theme is the need to streamline the definition of democratic consolidation, and particularly to distinguish it from the concept of institutionalization. To do otherwise invariably means drawing out the process of consolidation into a distant and open-ended future, where consolidation loses discriminant power—as if every new democracy, not just some, were destined to live for years under the pall of its first jarring days. The role of institution-building is not to secure otherwise shaky democracies—a matter which is either decided before institutions are put to work, or else will stalemate institution-building itself. The role is to verify and reproduce the original agreement between competing players, if and when a tolerable agreement has emerged.

This brings me to the second theme: the possibility that the original agreement be altered or adjusted during the life of democratic institutions, and even improved upon. To say that consolidation has to occur quickly if it is to be successful is not to say that what follows is irrelevant. I have offered sufficient evidence from a number of new European democracies to suggest that maintaining consent is a continuous process, and that institutions can improve on that process in unanticipated and at times counterintuitive ways, even if the original agreement had been grudging. Since the fact remains that these later developments should not be confused with aspects of consolidation, this theme, like the previous one, justifies the minimalist view of consolidation which is the title of this chapter.

Notes

1. I am referring in particular to the work of Guillermo O'Donnell and Philippe Schmitter and their research groups. See G. O'Donnell et al., (1986). This is a series of five volumes, of which the most important for our present purposes is by O'Donnell and Schmitter and is subtitled *Tentative Conclusions about Uncertain Democracies*. See also O'Donnell, (1985); Schmitter, (1987); Morlino, (1986); Mainwaring, (1986).
2. Since I do not wish to select scapegoats, I will refrain from listing authors. Actually, more than a literature, we are talking about a whole paradigmatic view about new democracies, an orthodoxy implicitly reflected even in works that did not necessarily address issues of democratic development.
3. Since trial and error may be involved, it may take some time before rules and players mesh. But time is not irrelevant. We will see that a process that is too protracted can founder.
4. Insisting on the search for reliable and fail-safe indicators may involve us in stultifying, talmudic and reifying discussion, in which we lose track of our objective. Our objective is not to say exactly 'when' consolidation is present, as if consolidation were a clear-cut tangible end-state. Our objective is to give the concept of consolidation theoretical validity. Besides, there is general agreement, as stated in the text, that there are different paths to consolidation. Thus, an event that can be taken as an operational pointer of consolidation in one case would not serve the same purpose in another.

5. One interesting recent contribution to this revision is Joseph La Palombara (1987), *Democracy Italian Style*, New Haven, Yale University Press.

6. There is yet a fourth possibility (after the Greek, the Portuguese, and the Italian): contrasting interpretations lead to a subsequent breakdown. I am not including the case in the text because my topic is institutional adaptations and responses. None the less, if the terms of the compromise stay either fuzzy and controverted or detailed and constrictive, we must recognize that the chances of a breakdown are comparatively enhanced. Players involved in perfecting or renegotiating the original compromise, though eager and willing, may not be skilled at the task. Good as they may have been at the inception, they may be less adept in the phase of institutionalization. Lack of skills, sophistication, and understanding, inability to learn, lack of habituation to the give and take of democracy, excessive fear or boldness, may all carry heavy unanticipated costs. Democratic players may themselves set in motion, inadvertently, a breakdown spiral that other players will exploit. However, dramatic examples notwithstanding (the Spanish Republic being possibly one). I do not consider this scenario the most likely—once the players have entered even in the spirit of the democratic bargain. Therefore, *if* a breakdown occurs, I am also very sceptical of interpretations that play heavily on 'original sins'. It is still not useful to assume that a later breakdown was built in, and leave the analysis at that.

7. O'Donnell and Schmitter do make the assumption explicit.

8. Obviously, we cannot describe the founding elections of Portugal as irrelevant and overdetermining as to the outcome of the transition. Here is a case where the electoral victory of the democratic forces—strongly contested and by no means forgone—made a world of difference as to bringing the removal of breakdown games within close reach. Here, however, is also a case where it then took years and full constitutional revisions (rather than simpler and informal institutional accommodations) before parliament could be called to change the unwieldy constitutional stalemate which the military–civilian left managed to extract as a token of accepting defeat. And the process is not finished yet. Thus, though elections made a difference for democracy, institutional performance suffered in ways somewhat reminiscent of the Central American experience. See Opello (1987).

9. The consensual constitutional process of Spain is examined, Gunther (1985). In his conclusions, Gunther stresses the importance of speed in reaching a satisfactory constitutional compromise. See also De Vergottini (1978). For Greece, see Diamandouros (1987). For Italy see Di Palma, (1977, chap. 3) and (1987b).

10. In the Philippines, and in much of Latin America, a further element that undermines a clear definition of parliaments and parties as the institutions for processing conflict is presidentialism. On parliamentarism versus presidentialism in new democracies see Linz (1985). Another problem with parliament in the Philippines is that it had no role (it did not exist) in the drafting of the new constitution.

11. For a thorough treatment of why this institutional perspective should be considered obsolete, and for the elaboration of a correct perspective on parliament–government relations, from which I draw in the text, see Cotta (1987).

12. The emphasis reflects the sufficient decisiveness of the variable. Alternance is one factor significantly influencing the other two: the number of parties in government and especially their cohesiveness. See again Cotta (1987).

13. For further elaboration see Di Palma (1988).

References

Collier, D. and D.L. Norden (1986), 'Promoting Political Change in Latin America: The Strategic Choice Models of Hirschman, Przeworski, and O'Donnell' (mimeo), Berkeley.

Cotta, M. (1987), 'Il sotto sistema governo-parlamento' in *Rivista Italiana di Scienza Politica*, **17**, 241–83.

De Vergottini, G. (ed.) (1978), *Una costituzione democratica per la Spagna*, Milan, Franco Angeli Editore.

Diamandouros, N. (1987), 'The Politics of Constitution-Making in Postauthoritarian Greece in Historical Perspective', paper presented at the Annual Meeting of the American Political Science Association, Chicago.

Di Palma, G. (1977), *Surviving without Governing*, Berkeley, University of California Press.

— (1984), 'Government Performance: An Issue and Three Cases in Search of Theory', in *West European Government*, **7**.

— (1986a), 'Party Government and Democratic Reproducibility: The Dilemma of New Democracies', in F.G. Castles and R. Wildenmann (eds), *Visions and Realities of Party Government*, Berlin and New York, de Gruyter.

— (1986b), 'The European and the Central American Experience' in G. Di Palma and L. Whitehead (eds), *The Central America Impasse*, London, Croom Helm.

— (1987a), 'Parlamento-arena o parlamento di trasformazione?' in *Rivista Italiana di Scienza Politica*, **17**, 179–202.

— (1987b), 'Tout se tient: The Constitutional Culture of Italy', paper presented at the Annual Meeting of the American Political Science Association, Chicago.

— (1988), 'On Reforming the Grundnorm', paper presented at the Conference on Italy: Political, Social and Economic Change since 1945. Woodrow Wilson International Center for Scholars, Washington, DC.

Gunther, R, (1985), 'Constitutional Change in Contemporary Spain' in K.G. Banting and R. Simeon (eds), *Redesigning the State: the Politics of Constitutional Change*, Toronto and Buffalo, University of Toronto Press.

Hirschman, A. (1965), 'Models of Reform-Mongering' in A. Hirschman, *Journeys Toward Progress*, Garden City, Doubleday.

— (1971), 'Political Economics of Possibilism' in A. Hirschman, *A Bias for Hope*, New Haven, Yale University press.

Huntington, S. (1965), 'Political Development and Political Decay' in *World Politics*, **17**.

Karl, T. (1986), 'Democracy by Design: the Christian Democratic Party in El Salvador' in G. Di Palma *et al.*, op. cit.

La Palombara, J. (1987), *Democracy Italian Style*, New Haven, Yale University Press.

Linz, J. (1978), *The Breakdown of Democratic Regimes: Crisis, Breakdown, and Re-equilibration*, Baltimore and London, Johns Hopkins University Press.

— (1985), 'Democracy: Presidential or Parliamentary: Does it Make a Difference?' Woodrow Wilson International Center for Scholars. Washington, DC.

— (1986), 'Il fattore tempo nei mutamenti di regime' in *Teoria Politica*, **2**, 1, 3–47.

— (undated), 'Legitimacy and Efficacy' (mimeo).

— and A. Stepan, (undated), 'Political Crafting of Democratic Consolidation or Destruction: European and South American Comparisons' (mimeo).

Mainwaring, S. (1986), 'The Consolidation of Democracy in Latin America: Rapporteur's Report', Working Paper n. 73, The Helen Kellogg Institute for International Studies, Notre Dame, University of Notre Dame.

Morlino, L. (1986), 'Consolidamento democratico: definizioni e modelli' in *Rivista Italiana di Scienza Politica*, **16**, 197–238.

— (1986), 'Consolidamento democratico: alcune ipotesi esplicative' in *Rivista Italiana di Scienza Politica*, **16**, 439–59.

O'Donnell, G. (1985), 'Notes for the Study of Democratic Consolidation in Contemporary Latin America' (mimeo), Notre Dame.

—, P.C. Schmitter and L. Whitehead (eds) (1986), *Transitions from Authoritarian Rule*, Baltimore and London, Johns Hopkins University Press.

Opello, W. (1987), 'The Constitutional Settlement as a Cause of Political Instability in Post-Authoritarian Portugal', paper presented at the Annual Meeting of the American Political Science Association, Chicago.

Polsby, N.W. (1975), 'Legislatures' in F.I. Greenstein and N.W. Polsby (eds), *Handbook of Political Science*, vol. V. Reading, Mass., Addison-Wesley.

Rustow, D. (1970), 'Transitions to Democracy', in *Comparative Politics*, **2**, 337–63.

Przeworski, A. (1986), 'Some Problems in the study of the Transition to Democracy' in G. O'Donnell *et al.*, op. cit.

Schmitter, P.C. (1987), 'The Consolidation of Political Democracy in Southern Europe' (mimeo), Stanford University Press.

Part II   Parliamentary practice in southern Europe: some case studies

3 The 'centrality' of parliament in a protracted democratic consolidation: the Italian case

Maurizio Cotta

Introduction

The Italian case in a southern European perspective

Analysing the Italian case in the same context with the other southern European countries—Spain, Portugal, Greece and Turkey—raises some methodological problems that have to be solved before starting to discuss the substantial side of our theme. The crucial question relates to the time dimension, a tricky dimension whenever a comparative effort is pursued. The question that has immediately to be answered is: *Italy when?* At what point in time should the Italian case be analysed? The dilemma that faces the researcher in this as in similar cases is to choose between *calendar synchronism* and what we might call *substantial* or *developmental synchronism*. In our case the first choice would mean analysing the Italian parliament in the seventies or in the eighties as has been done in this book for the legislative institutions of the other countries. The second choice, which favours the analysis of similar phases in the development of a country, would mean going back to the period in Italy when the processes of transition to democracy and of consolidation comparable to those of the other countries in the group began (and to follow them until completion). The starting point for Italy would in that case be the fall of the Fascist regime in 1943, when transition to democracy began.

The substantial principle of comparing similar phenomena argues in favour of the second choice against the more extrinsic rule of absolute chronology. If we accept, as I suggest, the second point of view, two caveats should not be overlooked. The first is that calendar synchronism may have some substantial arguments on its side. In fact a number of events (variables), transcending the national context but affecting the countries examined, take place in 'calendar synchronism' for all countries and are therefore overlooked (unless explicitly taken into account) by the developmental time perspective. The most obvious example is that of changes in the international system that produce their effects in the internal politics of all countries at the same time. In our case, for instance, choosing to set aside synchronism and studying Italy in the forties (while the other countries are analysed in the seventies or eighties) means that important factors such as the state of East–West relations, the appeal of the Soviet Union for the left, the world economic situation, the ability to learn from past experiences (if any such thing exists) etc. have undergone significant variations. As a consequence they cannot go under the *ceteris paribus* label. This means also that the distinction between a formalistic (calendar) versus a substantial (or developmental) contemporaneity becomes a little more blurred than initially thought.

The second caveat has to do with the problem of identifying 'comparable phases'. Analysing countries during similar phases of their political development obviously requires that we use common definitions for concepts such as transition, instauration, consolidation etc. and also, something which may be more difficult, that we are able to apply these concepts with some degree of precision to the empirical phenomena they indicate. To put it more explicitly this requires that we are able to establish when a phase begins and ends for each country; when transition starts and when it is completed, when consolidation is attained etc. To some extent the choice between a formal and a substantial treatment of time again comes to the foreground. On one side the solution is to define conventionally in a specified number of years the duration of the political phase to be considered (for instance, to define transition as the first five or ten years after the demise of the authoritarian regime); on the other side the temporal extent of a political phase is identified on the basis of substantial indicators (Morlino, 1986: 216 ff.). In the second case the duration of the political phase being compared may obviously vary.

With these caveats in mind we may go back to our original question: 'Italy when?' My suggestion is that to discuss the theme 'parliament and democratic consolidation' in the Italian case it would be fruitful to adopt a long-term perspective. Instead of the 10–15 years after the demise of the authoritarian regime and the restoration of democracy that are being analysed in the other southern European countries,[1] I will, for Italy, take into consideration the entire period stretching from the transition to democracy in the forties to the more recent developments of the eighties.

The choice of such a long period of time spanning over four decades requires some explanation and raises some problems. The main reason for adopting such a time perspective is that the peculiarities in the evolution of the Italian parliament (both from a structural and from a functional point of view) have been to a significant point interconnected throughout the 40 years that have elapsed since the end of World War II — as I will try to show in the following pages — with the process of democratic consolidation, with its specific developments and with their consequences. In spite of all the tremendous changes that Italian society and Italian politics have undergone during this period, the impact of the formative years has not entirely vanished. The consolidation process stretches over a very long time-span and only in the eighties has the break with this past tended to become more evident both symbolically and substantially.

In the following pages I will try to show in more detail the peculiarities of the role of Parliament in Italian politics. To capture them in a few words we can say here that the parliamentary arena in Italy has been comparatively more important than in the other southern European democracies.

But before developing this analysis, a major problem raised by the adoption of such a long time perspective must be discussed. Can we really stretch the process of democratic consolidation over such a long period of time? A digression on the theme of democratic consolidation and on the problems encountered when applying this concept to the Italian experience is required here.

On the consolidation of democracy in Italy: successful persistence and conditioned consolidation?

Some attention must be paid to the content of the concept of consolidation due to its relevance for the chronological delimitation of the phenomena it describes. Once it is agreed that democratic consolidation entails essentially that fundamental democratic institutions and rules have become stabilized and that they are beyond dispute and fully accepted by all relevant political actors (Morlino, 1986), the typical question normally asked about the process of democratic consolidation is: 'when has it ended?' When is consolidation attained? Most of the time this way of formulating the question is based on a more or less explicitly accepted dichotomous logic. A democratic regime is seen as being either consolidated or not. If this is so, we should be able to ascertain with some degree of precision *if* and *at what precise point* a country has moved from one state to the other.

If such a perspective is adopted, the Italian case stands out as particularly paradoxical, and the answer to our question becomes rather controversial.

On one side it was common for a very long time to picture Italy as a democracy under threat. This threat was ascribed mainly to the existence of oppositions on the right and (more strongly) on the left sharing a dubious allegiance to the principles and rules of liberal (polyarchical) democracy. This dubious allegiance was also the strongest reason for disqualifying (at the electoral and at the parliamentary level) these political forces from aspiring to governmental roles for about forty years. This point of view was shared both by respected political scientists (Farneti, 1983; Linz, 1974; Sartori, 1966 and 1976) and by political actors involved at the elite and at the mass level in the Italian political game.[2] Just when such a peculiarity lost its relevance is a much more controversial question and would probably require differentiated answers at the elite and mass level if political actors were considered (Putnam et al, 1981). To what extent scientific observers and political actors have followed closely in their perceptions (or have lagged behind) the real changes taking place in the opposition parties (Sartori, 1974) might also be discussed. There is little doubt, however, that, for all the refinement needed on this question, this theme was alive until the seventies. The best proof of this is that its relevance was in some way acknowledged by the opposition parties themselves. In particular, the Communist proposal of the *compromesso storico* in the seventies was devised as a solution to the lack of legitimacy of the PCI.[3]

If we look at this aspect of the Italian case, we are induced to put the *when* of democratic consolidation rather late (at some point in the seventies perhaps?).

The other side of the coin is the undeniable persistence over a long period of time of the democratic regime. And if we add to this the ability of the political system to overcome some crises of significant magnitude (in particular, the terrorist outbreak of the seventies and the economic crisis of the same period), to deny consolidation may appear 'extravagant' (See Chapter 2 of this volume) or at least unwarranted.

If we adopt a black or white approach to consolidation, the two faces of the Italian case cannot fit together in the same picture. One of the two must therefore be discarded as irrelevant or false. The consequences are obviously opposed.

Persistence is seen as the best sign of (or made equal to) attained consolidation, and consolidation is therefore conceived as a process taking place in a relatively short time span and rapidly creating the basis for successful persistence. The definition of consolidation comes very near to that of the process ensuring the (minimal?) conditions for democratic persistence. Di Palma, for instance, proposes 'crafting', dissuading actors from playing breakdown games, as a good approximation of its meaning (See Chapter 2).

When this view is adopted, the 'negative' side of Italian politics is either looked upon with a more benevolent attitude—the PCI after all accepted the Constitution (La Palombara, 1978); it was not disloyal to democracy but simply in favour of a different version of democracy (Putnam, 1973: 182ff.; Pridham, Chapter 8 of this book); its radical stance was more for the consumption of the masses than really meant etc. Or it is considered relevant for the working, the institutionalization of democratic institutions but not for the consolidation of democracy for which it was never a real threat (See Chapter 2)?

Persistence and consolidation are treated as different and relatively autonomous phenomena (Morlino, 1986). Persistence is discarded as not being a clear sign of consolidation since it might be due primarily to expediency, to the interested calculation of the major actors. It would therefore be bound to endure or to end with the conditions that determined such calculation. On the other hand, consolidation is seen as a property of the regime requiring the attainment of more explicit structural, functional and cultural thresholds. The consolidation of Italian democracy is therefore to be placed at a rather late point in time.

Although both solutions strike some relevant points, they are not entirely satisfactory. Is there a solution that would enable us to take both points of view into account and the part of the truth they contain? A positive answer to this question seems possible if we adopt a less dichotomous approach to the problems of democratic consolidation and we see consolidation not as a question of *either/or* but rather of *more or less, strong or weak* (Morlino, 1981 and 1986).

In our specific case, such a view would make it possible to accommodate some of the paradoxes of Italian politics (long-term persistence and, at the same time, enduring exclusion of a large opposition from government and wide perceptions of a democracy under threat).

The ability of democratic institutions to survive over a long period of time without major deviations from democratic rules (persistence) would suggest that probably a first level of consolidation was reached rather early. Indeed, the acceptance of democratic rules and refraining from adopting breakdown games by the major actors soon gave some stability to democracy. Opportunist considerations may have entered into this but such soft elements as motives and intentions are perhaps not so relevant for the first consolidation when harder elements such as concrete behaviour are on the side of democracy.

On the other side we must add that this consolidation took place under conditions which seriously limited the political game. One could obviously object that no consolidation holds under 'any condition' (Di Palma, Chapter 2). Any of the democracies that we are used to labelling as 'solid' would probably fall, given certain conditions. This is true but not very illuminating. The interesting point is that the conditions under which consolidation may hold vary greatly in their chances of being fulfilled or not. Let us take, for instance, a conditional proposition of the following type which presumably applies to any democracy: the results of the democratic game are accepted by all relevant actors under the condition that no party wishing to change the fundamental rules of the democratic game will gain control over the government. This condition in a country where parties with this ambition are politically irrelevant has almost no impact upon political life (and in fact no one even cares to discuss it); for all practical purposes the consolidation of democracy is unconditioned. But in a political system where a party with such an orientation (or which is perceived—rightly or wrongly—by the other actors to have such orientations) reaches perhaps 20 or 30 percent of the popular vote, the limiting condition under which democracy works has a much more direct impact upon some crucial aspects of democratic political life (for instance, electoral competition and government formation). The chances that the condition—under which democratic rules are accepted and work—will fail are much greater than in the other case. The existence of such a condition cannot therefore be overlooked when analysing that political system and evaluating the degree of consolidation of its democracy.

If we go back to the Italian case, we can easily see that it is a good example of consolidation 'under limiting conditions' and, moreover, under conditions that have not had a purely hypothetical and unrealistic value. The likeliness of their failure was a conceivable possibility for a long period of time. The existence of a large opposition party that, even while accepting the Constitution, shared, both at the level of its mass following and of large sections of its elite, political values that were at odds with the substance of liberal democracy,[4] for a long time raised legitimate doubts about its foreseeable behaviour were it to come into power. At the same time this made questionable the acceptance of an electoral success on its part and of its access to government by the other political actors (both internal and international).

Whether these doubts were really justified may be an interesting question (although difficult to answer). But the answer may not be so relevant for evaluating the working of Italian democracy. Whether right or wrong, these perceptions became real facts when they influenced the actual behaviour of relevant political actors. It is a fact that until the elections of 1979 the issue of 'democracy in danger' played an important role in the electoral arena. The exclusion of the second largest party from governmental roles at the national level because of its international connections and of its ambiguous position *vis-à-vis* democratic values has been extremely difficult to overcome (even now when the access to power of that party is accepted in principle, it remains difficult to become a reality). At each of the party congresses up until the last one of 1989 the question of whether the PCI had 'changed enough' was raised by the press, by the other parties and even within the party itself.

When the overcoming of this situation of 'consolidation under conditions' took place is a point that may be debated, but it clearly required a longer time span than for the other southern European countries (excluding Turkey).

Levels and factors of democratic consolidation

To understand this ambivalent situation (where partial consolidation coexisted with elements of precariousness for a long time) and its evolution, an important perspective is revealed by the parliamentary institution and its development. There are good reasons for this: parliament is one of the crucial arenas where parties interact. And where, as in Italy, the question of democratic consolidation has hinged fundamentally on the party system and its specific characteristics, we can expect that most of these problems will show up in the working of Parliament.

But before looking more directly into the different aspects of the relationship between democratic consolidation and Parliament, something must be said about the role of the party variable. In particular, some attention must be given to the somewhat paradoxical links between the factors that led to the successful attainment of the first level of consolidation (and of persistence) and the factors that produced the delay in the completion of a higher level of consolidation.

To explain the successful attainment, in the years following World War II, of the first threshold of consolidation which made survival and persistence of democracy possible (a threshold that the first Italian mass democracy had not been able to reach after World War I), a crucial aspect was the new structuring of the party system after the fall of Fascism. At the same time we can say that precisely this aspect has been largely responsible for the extremely long and difficult process leading to a higher and less conditional level of consolidation.

The two most relevant innovations at the party level in the first years of the new democracy were the growth in the 'partyness' (Katz, 1986) of political life and the emerging of a large centre party (the DC) capable of ensuring the stability of the governmental process in spite of the instability of cabinets (Pasquino, 1985). Both aspects point to a significant change from pre-Fascist democracy.

We must remember that in the pre-Fascist democracy Italy showed very clearly the syndrome of a weak party government, both at the electoral and at the parliamentary level, and lacked a democratic party able to lead with some assurance the process of government formation. These conditions made the Parliament unable to fulfil what in a parliamentary form of government is its primary function: ie producing relatively stable governments (or at least a fairly stable governing elite) with a majority backing (Farneti, 1978).

After the fall of the Fascist regime the growth in the strength of party government was clear. Some aspects had been apparent since the very beginning of the democratic instauration, but others would be produced only with the second and third general elections (in 1948 and 1953).[5]

The three larger parties (DC, PSI and PCI) were able very early to mobilize a mass membership that was many times larger than in the pre-Fascist period. The party with the largest membership in the twenties, the PSI, had at that time only about 200,000 card-carrying members, while in 1946 the PCI had already more than 1,600,000 and the DC 600,000. To the strengthening of the extraparliamentary organizations of parties should be added the fact that 'partyness' became a dominant feature of elections. Although some local electoral labels persisted, especially in southern Italy, their success was limited and national party labels became completely dominant.

At the parliamentary level personalistic groupings disappeared and the control of parties over members of Parliament produced a stabilization of alignments. Here the turning point was the elections of 1948 (more than those of 1946). While in the Constituent Assembly (1946–8) party splits and the creation or disappearance of a few small parties produced a substantial number of changes of party labels by members of Parliament (touching about 17 percent of the members), in the first regular legislature (1948–53) only a dozen such changes took place (Lotti, 1963: 146ff.). The combined effects of the increased 'partyness' of political life and of the growth of a large centre party after World War II were particularly clear in the government-building process. In a strict sense the goal of governmental stability was not attained, but two major correctives counterbalanced the short duration of cabinets: the greater stability of government formulae (ie of the coalitional combinations of parties supporting cabinets) and the even more pronounced continuity of the governing elite. This improvement was clearly due to the fact that a very large party (the DC) with a level of 'partyness' surely higher than that of the liberal-democratic parliamentary groups of the pre-Fascist period had now gained control over the government-building process.

It is probably not unwarranted to relate the long-term *persistence* of the Italian post-Fascist regime (in contrast to the very short life-span of the first Italian experiment in mass democracy) to the fact that the centre and centre–right areas of the political spectrum have undergone, under the aegis of the Christian Democratic party, a process of more marked structuring along party lines.

To explain the at least partial consolidation of Italian democracy it is usual to stress the importance of the broad agreement of the first years among the parties (originating in the common battle against Fascism) that culminated in the near unanimous approval of the Constitution. There is no reason to underestimate the importance of this condition (especially if we compare it with other experiences of democratic restoration where a broad agreement on the constitution could not be reached as in the French Fourth Republic or in Weimar Germany). It was surely a favourable factor in ensuring a successful instauration of democracy. It is less common to look at the tense conflicts of the following years as factors of democratic consolidation. It is more obvious to see them as the origin of the problems that democracy had to face. This point of view is easy to understand but overlooks an important meaning of these events. The breaking up of the broad agreement of the previous years and the dramatic electoral confrontation of 1948, but also the enduring conflictuality of the following years, had a crucial impact in determining those innovations in the party dimension that we have been discussing. On one side they pushed the division between republican and monarchist orientations if not into oblivion at least into a secondary and marginal role. This is an important point since this division could have otherwise given a much larger following to parties of the right with a dubious allegiance to the new democratic republic.[6] On the other side, they made it possible for a party of the centre (the DC) to gain control over a large part of the traditional right and at the same time stimulated the same party to develop a higher degree of organizational strength.

The reaching of the first threshold of democratic consolidation became very clear with the elections of 1948. Starting from that moment there would be a partly clearly able to ensure (through coalitions with other smaller parties) a governmental majority free from the need to negotiate the support of parties with dubious democratic loyalty (See table 3.1). This does not mean that *legislative majorities* will never rely upon such support. Far from that! But it is obviously a different question from that of the majority needed to support the government as the leading state and political authority.

While the minimal level required for the persistence of the democratic regime was thus reached fairly soon, attaining a higher level of consolidation of the democratic regime proved, in the Italian case, a much lengthier process (and to some extent the consequences of this question are still lingering today). The great polarization of 1947–53, which played a crucial role in the structuring of the party system along lines that, as we have said, contributed to making the first level of consolidation possible, at the same time made the overcoming of the great division between government (and regime-loyal) parties and opposition (and anti-regime or perceived as anti-regime) parties an extremely difficult and length process. If we agree that the conditions required for the full consolidation of a democratic regime, as a regulated and accountable system of political pluralism are—(1) the acceptance of democratic rules by all major actors; (2) the mutual acceptance between major actors stemming from the confidence of every major actor that the others will comply with those rules—it becomes understandable why reaching a full consolidation has been difficult in Italy. A full reciprocal acceptance by the major parties would have meant a radical departure from the all-out confrontation that had established their fortunes at the electoral level.

But stressing the importance of mutual confidence and acceptance for consolidation is not superfluous. A political actor might be perfectly willing to play according to the rules, but a negative perception by other relevant actors

Table 3.1 The distribution of seats in the Constituent Assembly and in the Chamber of Deputies

Constituent Assembly	1946–8	1948–53	1953–8	1958–63	1963–8	1968–72	1972–6	1976–79	1979–83	1983–87	1987–
Radicals								4 (1%)	17 (2%)	11 (2%)	12 (2%)
PCI	104 (19%)	131 (23%)	143 (24%)	141 (24%)	166 (26%)	171 (27%)	175 (28%)	222 (35%)	193 (31%)	177 (28%)	157 (25%)
PSIUP				25 (4%)	23 (4%)						
PSI	115 (21%)	52 (9%)	75 (13%)	88 (15%)	62 (10%)	—	61 (10%)	57 (9%)	61 (10%)	73 (12%)	94 (15%)
PSI–PSDI						91 (14%)					
PSDI	—	33 (6%)	19 (3%)	17 (3%)	32 (5%)	—	30 (5%)	15 (2%)	20 (3%)	22 (3%)	17 (3%)
PRI	25 (4%)	10 (2%)	5 (1%)	6 (1%)	5 (1%)	9 (1%)	15 (2%)	14 (2%)	16 (3%)	29 (5%)	21 (3%)
DC	207 (37%)	306 (53%)	262 (44%)	273 (46%)	260 (41%)	265 (42%)	265 (42%)	262 (42%)	262 (42%)	226 (36%)	234 (37%)
PLI	29 (5%)	15 (3%)	14 (2%)	18 (3%)	38 (6%)	31 (5%)	20 (3%)	5 (1%)	9 (1%)	16 (3%)	11 (2%)
Mon.	10 (2%)	13 (2%)	39 (7%)	25 (4%)	8 (1%)	6 (1%)					
MSI		6 (1%)	29 (5%)	24 (4%)	27 (4%)	24 (4%)	55 (9%)	34 (5%)	29 (5%)	42 (7%)	35 (6%)
Others	66 (12%)	8 (1%)	4 (1%)	4 (1%)	7 (1%)	10 (2%)	9 (1%)	17 (3%)	23 (4%)	34 (5%)	49 (8%)
Total	556	574	590	596	630	630	630	630	630	630	630

Sources: *I Deputati e Senatori del Decimo Parlamento Repubblicano* (1987) Rome, La Navicella.

Notes: Starting with the fifth Parliament there has always been an early dissolution and the normal five-year term has never been achieved.

Key: Radicals = Radical Party; PCI = Italian Communist Party; PSIUP = Italian Socialist Party of Proletarian Unity (a left splinter from the PSI); PSI = Italian Socialist Party; PSDI = Italian Social Democratic Party; PRI = Italian Republican Party; DC = Christian Democratic Party; PLI = Italian Liberal Party; Mon. = Monarchist Party (at times there were more than one monarchist party); MSI = Italian Social Movement (a neo-Fascist party).

might be enough to induce the latter to adopt pre-emptive action to protect themselves from presumed anti-democratic behaviour of the former. This pre-emptive action might take the perfectly legitimate (from a democratic point of view) form of denying one's vote at the electoral level to the 'dubious party' or of refusing to enter a coalition with it at the parliamentary level, but in a more critical situation democratic actors might be tempted to leave the ground of democratic authenticity in order to 'defend democracy' (Linz, 1978: 70).

The reaching of an acceptable level of mutual confidence is particularly critical in order to make the exchange of governmental and oppositional roles an acceptable risk. In this perspective an important test of a full consolidation of the democratic regime will be a peaceful transfer of power between the governing parties and the major opposition parties. (Weiner and La Palombera, 1966: 412). This need not necessarily mean that the democratic regime had not become accepted before that event; but in the absence of such a test we lack strong proof both of the acceptance of the democratic rules by all actors and of the reaching of a satisfactory level of mutual confidence between them.

In the Italian case we have very clearly a situation where the (long) persistence of the democratic regime has been associated with the avoidance of that test. Except for the transitional stage between the authoritarian and the democratic regime (1943–7), a major political party with a share of the electoral vote ranging between 19 percent and 34 percent (1976) has not been able to move from an opposition to a governing role. This is a case almost unique in democratic regimes in terms of the length of the exclusion from power of such a large party. This exclusion (the end of which seems even today not so near) has been the product of two combined conditions: (1) the fact that the PCI has not reached a parliamentary majority alone; (2) the fact that this party has not been able to enter a parliamentary coalition commanding a parliamentary majority (Farneti, 1983). Both conditions can be interpreted as reflecting at least in part the lack of confidence of important political actors in that party. Large sections of the electorate have for a long time been unconvinced of the democratic character of the PCI (Sani, 1976). This has been shown by survey results but perhaps more convincingly by the fact that in spite of a diffuse dissatisfaction with the (permanent) governing parties, the largest opposition party has not been able to acquire the votes of unsatisfied electors beyond a certain point. Italy, one of the countries more heavily struck by the economic crisis in the seventies, has seen the governing parties able to escape 'punishment' and to maintain an electoral following giving them the control of a parliamentary majority. If the Communist party has not been able to make an electoral breakthrough, neither has it been able to attain a larger coalition potential at the parliamentary level. While in local politics the PCI after 1975 managed to win the confidence of the other parties on the left and even in the centre (from the PSI, to the PSDI, the PRI and even, in a number of cases, the PLI), thus finding its way into many local governments outside the 'red regions', it was not able to replicate such a strategy at the national level. Even if a parliamentary majority left of the DC has existed since 1976 in the lower chamber (PCI+PSI+PSDI+PRI+ other small leftist parties: See table 3.1) and since 1979 in the Senate, such a possibility has not been explored seriously either by the PCI or by the other leftist or centre–left parties. The latter have thought it more convenient to continue their traditional although far from peaceful alliance with the DC.

The only instance when the PCI came close to executive power was in the years 1976–8 and that took place under very special conditions: a grand coalition (stretching from the PCI to the Liberal party and thus making the PCI not numerically necessary to reach a parliamentary majority) and the exclusion of Communist politicians from the cabinet. The inclusion of the PCI in the governmental coalition took place therefore in a very cautious setting. As is well known, the Communist leadership itself explicitly (if *pro tempore*) accepted these very special conditions as an instrument for 'legitimating the party in the eyes of the other political actors. In this way it was acknowledged that mutual confidence among major political actors had not yet been reached. After the failure of that strategy, the PCI moved back to opposition roles. Since then, an increasing number of pronouncements by other parties have given credence to the acceptability of the PCI as a fully democratic actor, but, paradoxically enough, its ability to become part of governmental coalitions has declined rather than increased. In fact, since then, the relations with the Socialist party have been particularly strained. And of course it would be difficult to build an alternative majority without an alliance with the PSI.

Such a situation, or more exactly the prolongation of this situation over an increasingly long time span, raises a number of questions. The major one is the following: why, in spite of its remarkable success in establishing itself as a large and very influential opposition party, has the PCI not been able to cross the executive threshold?

The answer often given is that the other parties have adopted an exclusionary posture toward the PCI (the so-called *conventio ad excludendum*). This answer, however, does not bring us very far. We still need to know why they have adopted such a position and how they have been able to keep it in effect for such a long period of time. But there is a further question: why has the PCI not been able to overcome such an exclusionary attitude? Could we not advance the hypothesis that this simply has not been the first priority of the party leadership? Or, to put it another way, that adaptation to the environment (and particularly to the challenge of overcoming exclusion from government) has been subordinated to preoccupations about the maintenance of identity? It is true that the party has changed, but always within margins that allowed it to stress the continuity with its past.[7] The party seems to have been more concerned with the risk of losing its followers than with being kept out of executive power for longer. We may say that for a long time the Communist party has preferred to accept being confined to an oppositional role rather than face the risks of a bolder and more visible process of change such as would be required to open the path to a governing role.

To sum up briefly the results of this digression, we may conclude that:

(1) the first years of the transition and instauration of democracy produced the conditions for a first level of consolidation of democracy;

(2) these conditions rested at the same time upon a broad agreement (on the Constitution) and tense conflicts (over government formation since 1947 and at elections from 1948 onward) between the largest political parties;

(3) this first stage of consolidation was linked to the avoidance of the access of the Communist party to government;
(4) electoral and, in general, mass politics have been based upon the confrontation, centred on the question of regime loyalty, between the DC and PCI;
(5) the governmental and opposition roles of the two largest parties have been frozen and only smaller parties have been able to switch roles;
(6) the overcoming of this limiting condition has proven an extremely long process—in spite of very substantial changes involving all political actors and of some more or less explicit attempts, the overcoming of such conditions has not yet been accomplished in 1989;
(7) with the passing of time the meaning of this condition for consolidation has weakened but its impact upon the working of the political system has proven difficult to dispel entirely;
(8) the way in which the problem of democratic consolidation was faced in Italy in the forties has affected to a very significant degree the following 40 years of political life.

Given the peculiarities of Italian democratic consolidation examined so far, it seems meaningful with regard to Italy, to embrace a relatively long period of time when discussing the relationship between consolidation and a crucial institution of democracy such as Parliament.

In particular, the fact that the institutional roles of the two major parties (DC and PCI) have been frozen for a long period of time due to the nature of political competition has had important consequences for the role of Parliament. It has meant that, for the Communist party, Parliament has been the only institutional arena (at the national level) through which it could exert its influence—an influence that, thanks to the strong cohesion of this party and the fractionaliz-ation of the governmental majority, could become in that arena a significant power of veto and delay. For this reason the PCI has been consistently in favour of strengthening the role of Parliament and has strenuously opposed any limitation to its powers. On the other side the DC and the other governing parties have had a more ambivalent attitude toward Parliament. The reason is that they have played their game both in the executive and parliamentary arena. For them to have pursued to a greater extent an exclusionary strategy against the PCI would have required playing down the importance of Parliament in favour of the executive. Although some attempts in this direction were made (as we will see), significant opposition to them came also from within the majority ranks. In fact such a strategy would have also worked against sections of the Christian Democratic party that had no governmental roles and saw Parliament as their major resource and against some of the smaller governing parties that considered parliamentary action a safeguard of their autonomy vis-à-vis the dominating party.

Having given the crucial elements of the party background regarding the process of democratic consolidation, we can now move back to our specific theme. When discussing the relationship between Parliament and democratic consolidation we are confronted with two perspectives: the first looks at Parliament as the dependent variable—how the process of consolidation has shaped the structure and working of Parliament and how it has defined its functions; the second looks at Parliament as the independent variable — the role Parliament has played in the process of consolidation. Particularly in the second perspective care should be taken not to fall into the holistic view of Parliament as a unitary actor (King, 1976; Cotta, 1987). To talk about the influence of Parliament must be shorthand for referring, on one hand, to the impact of an institutional setting providing opportunities and restraints for different political actors and, on the other, to the influence of a set of specific actors that have in Parliament a privileged seat and can be distinguished from actors operating outside its boundaries.

In the Italian case the two perspectives have to be connected with the two stages of consolidation. From what we have already said, there are many elements suggesting that in both phases the parliamentary arena has been significantly linked with the process of democratic consolidation. Given their different time dimensions (short term the first, long term the second), the two phases will be discussed separately.

From transition to first democratic consolidation: the role of the parliamentary institution

If we look at the relatively short period during which transition from authoritarianism, instauration and first consolidation of democracy took place (a period that stretched in Italy from 1943 to the early fifties), the first question to be answered is: at what step of this crucial process did a parliamentary institution come into play and how was it shaped by the specific conditions of that moment? The second question is: how did this institution with its specific character affect that process? There is a clear link between the two questions. We may expect that the sooner a parliamentary institution is put to work, the greater will be its impact (positive, favouring certain developments; and negative, working as a limit to others) upon the making of the new democracy. But obviously the impact will depend also on the specific features of that institution.

The Constituent Assembly

In Italy the first parliamentary-like institution was the Constituent Assembly elected in June 1946, three years after the demise of Fascism and two years after the first party government.[8] Compared to ordinary parliaments this institution had two peculiarities: a *positive* one — it was devoted to the making of the Constitution; and a *negative* one — it had only limited powers in the field of law-making (which was left on the whole to the government except for international treaties and electoral laws).[9] In spite of this it could be considered from a political point of view a parliamentary body for at least two important reasons: (1) it was not composed mainly of constitutional technicians but rather of the political elite of the parties (its large size — 535 members — is a clear indicator of this); (2) the government had to have the political confidence (a majority) of that assembly.

The creation and the nature of this first (quasi) parliamentary body was at the centre of important political skirmishes between the monarchy and the parties and also among the parties themselves during the transition period (Piscitelli, 1975: 150 ff.). The opposition to the convocation of a constituent assembly was strongest from the political actors that wanted to reduce to a minimum the discontinuity with the pre-Fascist regime. Along this line some attempts were made by the first monarchial government after the fall of Fascism and also by some of the old politicians linked more to the past political experiences to preserve a continuity with the pre-Fascist constitution and institutions in particular by reviving the old Parliament (Bettinelli, 1982: 21 ff.).[10] This attempt was bound to fail since the old constitution and its institutions, which had not been abolished by Fascism but formally kept alive while substantially transformed according to the authoritarian model, had lost most of their legitimacy. Against this self-protecting attempt of the monarchy and of the old *notabili* who tried in this way to keep control over the transition to democracy in their hands, the opposition of the parties of the anti-Fascist coalition (CLN) was almost unanimous. Their own role in the transition was at stake. The parties' fight against the monarchy and the state bureaucracy for determining who would lead the transition (and that meant, among other things, who would convoke the first parliamentary body and choose the electoral procedure for electing it) saw a first victory in the spring of 1944 when they secured the control over the government, which pending the activation of elections and Parliament was the crucial actor in the first transition steps. But the parties themselves were not fully in agreement either on the powers of the Constituent Assembly or on the electoral system to be adopted. The solutions to these points were the result of a delicate and complex bargaining process between the existing parties (Catalano, 1980: 747 ff.; Gambino, 1978). The resulting agreements (on the electoral system, on the limitation of the powers of the Constituent Assembly and on the devolution of the choice between monarchy and republic to a popular referendum) had a crucial role in making the prosecution of democratic transition along consensual lines possible.

The compromise on the electoral system

As far as the electoral system was concerned, a number of factors combined to produce the choice: the nature of the first party governments composed of six parties (equally weighted), the uncertainties over the electoral perspectives of each of these parties and the political tradition of the largest ones (DC, PSI, PCI). All these conditions worked in favour of the decision to elect the new Constituent Assembly with a proportional representation (PR) electoral system.

The fact that the electoral law was to last only for the election of the Constituent Assembly and not for the following parliaments and the special nature of that assembly for which a high level of representativeness was particularly desirable contributed to overcoming the opposition of those favouring a more majoritarian solution (Bettinelli, 1982). The anti-party orientations of the right (the area of the political spectrum that had been more strongly in favour of a plurality system *à l'anglaise*) and of sections of the centre were in some way compensated by introducing the preference vote (ibid). The desire of the mass parties to have a stronger control over those elected was taken into account by creating the so-called Collegio Unico Nazionale with predetermined list orderings (for all the remaining seats not assigned at the constituency level). At the same time this provision increased the degree of proportionality of the electoral system. Finally, the left was able to win the battle against the compulsory character of the vote: the principle was kept but the strong sanctions asked for by the parties of the centre and the right (which feared the greater ability of the left to mobilize the electors) were abandoned (ibid).

The electoral law devised for the Constituent Assembly which was supposed to last only for that 'special assembly', was in fact followed almost exactly by the Constituent Assembly when its turn came to discuss the electoral system for the ordinary parliament.

An attempt by the government[11] to mitigate somewhat the degree of proportionality of the electoral system, thus favouring the largest parties, was promptly rejected (ibid.: 337 ff.). Although the choice of the electoral system did not become, as someone had asked, part of the formal Constitution, it is reasonable to see it as one of the corner stones of the *real* Constitution. This is true both from the point of view of chronology—the crucial decision on the electoral system antedates, as we have seen, the convocation of the Constituent Assembly—and of its importance: the electoral system defines some of the basic rules for the competition among parties. It was not by chance that the major attempt of the following years to change the real Constitution would be centred on the modification of this electoral system. The failure to implement successfully a more majoritarian electoral system and its abolition after the elections of 1953 was to sanction the PR system (with only minor changes of the original law regulating it) as a cornerstone of Italian politics. Only in the eighties will we again find significant sections of the political elite (particularly in the DC and in the PCI) ready to accept as legitimate and to discuss seriously the possibility of altering this first choice.

Looking back at this important decision of the transition years we can thus detect a sequence of causally linked events in the middle of which the inauguration of the first parliamentary body can be seen as an intervening variable reinforcing rather than altering the original trend of developments. First, a government based on a plurality of parties chooses an electoral (PR) system establishing a low threshold of representation; then the parliamentary body (Constituent Assembly) thus elected and seeing within its ranks a further increase of the fragmentation of parties cannot but reproduce the same electoral system. The first choice was not made by Parliament, but Parliament (or rather the actors represented in it) contributed to freezing that choice.

The powers of the Constituent Assembly

The second issue at stake between the parties had been the question of the powers to be assigned to the Constituent Assembly. Should it be allowed to decide on the hot issue of monarchy versus republic or should this choice be left to a popular referendum? Should it have full legislative powers or rather be confined to the drafting of the Constitution while the ordinary legislative power remained in the hands of the executive as it had been until that moment? If we leave aside the first question, one could be surprised by this dispute, given the fact that the government had worked until then on the principle of a grand coalition of (almost) all parties and not along a division between majority and minority. The government itself had been conceived as a representative body. What then would be the difference in assigning the legislative powers to one or to the other? Looking more closely a number of reasons both of a symbolic and of a more substantial nature concur to explain this *quérelle* and the strong opposition particularly from the parties of the right (PLI) but also of the centre (DC) against granting too extensive powers to the Constituent Assembly. On the cultural and symbolic side particularly relevant was the revolutionary halo—the idea of a break with the past that both from the right and from the left was attached—even if with opposing value judgements, to the Constituent Assembly. But there were also some more substantial reasons. A major one was the fear of the parties of the centre and right that while until then in the cabinet each party had more or less the same standing, a popularly elected Constituent Assembly would have produced a differentiated weighting of the parties (and all the forecasts suggested a success of the left). To counteract this strengthening, the only chance for the centre and right would have been to abandon at the government level the grand coalitional scheme and to follow a majoritarian course excluding the left (if it had not reached an absolute majority). But in any case in Parliament the left would have had a powerful influence, and given the wider spectrum of political positions even within the parties of the majority, probably the government would have had much greater problems in controlling the legislative process. Another important point was that while a parliamentary body would have felt the influence of popular mood and of mass movements more, the cabinet would have worked more closely with the state bureaucracy and with the international actors (and particularly the Western powers). Both could then have had a crucial importance as constraints against the left and as resources for the centre and right. Finally, there was a clear interest of the party (the DC) that, thanks to its pivotal position between left and right, had been able to gain firm control over the premiership[12] in strengthening the role of the cabinet. In fact all these elements were eventually to play an important role in the Italian situation. The difference between the political spectrum represented in the first parliamentary body (the Constituent Assembly) and in the governments of the same period had been of some relevance since the beginning, but gained a much greater political importance when the anti-Fascist grand coalition broke down and a centre majority government was inaugurated (May 1974). And finally the relations established by the government with the state bureaucracy and with the Western powers (particularly the United States) were to provide important political resources in the power game of those years for the leading governmental party (the DC).

The agreement reached among the parties after a long and heated political debate provided for some important limitations to the powers of the Constituent

Assembly. This agreement proved to be a significant political victory for the Christian Democratic party. Leaving the divisive choice between monarchy and republic to a popular referendum rather than to the Constituent Assembly meant that a centre party such as the DC could avoid having to campaign at the first popular elections (those for the Constituent Assembly) and take a clear and visible position on this issue (which would have meant losing important sections of its electorate on one side or the other). But it also meant for that party avoiding the risk of facing a split in the ranks of its members in the Constituent Assembly when voting on that issue.[13]

Depriving the Constituent Assembly of the legislative function and leaving it to the cabinet meant that although when drawing up the Constitution the practice of compromise among all major political parties was easily prevalent, in the field of ordinary law-making, a field far from unimportant in the crucial phase of post-war reconstruction, the governmental parties and, in particular, the DC could follow a less consensual and more 'majoritarian' course. This difference became particularly clear when, after the breakdown (spring 1974) at the governmental level of the anti-Fascist coalition of the three mass parties (DC, PSI and PCI), the cabinets were based on centre coalitions of a smaller size, dominated by the DC. With regard to hypotheses one could even go further and suggest that the fact that the government had these special legislative powers was an important incentive for the DC to disengage itself from a large coalition with the leftist parties and pursue through the government a much more distinctive policy course than in the past in order to strengthen its popular following. Such a course would have been much more difficult if the government had had to gain the support of Parliament for its legislative proposals.

The drafting of the Constitution

Having seen some of the problems connected with the inauguration and the powers of the Constituent Assembly, we can move to the field that was its specific domain: the making of the new Constitution. To what extent and in what direction was the drafting of the constitutional text affected by the fact that this task was accomplished by that type of constituent body?

There are two sides to this question. The first concerns the content of the Constitution. The making of the Constitution was assigned to a large, parliamentary-like assembly, elected via an electoral system with a low threshold of representation rather than to a smaller body, more technical and perhaps under stricter control of the government (as might hypothetically have happened). What impact, if any, has this fact had upon the substantial contents of the constitutional text?

The second and crucial aspect of the question is that of the acceptance of the new Constitution by the major political actors. To what extent did the way the Constitution was made contribute toward producing generalized support for it?

A satisfactory answer to these questions would require a comparative analysis of a number of constitution-making processes, which cannot be done here.[14] But even without such stronger analytic instruments, it is perhaps

possible to find some evidence supporting a number of hypotheses as to the
influence of the nature of the constitution-making body upon the two above-
mentioned aspects.

On the basis of our general knowledge about the structure and working of
parliamentary bodies, the following hypotheses can be put forward to see how
they fit the Italian case.

The stronger the role of a parliamentary-like body in constitution-making and
the weaker the role of a technical body and of the government, *then*

H.1.   The greater will be the chances of a constitutional text with less internal
        consistency, and which leaves greater space to compromises between
        different legal and political outlooks.
H.2.   The greater the likelihood of a constitution that is more parliament-
        orientated than government-orientated.
H.3.   The greater the chances of a more favourable treatment of individual
        parliamentarians.
H.4.   The greater the weight of 'principled' democratic proclamations against
        more technical and more 'cynical' (from the point of view of democratic
        ideals) rules.

Moreover, we might expect as all these hypothetical consequences are
strengthened, the larger and the more fragmented the constitution-making
body will be.

To these hypotheses bearing on the contents of the Constitution we could
add one concerning the problem of its acceptance.

The stronger the role of a parliamentary-like body in the process of
constitution-making and the less this body works according to a majoritarian
model, *then*

H.5.   The greater the chances that the Constitution will be accepted by all the
        relevant political forces.

If we look now at the Italian constitution-making process, what were the
conditions under which it developed?

A first point to be mentioned is that the government did not play an active
role in the process. There was no governmental project for the Constitution.
Moreover, the separation between the government and the Constitutional
Assembly increased with the passing of time. At the beginning the coalition
supporting the cabinet included, with few exceptions of limited weight, all the
major parties represented in the Constituent Assembly; after May 1947 and
until the end of the drafting of the Constitution, the government could count
only upon an uncertain majority.[15]

A second point concerns the role of (legal) technicians in the making of the
Constitution. The picture here is mixed. In fact, in the making of the Italian
Constitution it is possible to see the contributions of both technicians and
politicians. The Constituent Assembly was clearly a political, parliamentary
body rather than a technical institution. But it counted among its members an
important group of the best constitutional lawyers of the Italian universities.

These technicians, outnumbered by pure politicians in the plenum, played, however, an important role in the committee stage that produced the first draft of the Constitution and also took an active part in most of the discussions in the assembly. The Constitution was thus made by a 'Parliament' but a Parliament that to some extent was integrated by a more technical body of experts. Although the distinction is far from neat, we can distinguish between a first stage in the process (the committee stage) which saw the technicians play a larger role and a second stage (that of the discussion in the plenum of the assembly) that saw rather the dominance of the parliamentary and political climate. The distinction is not so neat because the so-called Committee of 75 (with its three sub-committees) which prepared the draft of the Constitution was not composed entirely of technicians (who in any case were selected on the basis of their party links), but also of politicians. Equally, some of the technicians also were very active in the assembly stage.

An attempt to check the validity of some of the hypotheses that we have formulated could be made by comparing the constitutional draft as it came out of the committee (and more technical) stage and the changes that were introduced in the plenary (and more political and parliamentary) stage.

It must be said, however, that the committee stage had already seen the search for compromises between the politically and technically divergent views that had been put forward by different sides. This was particularly clear when the central institutions of the democratic regime (parliament and government) were discussed. A major difference was that between the left, which wanted a unicameral and all-powerful parliament, and the centre and the right, which stood for a bicameral parliament and for the strengthening of government *vis-à-vis* parliament.

But the search for compromises was pushed even further in the assembly stage. An interesting point to be underlined is that these compromises followed extremely varied and shifting coalitional alignments. This is exactly as one would expect in a parliamentary situation where the government is not playing a leading role and the preoccupation with building an homogeneous and durable majority is outweighed by the interest of each party in obtaining the most favourable rules and institutions. We saw alliances of centre and right against left, but also the centre siding with the left against the right and, what is more, also coalitions of the right and left against the centre.[16] The problem of the second chamber and of its specific features was one of the themes over which such manoeuvering reached a particularly high level of complexity (Bettinelli, 1982: 295 ff.). The bicameral system that resulted from this process, where negative and occasional alliances were more easy to reach than positive and coherent ones, embodied an institutional model that did not correspond to any of the original schemes devised by the technicians[17] or to the specific intentions of any of the political forces that had taken part in its elaboration. Moreover, its political and constitutional meaning is cryptic.[18]

The evidence supporting the first hypothesis is thus not irrelevant. But there is some evidence also for the second and third hypotheses (that a parliamentary body will produce a more parliament-orientated than government-orientated constitution and more favourable conditions for individual members of parliament). As we move from the early work done by the sub-committees to the draft of the Committee of 75 and finally to the discussion in the plenary, we see a progressive watering down of all measures devised for strengthening the government (Amato and Bruno, 1981). A good example is that the number of members of parliament required to sign a motion of no confidence is progressively reduced from one stage to the other.

Another parliament-orientated innovation that was added in the plenary, and that was to have important consequences in the working of the law-making process, was the attribution to the standing committees of the chambers of the power to enact a bill definitively without the need of a vote in the plenary (as the original constitutional draft required).

A good instance of the influence of the parliamentary milieu upon certain constitutional issues is offered by the discussion on the size of parliament. The relevance of this point for the small parties and also for individual politicians is clear: the larger the number of seats, the lower the threshold of access. On this point there had already been different positions in the committee stage and the final result was the fairly large size of the first chamber: a deputy for every 80,000 inhabitants. In the plenary stage a proposal was advanced to reduce the number of deputies (to a ratio of one for every 150,000 inhabitants). But a coalition of the left with the small parties of the centre and the right (and favoured by the secret vote) was able to check these proposals. As a result of this decision and of the bicameral system, the size of the first ordinary parliament was thus much larger than that of the Constituent Assembly (the first chamber alone was to have more or less the same number of members as the Constituent Assembly; and then there was the second chamber). This offered the best chances for re-election to the members of the constituent body.[19]

Connected to this theme also was in some way the problem of how to elect the second chamber. While the first constitutional draft required that the senators be chosen only among members of very selective categories (high-ranking members of the judiciary, university professors, entrepreneurs, high-ranking politicians and bureaucrats etc.) according to a scheme that tried to introduce some elements of a corporatist representation, the plenary brought the senate back to the ordinary type of political and territorial representation. We do not want to discuss here the validity of the original scheme devised for the second chamber by some of the brightest constitutional lawyers of the time; the interesting point to be noticed is the fact that for a parliamentary-like body such as the Constituent Assembly it was easier to solve the dissensions existing on the point by adopting a model of representation less dissimilar from its own.

To sum up, even from a sketchy analysis such as the one presented here, there are some good reasons for saying that the peculiarities of the parliamentary body and of the parliamentary process through which the Italian Constitution was made have had a significant impact upon the contents and the quality of the constitutional text produced. And they provided some of the ground for the future developments of parliament along polycentric lines.

The legitimation paradox of the democratic regime: constitutional consensus and growing polarization

But as we have anticipated, the way the Constitution was made probably had important effects upon another crucial question in the instauration of democracy: the question of the legitimation of the new regime.

This question cannot be equated simplistically with that of the (more or less diffuse) acceptance of the constitutional text. We should probably say that this is a necessary condition but not a sufficient one. Surely the existence of a strong opposition to the fundamental law would mean a dubious and weak legitimation of the democratic regime. But the fact that all major political forces accept the Constitution may not be enough to establish a full legitimation of the new regime. The political interpretations they give to the legal text could be thoroughly opposed.

The Italian Constitution was indeed largely accepted by the political forces represented in the Constituent Assembly. The final vote (December 1947) saw 453 in favour, only 63 against (or 12 percent). This result is surprising if one thinks of the growing political polarization that the Italian political system had undergone in the previous months and that was to reach its climax at the elections of April 1948 only four months after the voting on the Constitution.

The near unanimous vote for the Constitution can be interpreted as the consequence of a constitution-making process that allowed a rather faithful representation of all political forces and where the accommodation of the conflicting demands stemming from all the parties prevailed over the attempt to maintain the purity of a coherent scheme. It cannot be said that one (political) side prevailed systematically over the other, but rather that, thanks to the frequent shifting of alliances, each party could feel it had been at least sometimes on the winning side.

The near unanimity in the acceptance of the Constitution was not enough to prevent or stop the growing polarization. It left, however, a link (thin but not irrelevant) between parties that subsequently were to be firmly divided by the freezing of the government–opposition cleavage.[20]

Out of this there developed in the following years a somewhat paradoxical situation: the parties of the leftist opposition that were excluded from government on grounds of their dubious acceptance of the substantial tenets of pluralistic (liberal) democracy became the strongest defenders of the Constitution and of its full implementation, while the parties in government soon became colder towards a number of constitutional guarantees (such as the Constitutional Court, regional devolution etc.) they had contributed toward introducing, against the opposition of the left (Rotelli, 1981).

In fact if we leave aside the small radical right that has always contested some of the central points of the democratic constitution, the only explicit attempt in the following years to change the institutional setting born out of the new Constitution (and perhaps the Constitution itself) came from the parties in power. This revisionist approach had two aspects. The first took the form of a delay in the implementation of some institutions mandated by the Constitution (the Constitutional Court and the ordinary regional governments) that would have limited the powers of the executive and increased the controls over its legislative powers (Cheli, 1978). The second was the already mentioned change of the electoral law (in 1953) in a more majoritarian direction. That change did not formally involve a revision of the Constitution, but was a way to alter the balance between government and Parliament (both from the point of view of the government–opposition and of the government-parliamentary majority relationship) that the Constitution had not clearly defined (Baget-Bozzo, 1974: 413 ff.). Moreover, a successful implementation of the new electoral system would have made the governmental majority able to change the Constitution more easily.

Parliament in the process toward a full consolidation

After having seen some of the problems connected with the transition to democracy and the inauguration of the parliamentary institution, we can move to the discussion of the subsequent stages of the democratic development. With the breakdown in 1947 of the anti-Fascist (and constitutional) coalition, and with the emergence of the great polarization at the electoral level that started in 1948 and until late in the seventies was to split the parties on the question of allegiance to the democratic regime, the political system developed in a situation of conditioned consolidation, that is, under the condition that the largest opposition party was to be excluded from government. The questions that from the point of view of our theme require an answer are two. First, what type of parliament has emerged from the instauration phase of the democratic regime and what changes has it undergone with time in the peculiar situation that we have mentioned? The second concerns the role that this type of parliamentary institution has played in the development of such conditioned consolidation into full consolidation.

In a synthetic and cumulative form the answer to the two questions could be the following. Under the combined influence of legal regulations and of political conditions the Italian Parliament has developed as a highly polycentric institution not easily amenable to majoritarian decisions and to firm leadership by the cabinet (Cotta, 1976). This organizational and working model, by lowering the threshold of incorporation, has proven very apt to favour a partial integration of the anti-regime opposition in the political process, thus compensating its persistent exclusion from government (and probably favouring a renunciation by it of more radical behaviour). At the same time it has provided limited incentives (and perhaps even some disincentives) for the opposition to pursue with more determination and coherence the goal of fuller integration. The parliamentary arena has probably worked as an important compensating factor in a situation of weak consolidation but not as a strong factor of change.

These statements require, however, more detailed discussion. And the starting point must be the type of parliamentary institution that has developed after the democratic instauration.

In order to determine the real structure of a parliamentary body we have to look at the cumulative effects of legal and political factors.

The legal framework

With regard to the legal side we must take into account both the constitutional text and the standing orders of the chambers. In our case the Constitution had introduced two major potential factors of polycentrism in the parliamentary model: (1) a perfect bicameralism according to which the two chambers have exactly the same powers, and the consent of both is required for supporting a government and for enacting bills; (2) the possibility of full delegation of the law-making competence to the permanent committees (with the consequence that a bill can be approved by a committee without a vote in the plenary).

As far as the standing orders of the two chambers are concerned, a diachronic analysis is needed since they have undergone important changes in the time span considered. Initially the chambers adopted the old standing orders of the pre-Fascist Parliament with some changes, but in 1971 new regulations were approved and since then a number of further modifications have been introduced. A number of these changes are relevant for our discussion and we will return to them. There are, however, other elements that do not change with time (or have changed only recently).

Two points deserve mention here: the role of the executive in parliamentary workings and the voting practices. With regard to the first point, the standing orders have not reserved a particularly favoured treatment for the government (compared to ordinary members of Parliament and to parliamentary groups) in the law-making process. Moreover, they offer only weak instruments to the majority for curbing obstructionist practices. The second and connected point is the privileged position that had been attributed until the reform of 1988 to the secret vote in the legislative process. On the latter point the Constituent Assembly had decided after some discussion not to include in the constitutional text the prescription of a secret vote for the final approval of a bill. But the standing orders of the first chamber made such a way of voting mandatory, while in the Senate it had to be adopted whenever asked for by at least 20 members (therefore whenever a medium-sized opposition party asked for it). Moreover, in both chambers a secret vote can be requested at any other stage of the law-making process (as for the voting on amendments) and can be stopped only by a request from the government for a vote of confidence. This peculiarity of the Italian Parliament has offered dissenters within the governmental majority protection against political sanctions and has become an instrument of leverage in the policy-making process for the opposition cooperating with what might be called the 'minorities in the majority', that is, those sections of the majority that feel less at ease with the policy orientations of the government and nearer to those shared by the opposition. The motivations behind the recourse to this covert dissent may obviously vary. But the chances that they pertain more to questions of interest or of parliamentary tactics rather than to questions of principle are high. The dissent on questions of principle normally requires publicity that the secret vote obviously does not allow.

If the standing orders of the two chambers have been, since the beginning, not particularly orientated in a 'majoritarian' direction, their reform in 1971 has undoubtedly seen an increase of polycentric and 'consensus' (Lijphart, 1984) elements.[21] Among the main innovations have been the role assigned in the drawing up of the calendar of parliamentary activities to the conference of the leaders of parliamentary groups (it should be added that for decisions of this body the rule of unanimity is prescribed); and the increased powers of inquiry and of governmental oversight given to the standing committees of parliament (Manzella, 1977: 147 ff.).

The political factors: weak majorities

But the impact of all these elements of a legal nature (both traditional and new) cannot be fully appreciated unless one takes into consideration the political factors that have been at work with them.

Particularly important for the 'real' structure of Parliament have been the characteristics of governmental majorities. A number of reasons have contributed to making the majority supporting cabinets a parliamentary actor with a relatively low degree of cohesion:

(1) The parliamentary majority has always been the result of a coalition of parties (Marradi, 1982; Pridham, 1983);
(2) The number of parties involved has always been high (typically four although not all sharing ministerial responsibilities) with a tendency to grow with the passing of time;
(3) The relative weight of the largest party (the DC) within these coalitions has declined (to a point that in recent years its claim to the premiership has been successfully contested);[22]
(4) After 1948 the governmental majority has never been faced by an alternative coalition that could represent a real threat to its control of the executive power—an important incentive for cohesion has therefore been absent;
(5) The leading party of the majority has always been highly factionalized (Zuckerman, 1979);
(6) The governmental coalitions have generally been rather heterogeneous in their policy orientations since their formation has been determined by reasons of democratic safeguard (the necessity to exclude parties of dubious democratic loyalty) rather than by a substantial policy consensus (Sartori, 1966).

This is not the place to discuss in detail these factors and their explanations, but it is easy to see that the characteristics of the majority that we have mentioned have been to a great extent linked to the conditioned consolidation of Italian democracy. As for the consequences, the weakness of the governmental majority as a cohesive actor in parliamentary life has helped to translate into reality the opportunities for polycentrism offered by the legal setting.

The institutional polycentrism authorized or required by the legal regulations of parliamentary life has made it particularly difficult to keep the majority united and has weakened the ability of the cabinet to exercise leadership over it. On the contrary, the plural components of the majority have found a favourable environment for safeguarding their relative autonomy.

Recruitment and career patterns of parliamentarians

But some further factors have converged to strengthen the role of other parliamentary actors besides the government and its parliamentary majority. An important one has been the evolution over time of the parliamentarians, of their recruitment and career patterns. Our attention should focus in particular on the contrasting characteristics of the parliamentary elites of the governing parties (and especially of the DC) and of the opposition parties, which have been the result of the differentiated impact of the electoral system and of the diverging party organization models upon recruitment and careers.

Table 3.2 New members of the Chamber of Deputies (%)

| | Legislatures | | | | | | | | | |
	1	*2*	*3*	*4*	*5*	*6*	*7*	*8*	*9*	*10*
New MPs										
DC	46	30	35	22	31	22	37	19	27	26
PSI	60	47	38	31	36	28	26	45	43	32
PCI	67	28	37	49	46	47	57	23	50	45
Total 1st Chamber	56	37	36	35	36	33	42	27	40	33

Sources: Cotta (1976 : 317ff.) and Camera dei Deputati, *Elenco dei Deputati* (a publication issued for each new Parliament). The first Parliament is the one elected in 1948 (not all are new Members since 44% were previously members of the Constituent Assembly.

Table 3.3 Senior members in the Chamber of Deputies (%)

| | Legislatures | | | | | | | | |
	2	*3*	*4*	*5*	*6*	*7*	*8*	*9*	*10*
DC	36	44	49	53	48	46	53	55	54
PSI	12	30	39	33	47	54	34	27	43
PCI	24	39	24	20	18	18	28	28	17
Total 1st Chamber	30	41	40	40	42	37	39	39	40

Sources: Cotta (1979 : 326) and Camera dei Deputati, *Elenco dei deputati* (various issues). Deputies at their third (or further) mandate (membership of the Constitutent Assembly was counted as a mandate) are counted as 'senior members.'

With the passing of time there has been a strong decline in the turnover of DC parliamentarians and a steady growth of their tenures (see Tables 3.2 and 3.3). To better understand the meaning of this we must remember that, since the Italian electoral system assigns the seats won by a party list to the candidates that have collected the largest shares of preference votes, the gaining of a parliamentary seat has in most parties become the object of an open intraparty competition.[23] The long tenures in parliament and the limited turnover of Christian Democratic politicians mean therefore that they have built an electoral following of their own (on an individual basis or thanks to the links with a party subgroup, a *corrente*). This has given them a significant autonomy *vis-à-vis* the central party leadership and has introduced a strong degree of individualism within the ranks of the parliamentary majority (Di Palma and Cotta, 1986).

Quite a different outlook has prevailed in the largest opposition party, the PCI. Thanks to a very centralized and hierarchic party organization the use of the preference vote as an individual resource for the candidates has been, until recently, radically curbed (Cotta, 1979; Katz and Bardi, 1979: 85 ff.). In addition a deliberate policy of short tenures and high turnover has been applied for the largest part of the parliamentary group (see Tables 3.2 and 3.3). This has produced a parliamentary party with limited weight and autonomy *vis-à-vis* the party apparatus and which acts in the parliamentary arena as a highly cohesive actor under the guide of the party leaders. (Cotta, 1979: 307 ff.).

As a consequence of these divergent developments, the government has had to face in the parliamentary arena both a cohesive opposition, and sections of its own parliamentary following often showing autonomous and dissenting orientations.

The legislative process

The law-making process and its outputs bear some relevant evidence of the qualitative and quantitative effects of the polycentric structure of the parliamentary arena. On the basis of empirical studies on the Italian law-making process (Cantelli, *et al*, 1974; Cazzola, 1974; Di Palma, 1977; Cazzola and Morisi, 1981; Motta, 1985), its main features are the following (see Table 3.4):

1. An extremely high number of bills is introduced every year by members of Parliament and by the government.
2. The number of bills enacted, although only a small percentage of all those introduced, is in absolute number very high.
3. A large share of the bills are passed in the committees (following the special procedure that gives them the power to legislate directly).
4. The success rate of bills introduced by members of Parliament, although rather low, makes the legislation not originated by the executive substantial in absolute terms.
5. The success rate of government bills is higher than that of private members' bills but lower than in most other European countries (Inter-Parliamentary Union, 1986: 910 ff.).
6. Government bills are subject to relatively frequent amendments both from the majority and from the opposition in the parliamentary arena (and particularly in the committee stage) (Di Palma, 1977: 60 ff.).
7. With the passing of time the government has made increased recourse to decrees (originally conceived as an emergency way of legislating) which require only subsequent ratification by Parliament. But Parliament has also made increased use of its powers to reject or to alter these decrees (Cazzola and Morisi, 1981).[24]

8. The content of the legislative output has had a high level of disaggregation (most of the legislation concerns small, sectional interests and categories) (Di Palma, 1977: 72 ff.).

This type of law-making process has provided opportunities for participation to actors other than the government and its majority: in particular, to parliamentary backbenchers and dissenting groups within the majority and to the opposition. This point leads us to the more general question of the integration of the opposition in the political process and to our second question (about the role of Parliament in overcoming the conditioned character of the consolidation of Italian democracy).

From exclusion to integration: a non-linear path?

The dilemma between exclusion and integration of the largest opposition party (the PCI) has played (even if with changing tendencies) a central role in Italian political life after World War II. And it is still relevant today. As we have seen, the exclusion from government of that party has probably been a condition for reaching a first threshold of consolidation of the democratic regime, but at the same time it has also meant a limitation of that consolidation. Moreover, it has deeply affected the functioning of central political institutions.

After the failure of the attempt pursued between 1948 and 1953 by the governing parties to limit the influence of the oppositions and in particular to make the exclusion of the PCI from decision making more rigid through a more majoritarian interpretation of the Constitution (and with the help of some institutional reforms as that of the electoral law) (Baget-Bozzo, 1974; Rotelli, 1981), the need for the majority to find a *modus vivendi* with the opposition parties has become greater. The main reason for this has been the precarious cohesion of the majority and the problems that it has had to face given the nature of the institutional setting.

As a consequence, the sharp confrontation at the electoral level and the exclusion at the governmental level have been to some extent balanced in other political arenas (and particularly in Parliament) by a less rigid relationship between majority and opposition.

As might be expected, integration has been easier and earlier where the political stakes have been lower and also where integration has been less visible for the electorate. As it has been underlined (Sartori, 1976: 143 ff.), the problem of visibility is particularly crucial in a situation where the electorate has been for a long time strongly imbued by messages by the governmental parties about the risks for democracy coming from the Communist party and by messages from the Communist opposition delegitimating bourgeois democracy and the governing parties as subordinate to international capitalism (Barbagli and Corbetta, 1978). In the case of a too visible compromise such methods of indoctrination, which had been used by both sides to strengthen their electoral following, would obviously backfire.

In fact the political arenas where the integration of the PCI has gone further have been local and regional government (Motta, 1988: 488 ff.)[25] and

Table 3.4   Legislative output in nine legislatures

	First legislature (1948–53)			Second legislature (1953–8)		
	Introduced	*Passed*	*%*	*Introduced*	*Passed*	*%*
Government bills	2,287	2,054	90	1,667	1,414	85
Members' bills	1,375	260	19	2,514	480	19
Total	3,662	2,314	63	4,181	1,894	45
(per year)	(732)	(463)		(836)	(379)	
Members' bills over total (%)	38	11		60	25	

	Third legislature (1958–63)			Fourth legislature (1963–8)		
	Introduced	*Passed*	*%*	*Introduced*	*Passed*	*%*
Government bills	1,569	1,300	83	1,569	1,240	79
Members' bills	3,688	481	13	4,414	771	17
Total	5,257	1,781	34	5,983	2,011	34
(per year)	(1,051)	(356)		(1,197)	(402)	
Members' bills over total (%)	70	27		74	38	

	Fifth legislature (1968–72)			Sixth legislature (1972–6)		
	Introduced	*Passed*	*%*	*Introduced*	*Passed*	*%*
Government bills	977	691	71	1,235	850	69
Members' bills	4,189	250	6	4,597	272	6
Total	5,166	941	18	5,832	1,121	19
(per year)	(1,291)	(235)		(1,458)	(280)	
Members' bills over total (%)	81	27		79	24	

	Seventh legislature (1976–9)			Eighth legislature (1979–83)		
	Introduced	*Passed*	*%*	*Introduced*	*Passed*	*%*
Government bills	1,001	567	57	1,328	755	57
Members' bills	2,646	99	4	3,980	287	7
Total	3,647	666	18	5,308	1,042	20
(per year)	(1,216)	(222)		(1,327)	(260)	
Members' bills over total (%)	73	15		75	28	

Table 3.4 cont'd.

	Ninth legislature (1983–7)		
	Introduced	Passed	%
Government bills	1,331	567	43
Members' bills	4,653	221	5
Total	5,984	788	13
(per year)	(1,496)	(197)	
Members' bills over total (%)	78	28	

Sources: Di Palma (1977 : 44ff.); Senato della Repubblica, *Resocont dei lavori del Senato*, Rome (various issues).

Parliament. Of the two arenas the second is more important, given its national role and its greater proximity to the other arena (the executive) where exclusion has been strongest.

Up to a certain point a democratic parliament is always an instrument of integration for the opposition. It offers continuing participation in the national politico-institutional scene for the actors that are excluded from the central position of that scene, the executive. The nature of this participation (integration), however, may vary from symbolic to substantial, depending on the specific structure of the parliamentary milieu and the opportunities it offers. The more the parliamentary arena is structured along a majoritarian and dualistic model (and this in a parliamentary democracy means also a government-centred parliament) (King, 1976; Cotta, 1987), the more this integration will have a symbolic nature. It will mainly lie in the chance of acting as the prospective government. The less the structure of parliament is government-centred and the more it has a polycentric character, the greater will be the opportunities for substantial participation of the opposition in the decisional processes.

The fact that in a polycentric parliament such as the Italian one there are many decisional *loci* where the leadership of the government is not at stake encourages all the heterogeneous elements existing in the governmental majority to emerge and to search for contacts and alliances with the opposition. We may expect that such opportunities will be increased: (1) whenever a question is important for sectional interests within the majority that have been suppressed in the making of the governing coalition; (2) whenever the political game is played with limited publicity (with a secret vote or in less visible milieus such as the parliamentary committees); (3) when the safeguarding of the regime or other major social and international cleavages are not at issue. We must also remember that since the building of the governmental majorities has been heavily determined by the problem of loyalty to the democratic regime (and to international alliances) rather than by policy homogeneity, the components of the majority have often been anxious to find opportunities for reaffirming their specific identities and their policy preferences.

We have already seen that the law-making process has offered significant opportunities for overcoming the division between majority and opposition, but other important occasions have been stimulated by the electoral powers of the parliament. A major one has been that of the election of the head of state by the two chambers meeting together. In fact this is a situation where all the conditions mentioned above exist. Since the election of the first president of the Republic, the opposition parties (including the PCI) have played an important role. Sometimes it has been a negative one by contributing to the failure of a candidate proposed from within the governmental majority, and sometimes a positive one by adding their determinant support to a new candidate proposed by dissenters inside the majority. The highest level of this participation was reached in the election (1985) of the president now in office when the Communist opposition was publicly included from the start in the consultations for the selection of a common candidate.[26] For other high public offices of a collegial nature, the integration of the opposition has taken the form of a proportional representation within their membership. This has happened, for instance, in the elections by Parliament of a third of the members of the Constitutional Court and of the *Consiglio Superiore della Magistratura* (the highest body of the judiciary with disciplinary and career-regulating powers over the judges).[27]

An increasing integration can be seen also with regard to a number of positions of institutional leadership within the two chambers of Parliament. For the highest institutional office in the Chamber of Deputies—the presidency—a position of great importance in the working of Parliament and a stepping-stone for reaching the office of president of the Republic (all the presidents but one have been recruited among former presidents of one of the two chambers), the degree of integration of the PCI has grown more or less steadily. From proposing an alternative candidate (1948–55 and again in 1963), to abstaining (1958), to the positive support of a common candidate with the majority (1963 onwards), to the election of a Communist deputy to this office with the support of the governmental majority (1976 onwards). With the last stage the Communist party has for the first time (after the breakdown of the anti-Fascist coalition in 1947) been admitted to one of the highest constitutional offices of the state. At lower levels this had happened before: among the vice-presidents of both chambers one or two have always been Communist. However, the presidency of the Senate, because of its special role (in the case of death of the head of state the president of the Senate will take his or her place), had heretofore been refused to politicians of the PCI.

With regard to the legislative committees, the PCI until 1976 had been admitted only to the position of deputy chairman; in 1976 together with participation in the parliamentary majority it gained access also to positions of chairman in the committees. But after 1979 with the end of the governments of national unity it has again lost these positions[28] and has been able to keep only the chairmanships of a number of non-legislative committees of the two chambers.

Another point that deserves mentioning is that, with the creation in the seventies of a number of parliamentary committees that have what could be defined as 'governing powers' rather than purely legislating and oversight functions, the opposition has come, through Parliament, to share powers that in the past had been under the exclusive control of the cabinet. A major example in this field has been the important committee on radio and television (Baldassarre, 1985: 325).

By putting all these elements together, we can detect in the parliamentary arena a trend toward increasing institutional and functional integration of the opposition excluded from government. This means also that at the parliamentary level the majority–opposition cleavage has become more blurred with time. This trend reached its highest point in the seventies. First with the new standing orders of the two chambers (but particularly those of the Chamber of Deputies), then with the 1976–9 legislature when all the thresholds of integration in the parliamentary institution were overcome, even the threshold of greatest political relevance, that of integration in the parliamentary majority supporting the government.

The rules of proportional distribution of parliamentary offices and of 'broad agreements' and the disappearance of the majority–opposition dualism (except for the small parties of the extreme right and left) became the organizational principles of Parliament. Interestingly enough, during these years there became popular both in academic and political milieus the so-called doctrine of parliamentary centrality (*centralità del parlamento*). According to this theory, Parliament, rather than the executive, should play the leading role in the decision-making process; and the *consociational* rules of large coalitions and of proportional representation should prevail over the *majoritarian* principles of majority–minority confrontation and of 'government by the majority'.[29]

The participation of the Communist party in the parliamentary coalition supporting the third (1976) and fourth (1979) Andreotti cabinets was clearly the highest point of what we may call the 'parliamentary way' to the integration of the PCI in the Italian political system. After the abstention in the vote of confidence for the Christian Democratic government in 1976, the positive vote in favour of the government in 1979 put the once-excluded opposition party only a step away from full access to the executive.[30] The rather interesting point is that the last step did not follow and that parliamentary integration did not also become an integration in the executive. And at least until today the *Koalitionsfaehigkeit* (the ability to enter coalitions) (Farneti, 1983) of the PCI at the governmental level remains dubious.

Moreover, the failure to cross the threshold of governmental office and to have this sanctioned by the electorate seems to a certain extent to have backfired against the other forms of (parliamentary) integration. The renewed exclusion of the PCI from the governmental majority has brought about the loss of some important institutional positions that the party had gained in Parliament (most notably the chairmanships of the legislative committees, but not the presidency of the Chamber of Deputies). And, what is perhaps even more relevant for the opposition party, the years after 1979 have seen the strengthening of an anti-proportionalistic mood and of the support for more majoritarian solutions in the organization of Parliament (and also of the electoral system). This mood has not yet produced a full institutional *revirement*, but indicates an important change from the spirit of the seventies. Among the steps in the new direction one should mention the attempts to strengthen the cabinet both by creating a stronger bureaucratic apparatus at the disposal of the prime minister[31] and by giving a more favoured status to the government *vis-à-vis* other parliamentary actors in the law-making process. At a symbolic level (if not at the level of concrete effects) the most significant change in this direction has been the drastic limitation in 1988 of the secret vote which was the dominant voting practice in the law-making process. A clear attack has been made against the ability of the opposition to assert its influence by exploiting centrifugal forces in the governmental majority. Interestingly enough, while the previous important change in the parliamentary standing orders (1971) had been made after a broad agreement with the opposition, this time it was promoted by the majority *against* the opposition.

Paradoxically enough, the largest opposition party has been pushed to a more marginal position in the parliamentary arena and appears more distant from access to governmental office in the eighties than it was ten years before. And this is true in spite of the fact that its move toward the centre of the political spectrum (on the levels of ideological stances, international commitments and policy proposals) has become stronger in recent years, and that its acceptance by the other political actors as a loyal democratic player has deepened.

Concluding remarks

The events that we have resumed seem to indicate that the problem of the integration of a large and previously excluded anti-regime opposition cannot be easily and entirely solved through an incremental process of step-by-step institutional integration such as the one that has taken place in Italy and for which the parliamentary setting has offered an extremely favourable milieu for all the reasons that we have seen. The last step—full assumption of governmental roles—seems to be less liable to be reached through such a continuous process. The reasons are probably the particularly sensitive power implications of this step and its maximum visibility for the electorate.

If this is true one could add that from the point of view of the PCI the strategy of incremental integration through Parliament that this party has deliberately followed for a long time has had a mixed success. It has enabled the largest opposition party to move from exclusion to the position of playing an important role in Italian political life and to do this without having to put in jeopardy its more militant following by too abrupt a revision of its ideological and international identity. At the same time one could suggest that exactly this strategy with its successes, and the assumption that this strategy will develop in a linear way up to the point of full integration, have for a long time distracted the party from more boldly facing the problem of its image at the electoral level and of its *Koalitionsfaehigkeit* for the executive. And this has delayed in the long run the full access of the PCI to governmental roles. The party's revision of its strategy, which has taken place in recent years (and the shift of interest from the parliamentary to the electoral and executive arenas) indicates a growing awareness of the Communist party of the limitation of the previous strategy.

From the point of view of the political system as a whole the role played by the parliamentary arena during the first three decades of democratic life (1946–79) has probably reduced the risks of a breakdown by counterbalancing the electoral confrontation and the permanent exclusion from government of the second largest party. At the same time it has made change in the political system (and particularly in the governmental process) slower. The tempo of change has become quicker in recent years; is it by chance that the weight of the parliamentary arena has been declining?

Notes

1. Primarily because only this length of time is 'available' given the timing of these processes, but perhaps also for more substantial reasons if we agree that democratic consolidation was—at least in Spain, Greece, and Portugal—a relatively faster process than in Italy.
2. For a long time public opinion polls showed a significant part of the electorate sharing doubts about the full democratic integration of the PCI. It is obviously more difficult to evaluate to what extent similar doubts expressed by elites were sincere or had to do with reasons of propaganda for their parties.
3. The idea expressed by the leader of the PCI, Berlinguer, that it would not be convenient for the left to govern with a bare majority (51%) but it should enter a much larger coalition acknowledged implicitly the fact that the PCI still lacked a full legitimation (Gruppi, 1977: 309).
4. On the attitude of the PCI *vis-à-vis* the constitution see the following pages. On the political values of the followers of this party there are many empirical data collected in different periods of time (eg Alberoni, 1967; Barbagli and Corbetta, 1978); as for the elites a reading of the cultural weekly (*Rinascita*) and of some of the theoretical journals of the party shows at least until the seventies a generalized critique of formal democracy, little sympathy for party competition and stronger support for 'other forms' of democracy (economic democracy, direct democracy etc.). Similar results can be drawn by interviews with Communist MPs made in the late sixties (Putnam, 1973).
5. The elections of 1946 were for the Constituent Assembly and not for an ordinary Parliament, but for all practical purposes can be considered as the first elections.
6. One should remember that in the local elections that took place after the 1946 referendum over monarchy, the right made strong gains against the centre and particularly against the DC (Catalano, 1980; Gambino, 1978). The growth of the right which could attack on that occasion the DC as being an 'accomplice of the left' (in the executive), was stopped by the great confrontation of 1948 when the major dividing line was between left and centre.
7. It is interesting to note for instance that in spite of all the changes that have taken place in the seventies and eighties in the relationship with the CPSU, in the great annual summer *kermis* of the PCI (*Festa Nazionale dell 'Unità*) the exhibit of the Communist party of the Soviet Union retains a central place together with those of all the Communist parties in power. And also the idea of changing the name of the party has never been accepted.
8. In fact another assembly (*Consulta*) existed before the Constituent Assembly with the task of preparing the way to the first elections. This assembly, however, was not elected but nominated by the government. Its political role was therefore much more limited.

9. The Constituent Assembly tried, however, to exert some influence over the legislative process through its committees that had consulting powers.

10. The last attempt to preserve continuity with the past institutions was made by the second prime minister, Bonomi, an old politician of pre-Fascist democracy, who nominated the presidents of the two old chambers. But the two chambers themselves were not revived (Bettinelli, 1982: 21 ff.).

11. The proposal was put forward by the Christian Democratic minister of interior (Scelba). Only the three largest parties (DC, PCI, and PSI) belonged at that time to the government.

12. The Christian Democratic party had gained the premiership for the first time in 1945, when it could present itself as an arbiter in the increasingly sharp conflict between left and right.

13. The position of the DC on this issue was particularly delicate. Its leaders and political elite were predominantly in favour of the republican solution, but among its prospective voters (particularly in the south) a large number would have been in favour of the king. And also important sections of the Catholic Church favoured the monarchy (Baget-Bozzo, 1974).

14. The other four countries considered in this book could offer some interesting evidence given the rather different processes through which their democratic constitutions were adopted.

15. While the second De Gasperi cabinet (July 1946–February 1947) had the full support of DC, PCI and PSI and PRI, and the third De Gasperi cabinet (February 1947–May 1947) still enjoyed the support (although weaker) of the three largest parties, the fourth De Gasperi cabinet (May 1947–May 1948) was in practice a purely Christian Democratic cabinet and had the parliamentary support of the Republican and Social Democratic parties.

16. For instance the DC and PCI sided together on the vote for article 7 (Church–State relations) against other left and centre parties. But the DC voted with the right in favour of a second chamber. And part of the right helped the left to defeat the Christian Democratic proposal to have a second chamber based on the principle of functional representation.

17. At the end of the committee stage there was still the idea of a second chamber based on the principles of functional representation. (Amato and Bruno, 1981).

18. In the end the main differences between the two chambers are the following: 1. the second chamber is half as big as the first; 2. the second chamber is elected via a PR electoral system that allows for no preference voting and is slightly less proportional than that of the first chamber since it does not provide for the counting of remainders at the national level. So all the battle for having a second chamber that in some way would equilibrate the first produced a second chamber that is more or less a replica of the first.

19. Of the members of the Constituent Assembly 45% were re-elected to the Chamber of Deputies and 25% to the Senate in the first ordinary Parliament.

20. The participation in drafting the Constitution and the common vote in its favour became a symbolic theme (the so-called *arco costituzionale*) of some importance in the seventies, preparing the ground for bridging the gap between governing parties and opposition.

21. It is interesting to underline the fact that the new standing orders of 1971 were drafted on the basis of a broad agreement between majority and opposition.

22. The largest party (the DC) lost the premiership in 1981 for the first time since 1945. The cabinet leadership went to a small centre-left party (PRI). In the following Parliament (1983–7), the PSI kept uninterruptedly that position. Only in 1987 did the DC gain back the cabinet leadership.

23. It is common for candidates to stage a highly visible personal campaign (with TV commercials, newspaper ads, stickers etc.).

24. The legal effects of these decrees begin from the day of their issuence by the government. But the decrees become void of effects unless they are ratified by Parliament within 60 days. The recourse to this instrument has become more frequent with time. Particularly after 1976 it has become an ordinary rather than an exceptional instrument for legislating (Cazzola and Morisi, 1981; Motta, 1985).
25. The Communist party has always had regional strongholds where it controlled local government alone or together with the Socialist party. But in the seventies it had a strong growth also in other areas of the country and became able to build alliances with parties traditionally nearer to the DC (eg the PSDI and PRI and in some cases even the PLI).
26. Also Pertini was elected (in 1978) with the votes of the PCI but without such formal consultations. It is interesting to note that with the exception of the last presidential election (Cossiga in 1985), in no case was the first candidate of the DC elected. The largest party always had to bow to a second choice (Baget-Bozzo, 1974 and 1977).
27. The original attempt to adopt a strategy of exclusion of the oppositions in this field failed. After a stalemate of nearly two years, between 1953 and 1955, an agreement was finally reached to elect also some candidates that could be accepted by the opposition. Since then the practice of proportional representation of the major parties in these bodies has become increasingly clear.
28. A heated debate developed on this subject. But the point of view of the PCI that committee chairmen should not necessarily belong to the parties of the governmental majority was finally defeated.
29. A reading of *Democrazia e diritto*, a semi-academic journal of the PCI in the fields of constitutional law and political science, during the seventies is particularly fruitful for appreciating the contents of this doctrine. The limits and the decline of this doctrine and of its practical implementations were the object of a broad discussion in the eighties (Onida, 1981; Cheli, 1981; Baldassarre, 1985; Cotta, 1987).
30. While the third Andreotti cabinet of 1976 rested upon the positive vote of the DC and the abstentions of PCI, PSI, PSDI, PRI and PLI, the fourth Andreotti cabinet of 1978 had the votes of DC, PCI, PSI, PSDI and PRI. The PLI did not give its support and there was also a strong dissent within the Christian Democratic parliamentary party. Only a dramatic speech of Moro (his last political act before being kidnapped) overcame the doubts of the DC. Both governments had only Christian Democratic ministers.
31. With the De Mita cabinet of 1987, a cabinet secretariat was created. This was the consequence of the approval by Parliament of a bill that was introduced for the first time in the early eighties by the Spadolini government (the first cabinet not headed by a Christian Democratic prime minister.

References

Alberoni, F. (ed.) (1967), *L'attivista di partito. Un'indagine sui militanti di base nel PCI e nella DC*, Bologna, Il Mulino.
Amato, G., and F. Bruno (1981), 'La forma di governo italiana. Dalle idee dei partiti all Assemblea Costituente', *Quaderni Costituzionali*, **1**, 33–85.
Baget-Bozzo, G. (1974), *Il partito cristiano al potere*, Florence, Vallecchi.
—(1977), *Il partito cristiano e l'apertura a sinistra*, Florence, Vallecchi.
Baldassarre, A. (1985), 'Le "performances" del Parlamento italiano nell 'ultimo quindicennio' in G. Pasquino (ed.), *Il sistema politico italiano*, Bari, Laterza.

Barbagli, M. and P.G. Corbetta (1978), 'Una tattica e due strategie. Inchiesta sulla base del PCI', *Il Mulino*, **27**, 922–67.

Bettinelli, E. (1982), *All 'origine della democrazia dei partiti*, Milan, Comunità.

Cantelli, F., V. Mortara and G. Movia (1974), *Come lavora il Parlamento*, Milan, Giuffrè.

Catalano, F. (1980), *Una difficile democrazia. Italia 1943–1948*, Messina, D'Anna.

Cazzola, F. (1974), *Governo e opposizione nel Parlamento italiano*, Milan, Giuffrè.

—and M. Morisi (1981), *L'alluvione dei decreti. Il processo legislativo tra settima ed ottava legislatura*, Milan, Giuffrè.

Cheli, E. (1978), *Costituzione e sviluppo delle istituzioni in Italia*, Bologna, Il Mulino.

—(1981), 'La "centralità" parlamentare, sviluppo e decadenza di un modello', *Quaderni Costituzionali*, **1**, 343–50.

—(1979), *Classe politica e parlamento in Italia. 1946–1976*, Bologna, Il Mulino.

—(1987), 'Il sotto-sistema governo-parlamento', *Rivista Italiana di Scienza Politica*, **17**, 241–83.

Di Palma, G. (1977), *Surviving without Governing'. The Italian Parties in Government*, Berkeley, University of California Press.

—and M. Cotta (1986), 'Cadres, Peones and Entrepreneurs: Professional Identities in a Divided Parliament' in E.N. Suleiman (ed.), *Parliaments and Parliamentarians in Democratic Politics*, New York, Holmes and Meier.

Farneti, P. (1978), 'Social Conflict, Parliamentary Fragmentation, Institutional Shift, And the Rise of Fascism' in J.J. Linz and A. Stepan, (eds), *The Breakdown of Democratic Regimes: Europe*, Baltimore, The Johns Hopkins University Press.

—(1983), *Il sistema dei partiti in Italia 1946–1979*, Bologna, Il Mulino.

Gambino, A. (1978), *Storia del dopoguerra. Dalla Liberazione al potere DC*, Bari, Laterza.

Gruppi, L. (ed.) (1977), *Il compromesso storico*, Rome, Editori Riuniti.

Inter-Parliamentary Union (1986), *Parliaments of the World*, Aldershot, Gower.

Katz, R. (1986), 'Party Government: A Rationalistic Conception' in F.G. Castles and R. Wildenmann (eds), *Visions and Realities of Party Government*, Berlin and New York, de Gruyter.

—and L. Bardi (1979), Voti di preferenza e ricambio del personale parlamentare, *Rivista Italiana di Scienza Politica*, **9**, 71–96.

King, A. (1976), 'Modes of Executive–Legislative Relations: Great Britain, France, and West Germany', *Legislative Studies Quarterly*, **1**, 11–35.

La Palombara, J. (1978), 'Il PCI in una società in trasformazione' in J. La Palombara, G. Sani and G. Sartori, *Il PCI dall 'opposizione al governo e dopo?*, Torino, Quaderni di Biblioteca della Libertà, n.11.

Liebert, V. *Parliament as a Central Site in Bureaucratic Consolidation: A Preliminary Exploration*, in this volume, chapter 1.

Liebert, U. (1988), 'Parlamento y consolidación de la democracia en la Europa del Sur', *Revista Española de Investigaciones Sociológicas*, n. 42.

Linz, J.J: (1974), 'La democrazia italiana di fronte al futuro' in F.L. Cavazza and S.R. Graubard (eds), *Il caso italiano*, Milan, Garzanti.

Linz, J.J. (1978), 'Crisis, Breakdown and Reequilibration' in J.J. Linz and A. Stepan op. cit.

Lijphart, A, (1984), *Democracies, Patterns of Majoritarian and Consensus Government in Twenty-One Countries*, New Haven, Yale University Press.

Loewenberg, G. and S.C. Patterson (1979), *Comparing Legislatures*, Boston, Little, Brown and Company.

Lotti, L. (1963), 'Il Parlamento italiano 1909–1963'. Raffronto storico'in G. Sartori (ed.), *Il Parlamento italiano. 1946–1963*, Naples, Edizioni Scientifiche Italiane.

Mammarella, G. (1976), *Il Partito Comunista Italiano 1945/1975*, Florence, Vallecchi.

Manzella, A. (1977), *Il Parlamento*, Bologna, Il Mulino.

Marradi, A. (1982), 'Italy: From "Centrism" to Crisis of the Center–Left Coalitions', in E.C. Browne and J. Dreijmanis (eds), *Government Coalitions in Western Democracies*, New York, Longman.

Morlino, L. (1981), 'Del fascismo a una democracia débil: El cambio de régimen en Italia (1939–1948)' in J. Santamaria (ed.), *La transicion a la democracia en el sur de Europa y America Latina*, Madrid, Centro de Investigaciones Sociologicas.

— (1986), 'Consolidamento democratico: definizione e modelli', *Rivista Italiana di Scienza Politica*, **16**, 197–238.

Motta, R. (1985), 'L'attività legislativa dei governi', *Rivista Italiana di Scienza Politica*, **15**, 255–92.

— (1988), 'Le coalizioni regionali in Italia', *Rivista Italiana di Scienza Politica*, **18**, 447–86.

Onida, V. (1981), 'Recenti sviluppi della forma di governo in Italia: prime osservazioni', *Quaderni Costituzionali*, **1**, 7–31.

Pasquino, G. (1985), 'Partiti, società civile e istituzioni' in G. Pasquino (ed.), *Il sistema politico italiano*, Bari, Laterza.

Piscitelli, E. (1975), *Da Parri a De Gasperi. Storia del dopoguerra 1945/1948*, Milan, Feltrinelli.

Pridham, G. (1983), 'Party Politics and Coalition Government in Italy' in V. Bogdanor (ed.), *Coalition Government in Western Europe*, London, Heinemann.

Putnam, R. (1973), *The Beliefs of Politicians: Ideology, Conflict and Democracy in Britain and Italy*, New Haven, Yale University Press.

— R. Leonardi and R. Nanetti (1981), 'Polarization and Depolarization in Italian Politics 1968–1981', paper presented at the 1981 annual meeting of the American Political Science Association, Chicago.

Rotelli, E. (1981), 'La prima legislatura repubblicana e il ruolo del Parlamento', *Quaderni Costituzionali*, **1**, 87–113.

Ruffilli, R. (ed.) (1978 and 1979), *Cultura politica e partiti nell 'età della Costituente*, 2 vols, Bologna, Il Mulino.

Sani, G. (1976), 'Mass Perceptions of Anti-System Parties' in *British Journal of Political Science*.

Sartori, G. (1966), 'European Political Parties. The Case of Polarized Pluralism' in J. La Palombara and M. Weiner (eds), *Political Parties and Political Development*, Princeton, Princeton University Press.

— (1974), 'Rivisitando il Pluralismo polarizzato' in F.L. Cavazza and S.R. Graubard (eds.), *Il caso italiano*, Milan, Garzanti.

— (1976), *Parties and Party Systems. A Framework for Analysis*, Cambridge, Cambridge University Press.

— *Teoria dei partiti e caso italiano*, Milan, Sugarco.

Scoppola, P. (1977), *La proposta politica di De Gasperi*, Bologna, Il Mulino.

Weiner, M. and J. La Palombara (1966), 'The Impact of Parties on Political Development' in J. La Palombara and M. Weiner (eds), *Political Parties and Political Development*, Princeton, Princeton University Press.

Zuckerman, A.S. (1979), *The Politics of Faction*, New Haven, Yale University Press.

4 By consociationalism to a majoritarian parliamentary system: the rise and decline of the Spanish Cortes

J. Capo Giol[†], R. Cotarelo,*
*D. Lopez Garrido** and J. Subirats[‡]*

Introduction*

After the death of Franco in November 1975, Spain, which was among the last dictatorships in Europe, became a democracy. The process by which this took place has been dubbed 'transition' and began to be studied as if it were a mechanism that could later be applied in other contexts.[1] When the evolution of the three cases of Spain, Portugal and Greece was considered, it was feared that democracy could turn out to be ephemeral in countries without a firm tradition of democratic government. It is true that, in the past, the three countries have shown a tendency to resolve politics 'by other means' as Clausewitz would have said. But it is not true that they 'lacked a democratic tradition'. In the nineteenth century, from 1834 onwards, Spain had a political system similar to those of other countries in Europe, and after 1876 the system was clearly democratic. The dictatorship from 1936–9 to 1975 was an exceptional period whose shadow, because it is so recent, tends to be projected backwards in time; thereby, one is encouraged to think that the past was the same. However, a country's political traditions are established over centuries, not decades. Even the dictatorship of Primo de Rivera, in the twenties, was not a totally authoritarian regime.[2] Thus, the transition to democracy in Spain did not entail trying out a new, unknown form of government, but rather, the return to a political system that the country had already experienced in the past, whether with stability or without it. This may, in part, explain why the anti-liberal, anti-parliamentary culture inherited from Francoism could co-exist with the rapid restoration of democratic political institutions.

It should also be remembered that, in Spain as well as in Portugal, Greece and Turkey, the re-establishment of democracy took place under conditions of widespread economic crisis.[3] Such conditions make democratic reform of the political system difficult. In the case of Spain this was particularly true given that during the years of economic development from 1960 to 1973, the dictatorship had managed to identify itself with security and prosperity. Democracy, unfortunately, seemed to many to be linked to high inflation and unemployment, economic recession and a drop in purchasing power, not to mention disagreeable measures of economic adjustment.

In Spain, transition was basically peaceful,[4] and this was an important contributory factor to the legitimization of the proposals for democratic transformation: one of the means by which earlier dictatorships had attempted to legitimize themselves was by arguing that they gave their people peace.

Despite the operation of a range of contrary factors, Spain seems to have established a stable democratic system. In the Spanish case, we can discern a classical political regime in which the traditional state powers have, to different degrees, contributed to the consolidation of democracy.

The organization and workings of the public powers in Spain have achieved characteristics which appear common to all parliamentary democracies, together with certain elements which are specific to Spain. To be emphasized is the special importance of one institution in particular in the Spanish political system, namely, the monarchy.[5] Although the Crown's role in Spain's parliamentary system is purely ceremonial, none the less, at the most delicate moment in the new Spanish democratic experience ie during the attempted *coup d'etat*, the Crown's influence was decisive.[6] So much was this the case that the king's actions at that time brought about a definitive re-legitimization of the Spanish monarchy and a long-awaited recovery of the loyalty that his subjects had refused his grandfather.[7] In these circumstances, there is practically nothing to distinguish the Spanish political system from those of other democratic monarchies.

It is, however, interesting that, in the Spanish case, the political device that had originally served to re-establish democracy and to provide the country with a constitution—the strategy of consensus politics—[8]is one of the bugbears of anti-parliamentary critics in Spain. Indeed, when there was a desire to take such policy beyond the constituent legislature, (1977–9), it was subjected to a criticism which accused the consensus style of being responsible for the irrelevance of parliament.[9]

In Spain there is a strong tendency to criticize public institutions in general, and Parliament is second only to the government in the degree of criticism it attracts. After the consensus period came to an end, the legislative body lived through a hazardous period in which, during the first legislature from 1979 to 1982, the government lacked an absolute majority and, with regard to the most important measures, was obliged to arrive at agreements on the margins of of Parliament. The reaction to this was a widespread feeling of mistrust of the efficiency of the representative institutions. During the first legislature, criticism manifested itself in a variety of ways, from peaceful declarations of discontent all the way to the attempted coup mentioned above.[10]. Since then, the second and third legislatures have had governments with comfortable absolute majorities in both chambers. This, however, has led to a re-manifestation of a phenomenon that could be termed, the 'return in the opposite direction': whereas Parliament had been accused of being inoperative because parties agreed to measures on the margins of Parliament, now it is said that Parliament is inoperative because the party in power has no need to reach such a consensus with other parties. In this way it is assumed that Parliament is used as a mere sounding board for parties' own interests and that it has, as a consequence, become 'denaturalized'.[11] The fact that, both when the governing party has an absolute majority and when it does not, Parliament is criticized for being unworkable, proves that its inoperativeness does not depend on majorities or minorities, but on the control that the parties exercise at any given time.

The impact of these criticisms was heightened by the specifically Spanish factor, generated during the Franco regime: a political culture with anti-parliamentarism as one of its central elements. The starting points for this political culture were the assumptions that political parties are really interest groups without any concern for the good of the nation and that parliaments are places in which the *national* interest is manipulated for the benefit of other *partial* and/or *spurious* interests. This conception, which finds its origins in the Francoist notion of an 'organic' parliament, had negative effects on the prestige of Parliament as a democratic institution. The latter, nevertheless, as we shall see, carried out an important task in the process of consolidating democracy in Spain.

The constituent Cortes and the instauration of a majoritarian parliamentary system[†]

Introduction

Of all state institutions parliament is perhaps the one most shaped or governed by the constitution. Therefore, research on the parliamentary institution (unlike research in other fields, such as electoral behaviour or the organization and activities of interest groups) must normally start with the study of its constitutional and house rules in order to be able to evaluate their performance.

This by no means implies that empirical analysis of parliamentary behaviour should be avoided. Although individual members of Parliament and parliamentary groups may be subject to the same rules, they are likely to have different concepts and perceptions about their roles and functions as representatives. In fact, studies of the nature of parliamentary representativeness and decision making often reveal more of the legislature's real performance than essays on the jurisprudence of parliamentary standing orders.

However, it is parliamentary activity in particular that subjects individual and collective behaviour to detailed formal or informal rules, prescribing how differing demands should be articulated and setting limits on the decisions that authority may make to express the general will. For instance, as compared to the secret deliberations of government and its collective accountability, internal regulations require parliamentary debates to be open to the public; and while court decisions remain highly arbitrary, rigid parliamentary procedures regulate legislative decision making as well as methods for monitoring the government of the day.

The case of the Spanish Cortes during the constituent legislature and the three subsequent ones (1977–89) is especially revealing as regards the interplay of both the normative order and political dynamics. Among the most telling features are the change in the predominant figures in Parliament and the varying interrelations between them, both in Parliament and elsewhere. An explanation of the role of the Spanish Cortes and of how it has evolved during these four legislatures must aim equally at identifying juridical and political elements. A detailed study of the normative basis, which has remained stable for approximately ten years, must be complemented by an analysis of the political process and the several ruptures it has suffered during the past decade. This seems to be the only way to account for the major changes in Parliament's image during this period.[12]

Transition from the Franco regime

With the elections of June 1977, Spain turned its back on the former Franco apparatus, based on an organic, corporatist parliament anchored in an authoritarian system, and adapted itself to a multi-party, parliamentary mode of existence. As everyone knows, the transition was a peaceful one, steered by a reformist elite which, from within the Franco establishment, was able to reach agreement with the democratic opposition.

The reasons why such agreement was possible are too complex to analyse in these brief pages. However, it should be recalled that from the very outset the followers of Franco were a heterogenous grouping and that there had long been strain between various factions such as the Falangists, monarchists, Carlists, etc. The strain became even more pronounced with the enactment of the 1967 Organic State Law which enshrined both a reactionary and a reformist faction (Santamaria, 1981: 376). All this took place within an economic context in which Spain had gone from being an agricultural to an industrial country aspiring to join the Common Market, and within a climate of radically changing social customs (which were scarcely compatible with the preservation of the ideological values of the Franco regime).

These economic and social transformations gave impetus to the reformist faction, led by President Adolfo Suárez whose modernization strategy required him to enter a pact with opposition parties (Liberals, Christian Democrats, Socialists, Communists). Although these parties were relatively weak in terms of popular support, they were well connected to the reigning political forces in Europe and, consequently, their validation of the new government's democratic credentials was absolutely necessary.[13] Unable to impose its strategy of political 'rupture', the opposition accepted the pace and procedures for reform set by the Suãrez government. They accepted the referendum in 1976 on the Political Reform Bill and parliamentary elections according to the terms of this organic law. Parliament was to have two chambers and a considerable number of Senators were to be appointed by the Crown. In addition, the electoral system favoured the less-industrialized and urban areas where the democratic opposition was not as strong and the 'constituent' nature of Parliament was not clearly defined (although neither was it definitely discounted) (Lucas Verdú, 1976).

The constituent Cortes

Spain's political scene underwent a radical change after the first elections, held in 1977. The elections revealed just how little support the old regime enjoyed and attested to the existence of a sizeable electorate which favoured centrist and moderate parties (Marvall, 1984; Linz, 1981), capable of supporting the pact that had been made and broadening it by helping to draft a constitution based on consensus.

Thus, Parliament played a majority role in institutionalizing a democratic system. Not all parts of the Franco apparatus broke down simultaneously:

the crisis of the Franco regime did not affect all state institutions in the same way. While those which were most closely linked to the Franco years (such as the Movement, and the 'vertical' trade unions) have died with him, others, (such as the Army, the police and a substantial part of the administration), have survived almost intact. [Solé Tura and Aja, 1977: 2]

Parliament was the only state institution which was made democratic and the only one capable of fostering understanding among all those groups which favoured democratization.

The relative weakness of each group participating in the process facilitated this understanding. The Uniõn de Centro Democrãtico (UCD), the reform party led by Suãrez, needed to enter a pact with the opposition in order to weaken the sectors which resisted change and to demonstrate that the people were massively and uniformly in favour of democracy.

Meanwhile, the democratic opposition had little more than a single weapon in its arsenal: the electorate's support. The parties themselves were weak and in many cases were still in the process of being formed and/or reformed. The trade unions had few members and the employers' associations had just begun reorganizing; local government was still in the hands of Franco loyalists etc. In fact, it can be safely said that Parliament was the only meeting place for the democratically minded. (Since then, the consolidation of regional, municipal, union and other systems has caused power to spread to a larger number of institutions and individuals.)

But at the outset of democracy, Parliament was the place where all the advocates of renewal met. Thus, the Moncloa Pacts were ratified by parliamentary party leaders and not by representatives of the trade unions.[14] At another level, temporary systems of regional autonomy were forged through the efforts of Deputies and Senators from the regions concerned.

Still, despite their shared interest in democratizing and modernizing the system, not all the parliamentary parties were equally powerful nor were their objectives the same. Table 4.1 shows the results of the 1977 elections and the make-up of Parliamentary groups at the beginning and end of the legislature.[15]

Table 4.1 Composition of the constituent Cortes (general elections 1977)

	Party results			Strength of parliamentary groups	
	%	Seats		B	E
AP	8.3	16	AP	16	16
UCD	34.7	165	UCD	166	157
UDC	0.9	2			
PSOE	29.2	118	PSOE	103	106
			PSC	15	18
PCE	9.2	20	PCE	20	20
			MVC	20	–
CiU	2.8	11	MC	–	9
PNV	1.6	8	MV	–	8
EE	0.3	1			
ERC	0.7	1			
PSP	4.5	6	MX	9	15
Ind.	0.3	2			

B: Beginning of legislature/June 1977
E: End of legislature/March 1979

Source: Cortes Generales, Congresso de los Diputados. Legislatura 1977–1979 Memoria: Madrid, March 1979.

Conflicts and alliances

Table 4.1 reveals the basic cleavages which could have been an obstacle to consolidating democracy. The Franco regime versus democracy became a game of musical chairs played with the so-called *'de-facto* powers'. In Parliament, the weakness of Franco's followers, most of whom had joined the ranks of Alianza Popular (AP) (Lõpez Nieto, 1988), proved helpful to the government's blueprint for reform. The left–right conflict was mitigated by Suãrez's middle of the road strategy for UCD (Huneus, 1985); Social Democratic ideas were the point of departure for the Catalan nationalist party (Marcet, 1984); the Partido Socialista Obrero Español (PSOE) aimed for a moderate electorate (Tezanos, 1981; Maravall, 1984) and the Partido Comunista de España (PCE) defined itself as Eurocommunist.

The principal problem was not disagreements over what should be the socio-economic focus of the new system nor was it differences of opinion as to whether the system should be a monarchy or a republic. Opinions on issues like this were simply rhetorical statements symbolizing what the electorate expected each party to stand for. The political leaders were well aware that it was compromise which had kept the transition period under control.

The real discussion was about democratizing the institutions and their practices, (which explains why so much emphasis was placed on the Constitution's containing a declaration of rights), the actual make-up of the parliamentary system and the design of a system of regional autonomies rather than the traditional state centralism. This latter was the issue most likely to upset the fragile balance of democracy: defenders of the Spanish nationalism on which the state was founded and Catalan and Basque nationalists (the latter include the armed radicals of ETA) are unyielding in their opposition to one another.

The only way in which the fledgling democracy could be consolidated was by parliamentary negotiations between the different political groups, thus smoothing over differences that had not been settled in previous democratic experiments due to a paucity of general agreements between the various political alternatives (Solé Tura and Aja, 1977). The very memory of the failure of the Second Republic and its consequences now spurred political leaders to adopt a consensus strategy.[16]

'Consensus' was manifested in two ways. As far as content was concerned, it meant that the parties stressed points of agreement over those which might have led to divisions. In terms of procedure it meant restricting discussions about the Constitution to a limited number of members of Parliament. An *ad-hoc* committee, with representatives from AP (1), UCD (3), PSOE (1), PCE (1) and Minoria Catalana (MC) (1) (which also represented the Basque minority), was charged with writing a first draft of the Constitution. In fact, the committee served as a watchdog during the entire process of the drafting of the Constitution, making certain that the basic framework it had designed was adhered to.

This small group was a living example of one of the great truths behind the success of the consensus strategy:

the likelihood of success in settling disagreements which arise during a constituent process is greater . . . when the negotiations take place privately between a relatively small number of representatives of the parties (but without neglecting those groups whose final approval will be essential), who are empowered to make binding agreements for their respective political clientele. [Gunther, 1986: 61]

Nevertheless, there was frequent criticism of the fact that the representatives were not allowed to express themselves as individuals.

Guaranteeing the internal discipline of the different groups was essential to reaching a consensus. Indeed, the ideologies and political values of the different parties were so diverse that at first it seemed as though the Constitution would be quite unlike what it subsequently proved to be. One hypothesis—and it enjoyed some active support—was that UCD and AP would form a stable coalition, and, by achieving a parliamentary majority, put a brake on the democratization process.

In fact, consensus meant splitting this possible majority (considered 'natural' by the sectors on the far right of the political spectrum) and reaching, between UCD and PSOE, agreements that enjoyed a varying degree of support from the remaining parties, depending upon the specific issues involved.

Constitutional design of the parliamentary model

The design was particularly evident in discussions about the institution of Parliament itself. Examination of the various amendments presented and the votes cast by the individual groups and representatives during the first *ad-hoc* committee discussions on the Constitution, and a review of the discussion (which was largely a preview of subsequent discussions) about the regulations by which Parliament should be governed, reveals that the parliamentary models presented by AP and UCD were very similar: the legislative branch was to be just another state agency, subordinate to the executive branch. PSOE and PCE, on the other hand, insisted that, in the tradition of parliamentary sovereignty, the legislative branch be central (Capo, 1983).

Consensus managed to eliminate the inflexibility of the two models—the general contours of which reflected the right–left cleavage—by bringing in other issues which crossed ideological lines: nationwide parties versus regional parties; big parties versus small parties, etc. This made it possible to find some common ground—particularly in the case of UCD and PSOE—and also allowed the other parties to integrate to a greater or lesser extent, depending upon the particular issues involved.

Thus, it was not a single alliance that institutionalized Parliament. Rather, various alliances were formed around each specific aspect of the Constitution. In this way, the aspirations of every group were at least partially realized. Though drafting the Constitution was a long and arduous process, it bore fruit: the Constitution was almost unanimously approved by Congress (258 votes in favour, 2 votes against and 14 abstentions, the latter being cast largely by AP and the Partido National Vasco ÄPNVÜ). This breakdown of the classic right–left cleavage—which translated into a concept of Parliament as either a rationalized agency (AP and UCD) or as a central, sovereign institution (PSOE and PCE)—can be seen in two of the issues which have traditionally been among the most controversial: the upper house and the system of checks and balances.

In the case of the upper house the left did not so much fight to suppress the Senate as attempt to give it a specific function in relation to a state made up of autonomous regions. However, an early, ambitious proposal for a Senate consisting of representatives of Spain's different nationalities and regions was, under the joint pressure of AP, UCD and PSOE working against the interests of the regional parties and PCE, gradually whittled down to a modest chamber of territorial representatives. Still, the Senate's political power was effectively neutralized because the left was reluctant to accept a chamber that would be elected under a system that favoured the more conservative areas of the country.

As far as the system of checks and balances was concerned, the need to stabilize the democratic system meant that it was also essential to assure governability. Thus, both Suãrez's minority government and PSOE, which seemed very likely to find itself in a similar minority position in the future, were interested in seeing to it that both houses of Parliament were built on the idea of two majority parties in order to protect the government (which, given the party system in 1977, could presumably be only one or the other of them) from the danger of a parliamentary crisis.

In this way, they were able to overcome such differences of opinion dividing the left and right as majority versus proportional electoral systems. Until almost the very end of the congressional discussions it appeared that UCD would cast its vote for a majority system (as proposed by AP). However, UCD finally aligned itself with PSOE in favour of maintaining the basic norms of the March 1977 decree which, though nominally a proportional system, has some extremely distorting effects (Vallés and Carreras, 1977; Vallés, 1977; Pallarés, 1981) of benefit to the two major parties (Centrists and Socialists), as well as to the Basque and Catalan minorities which were majoritarian in their regions.

The same bipartisan approach was apparent in the formation of parliamentary groups and in the establishment of the competence of members of Parliament.[17] In order to prevent fragmentation of the UCD party/coalition as well as to make it difficult for non-PSOE socialist groups to act (Capo, 1981), obstacles were placed in the way of the formation of groups having only a few representatives. Furthermore, individual representatives were strictly controlled—through restrictions on their rights to present amendments or request the floor—and their voting behaviour was closely monitored.[18] These restrictions were not just evident during the constituent legislature but became almost institutionalized in 1982 when the final Parliamentary Regulations were passed (Capo, 1984), thus proving that they were by no means simply a product of the times but were, in fact, part of a longer-range plan.

The truth of the matter is that although UCD and PSOE differed in terms of their models of an ideal parliament, they shared the same views regarding the most desirable type of party system and both aimed for the same kind of democratic stability. Although seeming to contradict the consensus principal reflected during the drafting of the Constitution, the two leading parties preferred to enforce the law to its letter rather than becoming involved in any form of democracy which would require a greater degree of consensus. In this way they would achieve a system that would be as close to bipartisan as possible, and in which maximum stability of the executive branch would be assured, rather like in the British system. The basis of what was later to be labelled 'the antagonistic policy of the emerging Spanish political system' was laid down during the constituent process in 'the conviction that political issues are easier to resolve if there are two—and only two—contrasting alternatives' (Vallés, 1986: 18).

Thus did UCD and PSOE reach agreement on the system of checks and balances. Investiture proceedings make it easier to form governments[19] which, though they do not have a parliamentary majority, can resist crises, thanks to the Constitution's recognition of motions of constructive censure (Solé Tura and Aparicio, 1984; Montero and Garcia Morillo, 1984; Molas and Pitarch, 1987).

Fear of multipartisanism (Montero, 1979; 302) made it possible to diminish the gap between what had seemed to be radically opposed positions in the debate on the Government/Parliament Relations Bill of November 1977.[20] UCD guaranteed the stability of its minority government while PSOE was the only group with sufficient members of Parliament to be able to bring a motion of censure, with all the advantages this involved as regards the other parties and the electorate.

Parliamentary negotiation thus proved to be an efficient means for diminishing the traditional conflicts between Spain's left and right and its regionalists. Because the regional parties were appeased by a system of autonomous regions and the major leftist party was provided with a stable framework that would make its subsequent ascent to power feasible, the discussions on the Constitution were not a fight between diametrically opposed political and ideological alternatives. Social factors which might have led to polarization were mitigated by a group of skilled parliamentarians who made negotiation the symbol of the tolerance which had been missing from Spain throughout the country's entire constitutional history.

The representativeness of the Cortes[†]

The crisis of parliamentary representation

The Spanish Constitution envisages the Cortes as an institution designed to aggregate those interests which are represented by political parties and parliamentary groups. According to the principles of proportionality and qualified majorities, the Cortes' function is precisely that of facilitating negotiation between different societal groups and political alternatives. One may say that, owing to the changes brought about by political evolution, the design of parliamentary rules was intended to encourage a 'pactist' style of decision-making.

The intention behind this design was not to achieve a 'photographic' representation of political and social interests, but a parliamentary model which would privilege an exchange between majority and opposition and thus safeguard negotiation between the basic interests of society.

Now, in order to demonstrate the relevance of the Cortes within the Spanish decision-making process, it would not be sufficient to limit ourselves to a consideration of juridical and political factors. The constitutional and house rules of the Cortes were the product of specific political conditions, and once these conditions had changed, the gap between parliamentary practice and the conception which had inspired its design grew, and it was no longer able to bring about a balance between competing interests.

In fact, the constituent legislature (1977–9) presents two characteristics which gave a special force to parliamentary life but which ceased to exist during subsequent legislatures, thus creating serious representation problems.

The first of these characteristics is the dynamic of the constituent process. Collaboration between parliamentary elites was realized by excluding those political forces not having parliamentary representation from decision-making on all crucial issues. In order to settle such issues, the Unión de Centro Democrático (UCD) made use of different parliamentary alliances at different times. For example, the governing UCD allied itself with the rightest Alianza Popular (AP) on certain issues during the constituent debate and on issues such as the design of the Senate. Agreements with the Catalan minority (CDC), the PSOE or the PCE were generally made either with one of these parties singly, or else with all of them together. While other authors have stressed the role of negotiation between elites during the constituent process in Spain, for my part it is necessary to underline the importance of a plurality of alliances which allowed all groups to participate in the drafting of the Constitution. In this sense the first legislature reinforced the image of Parliament as a negotiating and balancing centre for the different interests.

The second characteristic of the constituent legislature is the non-existence of other political elites except for the parliamentary ones. In fact, Parliament and democratic life coincided at that moment. On the one hand, Parliament was the only institution having democratic legitimation—though we can note that Prime Minister Suárez (who had been appointed in 1976 by the king), and King Juan Carlos (who owed his position to Franco), enjoyed widespread popularity. On the other hand, all the relevant political leaders were in the parliament.[21] The political parties themselves were in a process of foundation or reconstitution which prevented them from functioning as centres that had autonomy and independence *vis-à-vis* their respective parliamentary groups. As a consequence, almost all the political life of that period was related to the Cortes given that regional governments hardly existed, that there hadn't yet been local elections and that trade unions and employers' organizations were so weak that the famous socio-economic and political agreements (*Pactos de la Moncloa*) had to be signed by parliamentary elites.

The predominance of consensus politics and the fact that the Cortes was the unique arena for the representation of political elites during the constitutent period, gave it a prestige which it was not to have subsequently. In theory, it continued to be the site of the aggregation and intermediation of interests according to the Constitution. However, since there has not been any corresponding adaptation of juridical regulations to new social and political conditions, the Cortes has been unable to fulfil these functions in the way the Constitution foresaw. The modifications in the party system played the major role in this process of marginalization. While both the Constitution and parliamentary standing orders require absolute majorities as an incentive to the building of alliances between different minority groups, since 1982, the presence of a solid—absolute and cohesive—PSOE majority has made such requirements superfluous. For instance, the instruments of control over government which could set limits on weak and minoritarian executives but which at the same time safeguarded their stability, after 1982 became superfluous. The ruling party can seek agreements with other groups, but it is not obliged to do so. In this way the Cortes has ceased to be a centre for negotiation between political groups and has rather become a chamber for the recording of governmental decisions and to some degree a forum for the opposition.

The process of change from consensual to majoritarian politics has taken place at the same time as a variety of institutions, assuming a varying degree of social representativeness, have been established: among these elected bodies we can note local government organizations and parliaments in the 17 Spanish regions, the more than one thousand municipal bodies and trade unions. This 'map' of representative bodies illustrates that the Constitution drafters did not intend the monopoly on representativeness which the Cortes enjoyed during the constituent period, to be permanent. Social interests have started to be active outside Parliament through other organizations and institutions. We are not now about to state a theory of neo-corporatism in Spain, but, in the context of this chapter we should just remember the various social and economic agreements between trade unions, employers' organizations and government between 1979 and 1985. Whether Spain is or is not a neo-corporatist society, what is true is that Parliament's function in balancing interests foreseen by the Constitution has moved to other actors and arenas, such as, for example, the 'mixed committees' between central and regional governments, or central and regional administrations and interest groups. In the light of this we should conclude our analysis of parliamentary representation by pointing to the fact that its crisis finds its origin in certain factors that have derived, not only from outside, but also from inside Parliament, ie its failure to adapt certain provisions of its house rules to a radically new political balance of forces.

Territorial representation and the problem of the Senate

We have already pointed to the shift of decision-making on centre-periphery relations and issues from the Cortes to extra-parliamentary organisms and procedures. Insofar as the drafters of the Constitution designed a hybrid Senate with hardly any functions in regional representation, the national parliament was incapable of articulating and mediating central and regional interests after the end of the constituent legislature. Because of this, important negotiations such as those concerning the finances of the 'Autonomous Communities' must be resolved at the administrative level before being passed to the Cortes for final approval.

The non-existence of a Senate based on a federal model places obstacles in the way of a more active intervention of Parliament in the process of the state's decentralization, even though the Senate occasionally takes symbolic action such as the creation of committees on regional issues, or inviting regional presidents to appear before the chamber.

We should also point out that the Spanish Senate, which is elected according to a majority system, also fulfils the requirements of representativeness badly because fewer groups achieve representation within it than within the Congress. This fact acquires even greater significance when it is borne in mind that recent electoral trends, specifically those relating to the latest regional elections, show a growing divergence in individual voting choices between national and regional elections. We cannot go into detail, but we should bear in mind that at present over 20 per cent of the regional parliamentarians belong to regional parties having no chance of achieving representation in the Senate. We observe, hence, that regional political dynamics are affected by local communities which put pressure directly on central government and are not able to act through representation in the Cortes.

Therefore, it can be concluded that problems of representativeness prevent the Senate from carrying out its function, as a territorial chamber, of overseeing the process of regional devolution still underway in Spain.

Political representation in the Congress

As for the representativeness of the Congress, this is a function of both the electoral law and the Cortes' standing orders governing the formation of parliamentary groups. Both have tried to restrict the great many parties to working formulas which involve a minimum number of parliamentary groups within the pluralist framework. The intention behind the electoral law was that big parties would enjoy the benefits of the d'Hondt system in districts having a small number of deputies. Since this system has been widely analysed we will not go into further detail. Although the Cortes has had the opportunity to discuss this problem on several occasions, it has never modified the initial framework of the current electoral system which was established during the transition period by a decree of 18 March 1977.[22] Afterwards, the relevant items were drafted during the constituent debate in 1978 and again during the elaboration of the electoral law of 1985 without the parliamentarians making use of the possibilities to strengthen the proportionality element allowed for by the Constitution.

There has been a desire on the part of all major political actors to carry on representation within the parameters of a two-party system. Thus, since the PSOE enjoyed a comfortable majority in the Cortes when the electoral law was drafted, it could have modified these criteria in favour of a more representative system.

At the same time, the standing orders of both chambers and their interpretations on certain occasions, have served to increase the difficulties for the activity of the parliamentary minorities. For instance, the substitution of the provisional regulation from the constituent period by the actual regulation from 1982, introduced rules which provided that: (1) parties — such as the Partido Socialista de Andalucia (PSA), for example — even though having five deputies, might not be able to form a parliamentary group; (2) deputies from the same party or from different parties, could not form parliamentary groups different from those of the parties which had included them in their electoral lists.

This rule prevented the formation of a Catalan Socialist (PSC) group and inhibited electoral coalition parties from forming different parliamentary groups, as was the case with AP and Partido Democrata Popular (PDP), for example. Additionally, the *mesa del Congresso* (board of Congress) at the height of the crisis within the governing UCD in 1980–1, had given an interpretation of the standing orders such that deputies who left the UCD were unable to form groups of their own.

These restrictions find an obvious theoretical justification in the desire to appear united before the electorate. Nevertheless, we could point to other motivations, such as the non-recognition of an individual mandate allowing the deputy to organize and act autonomously of the party. We cannot go into this debate fully. What really matters here is to point out that existing rules are much too rigid to enable Parliament to reflect modifications of, and to cope with the crisis in, the Spanish party system.

Electoral rules favour a bi-party system; standing orders make expression by minority groups which are unhappy with this situation, difficult. Parliament has not adopted procedures improving its representative capacity precisely at a time when other entities, representative of the citizens of their community or their members, have emerged with growing negotiating potential.

Conclusions

Conditions as favourable to Parliament as those which existed during the constituent period are unlikely to recur. Still, after ten years of a stable democracy, the time may well have come to begin thinking about eliminating all those features of the system which were deliberately used to prevent instability, fragmentation and even a breakdown of party discipline.

The current public debate on the advisability of changing the closed list electoral system and permitting preferential voting is a step in this direction. The media make veiled references to the current system as a 'partitocracy' and favour a system which would rob the omnipotent party leaders of some of their power.

Although this can be taken as no more than a complaint from citizens who do not feel that they are well represented in Parliament, it becomes more important when viewed in relation to the system's general defects in terms of proportionality and the extreme subordination of individual deputies to parliamentary groups.

Thus, improved representativeness of the Spanish parliamentary system should go hand-in-hand with reform of the electoral system. Futhermore, certain changes in Spanish political leaders' 'parliamentary culture' should be made. Currently, these leaders tend to consider the houses to be entitled to act quite independently of the aims of the executive branch. Steps should be taken to eliminate: controls over individual deputies, restrictions on the formation of parliamentary groups, obstacles to the presence of special interest groups in parliamentary information sessions and decision-making processes etc.

The Senate should become a genuine house of regional representation not only in terms of its electoral system but also in terms of its actual functions. No voice has hitherto been raised in favour of the current make-up of the Senate, and the political, journalistic and academic worlds all agree that it needs to be reformed. The question now is whether a constitutional reform of this type might not trigger demands for reforms involving other, much more conflictive issues, such as the very design of Spain's system of Autonomous Regions.

However, the Spanish Parliament has no other choice if it wishes to increase its power in relation to political parties, the government, the system of regional government, interest groups etc. The Constitution formally attributed certain functions to the Cortes; now it is time to bring them in line with a political process in which there are far more relevant and pressing issues than existed in 1972. The precautions taken during the transition period should not be permitted to act as brakes on the future.

Party dynamics and the evolution of Parliament–government relations**[††]

In spite of the fact that ten years have now passed since the first democratic elections were held, the political science literature on the Cortes is not particularly copious. With a few exceptions[23] it is difficult to find studies of the socio-professional background and evolution of Spanish MPs in the different legislatures, of the degree of continuity and change in representation, of the mechanisms of control of deputies exercised by the various party and party-group leaderships, of legislative production and parliamentary control of governmental activity etc. Without claiming to fill this gap, we want here to offer an account that might serve as the basis for future, more systematic, empirical studies within a political science framework.

UCD and PSOE: the hegemonic parties in the Spanish legislatures

During the first two legislatures, between 1977 and 1982, UCD commanded a relative majority in both houses. UCD comprised a medley of groups ranging from liberals to the odd social democrat, via others with Christian democrat leanings (Esteban and Lopez Guerra, 1982). Of the clashes which took place between these groups, some were for ideological reasons, but the great majority were due to personal differences and the struggle for power among the groups' leaders. Disputes such as these undermined UCD's strength throughout the life of the first two legislatures (1977–9; 1979–82) and led to the party's disintegration.[24] As is apparent from Table 4.2 showing the composition of the two houses, in spite of being the leading party, UCD lacked an absolute majority in the Congress (and the same was true for the Senate). In order to form successive governments, to get its bills passed and to defeat the motion of censure tabled by the PSOE in 1980, UCD was thus obliged to enter into pacts with forces of variable affinity to itself, such as Minoria Catalana (MC) or Coalición Popular (CP).

The general elections of 1982 gave an absolute majority in both houses to the PSOE. The most recent general election (in June 1986), produced

Table 4.2 Electoral results and party composition of the Spanish Parliament (1977–86) (lower house)

	Legislative Elections											
	June 77			March 79			October 82			June 86		
Party	Votes*	%	Seats	Votes	%	Seats	Votes	%	Seats	Votes	%	Seats
Centre (UCD)	6,309	34.7	165	6,228	34.3	168	1,494	7.1	12	–	–	–
Socialists (PSOE)	5,240	29.2	118	5,469	30.0	121	10,127	48.4	202	8,887	44.0	184
Communists (PCE)	1,655	9.2	20	1,911	10.5	23	865	4.1	4	930	4.6	7
Conservatives (AP)	1,503	8.3	16	1,067	5.8	9	5,478	26.2	106	5,245	26.0	105
Democ. Centre (CDS)	–	–	–	–	–	–	604	2.9	2	1,862	9.2	19
Basque Nationalists	304	1.6	8	275	1.5	7	395	1.8	8	308	1.5	6
Catalan Nationalists	666	2.8	13	483	2.6	8	772	3.7	12	1,012	5.0	18
Others	–	14.2	10	–	15.3	14	–	5.7	4	–	10.7	13
TOTAL		100	350		100	350		100	350		100	350

* number of votes in thousands

the same result despite the fact that the Socialists lost some votes (see Table 4.2).

PSOE has a long history. When it emerged from illegality during the Franco regime it had both a group of young leaders and an up-to-date programme which resembled those of Europe's modern and powerful Social Democratic parties. Following a period of greatly accelerated growth during the transition years, the party was torn by controversy over whether or not it should be Marxist in nature. This led to a confrontation between the 'critical' faction and the party leaders, headed by Felipé Gonzalez and Alfonso Guerra. Following Gonzalez's dramatic resignation at the 28th Party Congress in May 1979 and his clamorous re-election in September of the same year, the 'critical' faction of the party was left weakened while the Gonzalez–Guerra team was firmly entrenched in terms of both organizational and political strategies. PSOE's success in the 1979 municipal elections, the impressive public image of Felipé Gonzalez and the Socialist alternative, and the debate following the Socialists' motion to censure the Suãrez government in 1980 all presaged the 10 million votes cast in 1982 for PSOE and its much advertised *cambio*.

Since 1982, the Socialists have had an absolute majority in both houses of Parliament and they govern in the majority of the country's 17 regions (in 12 before 1987; in nine since the 1987 regional elections), as well as in all the leading cities of Spain. This situation, together with the difficulties experienced by the remaining political forces—dispersed and without efficient leadership— in finding ways of mounting effective opposition, has notably reduced the role of Parliament, with respect to that of the government, in policy-making (Subirats, 1989).

Parliament–government relations under the UCD government

The lack of unity in UCD was reflected both in the relationship that existed between the UCD government and its own parliamentary group, and in the general mechanisms of decision-making. Although many ministers and members of Parliament had similar political views, this was of little use given the lack of unity both within the cabinet itself and within the parliamentary group. In addition, political offences and responsibilities were handed out among the different 'families' that made up UCD, according to their relative power; this meant, for example, that the prime minister and the party secretary general had nothing in common either personally or politically, and that neither of them shared the viewpoints of the parliamentary whip. This naturally caused problems within the party.

A look at the legislative process during this period reveals a consistent lack of cohesion (see Figure 4.1). Every minister searched within 'his' parliamentary group for 'his' spokesman to defend a particular bill. General discussions between the government and UCD's parliamentary group were deliberately avoided in order to keep latent differences of opinion from coming to the surface. Only when the differences were so great that the very viability of a bill was threatened would an arduous process of negotiation begin between the government and its own members of Parliament. (This was the case with the

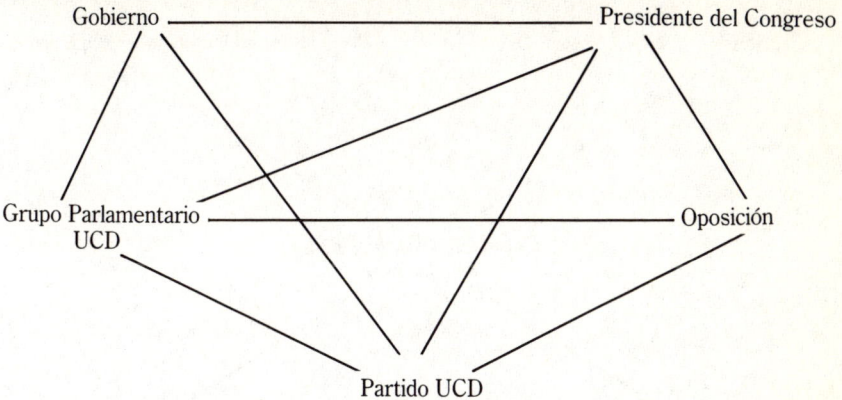

Source: Lopez garrido 1985

Figure 4.1   Relationship between different UCD parliamentary actors (1979–82)

University Reform Bill, the Divorce Bill and even the 1981 budget.) Further-more, the fact that UCD did not have an absolute majority in either house meant that the government was continually obliged to negotiate and make deals with other parliamentary groups. This put a further strain on the party as the different factions accused one another of being weak or of making too many concessions either to the right or the left. The opposition put pressure on the government, criticizing its inconsistency and lack of resolve, and made it increasingly difficult for Suárez or Calvo Sotelo, harassed by inner party problems in addition to being under constant attack by the opposition, to continue leading the country. This situation was maintained in spite of UCD's surviving the motion of censure promoted by PSOE in May 1980. UCD retained the support of other parliamentary groups in the motion of confidence presented and won by Suárez in the autumn of the same year, only a few months before his resignation and the attempted *coup d'etat.*

The centralization of Parliament–government relations under the Socialist government

Since the Socialists came to power, decision-making mechanisms have been as different as the political situation. While UCD was split into many different factions, PSOE is a highly centralized party in which the secretary and vice-secretary general have the most important roles. These offices are held by Felipé Gonzalez and Alfonso Guerra who also happen to be respectively, prime minister and deputy prime minister. Since none of their cabinet ministers are simultaneously members of the party's Executive Committee, this makes the position of Gonzalez and Guerra even stronger.

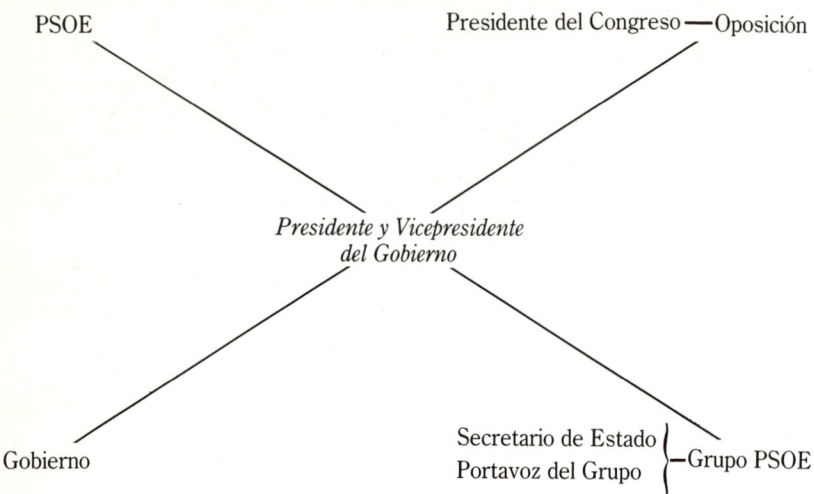

Figure 4.2 Relationship between different Socialist parliamentary actors (1982–6) (Lopez Garrido, 1985)

A look at the government's relations with Parliament in general and with the Socialist deputies in particular (see Figure 4.2) also reveals this centralization of decision-making. Every single bill drafted by the government is jointly discussed by the minister or ministers responsible and those Socialist members of Parliament who are specialists in the particular subject of the bill. These discussions result in an agreement to which amendments can be put. In the event of disagreement on an amendment, the opinion of the prime minister or deputy prime minister is decisive. The sort of relationship that exists between the PSOE government and its parliamentary group is echoed throughout the legislative procedure, disciplining the parliamentary group and assuring its loyalty, but also disciplining the government as well, because it no longer has as much freedom to designate spokesmen or present amendments as was the case during the UCD era.

All of the foregoing is intended to highlight the government's leading role in political relations and the great extent to which decision-making is concentrated in the hands of the prime minister and deputy prime minister. In June 1986 this concentration was added to when it was decided that Alfonso Guerra would preside over the Commission of Sub-Secretaries—from each ministry—which meets prior to any meeting of the cabinet. This decision robs the cabinet itself of some of its power and gives the deputy prime minister tighter control over the entire decision-making process. The party, the government and Parliament all converge and intersect in this team of leaders who, incidentally, have a close personal relationship (Lopez Garrido, 1985). Let us look at the legislative procedures in order to establish the impact which this symbiosis has on political decision-making.

Legislative process and output

Proposals   In Spain, the process whereby laws are drafted normally begins in the lower house. Bills may be introduced by the government, by the different parliamentary groups in the lower house, by the upper house, by the legislative assemblies of the regions and by so-called 'popular legislative initiative'.[25]

Table 4.3   Origin and success rates of bills

| | 1979–82 | | 1982–6 | |
	Introduced	*Passed*	*Introduced*	*Passed*
Government	287	207	200	183
Congress	200	33	109	13
Senate	7	6	1	1
Regions	1	–	17	6
Popular Petitions	–	–	3	–

Source: Own calculations.

Table 4.3 shows that the government is clearly predominant in terms of the number of bills actually passed. In the first Parliament, the Cortes Constituyentes (1977–9), 9 per cent of enactments originated in parliamentary initiatives. In the first ordinary Parliament (1979–82)—elected after the approval of the new Spanish Constitution—the proportion climbed to 16 per cent. This may be explained by several factors including the greater weakness of UCD, the end of the 'transitional' phase, and the decline in law-making initiatives on the part of UCD during the last stage of Parliament. In the last Parliament (1982–6), the proportion of enactments originating in parliamentary initiatives decreased to around 6 per cent. Again, the Socialist government's absolute majority and its strong centralization explained the change.

It can also be observed that bills introduced by the government are much more 'successful' than those submitted by Parliament. There is no restriction in Spain on the bills tabled by the government for discussion in the lower house: nor is there any period for public information, for consultation with sectors of society which may be presumed to have an interest in a bill or for prior examination by the upper house which, in theory, is supposed to represent the interests of the regions. If we consider bills introduced by the government, it is important to underline that in the UCD period, only 72 per cent of bills were passed, whereas in the Socialist period the number of bills passed reached 91 per cent.

Prior consideration   On the other hand, bills submitted by either of the chambers are subject to a process known as *toma en consideración* (prior consideration) during which the Congress, in plenary session, debates whether it is appropriate to commence formal discussion of a bill. It will be obvious from this that the majority group possesses a powerful weapon for curtailing parliamentary legislative initiative by the opposition. For example, the government often opposes initiatives by arguing that it is planning, or preparing, to introduce a bill on the same subject. In other cases, proposals are opposed simply on the grounds of disagreement with their basic philosophy. The above-mentioned process also provides a good opportunity for the conclusion of pacts between a minority government and the group supporting it on the one hand, and other groups ideologically close to it on the other. In the 1979–82 Parliament, 32 per cent of the bills introduced by the different parliamentary groups were accepted in the *toma en consideración* phase, whereas in the 1982–6 Parliament only 15 per cent were accepted. This is yet another illustration of how, in the last Spanish Parliament, an opposition with little room for manoeuvre in a parliament tightly controlled by the Socialists' absolute majority, declined in influence.

The legislative activity of parliamentary groups   Table 4.4 shows the number of bills introduced in Congress, in the 1979–82 and 1982–6 parliaments, by the various parliamentary groups. The most noticeable difference between the two Parliaments is the sharp fall in the number of bills. The main reason for this is the reduction in the number of bills presented by the principal opposition group in the second Parliament as compared to the first. Thus, while the Socialist group introduced 84 bills between 1979 and 1982, the Coalición Popular group introduced only 48 in the last Parliament. It is important to notice the sharp reduction in the number of bills presented by the smaller groups: 44 bills in 1979–82, only four in 1982–6.

Table 4.4   Bills tabled and approved in Congress by party

	1979–82			1982–86		
	(a)	(b)	(c)	(a)	(b)	(c)
UCD	15	8	5	–	–	–
PSOE	83	23	10	5	5	5#
PCE	32	7	3	22	3	3#
Minoria Catalana	15	7	4	23	3	2
Coalición Popular	11	7	2	48	2	2
Others	44	12	9	4	2	2
Minoria Vasca	–	–	–	6	1	1
Total	200	64	33	108	16	13

(a) introduced
(b) *Toma en consideración* (prior consideration stage)
(c) passed
\#   one of the bills passed was an amalgamation of two similar propositions, the first having been introduced by the Communist group, the second one by the Socialist group.
Source: Own calculations

One point which cannot be omitted when examining parliamentary legislative initiative is that Minoria Vasca (MV), the group that represents members of the Partido Nacionalista Vasco (PNV), did not introduce a single bill during either of the first two Parliaments. This amounts to five years' presence in Parliament without a single legislative initiative. Such a record might be the expression of a policy which, far from focusing on the legislative organs of the state, focused exclusively on negotiation between the Basque regional government, which MV controlled, and the central administration. In the last Parliament, MV introduced six bills, thus showing a major integration into the Spanish political arena. The case of the Catalan Minority is very different in that from the very beginning the group played a much more active role in Parliament. In order to obtain support for its policies in Catalonia, it first of all supported UCD in its attempt to build majorities. Later, it allied itself with the Socialist group, in spite of the latter's absolute majority, and helped thus to avoid the isolation of the government over certain contentious issues.

The sub-committee phase   During the first two Parliaments, the *ponencia* or subcommission phase, was the most important and decisive step in legislative proceedings. Formed within the relevant committee, the *ponencia* is a sub-committee on which the various parliamentary groups are represented. The number of members ranges from four to ten, according to the importance of the bill. Its essential function is not merely to establish the order of amendments submitted; it can also modify the text of the bill on the basis of one of the amendments, and even modify any aspect of the original text according to the 'spirit' of various amendments. During the first two parliaments, documents drawn up by the *ponencia*—its report or *informe*—were often substantially different from the texts originally presented and had the backing of the representatives of most of the groups. One of the principal reasons why this phase had such a significant impact on proceedings is that the *ponencia* works behind closed doors. Being the only parliamentary body to do so, it is the ideal place for groups to agree to modify their positions or to trade concessions without running the risk of their attitudes becoming known either to the public at large or to their electorate. In this way the *ponencia* stage often provided a key opportunity for agreement and consensus. The make-up of this sub-committee and the way it operates are very similar to the *Ponencia Constitucional*, which consisted of seven deputies from different political parties who were responsible for drafting the text of the Spanish Constitution.

An examination of legislative practice during the 1979–82 Cortes reveals that the *ponencia* was by far the longest and most significant phase in the whole legislative process. In the case of certain controversial and complex bills, the *ponencia* stage took more time than the whole of the rest of the process, including the debate in the Senate. (This was the case with the divorce law and the reform of the code of military justice, for example) (Subirats, 1986). UCD's lack of an absolute majority in the 1979–82 Parliament was probably one of the principal reasons for the heightened role of the *ponencia* during this period.

Since 1982, the *ponencia* has no longer been an important locus of political negotiation or the revision and alteration of bills and proposals. As we have said, in the two previous legislatures, certain controversial bills took longer to pass through this preliminary stage than through the whole of the rest of the legislative process. However, with an absolute majority in both houses of Parliament, Socialist parliamentarians do not need to make any great effort to negotiate, nor to work hard to reach a consensus. In fact, bills are now generally introduced in their 'finished' state by the ministries involved.

The role of the standing committees   During the period covered by our analysis, the full committee did not play a particularly remarkable role in the general legislative process. Indeed, one might say that it was 'hemmed-in' between the important *ponencia* phase and the more political and public phase of the plenary debate. The key debate had already taken place and the work in committee had little impact on public opinion. But, in certain cases, the full committee enjoys complete legislative competence, and the texts that emerge from its discussions are sent directly to the Senate.[26] During the life of the first Parliament, 46 bills were passed in committee, whereas in the last one the number of bills on which discussion was concluded in the lower house at the committee stage came to 74. Generally speaking, all these bills were of very limited scope.

The plenary debate   There is no doubt that the part of the legislative process that is most directly exposed to public opinion is the plenary debate. The presence of the most powerful of mass media, television, is of prime importance in that it makes it possible to broaden parliamentary debate to a very considerable extent. The most controversial topics are those most thoroughly discussed, and ministers and other leading political figures are very frequent participants. During the first Parliament, the process of negotiation, agreement and political trade-offs, in which political leaders played the main roles, were often brought to a final conclusion after endless days of debate in the *ponencia* and the committee. In this respect, the role of 'transactional amendments' was fundamental. During the last Parliament, the Socialists' absolute majority and the lack of a strong opposition, reduced the importance of the committee stages.

The role of the Senate   The Senate has a very limited role in the Spanish parliamentary system. Although the Constitution established it as a forum for territorial representation, in practice its function basically duplicates that of the Congress. Its scope for legislative initiative is very small.

In the case of initiatives emanating from the Senate, advance approval by the whole of that chamber for submission of the proposal or proposals is required. Once this agreement is obtained, proceedings commence in the Senate and the bill is discussed, first in commission and then by the chamber as a whole. Then the proposal is sent to the lower house where it is referred directly to the relevant committee. It will be clear that these proceedings in the upper house merely serve to avoid the prior consideration phase (*toma en consideración*) of the Congress, but that afterwards the lower house regains its predominant role. In the life of the 1979–82 Parliament seven bills were introduced by the upper house, and in the last Parliament (1982–6) the figure fell to just one bill. The small number of proposals originating in the upper house is unsatisfactory, and underlines the situation of near marginality towards which the Senate has been evolving.

In terms of its legislative function, the subordinate role of the Senate is obvious. It is only allowed two months during which to study, modify and approve texts passed to it by the Congress. If the Senate intervenes, the bill always ends up by being sent back to the Congress, which then has the last word. The above-mentioned period may be further drastically curtailed to 20 days if Congress decides that the matter is urgent. Such timing makes it impossible for the Senate to give serious reflection to texts approved by Congress. It cannot negotiate at its own pace and cannot leave the more controversial aspects to one side for later discussion. In short, its task cannot amount to much more than that of making technical corrections, rectifying oversights or reformulating aspects that fail to satisfy the majority group in either house. In the 1979–82 Parliament, only 30 per cent of the texts transmitted by the Congress were modified by the Senate. Generally, modifications were minimal and, as the figures show, usually not even a comma was changed. In the last Parliament the proportion of legislative texts modified by the Senate surpassed 50 per cent. However, this figure is indicative, not of a more important role of the Senate, but of an easy way to modify certain bills 'tested' in the Congress process. The Senate stage provides an opportunity for the acceptance of amendments that the Socialist group didn't want to accept before, and also allows more time for reflection.

The mechanisms which the Senate has at its disposal for controlling the government are few and infrequently used. It does not count leading Spanish politicians among its members. Government ministers only attend its sessions in response to a direct summons. The senators themselves have to go to the Congress if they wish to lobby ministers or party leaders. The senators from the regions[27] do not serve as intermediaries *vis-à-vis* the central administration. Government bills affecting regional interests are not subject to prior examination in the Senate (Solé Tura, 1982). In short, the Senate is located outside the country's two-fold centre of institutional and political attention: Congress and the government (Aja and Arbos, 1980).

The backbencher   The typical role of the Spanish MP is that of the *diputado llave* (backbencher).[28] Every parliamentary group and its leaders keep a tight rein on parliamentary initiatives. This is not only due to the internal logic of the parliamentary system, which consists of relatively well-defined and disciplined parties, but also to the very origins of Spain's constituent period. Aware of the weakness of the country's social structures, the authors of the Constitution tried to strengthen Spain's fledgling political parties. They enacted special measures which include an electoral system based on closed and blocked lists, and obstacles to grass-roots legislative initiatives, and which control the use of the referendum and the rules of Parliament itself. The aim was to strengthen political parties and institutions. The result is the weakness of the individual parliamentarian, who has little room for autonomous initiative.

Conclusion: the Cortes in the political process

Although Spanish parties in general are very strong in the institutional arena, their support within civil society is among the lowest for political parties in any political system in Western Europe (Linz, 1973, 1981). With the transition to democracy, there were moments of euphoria in which politics and the new political leaders were exalted and broad sectors of the population became politically active (Campo *et al.*, 1982; Maravall, 1980). But once the democratic novelty had worn off, Spain began to experience the same phenomenon that has occurred in the rest of the world, and particularly in Western Europe; ie the aura that had surrounded all kinds of political ideologies began to dim and Spain soon ended up with a few political parties that represented these ideologies in not more than a sceptical fashion. This generalized scepticism was further aggravated by Spain's long history of absolutism and authoritarianism, interrupted only by brief periods of open conflict. Thus the first period of intense political activity and participation was followed by widespread apathy as Spaniards engaged in a last ditch defence of their own individualism against possible political involvement. Currently in Spain there is an extremely low rate of union membership, a very small number of political militants, a definite tendency towards abstentionism (normal voter participation in elections being about 60 per cent) and a general lack of participation in public life (Tezanos, 1979, 1981; Perez Diaz, 1984; Maravall, 1982; Subirats, 1987).

The Cortes have suffered from this public disenchantment, for the new Constitution was drafted in such a way (via pacts and a consensus reached in meetings behind closed doors) that, although the final draft was probably improved thereby, the public became disoriented and any ideological passions the process might have aroused were eliminated.

The remarks presented in this last part should be taken as preliminary notes to be contrasted with future developments. If we confirm our analysis to the first constitutional legislature, we can conclude that the Spanish Parliament is relatively powerful and influential in the legislative and political process. Between 1979 and 1982 a large percentage of the most significant laws originated in the Cortes and, furthermore, all bills presented, underwent major changes in the *ponencia* phase which has an important role in the passage of legislation. During this period the weakness of both the government and the governing party's leaders and ideology, the democratic process's lack of stability and the maintenance of the constitutional consensus, all gave parliamentary activity an important role.

The Socialist victory in the October 1982, and in the June 1986 general elections brought about an important change in the way the Spanish legislative process works and in the Spanish Parliament's role as the political intermediary between the majority and the opposition. This change is largely due to a variety of factors: for example the Socialist party's absolute majority in both houses of Parliament, the particular relationship between the government and the Socialist members of Parliament and the obvious crisis in the leading opposition party.

Since 1982, the government has played a prominent role in Parliament. The strength and internal cohesion of the Socialist party and Parliament itself, and the fact that the Socialists have an absolute majority in Parliament, all combine to relegate the Socialist parliamentary group to a subordinate position in which its role amounts to little more than that of a privileged observer of the direct and intense relationships that exist between the government and the opposition. Accordingly it tends to limit itself to supporting dutifully whatever the government does or proposes to do. Clear indicators of this situation are given by the very limited part Socialist parliamentarians play in the process of drafting laws and their lack of room for manoeuvre as regards accepting amendments or altering bills. In all these situations, the role of the majority group is vague and it is the government itself that maintains a direct dialogue with the opposition (Jover and Marcet, 1985). This gives the government more space in the media while helping to maintain Parliament formally as a forum for political discussion.

The opposition has lost a good deal of impact and the crisis in the leading opposition group has only aggravated the situation.[29] During the 1982–6 legislature the Socialists, in an attempt to follow the British model, played up the importance of the main opposition group and its leader in order to promote a two-party image and the idea that a theoretical alternative existed. But since then, the leading opposition party has lost a good deal of power and has no real leader in Parliament. As a result, the remaining opposition groups (CDS, nationalist minorities, the Grupo Mixto, etc.) have been relatively reinforced in their position. Nevertheless, if a parliament is considered to be not only an organ of the majority, but an organ of both the majority *and* the opposition (Molas and Pitarch, 1987), our Parliament nowadays acts more as an instrument of the government than as a public platform which the opposition can use to set out its alternatives. No real negotiating takes place in Congress (particularly not regarding the legislative process) between the various groups representing different social interests. The real negotiations with people affected by proposed legislative measures take place at cabinet level. In fact, the *de facto* social powers usually agree on the contents of any bill before it even reaches Congress. The opposition has concentrated more on symbolic struggles with the government than on the representation of social interests. This partly explains why the opposition has lost a good deal of its strength in recent years and why the government can afford itself a certain arrogance in drafting, discussing and approving laws. The relationship between government and legislature is one of strong government—weak Parliament. The government is a decision-making centre where specific social interests are protected. Parliament has become a mere formality.

A tentative evaluation of parliamentary performance in Spain*

We will base our evaluation of the performance of the Cortes in democratic transition and consolidation on its major functions and tasks and on the problems they have met with so far.

With respect to the tasks of the Spanish Parliament, and its peculiarities, we must begin with *legislative activity*, which has been relatively intense over the last few years. This was to be expected, given that, apart from the complexity of modern societies, a Constitution had to be drawn up in order to provide the democratic system with juridical regulation in accordance with the values embodied in such a system. The legislative function has a very visible public aspect, which academics tend to deal with[30] by referring to legislation on 'public' issues relating to the organization of society. However, it also has a private aspect, to which authors tend to pay less attention, even though it is of crucial importance. The essential characteristics of the previous regime have penetrated and impregnated private social relations, giving them an authoritarian content that was more adapted to a state that had begun by proclaiming itself 'totalitarian'. Parliament's hard work in reforming the Civil and Criminal Codes governing court proceedings and a set of other provisions in different areas (commercial, labour, etc.)[31] has been essential to the consolidation of democracy in a positive sense within the ambit of a civil society that, bit by bit, is assuming the values of tolerance and liberty necessary for a democratic political system.

Control of the government is a task that has required special dedication from Parliament. Incidentally, we should point out that the 'motion of constructive censure' suitable for a rationalized parliamentarism, but which seems to have been invented more to prevent votes of no-confidence than for any other reason, has been applied twice in Spain so far. A cynical observer might remark that this fact is typically Spanish. If one adds the fact that in neither of the two cases was the vote successful, and that this was known before the vote was even suggested,[32] the same observer might add that this makes the example even more typically Spanish. Irrespective of the relatively frightful tendency to control the government by trying to throw it out or to get rid of its ministers, Parliament has also made intensive use of the possibilities afforded by the chamber's rules (questions, appeals, and investigation committees), although, as we shall show below, not totally successfully.

The *function of deliberation* is not completely carried out in the Spanish Parliament mainly because of the damage entailed by the inadequate organization of the Senate, which remains an essential area or forum for exchange and enlightenment about the one major problem that has yet to be resolved in the Spanish political system, that of the territorial organization of the state.[33]

As far as the *representation of interests* is concerned, the preponderance in the Spanish Parliament of the professional strata and classes shows a pattern close to that of other European countries, albeit with some variants. The liberal professions predominate, and among these, lawyers, who made up 21 per cent of the MPs in the second and third legislatures.[34] A characteristic, and significant, trait of the Spanish Parliament, and one which is of a certain interest, is the predominance of public officials. If we remember that teachers (accounting for 20 per cent of the second legislature and 24 per cent of the third, including both school and university teachers) are public officials in Spain, the percentage accounted for by public officials as a whole (including the elite corps and technical and administrative officials) was 33 per cent in the second legislature and 38 per cent in the third.[35] This predominance of representatives from the Civil Service is typical of the Western welfare states, run by enormous bureaucracies that have their own political interests, and incidentally also help to reproduce the new class.[36] In this light we might make the supplementary observation that the principal leaders of the national parties do not always have professions and activities that formally coincide with their professed politics. On the left, the leaders of the PCE (a 'liberated' ex-miner) and of the PSOE (a labour lawyer) have two professions typical of civil society; the same is true of the leader of the centre party (CDS). On the right, however, that is in the parties that believe in the reduction of the state's presence to a minimum, the leaders tend to belong to the elite corps of the Civil Service (lawyers serving the state council, state attorneys, parliamentary lawyers, etc.). This contradicts the neo-conservative criticism that all public officials are interested in an expansion of the welfare state.

In general terms, from a traditional class viewpoint, today's Parliament is definitely in the hands of the middle and upper-middle classes.[37] In accordance with most theories of democracy, this goes a long way to explaining democratic consolidation in Spain.

The importance of parliaments in democratic societies in the articulation and advance of the political careers of individuals is well known. Spain, however, seems to constitute a deviant case in this respect since careers are hardly made in Parliament, but rather within the parties. The technical needs, organization and the regulationary criteria of Parliament practically prevent any relevant participation on the part of new deputies. This means that, with a handful of exceptions, the latter cannot make themselves known to public opinion and their work is obscure and unrelieved. The politician who wants to make a career of politics, first has to cement it in the party he comes from before gaining parliamentary election.

Although the parties have been decisively incorporated into the running of the parliamentary regime, they have not yet managed to generate clear mechanisms by which the political careers that we referred to above become institutional careers. The method of appointment of ministers under different governments has been very different, according to whether UCD or PSOE has been in power. But there has also been something in common: people who had acquired their political stature through Parliament were hardly ever appointed.[38] This represents a vicious circle: parliamentary experience neither accommodates nor fosters political careers because it does not count in the formation of governments; and it does not count in the formation of governments because it does not foster political careers. In this respect, it is clear that the Spanish Parliament will have to develop customs, conventions or guidelines over time that enable it to make its importance in the composition of any government felt more strongly.

This aspect, which is also peculiar to the Spanish parliamentary system, leads us to another: the problem of the relations between parties and Parliament in Spain.

Spanish democracy cannot avoid the generalized contemporary paradox, mentioned above, that the current situation of weak parties coincides with an almost absolute predominance of parties in Parliament.[39] Even in the absence of other data, this predominance was clearly indicated by the legislators' interest in establishing public funding for parties (most of which are indeed much in need of cash), something that was finally achieved under the Organic Law of Political Party Funding.[40] The predominance of the parties is frequently criticized since it is understood that to a large extent they dominate Parliament by dominating the deputies and, at the same time, denaturalize it by turning it into a parallel mechanism of party machineries.

To the problem brought about by this double relationship of the parties to Parliament (parties are vital, but at the same time, counterproductive), we should add those brought about by the expansion of social communication media, which will bring about profound social changes. The generalization and intensification of the information media's influence undermines Parliament's old claim to be a sort of privileged spokesperson for the public. Nowadays, when any issue may be very quickly made the subject of direct, popular consultation, and of general and widespread debate, the relationship between Parliament and public opinion has altered substantially. Through its debates, Parliament used, to a large extent, to be a *generator* of public opinion. Nowadays, it is more than anything else, the *receiver* of a public opinion which, more often than not, is generated elsewhere. Awareness of this change can be perceived in the Constitution's acceptance of popular legislative initiative. To this, we can add an apparently trivial fact, which is actually quite important when it comes to understanding how Parliament works in Spain and what its relations to public opinion are: that all the social communication media have free access to the plenary session debates and commissions apart from those that are held behind closed doors. Media presence has contributed much more than anything else to the demystification of parliamentary procedures in the eyes of public opinion.

Apart from problems concerning the relationship between political parties and the mass media, we should also refer to the problems brought about by social conflicts of very varied sorts outside Parliament. The repercussions of social conflicts are the greater the more corporatized the society is and they usually give rise to direct negotiations and confrontation between the parties involved with or without the intervention of some sort of arbitration on the part of the public authorities. The clearest example is given by collective bargaining, but one could also include any direct relations established for whatever reasons between the government (and its administration) and specific corporations (for example doctors and teachers). The idea of removing direct negotiations between these two from parliamentary control (although, obviously, those occupying high posts from the administration will always make appearances in the Congress) basically responds to the intentions apparent in the proposal of the Spanish Constitution to establish an Economic and Social Council that could act as a sort of forum for issues of this specific type. The need for Parliament to recover the initiative in any important social debate gives way to reasons of survival of Parliament as an institution.

Having set out the disadvantages of and problems encountered by the Spanish parliamentary set-up, it would not be fair to let matters rest there; for in spite of its problems, Parliament has made a significant contribution to the consolidation of Spanish democracy. In the brief space of 10 years, it has made use of all the mechanisms provided for by the Constitution and the regulations (no-confidence votes, complaints about ministers or investigation commissions, for example)[42] to carry out its role as a check on government.[43] The check on administration activity in general is carried out, or so it seems, less efficiently than might be wished (perhaps because of a lack of resources) through the *Defensor del Pueblo* (People's Ombudsman), who is commissioned by Parliament for such purposes.

If an entirely satisfactory level has not been reached in parliamentary control of government, even using all the available resources,[44] the legislature has taken decisive measures to make itself independent of a judicial custodianship that it considers excessive and to affirm its supremacy over the third power.

The first of these objectives involved Parliament's passing an Organic Law which reformed the Organic Law of the Constitutional Court, and eliminated the prior appeal of unconstitutionality.[45] Through the appeal of unconstitutionality, the opposition had been largely able to paralyse the job of legislation. The second objective involved establishing that *all* the members of the General Council of Judicial Power were without exception to be appointed by Parliament. This eliminated the possibility of any sort of extra-parliamentary provision of members and any sort of co-optation.[46]

Nowadays, reconsideration of the work of Parliament in the context of advanced democratic societies is a necessity that is imposed both by the crisis of the welfare state[47] and by the exhaustion of criteria of procedural legitimacy.[48] Parliament was the quintessence of the rule of law and this was defined, in essential terms, by respect for the established procedures. In so far as the increased complexity of post-industrial societies leaves Parliament in a secondary or subordinate position with respect to the executive, a real danger arises of growing authoritarianism. The legislative, which continues to be the pivot around which any democratic organization revolves, needs to recover its old pre-eminence. This task entails great difficulties. For some, it is a matter of reinventing Parliament—no more, no less—[49] while others would be satisfied by the establishment of mechanisms which would guarantee a 'parliamentary recovery' in the democratic system. To such an end, it is thought that the very concept of procedural legitimacy must be overcome in order to arrive at a legitimacy of 'contents'.[50] In order to recover a function of guiding and orientating, which would serve to offer answers to contemporary societies, Parliament has, against the background of the crisis of the welfare state, to debate crucial, substantial issues again. Parliament has to recover the function of being the *indirizzo politico*[51] of the collectivity at all levels.

In order to carry out this task, at least in southern European countries, and definitely in Spain, parliaments must develop a degree of flexibility, initiative and inventiveness that they have not seemed to have had since World War II. In other words, the future consolidation of democracy in our countries will depend on whether our parliaments are able to institutionalize a new encounter between the state and civil society which, by liberating society from the constraints that hold it back, advances the social and economic rights of citizens.

Notes

1. The first to write on the transition to democracy in southern Europe was Nicos Poulantzas (1976) from a neo-Marxist point of view. The events, however, aroused the interest of social and political scientists, who elaborated a theory of political change—with the stages of establishment and consolidation—in general terms (cf. Morlino (1985, 1986); J. Linz; Santamaria (1981); Caciagli (1986); Maravall (1982); Maravall and Santamaria (1985); Vega Garcia (1983)).

2. On the peculiar nature of the dictatorship of Primo de Rivera, see various works by Javier Tusell, Garcia Canales, Ben Ami, etc. From our point of view, the work of José Andrés Gallego (1977) is of special interest, showing Primo de Rivera's interest in directing the workers' movement and coming to an agreement with the Socialists.

3. In the case of Spain, inflation became serious in 1973 with a rate of 11.4 per cent, which went up to 16.9 per cent in 1975 and 24.5 per cent in 1977, while the level of unemployment rose gradually from 3.84 per cent in 1975 to 11.6 per cent in 1980 (Aguirre, 1981: 38). In the case of Portugal, the economic ruin brought about by the 1973 crisis and the Portugese companies' overwhelming loss of competitiveness forced the International Monetary Fund to intervene with a stabilization plan in 1978. (Cravinho, 1982).

4. In the Spanish case, transition co-existed with an intense outburst of both political/social and nationalistic terrorism, which has always been assumed to be intentionally destabilizing, but which has never managed to achieve its aims. The incidence of 'leftist' and 'rightist' terrorism on the constitutional process is considered in the work by Mohedan and Peña (1978).

5. On the workings of the Crown in the Spanish political system, see Lucas Verdú (1983).

6. Although there are already numerous books on the attempted *coup d'état*, none the less, some time will have to pass before the obscure events of the coup can be fully clarified. However, one thing is clear: it was the decisive intervention of the Crown that managed to guarantee the loyalty of the military chiefs and put an end to the insurrection. See, among others: Oneto (1981, 1982) and Gilmour (1985).

7. One should not forget that questioning constitutional monarchy as a state form was an important part of the left-wing's programme at the beginning of the transition, especially in the Partido Communista de España. See Oneto (1985: 114).

8. Many authors and commentators point out that the Spanish Constitution of 1978 has one sole advantage over previous constitutions in the country's tortured history: the fact that it is the first Constitution not to be imposed on one part of the population by the other. (Tamames, 1982; Attard, 1983: 93).

9. Consensus would then give way to disenchantment. Excessive hopes had been placed in democracy and, it was said, the very praxis of consensus was responsible for the later parliamentary agony. Miguel Herrero Y Rodriguez de Miñon, for example, one of the most outstanding 'fathers' of the constitution, distances himself from consensus very early, as he states in: Martinez Cuadrado, (1982).

10. It is widely believed that Prime Minister Suárez resigned, above all, due to pressure from the military, apart from the uprising of important members of his party with whom he was forced into confrontation. Whatever the case, the causes of his resignation have never been totally clear, even to his supporters (see Navalón Guerrero, 1981).

11. From early on, there have been frequent criticisms of the unworkability of Parliament during the Socialist term in office with an absolute majority. Essentially, the complaint consists in showing that the Socialists impose their will, without coming to agreements with the opposition on important measures. (Fraile, 1984).

12. Specialized literature has concentrated largely on four subjects: the electoral system, the parliamentary groups, the motion of censure and the Senate. All but the first of these subjects have always been examined from a juridical point of view rather than from the standpoint of political science. In this chapter an attempt is made to describe the process of institutionalization and its consequences rather than provide a description of the most formal aspects of the Constitution and the regulations governing the two houses of Parliament. For a description of these, see Punset (1983) and Santaollalla (1984).

13. Spain's Communist party (PCE) was the best organized opposition to Franco. However, revision of its traditional ideological stances and adoption of the Eurocommunist line, together with a notable increase in the number of members as a result of the party's legalization, led to considerable internal problems only a few years later.

The Spanish Socialist party (PSOE) received a considerable boost from the 1974 Surenes Congress and at the outset of democracy PSOE's militants were young, closely united around a core of skilled leaders and capable of attracting other socialist groups. Still, its rapid growth was not without problems, particularly when Felipe Gonzalez called on the party to renounce Marxism.

The Unión de Centro Democrático (UCD) led by Adolfo Suárez, began as an electoral coalition of groups from the establishment's reformist wing and the moderate opposition. During the constituent legislature attempts to turn it into a real political party met with difficulties and internal strife, eventually causing the UCD to disappear from the Spanish political scene.

Alianza Popular was made up of various factions in the purest Franco style, all of which had different strategies. This was clearly revealed in the final voting on the text of the Constitution. Both the party and its electoral coalition of the same name were held together by Manuel Fraga, who from the very outset stamped the party's organization with his highly personal style of leadership. For a description of political parties in the early years of Spanish democracy, see Esteban and López Guerra (1982).

14. The Moncloa Pacts were both political and economic agreements, which were made before the final draft of the Constitution in order to announce: (1) reforms on such issues as the press, official secrets, state-owned organs of mass communication and the right to hold meetings and form political associations; (2) changes in specific articles of the Penal Code, the Public Order Act, the Code of Military Justice etc. The Pacts further aimed to improve the economic system by enacting monetary, fiscal and wage measures and by reforming the social security system.

The Moncloa Pacts were indeed the first realistic attempts to confront the economic crisis of the 1970s, which had been largely ignored in the paralysis of the Franco regime's final years. The move towards democratization of the system helped compensate for the austerity measures contained in the Pacts. (The text of the Moncloa Pacts was published by the Servicio Central de Publicaciones de la Secretaria General Técnica de la Presidencia del Gobierno).

15. There were two causes of these variations: first, shifts of individual deputies from one group to another as the party system became more stabilized. Second, the fact that UCD and PSOE pushed through a provisional regulation requiring a minimum of 15 deputies in order to form a parliamentary group. This forced the Catalan and Basque minorities to join forces in a single group. The final regulation, passed in a climate of consensus during the constituent period, permitted parties such as these to form their own groups if they had obtained 20 per cent of the votes in the districts where they had stood for election.

16. The Second Republic was polarized by religious, regional and agrarian conflict. At the outset of the democratic transition period, these three issues were a good deal less contentious. In fact, since the time Spain had become an industrial society and a pronounced level of emigration and migratory movement within the country had begun to take place, the agrarian conflict had all but ceased to exist and no one spoke out in favour of nationalizing the land.

Meanwhile, the Church, which had initially been a mainstay of the Franco regime, began gradually withdrawing its support in a process of post-Conciliate *aggiornamento*. Eventually, both reactionary and opposition factions (and even some more extremist viewpoints) coexisted within the Church. This led to the disappearance of the former anti-clerical cleavage and made it possible to include in the Constitution a declaration that Spain is a lay state while still maintaining special cooperative relationships with all religions, but particularly with the Catholic Church.

The regional conflict was by far the most serious. Despite the Franco regime's stern repression of Catalan, Basque and Galician 'nationalist' cultures, regional feelings by no means ceased to exist. On the contrary, regionalism became an important additional factor in mobilizing for democracy (further complicated in the Basque Country by the existence of ETA, an armed terrorist group which was well received by the Basque population). The 'pacted rupture', or controlled transition, forced nationalist leaders to moderate their claims, but also prevented state leaders from ignoring these claims if they wanted to stabilize the democratic system.

17. When the first democratic Cortes was constituted, it was impossible to apply the regulations which had governed the two houses during the Franco years because these rules had not even recognized the existence of political groups. Thus, the president of the Cortes enacted special provisions under the terms of which the political parties of coalitions represented in Parliament would decide the minimum number of deputies required in order to form a parliamentary group. An agreement between UCD and PSOE set the number at 15, forcing the groups within the centrist coalition to unite, impeding action by the Partido Socialista Popular and weakening the nationalist parties.

    Once the final draft of the Constitution was approved, the requirements for forming groups continued to be a controversial issue. Because such requirements placed obstacles in the way of the proliferation of small groups, they conflicted with the interests of splinter parties (PAD, DC), regional parties limited to a very small area (PSA), nation-wide minority parties (PCE) and regional groups (PSC) associated with a national party.

18. As an example, only parliamentary groups and not individual deputies can introduce proposals. Amendments proposed by deputies must be validated by the signature of the speaker. Furthermore, no deputy may switch from one parliamentary group to another during the life of a legislature unless he switches to the mixed group. All these rules complement the closed list electoral system whereby votes are cast for the party *en bloc* rather than for individual candidates, thus giving greater power to party officials.

19. The office of prime minister may be conferred if a simple majority is obtained in the second round of votes in Parliament. An absolute majority is required if the office is to be conferred in the first round. The government can only be toppled when an absolute majority approves a motion of constructive censure. This provided a certain guarantee of stability for minority governments such as UCD during the constituent legislature. It seemed likely then that this situation would be repeated due to the party system (in which the UCD and PSOE far outpaced the other parties) and the electoral system (with strong possibilities that the winner of the majority of votes might not necessarily win on the proportional basis on which the system is established), both of which combined to make it difficult for any party to obtain an absolute majority. Naturally, the Socialists' landslide victory in the 1982 elections invalidated this hypothesis.

20. The Political Reform Act had not provided means by which to hold the government liable for its actions. However, an incident involving the police and a PSOE deputy caused the Socialist group to try to bring action to prove that the ministry involved was liable for the incident. The governing party refused to accept the motion. This led to a meeting of the Association of Parliamentary Speakers, in which UCD was in the minority. The various groups then introduced a number of different motions on the same subject. So it might be said that the parliamentary regime emerged as a result of specific conduct in Parliament rather than as the result of any particular legal or constitutional regulations.

    UCD tried to counteract this *de facto* situation several days later by presenting a bill intended to regulate government–Parliament relations and limit the opposition's chances. Parliamentary debate on this bill coincided with the discussion on house rules (in which PSOE wanted to include the motion of censure) and with the final negotiations on the Moncloa Pacts.

All this combined to create an extremely fluid situation in which tactics (confrontation versus consent) proved more important than doctrine in debating the amount of control to be given to Parliament. In the specific case of the government–Parliament relations bill, UCD accepted the amendments proposed by the Catalan minority group in order to make the bill more moderate.

The bill was essentially a copy of French legislation, but with several important differences. Motions of censure were to be voted in both houses and required an absolute majority. No mention of the possible effects of such censure was made. The government could propose a vote of confidence in connection with the approval of any bill forming part of its platform, and this would be automatically approved unless a specific motion of censure was made. For a more detailed explanation of this, see De Arcenegui (1978) and Ripollés (1978).

21 In 1977, all the major political leaders were members of Parliament. This is in marked contrast with the situation in later years when members of Parliament might have been leading figures in only regional, local or union circles.

22. The 1985 Organic Law on general elections maintains the essential features of the electoral regulations of 18 March 1977, under the terms of which the first democratic elections took place. The 350 deputies are elected to Congress in representation of the various provinces of Spain. Each province is entitled to a minimum of two deputies and the remainder are assigned in proportion to the population of each province (reserving one deputy for the African cities of Ceuta and Melilla). The total number of deputies to which each province is entitled is calculated according to the d'Hondt system of highest averages. Preferential voting is not allowed.

The Senate is also elected by provincial districts (except in the case of the island provinces). Each province is entitled to four representatives. The electoral system is by majority vote with limited plurality. In addition, a small number of senators are appointed by the regional parliaments.

As has been pointed out by many authors (for example Vallés and Carreras, 1977; Martinez Sospedra, 1980), this system produces notable distortions in favour of the most sparsely populated provinces and tilts the scales sharply in favour of the majority parties.

23. In the references at the end of this chapter, see, in particular: Deputación de Barcelona (1985), Fundación Pablos Inglesias (1982), Universidad de Barcelona (1980), Congreso de los Diputados (1985), and the articles and parliamentary reports published by the Spanish Parliament as well as the different reports on each legislature which are published by the Congress and the Senate.

24. The UCD won over six million votes and 168 seats in Congress in 1979, as against only 1.5 million votes and 12 seats in 1982. It has now been dissolved.

25. In the 1978 Spanish Constitution, provision is made for the creation of 'autonomous communities' exercising legislative power within the areas under their jurisdiction. The Parliament of each region, in addition to passing laws of its own, can send bills to the central Parliament. The Constitution also allows the presentation of bills having the backing of petitions of at least 500,000 signatures. Prior to the collection of signatures, however, sponsors of bills require the sanction of the board of Congress.

26. The Constitution provides for a device called *reserva de pleno* (reservation for plenary debate) which applies to matters of constitutional reform, rights and liberties, general electoral law, regional statutes and the budget.

27. Each region can appoint one senator for every million inhabitants. The appointment is usually made by the regional Parliament.

28. That is to say his role is merely to turn the key of the automatic voting mechanism according to his parliamentary group's instructions.
29. Coalición Democratica has splintered into its different components, there have been major changes in the opposition's parliamentary leaders and the new leader of the main opposition party, Alianza Popular, is not even a member of Congress.
30. All legislation on public policy matters has been subjected to many studies by writers, academics, commentators and observers. However, little attention has been paid to legislation on private matters, which, none the less, have an immense influence on the organization of everyday life and on its absorption of the norms of democratic behaviour. On this, see the work by José Almagro Nosete and Francisco Fernández Segado on constitutional jurisdiction, or a variety of studies to be found in VVAA, *España diez años después de Franco*, Planeta, Barcelona, 1986, and VVAA, 10 años en la vida de los españoles, Plaza y Janés, Barcelona, 1986.
31. Between 1977 and 1979, five laws were approved amending the Law of Criminal Proceedings (legal aid and other issues) and six laws reforming the Penal Code (torture, adultery, common-law, marriage, contraceptives, recidivism). See *Memoria de Legislatura de 1977–1979*, Congresso de los Diputados, Madrid, 1979. In the following legislature, three laws were passed recognizing the rights of widows of civil-war veterans and those of ex-veterans themselves, one divorce law, one on under-utilized property, and later, reforms of the Civil Code and trial laws (sessions, court appearances, and provisional imprisonment). See *Memoria de Legislatura de 1979–1982*. We only have a memorandum for the first half of the second legislature (1982–6), but this also included much normative activity: one reform of the Civil Code, two of the Penal Code (among these one making abortion possible), one of the Law of Civil Proceedings, two of Criminal Proceedings, Law of *Habeus Corpus*, etc.
32. On the vote of no-confidence in Adolfo Suãrez in 1980, see Navalón Gerrero (1981: 98–9) where the authors admit that the winner was Felipe González, even though the vote failed.
33. Proof of the uncertain nature of the organization of the territorial distribution of power, is the recent petition by Catalan socialists for 'federalization' of the state. It is clear that the question of decentralization remains open in Spain, but, curiously, except for a recent debate in the Senate on the state of the Autonomous Communities, these issues have not been brought up in Parliament.
34. Data obtained from the *Guia del Diputado*, for the second and third legislatures, Congreso de los Diputados, Madrid, 1982 and 1986. Comparison with the interesting work by Jonás Condomines, 'Los diputado españoles Primeros análisis a partir del fichero ESDIP' in *Universidad y Sociedad*, no. 2, Madrid, 1981 shows in so far as possible a certain degree of consolidation of democracy with respect to the increase of 'pure' middle classes, so to speak, and the decreasing number of old Franco supporters. The liberal professions have grown: 33 per cent (1977), 32 per cent (1979), 26 per cent (1982) and 39 per cent (1986). The percentage of these who held political responsibilities during the Franco era, however, has gone down: 23 per cent (1977), 15 per cent (1979), 5 per cent (1982). We do not yet have data for 1986, but one can assume that the downward trend has continued.
35. We should not let these figures deceive us. The Spanish parliament is decisively in the hands of high-level bureaucrats. Administrative-level bureaucrats represented 2 per cent of the second legislature, and 3 per cent of the third, while elite public bureaucrats (upper corps of the state administration) were 13 per cent of the second legislature, and 11 per cent of the third (Guia, op. cit. percentages derived by author).
36. This is one of the neo-conservative criticisms of the welfare state. See, Milton and Rose Friedman, *La tirania del Statu quo*, Ariel, Barcelona, 1984; and Ramón

García Cotarelo, 'Socialismo y neoliberalismo' in VVAA, *Nuevos horizontes para el socialismo*, Sistema, Madrid, 1987.

37. The workers' representatives (also 'liberated', and in some cases without much contact with the rest of the workers' world for many years) were 3 per cent in the second legislature and 4 per cent in the third (Guia, op. cit.).

38. The UCD ministers came from different power centres within that conglomerate of parties forming the Spanish centre, such that each UCD government was really a balance of powers. The Socialist ministers are directly appointed by the president from the rank and file of the Socialists, or those closely related to them.

39. The figures for party membership (main indicator of strength) in Spain are low. Although now somewhat out of date, the report by Pilar Bravo, Castells and Carmen Ortiz on 'Militancia de los partidos politicos', Madrid, 1984, unpublished, continues to be the most comprehensive. It gives the following figures: PSOE−150,586; AP−150,905; PDP−20,277; PCE−79,990; CDS−6,630; PNV−50,035; EE−4,000. In some cases (CDS, PDP), the report is particularly out of date.

40. Public funding of parties has given rise to heated debate. See my article 'Las cuentas de los partidos' in *Cambio* 16, no. 788, 5 January 1987. However, as was to be expected, this draft bill was backed by almost all the parliamentary groups, including those that espoused the advantages to be had from the state's ceasing to subsidize activities in civil society.

41. Regulated by Organic Law 3/1984, 26 March, this is somewhat more restrictive than foreseen by the Constitution itself.

42. In this respect, one may remember the investigation committee into financial contributions to the political parties from abroad, as a result of the so-called 'Flick scandal' which gave birth to the above-mentioned Law of Party Funding.

43. On government control in the Spanish democracy, see Joaquin García Morillo, *El control parlamentario del gobierno en al ordenamiento español*, Congreso de los Diputados, Madrid, 1985. José Ramón Monero Gilbert and Joaquin García Morillo, *El control parlamentario*, Tecnos, Madrid, 1984.

44. Good proof of this is the complicated issue of the alleged sale of arms to Iran, authorized by the executive, which Parliament has not managed to clear up.

45. The opposition filed a prior appeal of unconstitutionality against this draft bill of the Organic Law designed to abolish prior appeal to unconstitutionality itself. The Constitutional Court found in favour of the parliamentary majority, in its judgement 66/1985, 23 May. The Court's line of argument was impeccably democratic: irrespective of other interesting and subtle questions, this body reasoned, since Parliament incorporates sovereignty, Parliament should have the power to decide, within the Constitution, how the Constitutional Court should work. A point of view favourable to the appeal can be found in Emilio Attard, *El cambio antes y después*, *op. cit.* 109 ff.

46. This measure was, at the time, subject to harsh criticism. It was felt in some quarters that it would put an end to the independence of the judiciary. See Fernando Vizcaino Casa, 'La justicia', VVAA, *España, 10 años después*, *op. cit.*: 37 ff.

47. This point is dealt with in Garcia Cotarelo, R., *Del Estado del bienestar al Estado del malestar*, CEC, Madrid, 1986.

48. On procedural legitimacy, see Niklas Luhman, *Rechtssoziologie*, Rowohlt, Hamburg, 1972, vol. II: 264 ff.

49. See Pierre Birnbaum *et al.*, *Réinventer le Parlement*, Flamarion, Paris, 1977, in which specific proposals are put forward to reform the representation system, leglislative procedure and control mechanisms.

50. The proposal is found in Norbett Reich, 'Forms of Socialisation of the Economy:

Reflections on Post-Modernism in Legal Theory', a paper presented at the Subcongreso de Derecho Publico de la Economia, at the 3rd Basque World Congress, Sept–October 1987.
51. See Andrea Manzella, *Il Parlamento,*, Il Mulino, Bologna, 1977: 261 ff.

References

Aguirre, J. (1981), *La política economica de la transición española*, Madrid, Union Editorial.
Aja, E., and X. Arbos (1980), 'El Senado. Cámara posibile de las autonomias', *Revista de Estudios Politicos*, **17**.
Attard, E. (1983) *La Constitución por dentro*, Barcelona, Argos Vergara.
Caciagli, M. (1986) *Elecciones y partidos en la transición española*, Madrid, CIS.
Campo, S., J.F. Tezanos and W. Santin (1982), 'La élite politica española y la transición a la democracia', *Sistema*, **48**.
Capo, Giol J. (1981) 'Estrategías para un sistema de partidos', *REP*, **23**.
—(1983). *La institucionalizacíon de las Cortes Generales*, Barcelona, Edicions de la Universitat de Barcelona.
—(1984) 'Consideraciones sobre los nuevos Reglamentos de las Cámeras en sus aspectos organizativos', in AAVV *Anuario de Derecho Politico*, Barcelona: Publicacions i edicions Universitat.
Cravinho, J. (1982) 'Portugal, um Pais em Crise entre o "Desplaneamento" e as Politicas de Estabilizacao' in *Pensamiento Iberoamericano*, no. 2, Madrid.
De Arcenegui, J.J. (1978) 'La Ley de relaciones Gobierno-Cortes de noviembre 1977 in M. Ramirez (ed.), *El control parlamentario del Gobierno en las democracias pluralistas. El proceso constitucional español*, Barcelona, Labor.
Esteban, J. and L. Lopez Guerra (1982) *Los partidos politicos en la España actual*, Barcelona: Planeta/Istituto de Estudios Economicos.
Fraile, M. (1984) 'Un año de gobierno socialista en el parlamento' in O. Alzaga (ed.), *Un año de socialismo*, Barcelona, Argos-Vergara.
Gallego, A. (1977) *El socialismo durante la dictadura, 1923–1930*, Madrid: Teba.
Gilmour, D. (1985) *La transformación de España*, Barcelona, Plaza y Janes.
Günther, R. (1986) 'El proceso constituyente español', *REP*, **49**.
Herrero, M. and R. De Minon (1982) 'Introducción general al contenido y a los principios de la Constituciòn' in M. Martinez Cuadrado (ed.), *La Constituciòn de 1978 en la historia del constitucionalismo español*, Madrid, Mezquita.
Huneus, C. (1985), *La Unión de Centro Democrático y la transición a la democracia en España*, Madrid, CIS Siglo XXI.
Jover, P. and J. Marcet, (1985) 'Teoria y realidad en las relaciones del gobierno con el grupo parlamentario y el grupo mayoritario' in *El Gobierno en la Constitución Española*, Barcelona, Diputación de Barcelona.
Linz, J. (1973), 'Opposition to and under an authoritarian regime. The case of Spain' in R.A. Dahl (ed.), *Regimes and Opposition*, New Haven: Yale University Press.
—(1981), 'Un secolo di politica e di interessi in Spagna' in S. Berger (ed.), *L'organizzazione degli interessi in Spagna*, Bologna: Il Mulino.
—et. al. (1981), *Informe sociológico sobre el cambio politico en España, 1975–1981*, Madrid, Euroamérica.
Lopez Garrido, D. (1982), 'La posición de las ponencias en al procedimiento legislativo del Congreso de los Diputados', *Revista de Derecho Politico*.
—(1985), 'Gobierno y Parlamento: dos modelos de relaciones internas' in *El Gobierno en la Constitución Española*, Barcelona, Diputación de Barcelona.

López Nieto, L. (1988), *Alianza Popular. La derecha conservadora española*, Madrid, CIS Siglo XXI.

Lucas Verdú, P. (1976), *La octava Ley Fundamental: critica juridico-politica de la Reforma Suárez*, Madrid, Tecnos.

—(ed.) (1983), *La Corona y la Monarquia Parlamentaria en la Constitucion de 1978*, Madrid, Facultad de Derecho, Universidad Complutense.

Maravall, J.M. (1980), 'Transición a la democracia. Alineamientos Politicos y elecciones en España', *Sistema*, **38**.

—(1982), 'Introduccion' in *Parlamento y Democracia. Problemas y perspectivas en los años 80*, Madrid, F. Pablo Iglesias.

—(1984), *La politica de la transición*, Madrid, Taurus.

—(1985), *La politica de la transición*, 2nd edition, Madrid, Taurus.

—and J. Santamaria (1985), 'Crisis del franquismo, transición politica y consolidación de la democracia de España', *Sistema*, **68–69**.

Marcet, J. (1984), *Convergéncia Democrática de Catalunya. El partito y el movimiento politico*, Barcelona, ed. 62.

Martinez Cuadrado, M. (ed.) (1982), *La Constitución de 1978 en la historia del constitucionalismo español*, Mezquita, Madrid.

Mohedan, J.M. and M. Peña (1978), *Constitución: cuenta atras. ETA, operacíon Galaxia y otros terrorismos*, Madrid, Casa de Campo.

Molas, I., and I. Pitarch (1987), *Las Cortes Generales en el sistema parlamentario de gobierno*, Madrid, Tecnos.

Montero, J.R. (1979), 'La moción de censura en la Constitución de 1978' in M. Ramirez (ed.), *Estudios sobre la Constitución española de 1978*, Zaragoza, Portico.

—and J. Garcia Morillo (1984), *El control Parlamentario*, Madrid, Tecnos.

Morlino, L. (1985), *Como cambian los regimenes politicos*, Madrid, Centro de Estudios Constitucionales.

—(1986), 'Consolidación democratica. Definición, modelos e hipotesis', *Revista de Investigaciones Sociologicas*, July–September 1986.

Naválon, A. and F. Guerrero (1981), *Objetivo Suárez*, Barcelona, Planeta.

Oneto, J. (1981), *La noche de Tejero*, Barcelona, Planeta.

—(1982), *La verdad sobre el caso Tejero*, Barcelona, Planeta.

—(1985), *Anatomia de un cambio de regimen*, Barcelona, Plaza y Janes.

Pallarés, F. (1981), 'La distorción de la proporcionalidad en el sistema electoral español. Análisis comparado y hipótesis alternativas', *REP*, **23**.

Perez Diaz, V. (1984), 'Políticas económicas y pautas sociales en la España de la transición: la doble cara del neocorporativismo', *España: un presente para el futuro*, Barcelona, Planeta.

Poulantzas, N. (1976), *La crisis de las dictaduras*, Madrid, Siglo XXI.

Punset, R. (1983), *La Cortes Generales. Estudios de Derecho Constitucional Español*, Madrid, Centro de Estudios Costitucionales.

Ripollés, R.E. (1978), 'La regulación vigente de las relaciones legislativo-ejecutivo (La Ley de 17 noviembre de 1977 y los reglamentos provisionales del Congreso y del Senado de 13 y 14 de octubre de 1977) in M. Ramirez (ed.), *El control parlamentario del Gobierno en las democracias pluralistas. El proceso constitucional español*, Barcelona, Labor.

Santamaria, J. (ed.) (1981), *Transición a la democracia en el sur de Europa y en America Latina*, Madrid, CIS.

Santollalla, F. (1984), *Derecho Parlamentario Español*, Madrid, Ed. Ecional.

Sole Tura, J. and E. Aja (1977), *Constituciones y periodos constituyentes en España (1808–1936)*, Madrid, Siglo XXI.

—(1982), 'Democracia y eficacia en las Cortes Españolas' in J.M. Maravall (1982), *Parlamento y Democracia. Problemas y perspectivas en los años 80*, Madrid, F. Pablo Iglesias.

—and M.A. Aparicio (1984), *La Cortes Generales en el sistema constitucional*, Madrid, Tecnos.

Subirats, J. (1986), 'An approach to the legislative production of the Spanish Parliament (1979–1982)', *European Journal of Political Research*, **14**.

—(1987), 'Monopolio Politico e Conflitto Sociale', *Micromega*, **2**.

—(1989), 'Political Change and Economic Crisis in Spain 1974–1987' in G. Damgaard and A. Richardson (eds.), *The Politics of Economic Crisis: Lessons from Western Europe*, Aldershot, Avebury.

Tamames, R. (1982), *Introducción a la Constitución española*, Madrid, Alianza.

Tezanos, J.F. (1979), *Estructura de clases y conflictos de poder en la España postfranquista*, Madrid, Edicusa.

—(1981), 'Identificación de clase y conciencia obrera entre los trabajadores industriales', *Sistema*, **43–4**.

Vallés, J.M. (1977), 'Desigualitats de representació en l'actual normativa electoral aspanyola', *Perspectiva Social*, **10**.

—and F. Carreras (1977), *Las elecciones*, Barcelona, Blume.

—(1982), 'Reforma electoral y coordenades politiques. Els condicionants de la normativa electoral a Espanya i Catalunya', *Estudis Electorals*, **6**.

—(1986), 'Sistema electoral y democracia representativa: nota sobre la Ley Orgánica de regimen electoral general de 1985 y su función politica', *REP*, **53**.

de Vega Garcia P. (1983), 'Constitucion y democracia' in A. Lopez Pina (ed.) *La Constitución de la Monarquia parlamentaria*, Fondo de Cultura Economica (FCE), Mexico.

5 The difficulties of 'rationalization' in a polarized political system: the Greek Chamber of Deputies

Nikos Alivizatos

Introduction

In the assessment of the role of the Greek Chamber of Deputies (*Vouli*) in the process of democratic consolidation, the weight of the institution's past seems decisive. This is mainly due to the fact that unlike the other southern European dictatorships that collapsed in the mid-1970s, the colonels' junta was short lived (1967–74); besides, it never succeeded in destroying the pre-existing political networks and eradicating the habits and attitudes of a long-established (130 years) virtually uninterrupted parliamentary tradition. It is not surprising therefore that, in spite of the constitutional innovations, the post-dictatorial Chamber maintained most of the characteristics of its predecessors in the newly born Third Greek Republic.[1]

The purpose of this chapter is to examine, using the available data,[2] the influence of continuity and change on the functioning of the Greek Chamber of Deputies since 1974. Before proposing an overall assessment of the role played by this unique representative body in the process of democratic consolidation, the Chamber will be examined in historical perspective, taking account of its constitutional framing and then in the light of the factors that have shaped its present composition and practices in its two traditional functions: the making of laws and the control of the executive.

The historical perspective

Like Spain, Italy and Portugal, Greece was one of the first European countries to establish a liberal constitutional regime as early as the first half of the nineteenth century. After the war of independence (1821–30) and a decade of absolutism (1833–43), the first Greek Parliament was elected following the 3 September 1843 liberal revolt; it drafted the 1844 conservative Constitution, modelled on the French and Belgian Charters of 1830 and 1831. This provided for a bicameral parliament, whose lower house was to be directly elected by quasi-universal male suffrage for a three-year term.[3] Although distorted in practice, the 1844 constitution was the first to permit the development of a primative parliamentarism.[4]

The centrality, however, of the Chamber of Deputies was confirmed under the 1864 liberal Constitution, one of the most egalitarian in nineteenth-century Europe.[5] The Constitution provided for a unicameral legislature, whose confidence, under a convention agreed upon in 1875, was necessary for the appointment of the cabinet by the king. Thus, parliamentary government, based on universal suffrage, was institutionalized at a comparatively early stage and the shift from constitutional monarchy to popular sovereignity was substantiated by holding general elections at regular intervals.[6] That tendency was further confirmed after the 1909 liberal revolt and the revision of the 1864 Constitution initiated by E. Venizelos in 1911. The Chamber's position was strengthened and the standing orders voted in the same year facilitated the unimpended functioning of the Assembly.[7]

The passage from oligarchic to mass politics was marked by the two major political crises that deeply divided Greece twice in the twentieth century: the 'national schism' in the inter-war period, and the second schism after World War II. Although the actors in and the object of those two major conflicts were far from being the same ones, the two schisms have had very similar consequences at the constitutional level: initially they caused a significant distortion, if not falsification, of parliamentary government and of the rule of law. Eventually, they both ended with the advent of dictatorships, in 1936 and in 1967 respectively, both of which owed their birth to the prolongation of the respective cleavages and to the subsequent attenuation of the legitimacy of the country's liberal institutions.[8]

Though formally defined by the constitutions adopted during those decades (in 1925, 1927 and 1952), the Chamber of Deputies — and to a lesser extent the Senate, from 1929 to 1935 — itself suffered the consequences of the two schisms, to the extent that it itself reflected the divisions of civil society. The unconstitutional reinforcement of the executive at the expense of the Chamber and the substantial restriction of parliamentary control and cabinet accountability were the most obvious signs of the Assembly's institutional decline. It is important to note, however, that in spite of that decline, the Chamber of Deputies, the only constitutional body to be directly elected by the people, managed to maintain much of its past symbolic value as the only legitimate — although not always authentic — representative of the electorate's will. Its apparent centrality, therefore, under all constitutional orders[9] should not be considered as a paradox.

The collapse of the colonels' regime on 23 July 1974[10] signalled the end of the institutional remnants of the second schism. Under the subtle circumstances of the very first phase of the transition to democratic politics[11], the so-called national unity government headed by Karamanlis immediately abolished the junta's constitutional order and revived the 1952 constitution, with the exception of those provisions referring to the king.[12] In less than two months, the same government legalized all political parties, thus putting an end to one of the major distortions of post-war Greek politics.[13] By the beginning of October 1974, martial law was lifted and civil rights were fully restored.[14] Under those circumstances, the first post-dictatorial Assembly was elected on 17 November, 1974.

The rules of the game

The conduct of the elections by the Karamanlis government less than four months after the July 1974 rupture was not seriously contested by the emerging political parties, despite an electoral law whose declared aim was to favour the over-representation in Parliament of the party which received the highest number of votes.[15] Under the 4 October, 1974 Constitutional Act, the new Assembly would have the power to revise all provisions of the 1952 Constitution with the exception of those referring to the republican or monarchical form of government. The latter issue was to be decided directly by the electorate through a referendum which was to be held within 45 days of the general elections.[16] For the drafting of the new Constitution, the same act provided that the Assembly would be assisted by the government to be formed after the elections which would submit a draft that had to be discussed and approved by the Assembly within three months. If that time limit was not respected, the government was to have the power to invite the electorate to approve, through a second referendum its own initial draft, amended in the meantime by the Assembly.[17]

The referendum giving a choice between a republic or a monarchy was held on 8 December 1974, and almost 70 per cent of the electorate voted for the republic.[18] It was only then that the newly elected Assembly met under the name of 5th Revisionary Chamber. Dominated by Karamanlis's New Democracy, which had won 75 per cent of the seats after obtaining 54 per cent of the votes, the Assembly's first task was to vote for a constitutional resolution that fixed the rules for its own functioning.[19] In fact, the pre-1967 standing orders were revived, and the only major innovation was the establishment of two legislative sections, each comprising half of the total number of the deputies, with the power to legislate on all matters. Another constitutional resolution fixed detailed rules for the framing of the new constitution. There was to be a special parliamentary committee, on which all parties would be represented in proportion to the number of seats they held in parliament which was to work on the draft that the government would submit; the committee's final draft was to be submitted for approval to the Assembly's plenum.[20]

Though the three-month dead-line was transgressed, the framing of the new Constitution was achieved in an unusually short period of time. Hundreds of amendments were submitted by the opposition parties as well as by individual deputies, both at the committee and the plenum stages of the deliberation. It is important to note that in spite of the governing party's overwhelming majority, consensual solutions were reached on many important issues.[21] However, there was one issue on which it very soon appeared that no compromise was possible: the status and prerogatives of the President of the Republic under the new Constitution. According to the majority, the latter should have a number of prerogatives such as the dissolution of Parliament, the holding of referenda 'on crucial national issues' and even the dismissal of the cabinet which could be exercised without the prime minister's consent. To quote well-known words of Karamanlis himself, the President of the Republic should have sufficient powers

to perform his regulatory role, that is to harmonize the relations between the people and the Chamber and between the Chamber and the cabinet, in order to ensure the normal course [of parliamentary government].[22]

In the view of the opposition, the head of state should have only nominal competences, while real power should lie with the cabinet and the Chamber, to which the executive should be directly accountable. Overdramatized, that debate led to a major clash, all opposition parties finally withdrawing from the Assembly in May 1975, denouncing the new Constitution as authoritarian.[23] As a consequence, at the final vote on 9 June 1975, the Constitution was approved only by the New Democracy deputies.

In the 1975 constitution, section III (comprising articles 51 to 80) the Chamber's status and competences primarily reflected pre-1967 rules and practices. However, a number of significant innovations were also introduced. Some of them were anticipated by practices adopted by the constitutional Assembly for the regulation of its own work and expressed Karamanlis's persistent search for greater efficiency in parliamentary procedure. They included simplification of the old rules on the Chamber's quorum as well as those pertaining to the deliberation and voting of bills by the deputies;[24] the provision for ensuring the deputies' continuous presence for all voting through the creation of the so-called 'vacations section' which operates between the Chamber's ordinary sessions;[25] the provision for a speedy procedure for the adoption of those bills designated by the cabinet as having an 'urgent nature' or 'special importance'. Such bills would be considered as passed even without a parliamentary vote, if the Chamber failed to discuss and vote on them within three to five sittings, irrespective of their length and importance.[26]

As regards the Chamber's second traditional function, parliamentary control of the executive, some major innovations were introduced: first, the Chamber was given a greater role in the appointment of the prime minister and of the other members of the cabinet by the head of state. The latter's position was considerably limited by a number of detailed rules which, in the event of a one-party majority in Parliament, made his role a mere formality.[27] This, however, was not coupled with a reinforcement of the Chamber's powers to exercise effective control of the executive in the day-to-day handling of public affairs, especially in the fields of foreign policy and national defence. Some interesting proposals aimed at establishing permanent committees, to which each corresponding ministers would be accountable, were rejected. It is also worth noting that the Constitution excluded the appointment of investigation committees in these two crucial areas without the consent of the majority of the deputies.[28] The cold-war practice of establishing 'impermeable' and 'out of bounds' areas of government action, where no true debate and no open action was admitted without the executive's consent, was thus perpetuated.[29]

The standing orders voted by the same Assembly, in October 1975,[30] confirmed the tendencies described above. While the cabinet's powers in the law-making function were considerably reinforced, no steps were taken to ensure its timely and effective accountability before Parliament. By maintaining rules and procedures dating from the inter-war years, if not from the beginning of this century, the 1975 standing orders ignored modern practices, such as committee work and public hearings, and adhered to a model of direct confrontation rather than of consensual agreement between the parliamentary majority and the opposition. Moreover, even from a purely technical standpoint, the post-dictatorial standing orders did not make it any easier for the deputies to perform their current duties and did little to ensure the Parliament's function as the nation's highest political forum.[31]

When the Socialist majority decided to proceed to the revision of the Constitution in March 1985, it declared that its main objective was to 'strengthen the role of Parliament', in order to reassert popular sovereignity.[32] In fact, the revision was limited to the prerogatives of the President of the Republic and not a single provision of section III of the Constitution was touched. With the unexpected assistance of the Communist party.[33] PASOK transferred most of the previously criticized prerogatives of the head of state to the parliamentary majority, ie into the hands of the prime minister, whose centrality was thus further confirmed.[34] That was the political and institutional meaning of the revision carried through by the '6th Revisionary Chamber' elected on 2 June 1985.[35] The new standing orders, adopted surprisingly enough by unanimous vote of the two major parties in June 1987,[36] were supposed, if not to counter-balance the prime minister's excessive weight through the reinforcement of the opposition's role in Parliament, at least to rationalize the Chamber's rules and procedures. Although some significant steps were made toward modern methods of work and toward institutionalizing some of the practices of the post-dictatorial Chambers, the supremacy of the executive remained intact.[37]

The composition of the Chamber

The major variable shaping the Chamber's character and position after the collapse of the dictatorship is connected to a factor which is in itself 'external' to the relevant constitutional rules, ie to the role of political parties in the emerging democracy. From the very first days of the transition and well before they were officially legalized, the parties played a very active role in mobilizing the population against the remnants of the colonels' regime. Moreover, their diverging attitudes on the nature and depth of the July 23 rupture did not

Table 5.1 Votes and seats, 1974–87

Parties	17 November 1974		20 November 1977		18 October 1981		2 June 1985	
	% of votes	no. of seats	% of votes	no. of seats	% of votes	no. of seats	% of votes	no. of seats
New Democracy	54.4	216 (72%)	41.8	171 (57%)	35.8	115 (38%)	40.8	126 (42%)
Centre Union	20.5	62 (21%)	11.9	16	–	–	–	–
PASOK	13.6	14	25.3	93 (31%)	48.1	172 (57%)	45.8	161 (54%)
Communist Party (Orthod.)	9.5[1]	8	9.4	11	10.9	13	9.9	12
Communist Party (Inter.)			2.7[3]	2	1.3	–	1.8	–
Other	2.0[2]	–	8.9[4]	7	3.9[5]	–	1.7	–
Total	100.0	300	100.0	300	100.0	300	100.0	300

1. United Left, including the orthodox Communist Party (KKE) (5 seats); the eurocommunist Communist Party of the Interior (KKEesoterikou) and the Unified Democratic Left (EDA) (2 seats and 1 seat respectively).
2. Including the National Democratic Union (EDE, extreme right) (1.08%).
3. Alliance of Progressive and Leftist Forces, which included the Communist Party of the Interior (1 seat); the Unified Democratic Left (EDA) (1 seat) and three minor groups.
4. Including the National Front (EP, extreme right) (6.82% and 5 seats) and the New Liberals (NF, centre–right) (1.08% and 2 seats).
5. Including the Progressive Party (KP, extreme right) (1.68%).

Source: Official Results, published by the Ministry of the Interior

Note: Percentage figures in parenthesis represent percentage of seats held by party.

prevent them from initiating a common action toward what they called 'securing and widening' the newly born democracy.[38] By October 1974, as we have seen, all legal restrictions on party activities were in fact abolished, and for the first time since the 1920s no persecutions whatsoever threatened party membership and affiliation.[39] It is not surprising, therefore, that political parties—starting chronologically from the left side of the political spectrum— organized themselves nation-wide and, in the months and years that followed, the partisan phenomenon acquired unprecedented dimensions in a society which was overpoliticized by tradition.[40] At the same time, this tendency prevented the development of collective action outside the strictly political arena (trade unions, local government etc) and as a consequence, to use a Gramscian term, it perpetuated the 'filigranic' character of civil society.

The development of mass parties—whose internal rules and practices did not always adhere, to say the least, to the purest democratic procedures—[41] significantly reduced the importance of traditional elites in the decision-making process. And it is worth noting that, with the exception perhaps of New Democracy, parliamentary groups and individual deputies lost much of their previous power *vis-à-vis* party leadership. There is no need to stress the structural importance of that development for parliamentary behaviour.[42]

Connected with the development of the partisan phenomenon is the polarization of the political conflict according to a right versus left pattern and the gradual disappearance of the centre as an independent political force.[43] The direct consequence of this trend was that all four of the Chambers elected after the fall of the dictatorship have seen one-party majorities, identified either with the centre–right or with the centre-left. Greek parliamentarism has remained majoritarian. Since 1981 it has also become 'rotational'.

As may be seen in Table 5.1, the differences between the percentage of votes and the percentage of seats of the largest party in all of the four post-dictatorial general elections (17.6 per cent in 1974; 15.2 per cent in 1977; 9.0 per cent in 1981 and 8.2 per cent in 1985) is due to the electoral system adopted. This is the so-called system of 'reinforced' proportional representation, which, with minor modifications, has maintained the pattern of Greek electoral history since 1958.[44] While encouraging the two-party system, reinforced proportional representation favours the party with the most votes since, in the normal course of electoral behaviour,[45] it is sure to gain at least 50 per cent of the seats, even if it achieves only 40 per cent of the votes.

This tripolar party system with bipolar competition,[46] shows an undeniable continuity with the political system of the pre-1967 period, in spite of the important internal changes within each one of the component parties. This has had very significant consequences for the functioning of the Chamber of Deputies.

A third feature affecting the composition of the post-dictatorial Chambers is connected with the extensive renewal of their personnel. While the pre-1967 party leaders reappeared on the political scene and remained practically unchallenged, the deputies themselves were now comparatively younger in age and hence more eager to adapt themselves to the new left–right competition (see Table 5.2).

Table 5.2 Age distribution of deputies

Age group	1964 Chamber		1974 Chamber		1977 Chamber		1981 Chamber		1985 Chamber	
	No.	%	No.	%	No.	%	No.	%	No.	%
25-9	1	0.3	7	2.3	3	1.0	6	2.0	1	0.3
30-9	25	8.3	45	15.0	57	19.0	51	17.0	30	10.0
40-9	65	21.6	78	26.0	95	31.6	115	38.3	102	34.0
50-9	120	40.0	83	27.6	68	22.6	68	22.6	91	30.3
60-9	68	22.6	71	23.6	56	18.6	42	14.0	59	19.6
70+	21	7.0	15	5.0	18	6.0	18	6.0	17	5.6
Not avail.			1	0.3	3	1.0				
Total	300	100.0	300	100.0	300	100.0	300	100.0	300	100.0

Sources: Metaxas, A.-I.D. (1981, 1985).

Still more eloquent are the conclusions that can be drawn from Table 5.3 which shows the deputies' length of parliamentary experience: In the 1974 and 1981 elections it was the first time since 1910, (when the newly founded Liberal party, under the leadership of Venizelos, removed from Parliament the old party notables[47]), that such high proportions of new deputies have been elected.

Table 5.3   The selection of deputies

Elected for	1964		1974		1977		1981		1985	
	No	%	No	%	No	%	No	%	No	%
1st time	37	12.3	184	61.3	115	38.3	123	41.0	38	12.6
2nd time	61	20.3	16	5.3	106	35.3	89	29.6	103	34.3
3rd time	41	13.6	25	8.3	13	4.3	44	14.6	88	29.3
4th or more	161	53.6	75	25.0	66	22.0	44	14.6	71	23.6
Total	300	100.0	300	100.0	300	100.0	300	100.0	300	100.0

Sources: Metaxas A.-I.D. (1981, 1985).

A high level of 'partyness' bi-polarization on the left–right continuum and deputy renovation were thus the three main parameters that characterized the post-dictatorial Chambers. It remains to be seen to what extent these have affected the working of parliament since 1974.

The law-making function

The majoritarian composition of the post-dictatorial Chambers has had a direct impact on the origin of the bills passed since 1974. Out of the 1,750 bills passed by June 1987, only one—which itself regulated a minor local issue—originated from Parliament.[48] In other words, government bills exceeded 99.9 per cent of the total number of laws, the highest percentage in any European country for which information is available including majoritarian democracies similar to Greece. (See Table 5.4)

The right of Parliament, ie of any individual deputy, to initiate legislation, which is in principle guaranteed by the constitution,[49] has consequently become a tool for controlling the cabinet instead of a means of reaching non-partisan solutions to pending issues.[50]

With regard to the time necessary for the adoption of bills, the Greek Chamber proved unusually fast. The committee stage seldom necessitated more than five to eight days, as the procedure involving the 20–5 parliamentary committees provided for by the 1975 standing orders[51] was generally considered as a mere formality. The committees, each composed of 30 deputies, at least 16 of whom belonging to the party in power, are presided over by deputies designated by the majority party leaders. The committees' competence was

Table 5.4   Number and origin of bills passed, 1978–82

Country	Total No. of bills passed	non-government bills No.	%
Austria	455	100	22
Belgium	965[1]	112	11.6
Cyprus	421	20	4.7
Denmark	782	25	3.2
France[2]	–	12	13.0
Greece	491	0	0.0
Italy	1,229	371	30.2
Netherlands	1,435	4	0.3
Norway	374	5	1.3
Portugal	216	130	60.2
Spain	361	38	10.5
United Kingdom	314	49	15.6

1. Including those referred by the House to the Senate and vice versa.
2. 1958–72.

Source: Interparliamentary Union (1986), *Parliaments of the World. A Comparative Reference Compendium*, 2nd ed., Vol. 2, Aldershot, Gower, 912–20.

restricted to preparing a report on pending bills falling under their responsibility.[52] It is significant although without practical consequences, that committee reports were not binding for the Chamber at the discussion stage, if the competent minister disagreed with any amendments proposed.[53] In all cases, the Chamber in plenary session as well as the legislative sections were required to deliberate on the original government bill. The 1987 standing orders were supposed to reinforce parliamentary committees, but their role continues to be restricted in the law-making area. Their number was reduced to six, following the French Fifth Republic model and, for the first time in Greek parliamentary history, they were empowered to decide, by simple majority to hold hearings, which, however, can never be public.[54] Although the procedure may thus become more elaborate, it remains to be seen whether, under the new rules, the committee stage will become more substantial.[55]

As for the next stage, legislative debate followed by voting either by the Chamber's plenum and the 150-member legislative section or—during the three summer months—by the 100-member vacations section,[56] it has been estimated that from 1974 to 1977 the entire procedure for a single bill lasted on average one day and, from 1977 to 1981, 11.1 days.[57] After 1981, according to our own estimates, the average time increased slightly, despite frequent use of the so-called urgent procedure, provided by article 76 of the constitution.[58] The same short time-scale applies to the debate and vote on the budget, for which the 1975 standing orders provided a maximum of four sittings, while the 1987 standing orders only five.[59] In any case, the changes observed from legislative period to legislative period are noteworthy, as can be deduced from Table 5.5.

Table 5.5   Legislative output 1974–87

Legislatures	Bills passed by Plenum and winter legisl. sections[1]		Bills passed by vacation section (summer months)		Total No. of bills passed	
	No.	Yearly average	No.	Yearly average	No.	Yearly average
1st (1974–7)	457	152	296	90	753	251
2nd (1977–81)	373	93	118	30	491	123
3rd (1981–5)	272	68	78	20	350	88
4th (1985–7[2])	146	73	26	13	172	86

1. Winter legislative sections functioned only from 1975 to 1980.
2. 30 June.
Source: Published and unpublished data from the Direction of Legislative Work of the Chamber of Deputies

The most striking tendency in Table 5.5 is the decrease in the average number of laws adopted yearly. Various reasons could be adduced to this interesting feature. First, the emergence of major opposition parties, namely PASOK and New Democracy (see Table 5.1) which, in appearance at least, differed fundamentally. This situation led to the prevalence of a bipolar type of ideological competition and impeded consensual policies within the Chamber. Second, obstructionism, although within the limits established by the standing orders in force,[60] became the standard mode of political behaviour, even in the absence of significant differences on the concrete measures to be adopted. Hence a relatively high number of government bills remain pending or are withdrawn by the competent minister.[61] Third, fewer laws were voted because an increasing number of bills contained disparate provisions, regulating issues which normally should have been the object of different laws. This practice of 'catch-all' laws was pursued through the adoption of last-minute amendments, without previous deliberation before the appropriate parliamentary committee, and inevitably resulted in a lowering of the standards of legislative work. Having in the last ten years become a normal procedure, that practice, although in principle forbidden by the Constitution,[62] has not been invalidated by the Courts, which follow the *interna corporis* theory and thus confirm it.[63]

At the same time, one should note an increasing tendency to transfer legislative matters from Parliament to the executive, via legislative delegations[64] and, to a lesser extent, through autonomous government legislation. This happens despite the fact that the Constitution allows it, in theory, only in emergencies.[65] There are no official statistics to show the exact dimension of this trend, but there is sufficient evidence that the law-maker's official intentions are very often altered and weakened, if not directly annulled, since the concrete regulation of more and more issues by the executive escapes any kind of overt public accountability.[66]

In short, the post-dictatorial law-making experience demonstrates that careful deliberation on substantive matters has not been the rule. On the contrary, with the exception of the years between 1974 and 1977, the parliamentary discussion of bills usually exhausted itself in ideological competition, aiming to impress public opinion rather than to deal with substantial issues and to promote consensual solutions to pending problems.

The controlling function

In the area of parliamentary control of the executive, the weight of tradition has been more perceptible. In spite of and perhaps due to the fact that the Constitution requires at least two weekly sittings in plenary session to deal with parliamentary control, the rules of the 1975 standing orders did not correspond to the need for publicity and timely accountability. As a result, entire sections of government activities escaped any kind of substantial control, while the cover-up of some of the most obvious deficiencies of the Chamber's controlling function was attempted through practices *contra legem*, inaugurated under pressure from the opposition.[67]

According to the 1975 standing orders, there were four means of parliamentary control: 'reports', 'questions', 'interpellations' and 'requests for document submission'. Any of them could be submitted by one or more deputies and only the Chamber's plenary session could discuss them. Specifically, reports, the milder form of parliamentary control, were expressions of a wish, aiming to draw the attention of the competent minister to a specific problem, usually of a local nature, and initiating legislative or administrative action for its solution.[68] In practice, they were submitted by opposition as well as by majority deputies but they seldom led to any sort of discussion.[69] Questions were basically requests for information 'on a public matter in general'; they were included in the agenda of the Chamber and eventually debated only if they were not answered, no matter how briefly and vaguely, by the competent minister within 20 days after they had been submitted.[70] Interpellations, which were not supposed to be submitted by majority deputies, sought the motives behind and scope of a specific government action or omission, and were in theory debated in the order they were submitted.[71] Finally, requests for document submission could be converted to interpellations and debated with priority, if they were not met within 20 days from the day they were submitted.[72] Table 5.6 shows the use of these means of parliamentary control since 1974.

During the 1981–7 period, for which more detailed statistical data are available, an average of 95–100 sittings per ordinary sessions (ie from October to June) with an average duration of 2.5 to 3.0 hours each, and with a usually small attendance, were devoted to parliamentary control. Half of these sittings dealt with the discussion of interpellations, 75–80 per cent of which had been submitted by one or more deputies belonging to the main opposition party.[73]

However, after 1974, wide publicity was given to a new means of parliamentary control, the so-called 'debates among party leaders'. Although the Constitution and the 1975 standing orders made no special provision for them, these debates took place twice a year at the initiative of the cabinet, ie the prime minster. They lasted four to five hours each and concerned 'national

Table 5.6 Means of parliamentary control, 1974–87

	1st Legislature 1974–7			2nd Legislature 1977–81			3rd Legislature 1981–5			4th Legislature 1985–7[1]		
	Submitted	Answered[2]	Discussed	Submitted	Answered[2]	Discussed	Submitted	Answered[2]	Discussed	Submitted	Answered[2]	Discussed
Reports	27,280	21,393	860	40,199	40,706	402	16,991	22,971	589	9,861	12,200	142
Questions	7,900	8,234	683	20,927	25,589	1,004	11,906	15,872	715	8,135	11,300	337
Interpellations	1,006	–	284	2,052	–	339	1,075	–	317	411	–	112
Requests for document submission	239	101	22	1,563	1,290	31	965	n.a.	32	1,142	n.a.	15

1. 30 June.
2. Written answers to a particular means of parliamentary control may be given separately by more than one ministry; hence in some instances the higher number of answers in comparison to the number of the respective means of parliamentary control.

Source: Published and unpublished data from the Direction of Parliamentary Control of the Chamber of Deputies.

issues', such as foreign policy, the economy and education. These debates were one of the rare occasions in which the prime minister personally participated in parliamentary work and extensive excerpts were broadcast nation-wide, usually the same evening, by the state television. After 1981, these debates were cancelled. They were reintroduced in 1985 by the PASOK cabinet, under pressure from the opposition as well as from public opinion. Recently, the 1987 standing orders have institutionalized these debates; they are to take place twice a year, once at the initiative of the cabinet and once at the initiative of at least two parties of the opposition.[74]

Discussions over motions of confidence and censure were infrequent. As for motions of confidence, with two exceptions, in 1980 and in 1987,[75] discussions took place only after general elections, on the occasion of the presentation of the new government's platform as provided by the Constitution.[76] With the exception of one instance, in 1988, no motions of censure have been submitted since 1974, although only 50 deputies' signatures are required, due to the certainty of being ultimately rejected by the majority.[77] Thus surprisingly enough, and contrary to what seems to be the rule in most Western European parliaments, motions of censure, which may lead to a three-day discussion of the cabinet's general policy, are not practiced.

The same applies to the establishment of parliamentary investigation committees in the post-dictatorial Chambers, since in view of the intentionally unclear wording of the relevant article of the Constitution, it was considered both before and after PASOK's advent to power that a majority vote was required for their creation.[78]

During the past 14 years, the main criticism of rules and practices on parliamentary control was that they were unable to allow timely as well as sufficiently documented discussion of crucial contemporary issues. This criticism is well-founded. By providing for the discussion of newly introduced 'questions' and 'interpellations of actuality' twice a week,[79] the 1987 standing orders aimed at remedying an obvious deficiency. Naturally, it remains to be seen whether a mere change of the relevant rules is sufficient to provide parliamentary control with substantial content in practice.[80]

Toward a general assessment

In order to assess the role of the Greek Chamber of Deputies in the process of democratic consolidation, one should seek the answer to a number of specific questions, in the light of the empirical data presented so far.

It is clear that the Greek Chamber is basically a 'talking' parliament as opposed to a 'working' parliament. This is true first from the point of view of its regulations which give the cabinet a privileged position in parliamentary work, while ignoring procedures that could lead to more consensual modes of competition. Aiming to ensure efficiency in government action at the expense, if necessary, of publicity and responsible control, both the Constitution and the standing orders now in force adhere to a model of spectacular confrontation, while making it difficult to adopt solutions which go beyond narrow party loyalties. A typical example is the fact that all the parliamentary control activity and the major part of the law-making process take place in plenary sessions and not in the parliamentary committees, which, by being smaller in size and having smoother rules, could obviously encourage consensual behaviour. The committees, although in theory upgraded by the 1987 standing orders, still assume a secondary role, and their role is restricted to the law-making field. Another significant example is the rules governing the role and competences of the Chamber's speaker. Despite the important steps made by the 1987 standing orders, the conduct of parliamentary work in fact remains in the hands of the governmental majority.[81] Besides the legal rules the talking shop character of the Greek Parliament has been enhanced in a decisive way by a political factor, namely the political configuration of the country since 1974 and principally after 1977. There has existed a primarily ideological conflict between right and left, between the so-called 'conservative' and 'progressive' forces, which certainly had never previuosly had the occasion to face each other openly within a framework of legal politics since the 1930s, the exchange of arguments and, in general, rational and pragmatic political discourse have been down-graded, to the benefit of over-simplified general statements. Only rarely have issues been faced by the deputies on the basis of technical and objective criteria; instead, as a rule, they have been seen as part of global conflicting socio-economic projects, which themselves were defined more in ideological than in political terms.

The way in which opposition was practiced in the Chamber after 1974 was the consequence of and at the same time the reason for the above-described symbolically orientated parliamentary process. With the significant exception of Greece's position in the international community, on which the two main parties have seemed increasingly to agree in recent years,[82] opposition has been basically destructive. After 1977, and within the limits tolerated by the standing orders in force, obstructionism has become an everyday parliamentary practice at the expense of constructive opposition. This opposition has taken the form of endless lists of speakers who make repetitive speeches which add nothing to what has already been said, endless speeches by parliamentary group leaders and ministers[83] and, especially, non-participation in or withdrawal from some critical debates as a sign of what has been described by a prominent PASOK leader as 'structural opposition'.[84] These tactics were used by PASOK until 1981 and by New Democracy since then. As for the Communist left, its small representation did not permit it to perform any substantial role in Parliament.[85] Thus, in spite of the fact that, with time, the points of real disagreement between the two major parties have become fewer and less evident—whether they had to do with the handling of the economy or with defence—parliamentary debate has remained destructively conflicting.

With regard to the 'partyness' of the Chamber of Deputies, the tendency has been for the parties to monopolize parliamentary activity at the expense of individual deputies. Party discipline, which in any case has always been stronger within the parties in power, has included restrictions if not prohibition of the use of certain means of parliamentary control by individual deputies, then restriction from the right to speak and, in general, ensured full dependence of the deputy on party and parliamentary group leadership.[86] This phenomenon was substantially enhanced by the abolition of the preferential vote in 1982, and by the provision of a 'closed list' of party condidates for each constituency, the drafting of which is by law the responsibility of the party leadership.[87] Dependence on the party leadership was recently reinforced in day to day parliamentary activity by the introduction in the 1987 standing orders of 'organized discussions' as the procedure for deliberation on a substantial portion of legislative work.[88] This means, as an opposition deputy put it, that all members of Parliament would from then on not only be anxious about their registration on the candidates' list of their own party for the next general elections, but also their place on the speakers' list of their group for the next parliamentary debate.[89] The dependence of individual deputies on party leadership reached the limits of draconian measures being introduced in certain instances. For example during the election by the Chamber of the President of the Republic in March 1985, in order to secure the positive vote of all its deputies for the only candidate, PASOK did not hesitate to make use of coloured ballots, in full violation of the Constitution, which at the time provided for a secret vote.[90] At the same time, small parliamentary groups, which were and still are not recognized as parties both by the 1975 and the 1987 standing orders,[91] have virtually the same rights as individual deputies. As a consequence, parliamentary activities have in fact been monopolized by the larger parties and, in practice, by the first and second, which also increasingly tend to agree on the destructive type of opposition, in terms both of rules and practices.[92] Thus, over the years, although not openly admitted, a kind of consensus seems to prevail between PASOK and New Democracy on how the parliamentary game should be played, a consensus which is more amazing if one takes into consideration the apparently imcompatible socio-economic projects of the two parties.

What could be said then about the specific role of the Greek Chamber in the process of democratic consolidation? The answer to this question seems to be two fold—institutional and political.

Institutionally the Chamber of Deputies after 1974 was overwhelmingly subordinate to the executive, namely the cabinet. The parliamentary groups of the parties in power never gained the slightest autonomy from the cabinet whose directives they obediently ratified. The opposition, on the other hand, did not even try to oppose specific issues as a general rule. Its discourse was ideologically orientated and almost never constructive. This was particularly true of PASOK until 1981, of New Democracy after PASOK's advent to power, and it is also to a considerable extent true of the Communist left, at least with regard to its principal component, the KKE. With the exception of the first post-dictatorial Chamber (1974–7)—the transitionary period when the New Democracy predominated—during which some consensual practices were observed,[93] the Chamber has functioned merely as a forum for vague, repetitive and usually outdated monologues, which, especially recently, have offered opposition only on an ideological-symbolic level. In view of its secondary role in the framing of the post-dictatorial institutions and in the way in which the country was governed, the Greek Parliament does not deserve consideration as a major protagonist in democratic consolidation. Has the Chamber's legitimacy suffered from this situation?

In my view, the answer to this question is not self-evident. During most of the twentieth century, Greek parliamentarism had been prone to tensions which reflected the acute polarization of a society that had gone through two major civil wars. The uniqueness of the Greek case does not lie in the breakdown of parliamentarism twice in less than four decades, but in the fact that, despite the two schisms, parliamentary government, even if sometimes distorted, has survived so long.

The fall of the colonels' junta meant the end of the remnants of the two civil strifes at the institutional as well as the political level. However, the politics of tension and ideological conflict has so deeply permeated political habits that transition to a model of milder confrontation has appeared unrealistic, even though the matters of dissention increasingly no longer seem to justify such an intense attachment to past and present symbols. From this perspective, by securing wide publicity for party conflicts, the Chamber of Deputies kept its legitimacy as the nation's major forum for political confrontation. And it is significant that a large portion of Greeks, which in the last elections exceeded 85 per cent of the electorate, seems to accept, if not actively endorse, bipolar confrontation and the two-party system, based on ideological battles instead of rational argumentation.

Nowadays, as the appeal of old ideological slogans seems to lose credence, it is uncertain whether the Greek Parliament will keep its legitimacy unless it adapts its rules and practices to the new challenges of our times.

Notes

1. Greece's First Republic is generally considered as covering the period of the War of Independence until the arrival of King Otto (1821–33). The Second Republic refers to the years from 1924 to 1935, while the Third, which is the present one, started with the fall of the colonels' junta or, to be more precise, with the referendum of 8 December 1974.
2. In general, parliamentary research in Greece is practically non-existant. Although provided for by the 1975 Constitution (article 65§5, see also article 108 of the Chamber's 1975 standing orders), the Parliament's scientific service was established only in 1988, under articles 160–3 of the 1987 standing orders; it is expected to start functioning by the end of 1988. Due to the lack of specialized studies, all data referred to in this article have been drawn either from empirical research, or from the Chamber's official and unofficial publications which cover only a small portion of parliamentary activities mostly in the law-making field.
3. On the drafting and content of the 1844 Constitution, see Kaltchas (1940), whose study remains the best English-language reference on Greek parliamentarism.
4. On the never-enforced constitutions of the revolutionary period (adopted by constitutional Assemblies in 1822, 1823 and 1827), which reflected the influence of the Enlightenment ideals on the new nation, see Kaltchas (*op. cit.*, I: 34 ff).
5. To the extent that it provided for popular sovereignty (article 21), at the same time introducing universal male suffrage (article 66) and guaranteeing the right to assemble (article 10) and to establish 'non-profit' corporations (article 11).
6. Every two to five years on average. It should be noted that despite the traditional underdevelopment of civil society in an almost exclusively rural country, the general conditions under which elections took place improved considerably throughout the last quarter of the nineteenth and the beginning of the twentieth century. See Sotirelis (1988).

7. The period from 1911 to 1915, which coincided with the Balkan Wars of 1912–13 and the doubling of Greece's national territory, can be described as the most productive in modern Greek history from the point of view of its institutional development. In a very short period of time an important set of legal measures was adopted with the aim of facilitating economic development within the rule of law. See Daskalakis (1938).

8. For an extensive account of the main institutional consequences of the two schisms, see Alivizatos (1979).

9. It is significant that although its competences had been substantially curtailed, the Chamber remained in the centre of the constitutional order provided by the colonels in their never-enforced Constitution of 1968–73; see Alivizatos (1979: 228 ff). The symbolic and legitimizing function of Parliament in modern Greek history has be underestimated, if not completely ignored by Legg (1969) whose model of analysis fails to take into consideration the impact of that decisive factor.

10. On the nature and depth of the rupture of 24 July 1974, a change from 'beyond', which initiated an important mass movement, see mainly Diamandouros (1986: 138–64).

11. Under the threat of an imminent war with Turkey—after the latter's invasion in Cyprus on 20 July, 1974—and while key positions in the army were still held by pro-junta officers, Karamanlis' transition strategy finally proved very successful since it managed to retain the dynamics of the political change until his position was sufficiently consolidated. See Diamandouros (1984: 50 ff).

12. Constitutional act dated 1 August 1974, as completed and amended by constitutional acts dated 7 August and 24 September 1974.

13. Legislative decree No. 59 of 23 September 1974. Under emergency law No. 509 of 1947, which was adopted during the civil war, the Communist party was outlawed and the cabinet was empowered to forbid any party it considered 'subversive'. On the importance of that exceptional measure, which was in fact abolished by the above legislative decree of the transition government, see Alivizatos (1981: 220–8).

14. Presidential decrees No. 615 of 29 September 1974 and No. 700 of 9 October 1974.

15. Legislative decrees No. 19 of 28 August 1974 and No. 65 of 25 September 1974 which fixed a strict version of 'reinforced' proportional representation. Also see note 44.

16. Article 1§1 of constitutional act of 4 October 1974.

17. Article 5§1 of constitutional act of 4 October 1974.

18. It was in fact the first referendum in Greek constitutional history whose result was not contested by the losing side; that was mainly because for the fist time the executive also abstained from supporting, directly or indirectly, either the 'yes' or the 'no' factions.

19. Constitutional resolution No A of 24 December 1974.

20. Constitutional resolution No C of 24 December 1974.

21. Such as for instance the obliteration of a provision contained in the initial constitutional draft, which provided for the possibility of outlawing 'subversive' political parties by a constitutional court (which itself was not finally established); the provision for equal rights for men and women; the adoption of a special article for the abolition of the 'exceptional measures' dating from the civil war period within a short period of time; the reinforcement of local government etc.

22. Official minutes of the Chamber, 7 June 1975, p. 1094.

23. For a succinct presentation of the opposition views, see Tsatsos (1982: 331 ff.); Official minutes of the Chamber, 21 May 1975, p. 963 & ff.

24. Articles 67 and 76§1 of the 1975 Constitution, which repeated the rules provided

by article 4 of the constitutional resolution of 21 December 1974.

25. Article 71 of the 1975 Constitution, modelled after the 'delegation committee' of article 35§2 & ff. of the 1952 Constitution.
26. Articles 76§4 and §5 of the 1975 Cosntitution.
27. Articles 37§2 and 84§1 of the 1975 Constitution.
28. Article 68§2 of the 1975 Constitution.
29. See Alivizatos (1987).
30. Approved only by New Democracy deputies, the new standing orders did not meet any serious opposition since their critics from the opposition parties contented themselves with some minor remarks mainly on the wide powers of the speaker and on the restrictions imposed on the length of speeches. See Official minutes of the Chamber, 13 and 14 October 1975, p. 26 ff.; 50 ff.
31. For instance, nothing apart from the Parliament's library was provided for the assistance of the deputies in terms of data nd technical information. On the other hand, 'debates among party leaders', which were to become the msot popular means of parliamentary control in the years that followed, were simply ignored by the new standing orders.
32. See primarily the proposal for the revision of the constitution, dated 9 March 1985 and signed by 161 PASOK deputies: Official minutes of the Chamber of the revision of the 1975 constitution, p. 5.
33. Whose support was necessary for the initiation of the revisionary process, according to article 110 of the Constitution which stipulates that 180 votes are necessary. The Communist party contented itself with a rather smooth denunciation of the limited character of the revision and abstained from bargaining for the inclusion of its own proposals in the revisionary process.
34. For an overall account of the 1985–6 revision see Manessis (1985: 772 ff.; 804 ff.); Manessis (1988: 5–102); Katsoudas (1987: 14–33).
35. The revised version of the 1975 Constitution came into effect on 12 March 1986.
36. Voted on in June 1987 (Official minutes of the Chamber, 1 and 3 June 1987, 6573 ff. and 6645 ff.), the 1987 standing orders came into effect on 5 October 1987.
37. Among the most important innovations of the 1987 standing orders were the provision for the election of two deputy-speakers (out of a total of five) from the two main opposition parties: the establishment of a new organ by the speaker, the board of the presidents, with a representative composition but with weak powers; the reduction of the total number of parliamentary committees to six; the institutionalization of the 'debates among party leaders', the introduction of 'questions' and 'interpellations of actuality' as new means of parliamentary control etc. See Voloudakis (1987: 52 ff.).
38. An action which was viewed as equally important as the rupture itself by Polantzas (1975: 105).
39. Under law No. 4229 of 1929, better known as 'idionym law', communist activities were penalized for the first time as such, though the Communist party was not itself outlawed. The main provisions of that law survived in various forms up until the fall of the colonels in 1974.
40. See Lyrintzis (1984: 99–118), who insists on the combination of new elements and old practices in the emergence of the partisan phenomenon, after 1974.
41. See Mavrogordatos (1981 149 ff.).
42. See below, section 5.6.
43. After obtaining a respectable vote in the 1974 elections (20.5 per cent), the Centre Union decreased to 11.9 per cent in 1977 and subsequently practically disappeared from the political scene in the years that followed. See Table 5.1.
44. For a detailed presentation of that peculiar electoral system, see Vegleris (1981: 21–48).

45. That in the event is a slight difference in the percentages achieved by the first and second parties.
46. To use Mavrogordatos' expression (*op. cit.*: 82).
47. On the August and November 1910 general elections, see Papacosma (1977: 159 ff.)
48. Ie, from the opposition, since the right to initiate new legislation, although guaranteed by the constitution for all deputies, has never in practice been exercised by majority MPs.
49. Although with some significant restrictions aimed at disouraging the discussion of bills involving state expenditure or connected to salary and pension issues, see articles 73 and 75 of the 1975 Constitution.
50. According to article 74§6, once a month a sitting is devoted to the discussion of bills originating from Parliament; between 1977 and 1981, out of 94 such bills submitted, 33 were effectively discussed and eventually rejected; the respective numbers for the period between 1981 and 1985 were 31 and 27.
51. Article 23 of those standing orders provided that one parliamentary committee was to be established for each ministry.
52. Within the time period fixed on each occasion by the speaker (article 77§3 of the 1975 standing orders). Should that time period be transgressed, the bill could proceed to the deliberation stage without any report (article 74§2 of the Constitution and 77§1 of the 1975 standing orders).
53. Article 79§2 of the 1975 standing orders.
54. Article 38 of the 1987 standing orders.
55. To our knowledge, the first hearing by experts from both the public and the private sectors of the economy occurred in Autumn 1988 on the occasion of the voting of a bill connected with the introduction of new auditing methods.
56. Due to PASOK's opposition to the principle of establishing the two 150-member legislative sections, no such sections have ever functioned since 1980.
57. See Drakatos (1986: 195–209).
58. While from 1975 to 1981 six bills in total were voted or using the so-called urgent procedure provided by article 76§5 of the 1975 Constitution (including two adopted with the so-called 'most-urgent' procedure of article 76§4), the number increased to 13 from 1981 to 1985 and to 16 from 1985 to the end of June 1987.
59. Articles 87–9 of the 1975 standing orders and 121–3 of the 1987 standing orders. No procedure whatsoever is provided for the control of the enforcement of the budget by the Chamber.
60. That is primarily through the various restrictions of speech time of the deputies. See article 48 of the 1975 standing orders and articles 97, 103, 128§3, 132§4, 137§2 etc of the 1987 standing orders (5–20 minutes as a general rule, according to the procedure provided for the specific stage and type of parliamentary work).
61. From the available data, 134 bills remained pending at the end of the four-year period of the 2nd post-dictatorial Chamber (1977–81, not including 14 that were withdrawn) and 63 at the end of the 4th (1981–5) not including 13 that were withdrawn).
62. While providing, in principle, that 'a bill or law proposal containing provisions not related to its main subject matter shall not be introduced for debate' and that 'no addition or amendment shall be introduced for debate if it is not related to the main subject matter of the bill or law proposal', article 74§5 of the Constitution paves the way for all sorts of abuses, by stipulating that 'Parliament shall resolve in case of contestation' (on whether an amendment or addition is linked to the main subject matter of the bill).
63. For an excellent review of the recent judicial experience on the issue by a supreme judge see Halazonitis (1984).

64. There are no official statistics, but the tendency is significant in recent years since the Constitution empowers the Chamber to delegate normative powers not only to the President of the Republic (that is to the cabinet) but also to subordinate administrative authorities: see Skouris (1987).

65. On the extent of that tendency in the subtle field of civil liberties see Pararas (1986: 367–89).

66. See Kassimatis (1981: 95–108).

67. Mainly through the practice of the 'debates among party leaders' (which were institutionalized only in 1987, see below) and through the raising of issues unrelated to the subject matter under discussion by the deputies.

68. Articles 95 of the 1975 and 125 of the 1987 standing orders.

69. Since in principle they were answered in writing by the relevant ministers within the time limit provided by the standing orders in force.

70. Within 25 days, according to the 1987 standing orders (article 126).

71. Articles 96–7 of the 1975 standing orders and 134–7 of the 1987 standing orders.

72. Articles 92 of the 1975 and 133 of the 1987 standing orders.

73. Unpublished data drawn from the yearly reports of the speaker.

74. Article 143 of the 1987 standing orders.

75. Once under New Democracy (on the occasion of Greece's reintegration in to NATO's joint military command) and once under PASOK (for the discussion of the government's general policy).

76. This stipulates that any new government should in principle seek Parliament's vote of confidence within 15 days after the appointment of the prime minister (article 84§1).

77. Article 84§2b of the Constitution. Since 1974, all of the main opposition parties have had more than 50 deputies: see Table 5.1.

78. See article 68§2 of the Constitution which provides that investigative committees are established, 'by a majority vote of two-fifths of the total number of deputies', ie by 120 deputies. Both the 1975 and the 1987 standing orders (articles 63§4 and 144§5 respectively) provided that for the establishment of the said committees a majority vote of the present deputies was required; the number of those voting in favour, however, should be equal to at least two-fifths of the total number of deputies.

79. Articles 129–32 and 138 of the 1987 standing orders.

80. The experience of the first ordinary session of the Chamber after the enforcement of the new standing orders (October 1987 to June 1988) was in principle positive. However it is too early to draw definite conclusions.

81. These aims and priorities are in fact shared—to say the least—by the speaker who was and, under the 1987 standing orders, remains the central organ for the functioning of the Chamber. For instance he is the only one who can fix the agenda, after some consultations that do not bind him (article 11). The five vice-speakers do not in fact have other powers except those delegated to them by the speaker.

82. Since 1981 and mainly since 1985, PASOK has reviewed its policies with regard to the EEC and NATO and more recently towards Turkey.

83. Under the 1975 standing orders, no time limits were provided for the speeches of the ministers and of party leaders; restrictions were imposed for the first time under the 1987 standing orders.

84. See Simitis (1979).

85. Apart from viewing it as a useful forum for the propogation of its platform. That was mainly the case of its principal component, ie the orthodox Communist party, whose tactics and strategy have always adhered to the 3rd International model of parliamentary behaviour. As for the eurocommunist left, despite the prestige of its main leaders, it has never had sufficient parliamentary representation to play an active role.

86. See, for instance, the rules and regulations of PASOK's parliamentary group dated 8 January 1982 and signed by Prime Minister Papandreou, which require the group leadership's prior approval and consent for all kinds of initiatives by the deputies, both within and outside the Parliament.
87. Law 1303 of 1982 which, however, is expected to be amended before the next general elections, in order to revive at least in part preferential voting.
88. Article 107 of the 1987 standing orders.
89. A. Pavlides, Official minutes of the Chamber, 1 June 1987, p. 6598.
90. Article 32§1 of the 1975 Constitution, which was amended in order to provide for a nominal vote after the unhappy events of March 1985.
91. The 1975 standing orders made the general provision that a parliamentary group could be recognized as such and benefit from the relevant privileges if (a) it comprised at least 15 deputies, or (b) it had obtained at least 10 per cent of the votes in the previous general elections (article 19). These rules were amended in 1986, and the 1987 standing orders provide either for 10 deputies, or for 5 deputies representing parties which in the last general elections have obtained at least 3 per cent of the votes and have had candidates running for office in at least two-thirds of the country's constituencies (article 15).
92. Apart from the unanimous vote of the two major parties in favour of the 1987 standing orders (see note 36), which is the most spectacular sign of that implicit agreement, one should add that all significant electoral law amendments adopted since 1974 have been supported by the two main parties.
93. The volume of legislation adopted during that period is the best sign of that climate: see Table 5.4.

References

Alivizatos, N. (1979), *Les institutions politiques de la Grèce à travers les crises, 1922–1974*, Paris, Librairie Générale de Droit et de Jurisprudence.
—(1981),'The "Emergency" Regime and Civil Liberties, 1946–1949' in J.O. Iatrides (ed.) *Greece in the 1940s: A Nation in Crisis*, Hanover and London, University Press of New England, 220–8.
Clogg, R., (1987), *Parties and Elections in Greece. The Search for Legitimacy*, London, C. Hurst & Co.
Daskalakis, G. (1938), 'Verfassungsentwicklung Griechenlands' in *Jahrbuch des öffenlichen Rechts*, 1938, (Greek translation, 3rd ed., Athens, 1952).
Diamandouros, N.P. (1984), 'Transition and Consolidation of Democratic Politics in Greece, 1974–1983: A Tentative Assessment in G. Pridham (ed.) *The New Mediterranean Democracies: Regime Transition in Spain, Greece and Portugal*, London, Frank Cass, 50–71.
—(1986), 'Regime Change and the Prospects for Democracy in Greece, 1974–1983' in G. O'Donnell, P. Schmitter and L. Whitehead (eds.) *Transition from Authoritarian Rule, Prospects of Democracy*, Baltimore and London, The Johns Hopkins University Press, 138–64.
Drakatos, G. (1986), 'Counting the Time for Law-Making Work', *To Syndagma*, 12, 195–209 (in Greek).
Halazonitis, K.M. (1984), 'Judicial Control of the Formal Elements of Acts', *Comptroller's Council Jubilee*, Athens, Ministery of Finance (reprint, in Greek).
Kaltchas, N. (1940). *Introduction to the Constitutional History of Modern Greece*, New York, Columbia University Press.
Kassimatis, G. (1981), 'The Enforcement of Laws as a Technique for Annulling the Legislator's Will' *Politiki-Political Science Review*, I/, 95–108 (in Greek).

Katsoudas, D. (1987), 'The Constitutional Framework', in K. Featherstone, D. Katsoudas (eds.), *Political Change in Greece Before and After the Colonels*, London and Sydney, Croom Helm, 14–33.

Legg, K. (1969), *Politics in Modern Greece*, Stanford, Stanford University Press.

Lyrintzis, C. (1984), 'Political Parties in Post-Junta Greece: A case of Bureaucratic Clientelism?' *The New Mediterranean Democracies, op. cit.*, 99–118.

Manessis, A. (1985), 'L'évolution des institutions politiques de la Grèce: à la recherche d'une légitimité difficile', *Les Temps Modernes*, No. 473, 772–814.

—(1988), 'The Legal and Political Significance of the Constitutional Revision of 1986. A General Critical Appraisal', *Dikaio kai Politiki*, No 13–14, 5–102 (in Greek).

Mavrogordatos, G.T. (1981), 'The Emerging Party System', in R. Clogg (ed.) *Greece in the 1980s*, London, Macmillan.

Metaxas, A.-I.D. (1981), 'Bio-Social and Cultural Chartography of the Chamber of Deputies, 1964–1974–1977', *Politiki-Political Science Review*, v. I, p. 11–56 (in Greek).

—(1981, 1985), *The 300 Deputies of the Chamber*, Athens, Kathimerini Press.

Papacosma, V. (1977), *The Military in Greek Politics. The 1909 Coup d'Etat*, The Kent State University Press.

Poulantzas, N. (1975), *La crise des dictatures: Espagne, Grèce, Portugal*, Paris; Maspero.

Simitis, C. (1979), *Structural Opposition*, Athens, Kastaniotis

Skouris, V. (1987), *The Crisis of the Legislative Function. Better Law with Fewer Acts*, Athens, Sakkoulas.

Sotirelis, g. (1988), *The Legal and Political Dimension of Universal Suffrage: Constitutional Problems From the First Parliamentary Experience, 1864–1909*, unpublished doctoral dissertation, University of Athens, School of Law.

Tsatsos, D. (1982), *Constitutional Law*, Athens, Sakkoulas.

Vegleris, Ph. (1981), 'Greek Electoral Law' in A. Penniman (ed.) *Greece at the Polls. The National Elections of 1974 and 1977*, Washington and London, American Enterprise Institute for Public Policy Research.

Voloudakis, V. (1987), *The 1987 Standing Orders*, Athens, Sakkoulas.

6 Revolutionary transition and problems of parliamentary institutionalization: the case of the Portuguese National Assembly

Manuel Braga da Cruz
Miguel Lobo Antunes

Introduction

Although Portugal has a long parliamentary tradition, it can nevertheless be said that a democratic parliamentary process, based on direct universal suffrage, was only established after 25 April, 1974.

The parliamentary system emerged in Portugal after the liberal revolution of 1820. The 1822 Constitution produced a parliamentary regime, with a single chamber of a distinctly liberal-democratic seal. Apart from symbolizing the sovereignty of the nation, the king had only the power of suspensive veto, institutional predominance being reserved for the Chamber of Deputies, which was elected by direct, universal suffrage.

Very soon, however, the 1822 parliamentary system would be amended by the Constitutional Charter issued by the liberal monarch D. Pedro IV in 1826, which reinforced the power of the Crown while minimizing popular sovereignty. Apart from conferring on the king a 'moderating power' by which he was able to sanction all decrees issued by the Cortes, the Charter introduced a bicameral system, with the creation of a Chamber of Peers, made up of both lifelong and hereditary members, and appointed by the king,[1] and abolished universal suffrage for elections to the Chamber of Deputies, replacing it with an indirect system, limited to voters with property qualifications.

The 'Septembrist' Constitution of 1838 attempted to balance out the two previous tendencies, abolishing the Crown's moderating power, but maintaining the bicameral system in which the Chamber of Peers was, however, replaced by a Chamber of Temporary Senators who were elected, just like the deputies, by direct but restricted suffrage.

However, throughout the second half of the nineteenth century, it was the Constitutional Charter which prevailed, until the establishment of the Republic in 1910, though amended by Additional Acts: the first (of 1852) widened the suffrage (which nevertheless remained limited to property owners), and made the election of deputies direct; the second (of 1885) abolished the hereditary rights of the Peers and gave the Chamber of Peers a mixed composition (part of its membership being appointed by the Crown, part by indirect election, besides those with automatic right), while at the same time restricting the moderating power of the Crown by limiting its right to dissolve parliament; the third (of 1896) practically revoked the changes brought about by the previous act when it once again abolished the election of Peers of the Realm and attributed to the Crown the right of dissolution.

Parliamentarianism in Portugal therefore fluctuated, throughout the nineteenth century, between repeated affirmations of popular sovereignty, and the maintenance of the power of the Crown. In fact, it was conditioned as much by partisan pressures and caciquism, as it was by the rotation of governments, while at the same time being inhibited both by the king's moderating power and the aristocratic power of the Peers.

With the 1910 republican revolution and the new Constitution of the following year, a system of parliamentary supremacy was established, with two chambers elected by direct suffrage (the Senate and Chamber of Deputies), and a president of the Republic elected by a congress of these two chambers and who possessed no power to dissolve them. The excessive parliamentary power provided for by the Constitution of 1911 was, in fact, largely responsible for the political instability which was ultimately to invalidate the regime. Efforts to correct this produced, as early as 1918, during the administration of Sidónio Pais, a change towards a presidentialist style of government, and culminated in the establishment of the military dictatorship in 1926 and the Salazar regime which followed in its wake (Caetano, 1971; Sousa, 1910).

Salazar's conservative authoritarianism, while denying democracy and political parties, nevertheless retained, in the ideological eclecticism of the 1933 Constitution, some liberal principles, among which that of political representation (which it did not confuse with corporative representation), and the electoral principle, which it would inhibit and limit in practice.

Consequently, the *Estado Novo* (new state) maintained in operation a National Assembly, elected by direct suffrage, and alongside it a Corporative Chamber. Likewise, the president of the Republic continued to be elected by direct suffrage, and only stopped being so from 1958.

Salazar's Constitution consecrated a system of diarchic presidentialism which, with the passing of time, came to be enshrined in the figure of the president of the Council of Ministers, not only because of the growing subordination of the president of the Republic to the head of government, but also because of the progressive subordination of the National assembly to the government and the transformation of the Corporative Chamber from being a consultative organ of the political chamber to effective cabinet status over the years (Cruz, 1988).

The parliamentary tradition was therefore not strictly speaking interrupted, but altered in a non-democratic manner, and was thus allowed to survive throughout Salazar's authoritarian regime.

It was this parliamentary tradition, adulterated in an authoritarian and dictatorial sense by the Salazar regime, which, after 25 April 1974, came to be resumed, but now in a distinctly democratic direction, based on a so far non-existent universal direct suffrage. However, the establishment of a democratic parliamentary system was not easy, given the troubled revolutionary transition to democracy.

The transition from authoritarianism to democracy began in an abrupt and radical manner in 1974, with the revolt of the Armed Forces Movement, caused by dissatisfaction among the military over the lack of a political solution to the wars in Africa. It was the colonial problem that made the democratic transition in Portugal unique in both its essence and form, for unlike what occurred in Spain, it was both a *revolutionary* transition and a *military* one.

This meant that democratic transition took place under military tutelage and by means of a political pact. The parties, as impotent agents of the break with the past, but indispensable for parliamentary democracy, negotiated with the military, the main protagonists of the revolution, over the democratic regime to be established. The transition to democracy in Portugal thus consisted in a preliminary revolutionary phase in which the institutions of the old authoritarian regime were dismantled and replaced by new institutions and by a Constitution, approved on 2 April, 1976. There followed a second transitionary phase, specifically stipulted by the Constitution, in which a democratic regime under military tutelage in the shape of a Council of the Revolution culminated in the revision of the Constitution of 30 October, 1982. A third phase of total institutional demilitarisation came to an end with the election of the first civilian president of the Republic on 16 February, 1986 (Cruz, 1986).

Parliament and the instauration of the democratic regime

The consolidation of the new parliament, just as in the case of other democratic institutions, did not take place in opposition to conservative authoritarian tendencies, as happened in Spain, but rather against revolutionary tendencies which either regarded the parliamentary form of government as an expression of bourgeois class power, or defended other forms of political representation, more specifically, direct representation. The revindication of parliamentary democracy, which during the dictatorship had been an expression of left-wing aspirations, was ultimately taken up by the forces of the right because of the revolutionary process. The revolutionary forces, defenders of direct or popular democracy, had strong military backing. Hence the reason why the institution-alization of Parliament, like that of the parties, had to be achieved by agreement with these revolutionary military forces, and consolidated gradually, through successive phases, until the military presence had been totally eradicated from the political institutions. The institutionalization of parliament therefore went hand in hand with the process of the demilitarisation of political institutions.

The revolution of 25 April, 1974, as carried out with the objective of decolonization and democratization. The initial idea of the Armed Forces Movement (MFA) was therefore to convoke by popular election a Constituent Assembly, which would elaborate a fundamental democratic law, and by so doing, take on the function of a Legislative Assembly.[2] It is thus easy to understand why this Constituent Assembly found itself shackled from the start by the transitory organs of sovereignty defined by Law 3/74, given that its sole function was to bring in the new Constitution, and it was destined to be dissolved as soon as the latter was approved.

But the sovereignty of the Constituent Assembly was also, from the onset, shared and divided, not only with the Junta of National Salvation which performed the additional function of a Council of State, and held constituent powers, but also with the provisional government, which possessed legislative powers. The Assembly was neither the only organ of sovereignty, nor was it alone in holding constituent powers. On the other hand, the only powers it did have were constituent. It lacked any legislative or fiscal prerogative.

In any case, it was the political radicalization engendered by the revolutionary process, motivated above all by decolonization and the advance of the theses of popular democracy, with the subsequent curtailment of parliamentary democracy, which more seriously countered and even threatened the installation and the work of the Constituent Assembly.

With the events of 11 March and the ensuing acceleration of the revolutionary process, the framework of the organs of sovereignty was altered with the institutionalization of the MFA, expressed in the creation of the Council of the Revolution and the Assembly of the MFA, which was made up of representatives of the three branches of the armed forces. The Movement assumed the role of vanguard of the revolution, and its own revolutionary aims seemed to collide with the democratic parliamentary objectives of the largest parties.

Hence the establishment of the First Pact between the MFA and the parties, signed when the revolution was in full swing, on 13 April 1975, and which in effect formally paved the way for the two forms of representation to coexist. The signing of the pact by the parties was in fact the condition imposed by the military for the holding of general elections and the formation of a Constituent Assembly, and already outlined the most important features of the future constitutional text. Combining the concept of revolutionary legitimacy with that of electoral legitimacy, and forms of direct democracy with those of representative democracy, the First Pact between the MFA and the parties allowed for the future coexistence of an Assembly of the MFA, established after 11 March, with an Assembly of the parties. The president of the Republic would be elected by an electoral college formed from these two Assemblies. The Constituent Assembly would furthermore be accompanied in its functions by a Commission of the MFA, and once the text of the Constitution was approved, it would only be promulgated after the Council of the Revolution had given its verdict. Moreover, the results of the elections would not have immediate and direct effect on the composition of the provisional government. In this manner, the constituent power of the Assembly elected in 1975 was, from the outset, limited.

Once elections had been held on 25 April, 1975, the results, beyond proving that the appeal to voters to return a blank ballot as a vote for the MFA had been largely ignored, confirmed the victory of electoral legitimacy, and marked the start of a process of integration into the democratic legality of the revolutionary forces, and of the Communist party (PCP) for the first time.

The installation of the Constituent Assembly did not, however, take place without resistance. Once a commission had been created for this purpose, with a chairman from the military, though under the responsibility of the Minister without portfolio Magalhaes Mota, and consisting of functionaries from the extinct National Assembly and Corporative Chamber,[3] it had to overcome various obstacles, from the problem of deputies' salaries, which the military at first thought too high, proposing to remunerate deputies on the basis of an attendance register, to the problem of the establishment of the Constituent Assembly in the Palace of São Bento, which had been occupied by the MFA and by the provisional government.

Once the Constituent Assembly had begun to operate, considerable debate occurred over the role the Assembly and the Constitution were to have. With regard to the former, the law had only given it responsibility for drawing up the Constitution, without any possible intervention in government. Much advantage was however taken of a special provision for a 'period before the order of the day', when the deputies would comment on political events. The Regulation of the Constituent Assembly allowed for such a period, and it became a frequently used platform for its members to intervene in the political course of the revolution.

As for the importance of the Constitution, the position of those parties which saw the Constitution as institutionalizing the revolution began to prevail over those which merely saw it as an instrument of the revolution (Miranda, 1978).

The Regulation of the Constituent Assembly immediately confirmed some decisive aspects not only of the Constitution itself, but also of parliamentary life, and for this reason can justly be considered the 'fountainhead of the new parliamentary law in Portugal' (ibid: 83). Among these, of special importance were the relations within Parliament, in particular relations between deputies and parties, as it laid down the loss of mandate for deputies who joined a different party from the one to which they were affiliated when elected. Similarly, it established proportional party representation in the composition of committees, giving representatives the possibility of forming parliamentay groups. This incipient party supremacy in parliamentary life merely reflected the gradual rise to prominence of the parties in political life, and can be explained by the very genesis of the party system and justified by the gradual consolidation of democracy. The affirmation of democracy after 25 April is closely related to that of the parties, not only in the face of the military, but also in that of the attempts of unitary 'movements', led by or subordinated to the revolutionary interests of the communists, the most obvious case in point being the MDP–CDE.[4] Because of this, independent movements and candidates were marginalized from the beginning, sacrificed to the electoral monopoly of the parties.

The balance of legitimacies and forms of democracy consecrated by the First Pact between the MFA and the parties was, however, being increasingly questioned as the revolutionary process became more radical. The Document-Guideline of the 'People'-MFA Alliance, approved by The Assembly of the MFA in July 1975, gave official blessing to the organization of popular power in successive assemblies, from the grassroots right up to the People's National Assembly, with the Council of the Revolution being then defined as 'the supreme organ of national sovereignty'. The concept of electoral legitimacy and the Constituent Assembly were thus subordinated, and their survival was even called into question and threatened on 12 and 13 November, with the seige of the Palace of São Bento, where the Constituent Assembly was gathered. Most of the deputies, as soon as the siege was over, withdrew to the north of the country, with the intention of proceeding with their activities there, if conditions could not be guaranteed in Lisbon.

The change of political direction brought about on 25 November 1975 enabled the first pact to be revised and saw the signing of a second pact between the MFA and the parties, in which coexistence was abandoned and replaced by the establishment of a transitional period of military tutelage over political institutions, the Parliament among them, to remain in effect until the first constitutional revision. This tutelage would be exercised through the constitutionalization of the Council of the Revolution, which was to be empowered with the supervision of constitutional and judicial matters, and which was given added weight with the election of the Chief of Staff of the Armed Forces to the presidency of the Republic who was at the same time president of the Council of the Revolution.

Such was the structure given to the organs of sovereignty which came to prevail transitionally in the Constitution until 1982. With the constitutional revision of that year, the tutelage of the Council of the Revolution ended, and with the election of the first civilian president of the Republic in 1986, this period of transition came to a definitive conclusion with the total demilitarization of the political institutions.

Once parliamentary democracy was established, another important question emerged during the transition: the role of Parliament in the system of government.

Between the presidentialist authoritarianism of the outgoing regime and the exaggerated parliamentarianism of the First Republic, the Constitution eventually produced a semi-presidentialist system (Sousa, 1984), distributing the political responsibility of the government between Parliament and the president of the Republic, both of these being elected by direct universal suffrage.

It became the president of the Republic's function to appoint the prime minister, 'bearing in mind the result of the election', and to dismiss the government, also veto laws and dissolve Parliament after obtaining the favourable opinion of the Council of the Revolution.

The Assembly of the Republic, or National Assembly, then assumed the role of legislating and controlling the executive, with an exclusive right to legislate on a wide variety of matters. The government's programme came to depend on its approval, and if rejected, the executive was dismissed, which could also occur when motions of confidence were rejected, and in the original version of the Constitution, when two motions of censure were approved.[5]

The constitutional system in this way facilitated the formation of minority governments, and along with them a certain instability, in not institutionalizing the approval of the government's programme, but only its rejection. Governments therefore did not need parliamentary majorities for permanent support, just as it was not obligatory for the head of the government to be the leader of the party with the largest parliamentary representation.

This came to favour the emergence of presidential governments, that is governments with a leadership which had the confidence of the president of the Republic, without a lasting parliamentary majority. This had an effect of sharpening the institutional conflicts between the president of the Republic and the Council of the Revolution, and with the government and Parliament, throwing into conflict in this way, above all, the 'military', who occupied the most important seats of power, and the 'parties', who occupied the second rank.

With some diffusion and reduction of the powers invested in the president during the period of transition ushered in by the constitutional revision of 1982, namely, with the limitation on the power of the president to dismiss government, possible only 'if necessary to the smooth running of democratic institutions', the system of government shifted suddenly towards parliamentarianism.

The constitutional revision of 1982 indeed altered the dual political responsibility of the government, maintaining it before the National Assembly, and making it more of an institutional responsibility before the president (art. 194). This had the effect of reinforcing the dependence of the government on Parliament, a dependence which had been intensified as a result of the possiblity of the government being dismissed by only one and not two motions of censure (Sousa, 1984).

Parliament therefore saw its role reinforced throughout the process of transition and with it, the role of the parties too. The general demilitarization of the institutions meant that they now fell under the influence of the parties, and this was true of Parliament itself, as we will try to demonstrate in the next section.

Parties and Parliament

The last ten years have witnessed the growing supremacy of the political parties in the formation of electoral and parliamentary policy in Portugal.

The electoral and party system

The 250[6] deputies of the Portuguese parliament are elected by lists, in accordance with the system of porportional representation and d'Hondt's method of the highest average. Constituencies correspond to each of the administrative districts. There is no special drawing of boundaries for electoral purposes.

The number of deputies per constituency depends on the number of voters. An independent organ, the National Electoral Commission, presided over by a judge and with representatives of the five largest parties, stipulates, at each election, the number of seats for each constituency, depending on fluctuations in the numbers of voters.

The constitution states — of course, unnecessarily — that only political parties may present candidates for parliament. In each party, candidates are chosen through a process of negotiation between local and national organs. The national organs, however, have priority in their choice over the local, and at the very least retain for themselves the right to designate the first candidates in each list.

Tension between local and national organs is not uncommon over the matter of the choice of deputies. This tension, which is often reported in the press, is all the more notorious in parties with larger parliamentary representation — in which there is more likelihood of 'backbenchers' of predominantly regional origin being elected — and at times when the authority of central government has been weakened, when pressure from regional organs consequently increases.

The first candidates on each list are usually the national party leaders. Traditionally, the first on the list for the Lisbon constituency is the highest authority in the party, and a candidate for prime minister.

Sometimes candidates are placed on the lists not in order to be deputies, but for either internal party reasons — for example, to influence the balance of power among different personalitites — or for external motives, for example to attract more votes to the list. This is particularly the case with certain national leaders who, although elected, never get to taking their seat in Parliament, but are replaced by others, or with current ministers who expect to remain so, and also never take their place in the Assembly, or with personalities placed on lists in areas where they have no chance of being elected.

In the composition of the lists, parties have increasingly sought to guarantee the election of specialists in the various areas relevant to the work of Parliament. This obliges them to reconcile criteria of internal party interests — such as the party hierarchy — with institutional criteria, directed towards the efficiency of the group in Parliament.

It is possible to detect the beginnings, albeit gradual, of a process of parliamentary professionalization, which embraces all parties and which may be seen both in the increasing tendency for deputies to be re-elected, and in the growing age of the membership of the house.

Despite factors contributing to instability, such as splits in parliamentary groups,[7] changes in party leadership, changes in party structure (induced by the changes in party alliances, the emergence of new parties), one can note a slight increase in the percentage of deputies re-elected from one legislature to the next,[8] and a corresponding decrease in the percentage of 'new deputies'.[9] Such a process of professionalization is more apparent in parties with less representation, as can be seen in Figure 6.1.

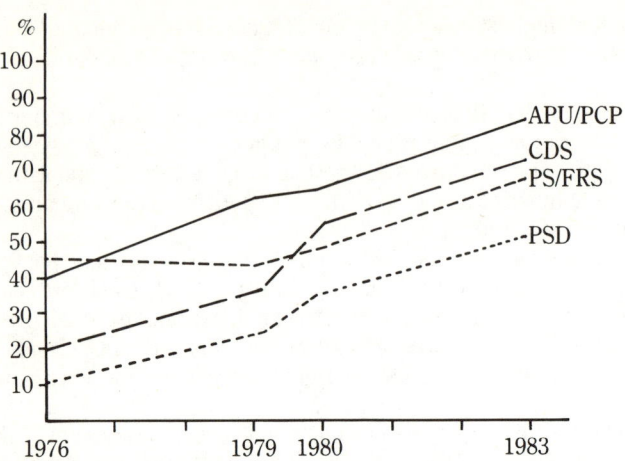

Figure 6.1   Deputies re-elected in 1985, by party, already previously elected in 1976, 1980 and 1983

A consequence of these declining turnover rates of mandates is the increase in the age of the members of Parliament from an average of 40.3 years in 1976 to 43.5 in the fourth legislature.[10] This is particularly true of the parties with the weakest parliamentary representation.

While candidates for Parliament may be put forward by political parties, those for the presidency of the Republic have to be endorsed by a minimum of 7,500 voters. Candidates have emerged who, though without the support of a particular party, have obtained significant numbers of votes. And all candidates have claimed the support of a wide variety of independent personalities. Nevertheless, all the elected candidates have benefited from the open support of at least one party.[11] However, they have very quickly distanced themselves from the majority which elected them, taking particular care to remove themselves from the influence of political parties, if not as a condition of their legitimacy, then certainly as a requirement for the fulfilment of their duties.

Until October 1985, the Portuguese party system was dominated by four parties, two on the right and two on the left. In each of these blocks, one party predominated: the PSD on the right, and the PS on the left (see Table 6.1).

Other smaller parties had parliamentary representation, but only when they entered into alliances with the big parties. When they ran by themselves, they failed to have any deputies elected. As for the rest, their degree of independence in parliamentary ativity was reduced. There was one exception: between 1976 and 1983 a small party of the left, the UDP, managed to have one deputy elected thanks to a concentration of votes in the Lisbon constituency.

In October 1985, the first major change in the number of parties occurred. Out of the four main parties, there emerged a fifth, the PRD, yet another party of the left, which attracted one million votes.

Table 6.1   The Portuguese Assembly Electoral Results, 1976–87

	1976–9			
Party	*Votes*	*%*	*Seats*	*%*
CDS	877,494	16.00	42	15.9
PPD/PSD	1,336,897	24.38	73	27.7
PS	1,911,769	34.87	107	40.6
PCP	786,701	14.35	40	15.2
UDP	91,691	1.67	1	0.3

	1979–80			
Party or coalition	*Votes*	*%*	*Seats*	*%*
AD (PPD+CDS+PPM)	2,554,458	42.52	128	51.2
PS	1,642,136	27.33	74	29.6
APU (PCP+MDP)	1,129,322	18.8	47	18.8
UDP	130,842	2.18	1	0.4

	1980–3			
Party or coalition	*Votes*	*%*	*Seats*	*%*
AD	2,706,667	44.91	134	53.8
FRS (PS+UEDS)	1,606,198	26.65	74	29.6
APU	1,009,505	16.75	41	16.4
UDP	83,204	1.38	1	0.4

	1983–5			
Party	*Votes*	*%*	*Seats*	*%*
CDS	716,705	12.56	30	12.0
PPD/PSD	1,534,804	27.00	75	30.0
PS	2,061,309	36.12	101	40.4
APU	1,031,609	18.07	44	17.6

	1985–7			
Party	*Votes*	*%*	*Seats*	*%*
CDS	577,580	9.96	22	8.8
PPD/PSD	1,792,288	29.87	88	35.2
PRD	1,038,893	17.92	45	18.0
PS	1,204,311	20.77	57	22.8
APU	898,281	15.49	38	15.2

continued/

Table 6.1   continued

		1987–		
Party	*Votes*	*%*	*Seats*	*%*
CDS	251,987	4.44	4	1.6
PPD/PSD	2,850,784	50.22	148	59.2
PRD	278,561	4.91	7	2.8
PS	1,262,506	22.24	60	24.0
CDU				
(POP+'Os Verdes')	689,137	12.14	31	12.4

Less than two years later, there was another change. For the first time, one party by itself obtained an absolute majority of votes and seats—a larger majority than the one obtained in 1979 and 1980 by the same party, but in a coalition. At the same time, apart from the PSD, all the other parties experienced a severe decrease in their number of votes. Elections to the European Parliament carried out at the same time confirmed the trend of the parliamentary elections, albeit far less dramatically.

The parliamentary groups

The Portuguese parliament, as in the case of most Western democracies, is not an inorganic collection of deputies, but an assembly of parliamentary groups with their own structural coherence.

Through organization and control parliamentary groups possess the same capacity to influence as deputies on an individual level, such as in the question of initiating legislation. But they have other powers exclusive to them. In this latter category, one can include, apart from the right to attend the conference of leaders,[12] the right to establish the agenda of a certain number of meetings (the number at present varies depending on whether the party is in the government and on its representation in Parliament); the right to present motions rejecting the programme of the government (which, if approved, can force it to resign); the right to request the setting up of committees of inquiry or to intervene in plenary meetings.[13]

Parliamentary groups coordinate and control the activity of deputies. This control manifests itself, of course, in voting discipline—expected in the regulations of these groups and in the party statutes—and in the way this practice is widely observed. The direction of the vote is decided either by the group leaders, or in plenary session, or, in crucial political issues, by the leadership of the party. It is the group leaders, moreover, who decide which deputies are to intervene in each debate and in some cases may even control the content of a deputy's speech. It is the group which determines what legislative or policy initiatives should be taken, or what stance should be adopted regarding the proposals of other groups.

The subordination of deputies to parliamentary groups reveals, in the final analysis, the subordination of deputies to the parties they belong to and by which they were elected.

In fact, parliamentary groups are more the instrument of the party in Parliament than the autonomous 'organ' outlined by the statutes or internal regulations of some parties. They are the parliamentary mouthpiece of the party rather than a free articulation of Parliament; they represent the party in Parliament rather than the opposite.

According to most of the internal regulations of the parliamentary groups, the party leadership either has the right to participate in group meetings, albeit without a vote, or is an integral *de jure* part of the parliamentay group. Groups are also required to follow the political guidelines laid down by the party leadership, namely in matters which it considers essential. In some cases, plenary speeches made in the name of or at the behest of the party leadership do not require the authorization of the parliamentary group and enjoy priority over the other interventions by that group.

Pressure from the most powerful interest group, as well as the main para-legislative negotiations are for the most part carried out at party headquarters. It is there that the most important decisions are taken. It is an acknowledged fact that the major laws passed by Parliament, and obtained as a result of wide-ranging inter-party consensus, are negotiated outside it, as was for example the case with the Agrarian Reform Laws, the Law of National Defence, that of the Constitutional Tribunal, and the revision of the Constitution.[14]

Initiative for legislation from parliamentary groups most frequently originates at party headquarters, more specifically in its research departments rather than within the group itself. This is largely because individual deputies, and even the groups themselves, do not have at their disposal the technical means with which to elaborate projects. The party and the parliamentary group therefore also function as a vital support structure for the activity of deputies.

This influence or predominance of the party leadership over the parliamentary group tends to be greater in less-well-represented groups, in which there is a preponderance of party leaders among the deputies. It is less evident in well-represented groups, in which there are correspondingly more deputies who are not in the leadership. Splits in parliamentary groups occurred partly because this type of predominance was not accepted.[15]

The committees

The predominance of parties over deputies is to some extent less evident in the activities of the committees. As with most parliaments, the National Assembly operates through committees. It is here that all legislative proposals are considered before being debated on the floor. It is here that most specialist documents are analysed and voted on. It is at committee level that petitions to Parliament from private citizens, institutions or groups are dealt with and that the administrative acts of the government are scrutinized. Here too, enquiries are set up to examine both the activities of the administration and the government and those of public corporations.

Apart from the Permanent Committee—which is like a mini-parliament without deliberative functions and which meets outside the period when the full house meets or when the Assembly has been dissolved—and the Committee on Administration and Mandates which verifies the powers of the deputies and has other functions to do with the Statute governing deputies and the administration of the Assembly, there are various permanent specialist committees. In 1977 there were 11; in 1980 they had increased to 19; since 1983 they have stabilized at 13 (see Table 6.2).

It may be said that each committee corresponds to a particular area of government activity with two exceptions: the first, on constitutional affairs, addresses a specific need related to the legislative work of Parliament (and is the one that meets most frequently), while the 12th committee addresses a political need, without direct correspondence to the activity of Parliament (and is the one which meets least).

These permanent committees have, in turn, spawned within themselves sub-committees, either for the scrutiny of certain laws, or to set up enquiries into the activity of the government, of the administration or of public corporations.

The chairmanships of the various committees are attributed to the various parliamentary groups in proportion to their number of deputies. This does not always allow for a choice to be made using institutional criteria, but forces a change in the chairmanship every time there are changes in the number of deputies from each parliamentary group. But parliamentary groups do not only determine committee chairman. They also nominate their representatives on the different committees. Gradually, however, the number of deputies repeatedly nominated by their parliamentary groups has increased. In 1980, only 32 deputies belonged to committees on which they had already previously sat. By 1983 this number had risen to 57, and by 1985 to 72, which is another indication, albeit modest, of the professionalization of parliamentary activity.

Committees function according to an unwritten rule upheld in their meetings. If a deputy defends a certain opinion on a committee, affirming that this is his party's position, this guarantees that his final vote in the plenary will correspond to the stated opinion. Violations of this rule are very rare and are universally censured.

The decrease in the predominance of parliamentary groups over the activity of deputies on the committees, stems from the nature of the work which they undertake: parties do not give detailed reports on the different matters debated in committees. The deputy therefore has a certain margin for manouevre both in his negotiations with partners and in the defence of the solutions he envisages for problems. In any case, there is always a latent control (quite apart from self-control: the deputy knows that over and above his personal opinion, he must defend that which he perceives to be the opinion of his party). A parliamentary group may oblige a deputy to rectify the opinion he has defended while still at the committee stage. It is not uncommon for a deputy to reserve his position on a given question in order to discuss the matter later with the leadership of his parliamentary group.

Table 6.2 Permanent parliamentary committees

1976	1980	1983
1. Constitutional affairs	1. Constitutional affairs	1. Constitutional affairs, civil rights and liberties
2. Civil rights and liberties	2. Civil rights and liberties	2. Health, social security and family
3. Labour	3. Social communication	3. Labour
4. Social security and health	4. Social security, health, family	4. Education, science and culture
5. Education, science and culture	5. Labour	5. Economy, finance and planning
6. Economy, finance and planning	6. Education	6. Agriculture and sea
7. Agriculture and fisheries	7. Science research	7. National defence
8. National defence	8. Economy, finance and planning	8. Foreign affairs and emigration
9. Foreign affairs and emigration	9. Trade and tourism	9. Social infrastructure and environment
10. Equipment and environment	10. Industry, energy and transport	10. Internal administration and local government
11. Internal administration and local power	11. Agriculture, forests and fisheries	11. European integration
	12. National defence	12. Women's affairs
	13. Foreign affairs and emigration	13. Youth
	14. Public works and housing	
	15. Culture and environment	
	16. Internal administration and local government	
	17. European integration	
	18. Women's affairs	
	19. Youth	

Table 6.3 Indicators of distance (all voting sessions)[1]

First government			Second government			Fourth government[4]		
PPL[2]	PJL	RAT	PPL	PJL	RAT[3]	PPL	PJL	RAT
PSD/CDS 13	PSD/CDS 3	PSD/CDS 4	PS/CDS 0	PS/CDS 7	PS/CDS 0	PS/PDS 10	PSD/CDS 13	PS/PCP 13
PS/PSD 19	PS/PSD 28	PS/CDS 20	PS/PCP 39	PS/PCP 40	PSD/PCP 10	PSD/CDS 10	PS/PCP 29	PSD/CDS 27
CDS/PCP 23	PS/PCP 28	PS/PSD 27	CDS/PCP 39	CDS/PCP 43	PS/PSD 50	PS/CDS 14	PS/PSD 38	PS/CDS 33
PSD/PCP 26	PS/CDS 29	PS/PCP 34	PSD/PCP 42	PSD/PCP 54	CDS/PSD 50	PS/PCP 52	PS/CDS 38	PS/PSD 40
PS/CDS 28	PSD/PCP 42	PSD/PCP 39	PS/PSD 65	CDS/PSD 59	PS/PCP 70	PSD/PCP 57	PSD/PCP 58	CDS/PCP 47
PS/PCP 31	PCP/CDS 43	PCP/CDS 39	CDS/PSD 65	PS/PSD 63	CDS/PCP 70	CDS/PCP 67	PCP/CDS 59	PSD PCP 53

Sixth government			Seventh government			Eighth government		
PPL	PJL	RAT	PPL	PJL	RAT	PPL	PJL	RAT
PS/PCP 31	PS/PCP 8	PS/PCP 8	PS/PCP 22	PS/PCP 15	PS/PCP 5	AD/PS 28	PS/PCP 5	PS/PCP 21
AD/PS 48	AD/PCP 43	AD/PS 13	AD/SP 63	AD/PS 41	PS/AD 68	PS/PCP 35	AD/PS 45	AD/PS 74
AD/PCP 74	AD/PS 50	AD/PCP 17	AD/PCP 18	AD/PCP 48	PCP/AD 73	AD/PCP 63	AD/PCP 45	AD/PCP 94

Notes:
1. Compare the behaviour of parties in twos. When the two parties vote the same way the score is 0; when one abstains and the other declares itself, the score is 0.5; when one votes for and the other against, the score is 1. The scores are then added and divided by the number of voting sessions. The quotient is then multiplied by 100. The indicator can go from 0 (complete common agreement) to 100 (complete opposition). Only the votes in which there is the most obvious divergence of principles have been chosen. See Pederesen, (1967) Consensus and Conflict in the Danish Folketing, 1945–1965, *Scandinavian Political Studies*, **4**, 143–66.
2. PPL = legislative proposal, or bill; PJL = legislative project, or private member's bill; RAT = ratification.
3. Only considers five voting sessions.
4. The third government saw its programme rejected by the Assembly. Neither before nor afterwards did it have any dealings with Parliament.

| Ninth government | | | Tenth government | | |
PPL	PJL	RAT[6]	PPL	PJL	RAT
PS/PSD 0	5	PS/PSD 0	PSD/CDS 1	PSD/CDS 11	7
PS/PSD/CD 41		PS/PSD/CDS 29	PS/PRD 6	PSD/PRD 13	
CDS/PCP 41		PCP/CDS 57	PSD/PRD 19	PRD/PCP 18	
PS/PSD/PCP 77		PS/PSD/PCP 71	CDS/PRD 20	PS/PCP 19	
			PSD/PS 24	PSD/PS 20	
			CDS/PS 25	CDS/PRD 20	
			PS/PCP 30	CDS/PS 21	
			PRD/PCP 34	PSD/PRD 24	
			PSD/PCP 54	CDS/PCP 31	
			CDS/PCP 55	PSO/PCP 38	

5. More than 200 projects were voted on, but the overwhelming majority concerned the creation of towns, parishes and other local administrative districts. The logic of approximating and distancing votes in these cases is completely different from others. For this reason we chose not to show the scores obtained here.
6. Only 7 voting sessions are considered.
7. Because of the change in administrative procedures, the custom of having a general vote to agree to or reject ratification was dropped.

Up until 1985 committees only met once a week, and in theory were unable to meet when the house was sitting. At that time, it was the work of the plenary assembly which held sway. After the great revision in the administration of 1985, and in response to the stated need to give priority to the work of the committees, the rules were changed. From then on, committees were allowed to meet while the plenary assembly was sitting. Voting in the plenary is set for a particular hour and the deputies who are working on committees are summoned to vote[16].

This system increased the number of committee meetings. Indeed, according to available information, in 1983–4, the different committees[17] met 452 times while in 1984–5 (it was during this session that the new regime came into force) they met 584 times, and in 1985–6, 745 times. In comparison, during the same periods the plenary met 141, 107 and 103 times respectively. The numbers—and the change in rules—point to a progressive increase in the activity of committees in parliamentary work and, in this way, and in the limited terms set out here, to a slight decrease in the predominance of the parties in parliamentary groups.

Government and Parliament

From June 1976 to August 1987, Portugal had 10 governments. If we consider the relations between these governments and the parliamentary oppositions, we may conclude that there were three types of executive:

— Governments without a party base,[18] led by a prime minister without party following and without any party taking responsibility for their formation and activity, in this case any party represented in Parliament can be the opposition;
— Governments with a party base, either with a minority backing, in this case the opposition will be, or may be, the majority in Parliament; or
— Governments with a majority following when the opposition will, of course, be the minority.

Whether governments enjoy support in Parliament or not, and the degree of such support, must clearly influence relations between the government and the Assembly. It is this possibility which we shall attempt to prove or disprove.

The following analysis will take into account each one of the three types of government and the legislative activity of the Assembly as well as its direct control over the executive.

Governments without a party base

There were three governments without a party base: the third, fourth and fifth. The third government under the leadership of Nobre da Costa saw its programme rejected by the Assembly. It was in power for only three months and its situation was always precarious. Its relations with Parliament practically limited themselves to the presentation and rejection of its programme.

The fifth government of Maria de Lourdes Pintasilgo had a unique working relationship with the Assembly. The Assembly met over the recess merely to debate the programme of the government and 15 legislative proposals (*propostas de lei*).[19] Immediately after this it was dissolved. The government's principal mission was to prepare elections. It was dismissed the moment the newly elected Parliament had been formed. The proposals which had been approved related to international loans, tax benefits and other politically insignificant matters which were nevertheless necessary for continuity in the running of the Assembly.

The fourth government, led by Mota Pinto, lasted for nine months and coexisted with the Assembly for its whole term. However, relations were anything but harmonious. The government's two fundamental legislative instruments, the budget and the economic plan, which it proposed, were rejected at once. The second version of the budget was passed, but the second version of the plan was once again rejected. Eventually the government resigned when the Assembly was preparing to vote on a motion of censure which would certainly have been approved. It was therefore only through anticipation that the government did not fall as a result of the direct action of Parliament.

The government did not obtain open or consistent support from any party. For this reason it had considerable difficulty in controlling parliamentary activity. Its legislative initiatives were few and were almost only restricted to what was essential for the day-to-day running of government. Here, it obtained the sympathy of the Assembly, which approved all proposals (with the crucial exception of the budget and the plan). Only the Communist party (PCP) systematically voted against it or abstained. The legislative proposals of the deputies were far more abundant, and at that stage it could be said that an opposition no longer existed.

At that point in time, the Socialist party (PS) held a key position in Parliament: it could have formed a majority with any party and was only defeated by the combined votes of all the other parties. To this extent the situation was identical to that which had existed at the time of the first government: the PS formed majorities with any one of the other three parties. This possibility resulted from the numerical distance between parties. See Table 6.3: the PS is equidistant from the other parties. Also significant is the proximity of the two parties of the right and the isolation of the PCP.

To the greater legislative initiative of the deputies during this period, there corresponds a greater legislative output originating from legislative projects (*projectos de lei*) (see Table 6.4), a situation which is unique both in the Portuguese and the international context (see Table 6.5).[20]

The control of government activity at the legislative level is exercised mainly through the process of ratification.[21] During the term of the fourth government 30 bills were subject to ratification, 26 of which originated from that government, it is a record (see Table 6.5). In eight cases, ratification was refused. In this domain one notes the approximation of the PS and the PCP. Opposition to the government was formed in this case by the PS and the PCP and not the PCP alone. The fourth government therefore found itself in the stranglehold of Parliament. It governed only when and how the Assembly so desired, despite the support it was given by the president of the Republic. This proves that if it was not easy to govern against the wishes of the president, it was impossible to do so against those of the Assembly.

The failure of the presidential governments was a landmark in the evolution of the regime, opening the way for the gradual strengthening of the parliamentary component. Because he never had a majority which might support a government of his making in Parliament, the president of the Republic tended to distance himself from the issues of government, limiting himself to the role of guarantor of the system and mediator in conflicts which occurred within it. Parliament itself came to dictate the formation of executives which derived their legitimacy from the Assembly. This meant that, in concrete political matters, presidents openly emphasized their unwillingness to identify with government opposition. It also meant that in the last two elections, the

Table 6.4   Origin of the laws of the National Assembly published during the terms of the different governments (in %)

Origin of laws	1st gov.	2nd gov.	3rd gov.	4th gov.	5th gov.	6th gov.	7th gov.	8th gov.	9th gov.	10th gov.
Legislative proposals (govt. bills)	69.4	69.8	28.6	41.3	26.9	71.4	56.2	76.1	27.4	30.6
Legislative projects (private members bills)	17.5	12.6	57.2	48.2	14.2	6.1	22.9	11.9	69.8	47.7
Ratifications	11.1	15.8	14.3	17.2	58.9	22.4	20.8	7.1	2.2	15.9
Other*	1.8	1.5	–	–	–	–	–	4.7	0.3	5.6

Notes: As the title of Table 6.4 indicates, it concerns laws published during the terms of each government. The legislative process of some of these bills, however, began during the previous administration. This explains why, for example, there is a reasonable percentage of laws originating from the government during the term of the Third Government, although it did not initiate any legislation in Parliament.

* The term 'other' refers to laws originating simultaneously in legislative proposals and projects.

Table 6.5   Percentage of government bills passed by Parliament

Percentage of bills passed	Number of countries	Percentage of countries
90–100	42	70
80–9	9	15
70–9	4	6
60–9	1	1.6
50–9	3	5
49% or less	1	1.6

Source: Inter-parliamentary Union (1986), *Parliaments of the World*, vol. II, Aldershot, Gower, 911.

successful candidates relied largely on the votes of opposition parties which remained in opposition.

Minority governments

The first and tenth governments were minority one-party administrations. The first was of the PS, the tenth, the PSD. While the first embarked on a practice of systematic negotiation with the other parties, the tenth adopted a confrontational posture. For this reason the first government was frequently able to use its power to initiate legislation (83 legislative proposals were voted on in all)—and with some success: the government only saw 4.8 per cent of its proposals rejected, and succeeded in getting unanimous agreement on 44.5 per cent of them (see Table 6.4). On the other hand, the tenth govenment only saw 41 of its proposals voted on, of which 9.7 per cent were rejected (among these the economic plan), obtaining unanimity on 31.7 per cent.

Table 6.6 Government requests for ratification of bills by party (%)

	1st legislature				2nd legislature			3rd legislature		4th legis.
	1st session	2nd ses.	3rd ses.	4th ses.	1st ses.	2nd ses.	3rd ses.	1st ses.	2nd ses.	1st ses.
PS	–	–	24.6	5.3	25.0	32.3	18.8	–	–	6.8
PSD	42.1	56.2	19.3	47.9	–	–	–	–	–	–
CDS	21.0	18.8	8.8	6.6	–	0.6	–	15.3	9.4	3.4
PCP	31.6	25.0	45.6	11.1	57.0	56.5	68.8	83.9	86.8	70.8
AD				28.7						
PRD										13.5
TOTAL (absolute figures)	19	18	57	244	100	124	16	118	53	89

It was not only in the quantity of legislation approved by Parliament, and initiated by government that the two administrations differed, but also in the political importance of the laws which were approved. While the tenth government did not manage to have any politically relevant law approved, the first government passed some laws which were fundamental to the definition of its economic policy,[22] a matter which was particularly controversial at the time. The first government therefore governed with Parliament. It managed to do so by means of constant negotiation with the other parties, with a slight preference, in the field of legislative proposals, for the PSD (see Table 6.3). An indication of consensus is the relative equidistance of all the parties; the indices of distance, in this particular area, vary between 13 and 31 on a scale from 0 to 100.

It is true that whereas during the first administration the PS could form a majority with any party, during the tenth the PSD needed the support of the

CDS and at least the abstention of the PS or the PRD (given that that of the PCP was unlikely), that is, it had to always negotiate with two parties. The indicators of distance demonstrate precisely this: approximation with the CDS is almost total and it is considerable with the PRD and the PS. When the parties are looked at as a whole, the indicators which vary here from 1 to 55, reveal the absence of consensus over the government's initiatives at legislation.

With regard to legislative projects, we see that during the first government 49 bills were voted on in all, only 19 of which became law. During the term of the tenth government, the figure was 131. It is clear, then, that the first government controlled the activity of the Assembly more effectively than the tenth, just as it is true that in both cases, private members' bills came overwhelmingly from the opposition.

The indicators of distance for the period corresponding to the first government reinforce the indications of consensus on the part of the PS, accentuating the distance between the PCP and the right (which is understandable, given the origin of private members' bills, which did not generally come from the ranks of the PS), those relating to the tenth government show figures which are closer together, indicating a greater degree of consensus, but also reveal that the PRD was further removed from the PSD.

If a global comparison of indicators relating to bills and private members' bills (legislative proposals and legislative projects) is made, it can be seen that the PS had a more disparate, more disorganised opposition, balanced by the various parties represented in Parliament; it was not a stable opposition, rather there were various potential oppositions, but also various possible sources of support. The PSD, for its part, had the consistent support of the CDS, and was systematically opposed by the PCP, with sporadic support from the PRD and the PS, meaning that here too opposition to and support for the government underwent some fluctuation, albeit to a lesser extent.

With regard to legislative output, differences may also be noted between the two minority governments. In the case of the tenth government, laws originating from private members' bills predominated over those originating from the Government, while exactly the opposite occurred in that of the first (see Table 6.4). This also supports the conclusion that the first government had a better working relationship with Parliament. In the first government, 22 bills were subject to ratification, of which two were refused; in the tenth, 24 decree-laws were scrutinized, of which four were refused. Quantitatively, these figures are similar. However, the bills presented to Parliament by the first administration related largely to questions of no great importance for government policy, and the decree-laws produced insignificant changes from the point of view of general policy. This was not the case with the tenth government whose bills related to fundamental areas, such as economic policy, health and information; and some of the changes introduced were of great importance, reducing the power of the government, submitting its activity to a much tighter parliamentary control. In fact, in other bills approved by the Assembly, one notes something of an invasion by Parliament of the powers of the executive. In this trial of strength between the Assembly and the tenth government, the Assembly would appear to have won: the government eventually fell after the Assembly approved a motion of censure. But it was the government that won in the end. In the subsequent elections, the PSD obtained that which no other party had previously managed—an absolute majority.

The first government did not confront the Assembly, as we have seen. Rather, it sought its collaboration. But it was brought down in the end by Parliament after its request for a vote of confidence was turned down. Certainly, the government assumed that it would win the vote—and the result was uncertain right up to the end—but it lost. The strategy of collaboration ultimately reaped no better results than that of confrontation. However, the two strategies were not in themselves avoidable. The political, economic and social reality of 1976–8 was very different from that of 1985–7.

Majority governments

Until August 1987, all governments which benefited from majority support in the Assembly were coalition governments. Examples of post-electoral coalition were the second government, formed by the PS and the CDS, or the ninth, formed by the PS and PSD; examples of pre-election coalitions were the sixth, the seventh and the eighth governments, all supported by the Democratic Alliance (AD), which incorporated the PSD, the CDS and a small party, the PPM.

All these coalitions demonstrated cohesiveness, invariably voting in the same way. There were very few exceptions and these only arose when there was a vote on legislative initiatives from deputies concerning questions not covered by coalition agreements. Government initiatives always received the support of all the coalition parties. This did not prevent the second and the sixth governments from losing in voting sessions—the second in two, and the sixth in one—because of the momentary absence of the deputies at voting time.

If the majorities supporting the government remained united, the same could not be said of the opposition. The opposition to the second government was led mainly by the PSD, as shown by the indicators of distance in Table 6.3. The constant remoteness of this party, in voting sessions, from the PS and CDS has nothing to do with the nature or the content of the bills, but with its strategy of open opposition to the PS/CDS coalition. The PCP, for its part, had a more constrained attitude, also for reasons which had to do with the general political climate of the time.

Opposition to the sixth, seventh and eight governments was provided by the PS and PCP, the latter more than the former. The opposition was more united when it voted on private members' bills than when government initiatives were being scrutinized, quite a few of which the PS supported. When one reads the figures referring to the eighth government, in which it is possible to discern the proximity of the PS to the government coalition on the matter of legislative proposals, it should be recalled that at this stage the PS agreed with the AD over the revision of the Constitution and the elaboration of fundamental laws relating to national defence and the constitutional tribunal.

The number of bills subject to ratification suffered a noticeable decline which is understandable: the government had a majority which meant that it was unlikely to drop or alter its own bills in any major way. Consequently, in the second government only five decree-laws were subject to ratification; in the sixth, 22 (but only three of these originated from the sixth government, the others were bills from the previous administration); in the seventh, 9; in the eighth, 15 and in the ninth, 6. The cohesion both of the majority and of the opposition is much more clear-cut in these voting sessions.

As might be expected, it is during the term of majority governments that a certain predominance of government over Parliament may be noted. This predominance was particularly evident during the term of the sixth government, when the majority, on various occasions, showed intransigence and little willingness to negotiate. But the AD lost its charismatic leader and entered into decline, culminating in the president of the Republic's refusal to accept the nomination of one of its more radical leaders to form a government (which would have been the ninth), even though it still had a parliamentary majority. And there is no doubt that the persistence of the opposition in Parliament contributed significantly towards accelerating the disintegration of the majority.

A reading of the figures concerning the legislative output (Table 6.4) reveals that in the Parliament with the largest ever majority, laws deriving from private members' bills (legislative projects) predominate over those originating in government bills (legislative proposals). This can probably be explained by the fact that the coalition parties preferred to negotiate certain laws in Parliament rather than with the government. Without doubt it was a coalition torn by conflicts: it was made up of the two largest parties, mutual rivals, with a largely similar social base and each with its own interest groups to satisfy. It was therefore a coalition which survived by means of constant negotiations, and not all of these could be carried out in the government.

Parliamentary control

During the term of majotiry governments, the opposition, without great hopes of seeing its legislative initiatives approved, or the corrections it wishes to make to others carried out, turns to other forms of control over government activity. One notices, for example, in those periods when requests for the ratification of bills increased, that these were presented exclusively by the opposition (see Table 6.7).[23] It is true that these requests for ratification never got as far as being considered (there was certainly collusion between majority and opposition, albeit for different reasons). Whatever the case, disagreement with government policy was registered and communicated to the voters.

The institution of eventual committees of enquiry increased during the second and third legislatures from 19 to 27 respectively, while in the first legislature, when minority governments predominated, there were only three. Although not all committees scrutinized government activities, but also analysed those of central and local administration and events in public life generally, it was the government which was the main target of such committees.

Table 6.7 Interpellations of government

Year	Number	Average per year
1976–9	2	0.66
1979–80	4	4
1980–3	10	3.3
1983–5	7	3.5

A more visible and effective form of political criticism and parliamentary control were the 'interpellations to the government'—debates solicited by one party on an area of government activity, normally given high profile by the media, including television—which increased from the first to the second legislatures, occurring with frequent regularity (see Table 6.7).

The same has not occurred with the government's so-called question times. In the rules governing Parliament, allowance is made for these to be held weekly, and at present fortnightly, but the truth of the matter is that these question times are occurring with more and more infrequency.[24] One of the likely reasons is that questions have to be formulated in advance and the government can choose those it wishes to answer.

The most important moment in relations between the government and its majority, and the opposition, is when motions of confidence or censure are being debated and voted on. But their presentation is obviously more or less significant depending on whether the direction of the vote is known beforehand. The first minority government fell, as we have seen, through the rejection of a motion of confidence which it hoped would be approved. The tenth government, also a minority one, first saw a motion of confidence approved, because the PRD abstained. Months later, it was the PRD which proposed a motion of censure that was approved, with the result that the government fell.

From the sixth government onwards, a practice was begun, and then continued, of governments with majority support requesting the vote on a motion of confidence directly after the presentation and non-rejection of their programme. As already mentioned, governments did not need a positive vote on their programme. The presentation of a motion of confidence straight after the non-rejection of its programme meant a positive vote on the future activity of the governemnt, thus providing evidence of the majority support it enjoyed. Some majority governments, however, have also presented motions of confidence, and had them approved. These have had the function of showing up growing internal dissatisfaction among government supporters, and have therefore become instruments of government control over its parliamentary support rather than of parliamentary control over government.

Conclusion

In an unstable, decentralized political system there is no single dominant centre of power. In Portugal, political power has been dispersed among people, organs, groups and institutions without it being possible to pinpoint one principal protagonist. At present, there is a majority party in the Assembly which supports a government. But the president of the Republic was elected against the leader of this majority. It is still not possible to know if the cohabitation will be a peaceful one—as some insist it will be, and as it has indeed been up to the moment of writing—or whether it will be riven by conflict and rivalry.

If Parliament has not been *the* hegemonic centre of power, it has never played a secondary role, and has frequently been the protagonist in the most important scenes in the political drama. Even when governments had the support of the majority, Parliament was very often the focal point for negotiation,[25] or for opposition to or attack on the executive. In comparative terms, the National Assembly shows a lesser degree of government influence than most other European parliaments. The legislative output is one such indicator, and we have seen how significant it is.

Seldom have governments encountered a cohesive and systematic opposition, closed to dialogue. There have always been different shades of opposition, and consensus has been frequent. One minority government managed to have fundamental laws approved in particularly sensitive and controversial domains. And when it was necessary—for the revision of the Constitution, and for the elaboration of the Law of National Defence, or the Law of the Constitutional Tribunal—agreement with two-thirds of the deputies was rapidly reached.

The political parties dominate parliamentary activity through parliamentary groups. Party discipline is respected. However, sometimes the frailty of the party structures, above all those of the largest parties, has allowed deputies a margin of autonomy. The increase in committee work has also conferred more autonomy on deputies, particularly in technical matters (which of course are always political too).

There have been times when politicians, above all dissidents, have rebelled against the obligations of party discipline and the lack of autonomy among deputies. Today, it would appear that there is greater acceptance of this discipline as a necessary, albeit sometimes painful rule of the parliamentary game.

The work of the Assembly has been the object of successive improvements. In this sense, the far-reaching changes in parliamentary rules, initiated in 1983 and concluded in 1985, during the PS/PSD coalition, are of particular significance. The changes introduced, which merited wide consensus among members of Parliament, enabled the work of the plenary to be rationalized and subject to greater discipline, and that of the committees to be increased. The fundamental objective of this revision of the rules, an objective which was shared by all parliamentary groups, was to improve the functioning of the Assembly. Committees have met more often, and the quality of their work has improved. The testimonies of deputies whom we were able to interview all agree on this point. The National Assembly is thus less of a 'talking parliament' and more of a 'working parliament' than it was in 1976.

Evidence of the as yet incipient professionalization of deputies also supports this notion of an improvement in the activity of the Assembly. The steady increase in the activity of the various parliamentary mechanisms—committees of enquiry, requests to government, interpellations, motions—provide deputies and the Assembly with invaluable experience. The unwritten rules of parliamentary behaviour—whether they refer to the confidence to be placed in the assumed position of deputies acting on behalf of their parliamentary group, or whether they address relations among deputies in the course of their work—are beginning to emerge and to be respected. The Portuguese Parliament is a young parliament. It has been in existence for as long as democracy, after a long authoritarian regime and an uncertain period of transition. In an unstable political environment one could hardly expect to see a rapid process of institutionalization.

There is still a long way to go, improving methods and procedures of work, and providing deputies with good working conditions—conditions which are at present still precarious. The turnover of deputies is still high, and this together with the frequent recourse to substitution, makes the parliamentary world still appear fluid in its characteristics,[26] reinforcing dependence on the parties and further delaying the professionalization of the deputies. It is still possible occasionally to note a lack of consensus over important rules of procedure in Parliament. However, it seems an indisputable fact that the consolidation of democracy, the growing sophistication of democratic rules, has been accompanied by the gradual strengthening of parliamentary institutions.

Notes

1. Apart from those with special right, were princes, heirs to the throne and bishops.
2. The programme of the Armed Forces Movement (MFA) in fact resolved, among its 'immediate measures' that the Junta of National Salvation should dissolve the National Assembly of the authoritarian regime and announce the 'convocation, within twelve months, of a Constituent National Assembly, to be elected by universal, direct and secret ballot, in accordance with an electoral law to be elaborated by the future Provisional Government'. And among 'short-term measures' it stipulated that the 'period of exceptional rule' would end when, 'in accordance with the new Political Constitution, the president of the Republic and Legislative Assembly had been elected, after which the Junta of National Salvation would be dissolved', and that the 'basic reforms' could only be 'adopted within the ambit of the future Constituent National Assembly' (Neves, 1975–6).
3. The institutional continuity between the National Assembly and the Corporative Chamber and the new constituent Assembly was not only expressed in the transfer of functionaries from one to the other, but also in the continuity of procedural rules (among which was the Rule on Policing and the Security of the Assembly which dated from 1911) and in the election of deputies who had been deputies during the previous regime (men such as Magalhães Mota, Sá Carneiro, Pinto Balsemão, Mota Amaral and others from the liberal wing of the old National Assembly).
4. The MDP–CDE was a broad front of democrats, socialists and communists which had stood against the ANP (National Popular Action) in the last elections of the authoritarian regime. After 25 April, it remained active, despite its split with the socialists, and ran in the elections as a type of 'civilian MFA', as Ferreira put it (1983: 109).
5. There are those who prefer to consider the system of government as being 'semi-parliamentary' or even 'Rationalized parliamentary' because they perceive the parliamentary elements as being more pronounced than the presidential in the

constitutional system of government, specifically the possibility of Parliament being able to dismiss the government and the absence of any powers invested in the president of the Republic to direct government policy (Lopes *et al.*, 1980; Canotilho and Moreira, 1978). There are those too who, after the 1982 revision, maintained that the system of government, defined juridically as semi-presidentialist, was in actual practice, 'a parliamentary system based on an assembly' (Amaral, 1985).

6. As a result of a temporary disposition of the 1976 Constitution, the Assembly elected in 1976 had 263 deputies.

7. The first party splits with parliamentary repercussions occurred in the PS when it was the party in power, and were directly connected with the agrarian and labour policies adopted. The first minister of agriculture in the PS, Lopes Cardoso, replaced in October 1976 by António Barreto (author of the later revision of the 1977 Law on Agrarian Reform) left the party in the summer of 1977 to found, along with two other deputies, the Union of the Left for Social Democracy, but remained in Parliament. Similarly, two Trotskyite deputies—Aires Rodrigues and Carmelinda Perei—also left the party in 1977 because they disagreed with labour policy, and formed the Workers' Party for Socialist Unity, likewise keeping their seats in Parliament.

Very different was the split caused by the so-called reformers among the socialist deputies. Two ex-ministers (António Barreto, of agriculture, and Medeiros Ferreira, of foreign affairs) disagreed with the position of the PS over the 'presidentialist' governments and the electoral law of 1978, and decided to leave the party, but resigned their seats. The 'reformers' only returned to Parliament after the intermediate elections of 1979 with five deputies on the AD roll, as a result of a political agreement with Sá Carneiro.

Perhaps more significant was the important split in the social-democrat parliamentary group in March 1979, when Sá Carneiro, having regained the leadership of the PPD/PSD, opposed the general budget proposal of Mota Pinto's 'presidentialist' government, and got the support of some 40 deputies. Organising themselves as a parliamentary 'splinter' group under the name 'Unavoidable Options', the PPD/PSD dissidents then sought to set up a parliamentary group, in an attempt to make possible a coalition government with the PS. However, they were prevented from doing so by the dissolution of Parliament and the calling of intermediate elections in 1979.

Equally important was the division which occurred within the PS, on the occasion of the presidential election of 1980, between the party leadership (the secretariat) which supported General Eanes, and the followers of the General Secretary Mário Soares, who had his support publicly withdrawn by the leadership. Once the 4th Congress of the PS had been won in 1982, the conflict between the parliamentary group, which for the most part remained loyal to the former secretariat, and the 'Saorist' leadership of the party became more acute. This conflict was only resolved when the minority refused to be included in the lists of candidates for deputy, as a result of which the parliamentary group came to be made up only of 'Soarist' deputies.

8. From 1976 to 1979, despite the split in the PPD/PSD parliamentary group, which excluded more than half of its deputies from re-election, the overall percentage of re-elections was 48 per cent. From 1979 to 1980, notwithstanding the short interval between elections, this number increased to 70 per cent precisely because there was no exceptional factor to interfere with the mechanism of re-election. From 1980 to 1983, because of the refusal of the socialist minority (which had been a majority in the parliamentary group elected in 1980) to agree to run again for election, the global percentage of those re-elected fell to 47.2 per cent. It is worth

noting that in these elections, the PS came to have the largest parliamentary group. Finally, from 1983 to 1985, in spite of the transformation in the PSD leadership and the appearance of the PRD, the overall number of re-elected deputies was 52.8 per cent.

9. The 'new deputies' decreased from 52 per cent in 1979 to 46 per cent in 1983 and 40 per cent in 1985.

10. In 1987, after the elections of 19 July, the average age increased to 47.9. At this point too, the smaller parliamentary groups (the PRD and the CDS) were particularly affected by the ageing trend.

11. General Eanes was re-elected against the majority parties in Parliament and was the historic leader and founder of the PS.

12. The 'conference of Parliamentary leaders', consisting of all the leaders of the parliamentary groups and in which the government is represented, plays a fundamental part in supervising the work of Parliament.

    It is the president of the National Assembly who sets the order of the day according to a list of priorities laid down by the administration. In this task, he is assisted by the conference of leaders which, in spite of having only a consultative function, has in practice shown itself to be capable of decisive influence. The conference is also frequently summoned by the president to resolve a wide variety of issues regarding either the method and procedure of debates or the submission of parliamentary questions or intepellations.

13. These interruptions constitute a fundamental instrument of parliamentary tactics: to hold up the vote or to ensure the way the group votes. From 1985, when voting began to take place on certain days and at certain times fixed in advance, these interruptions lost some of their importance.

14. See *A feitura das leis* (1986), Lisboa, Instituto Nacional de Administracao, vol. 1, in particular the articles by Antonio Barreto, Freitas do Amaral, Cardoso da Costa and Jorge Miranda.

15. See above, note 7.

16. Now, thanks to the use of closed-circuit television, deputies who are not in the plenary can know how work is proceeding and when their presence is required.

17. In these figures, we have not counted the meetings either of the Permanent Committee or of the Committee on Administration and Mandates.

18. In Portugal, these governments are commonly designated presidential. The denomination is not precise given that all prime ministers are appointed by the president of the Republic.

19. Legislative proposals (*Propostas de lei*) are so called because they are initiatives for legislation originating from the government (or the regional governments of Madeira and the Azores), while legislative projects (*projectos de lei*) are those initiatives originating from deputies or parliamentary groups. (Translator's note: the terms *bill* and *private member's bill* have been used.)

20. If one counts laws originating in ratifications as laws deriving from the legislative initiatives of deputies—which, in itself, is correct—the percentages in favour of parliamentary initiative are much higher, and even more exceptional in political terms.

21. In ratifications, Parliament, through the initiative of the deputies, calls upon itself to scrutinize a government bill (decree-law) which has already been published. As a result of its deliberations, Parliament may refuse ratification, thus eliminating the bill, or it may suspend it and alter it.

22. Such was the case of the law defining sectors of the economy barred from private enterprise, the one which established compensation to owners of nationalised assets and those concerning agrarian reform and rural land tenure, the latter being also the object of initiatives by individual deputies.

23. During the term of the sixth government, the parties of the coalition required the ratification of a large number of bills from the previous government, more than 80 per cent of the requests made during this legislative session. Such a situation, which was in fact exceptional, demonstrates above all that, at least at that time, there was little agreement on certain norms of parliamentary behaviour. The use thus made of the procedure of ratification was, without doubt, far removed from its object and *raison d'être*. For the rest, the majority parties ended up by removing almost all the requests that they had made, while those that survived did so because they were chosen as an instrument in the political strategy which had been adopted.

24. At present (1988), the reverse is the case. During the office of the first one-party majority government, the weekly session of questions to the government was taken up again with notable regularity.

25. The fact that this process of negotiation does not limit itself to the four walls of the Assembly, but is also carried out at party headquarters, does not contradict this affirmation: negotiation has as its objective the work of Parliament, and not that of government. Parliament is therefore the pretext for and context of negotiation.

26. In the National Assembly, it is very easy for a deputy to arrange to be replaced by a candidate on the same list, but who was not elected. These temporary substitutions, sometimes for very short periods, are justified on many grounds: because the substituted deputy does not wish to be present at a particular voting session, or because he has political, personal, or professional matters to attend to outside Parliament, or because it may be in the interests of the substitute, for whatever reason, to spend some time in the Assembly, etc.

References

Aguiar, Jaoaquim (1983), *A Ilusão do Poder. Análise do Sostema Partidário Portuguēs (1976–82)*, Lisbon, Dom Quixote.

Amaral, D. Freitas, (1985), *Uma solução para Portugal*, Lisbon, Europa-América.

Caetano, Marcelo (1971), *História Breve das Constituições Portuguesas*, Lisbon, Verbo, 3rd edition.

Catonilho, J.G. and Vital Moreira (1978), *Constituição da República Portuguesa Anotada*, Coimbra, Coimbra Editora.

Cruz, Manuel Braga da, (1986), 'A evolução das instituições políticas. Partidos Políticos e Forças Armadas na transição democrática portuguesa (1974–1976). *Povos e Culturas*, no 1, 205–15.

—(1988), *O Partido e o Estado no Salazarismo*, Lisbon, Presença.

Domingos, Ernesto da Veiga, (1980), *Portugal Político. Análise das Instituições*, Rolim.

Ferreira, José Medeiros, (1983), *Ensaio histórico sobre a Revolução do 25 de Abril. O Período Pré-Constitucional*, INCM–SREC.

Gaspar, Jorge and Nuno Vitorino (1976), *As Eleições de 25 Abril. Geografia e Imagem dos Partidos*, Lisbon, Livros Horizontes.

Lopes, P. Santana and J.M. Durão Barboso (1980), *Sistema de Governo e Sistema Partidário*, Lisbon, Bertand.

Lucena, Manuel de (1978), *O Estado da Revolução. A Constituição de 76*, Lisbon, Expresso.

Miranda, Jorge (1978), *A Constituição de 1976. Formação, Estrutura. Princípios Fundamentais*, Lisbon, Petrony.

—(1982), *Manual de Direito Constitucional*, 3 vols, Coimbra, Coimbra Editora.

—and Marcelo Rebelo de Sousa (eds) (1986), *A feitura das leis*, Lisbon, Instituto Nacional de Administração.

Neves, Orlando, (1975–6), *Textos Históricos da Revolução*, 3 vols, Lisbon, Diabril.

Pereira, André Gonçalves, (1984), *O semi-presidencialismo em Porgal*, Lisbon, Atica.

Sousa, Marcelo Rebelo de, (1979), *Direito Constitucional*, Braga, Livraria Cruz.

Sousa, Marcelo de, (1984), *O Sistema de Governo Português Antes e Depois da Revisão Constitucional*, 3rd ed., Actualizada, Lisbon, Cognitivo.

Sousa, Marnoco, (1910), *Direito Político*, Coimbra, França Amado.

Stock, M. José, (1986). *Os Partidos do Poder. Dez anos depois do '25 de Abril'*, Évora, Universidade de Évora.

7 Cyclical breakdown, redesign and nascent institutionalization: the Turkish Grand National Assembly

Ersin Kalaycioğlu

Introduction: cycles of democratization and the development of the Turkish Grand National Assembly (1946–1980)

In comparison to most Southern European parliaments the Turkish Grand National Assembly (TGNA) has experienced a different route from a single party to a multi-party assembly with a cyclical pattern of convocation, transition, suspension and reorganization.

The overall picture of the process of democratization and legislative institutionalization in Turkey seems rather bleak. Every trial since 1946 seems to follow a definite cyclical pattern: a new political regime, or a constitution that emphasizes multi-party parliamentarianism is initiated by the 'state elite'.[1] Conflict among the major contenders for power and political position, (or the political elite) gradually intensifies after two national legislative elections. The mounting tensions pave the way for political protests, demonstrations, strikes and even the use of firearms in the struggle for political power. The TGNA fails to perform as a conflict-resolving arena, and perhaps even helps to exacerbate political tensions. Finally, a praetorian interlude in multi-party politics occurs to restore law and order. The praetorian government tries to set up a new constitutional order; a new cycle starts to unfold.

This chapter sets out to examine the current democratization process and especially to scrutinize the role that the post-1983 TGNA performs in that evolution. The focus is on the post-1980 installation of the democratic regime and the restitution of the TGNA. The following background information is provided to give an understanding of the democratization process in Turkey, and the status that the TGNA occupies in that evolution.

Assemblies of the TGNA, 1946–60

In 1946, more than two decades of single-party rule ended, and a transition to multi-party politics was initiated by the pre-1946 single party, namely the Republican People's Party leadership. With this transition came the end of the era of elite consensus (Karpat, 1959: 176–95). The new political parties of the 1940s, and especially the powerful Democrat Party (DP), did not share the same goals, opinions and policy preferences as the RPP leadership nor those of the civilian and the military bureaucrats. The Democrats proposed to alter the centralist economic policies of the RPP, and also to revert to the socio-cultural policies of the single-party era. In fact, then the DP won the 1950 national legislative elections, it started to follow a liberal economic programme, to curb the influence of the civil and military bureaucrats in running the state machinery and specifically to revitalize what the latter considered to be anti-laicist religious activities. In the early fifties, a deep rift started to emerge between the RPP leadership, the civilian and military bureaucrats on the one hand, and the DP leadership, the emerging middle class and the rural masses on the other. The masses that supported the two parties were also infected by the sharp differences between the elites of these parties and the mounting tension between them. As an arena of interaction between the two leading parties, the TGNA was increasingly influenced by the existing political tension.

Gradually, the very bases of legitimate rule began to be regularly debated by both parties and their followers. The RPP and its supporters tended increasingly to disregard a government that deviated from the revolutionary policies of the 1920–40 era, and the principles of the founder of the Republic regime, Mustafa Kemal Ataturk, as illegitimate, even though it was legally and freely elected through competitive elections. The DP and its followers contended that a legally and freely elected government can have no restrictions imposed on its rule. Disagreements on the fundamentals of the political regime,such as those pertaining to the definition of legitimate political rule, eventually led to the intensification of conflict between the major political forces of the country. A financial and economic crisis and the DP's partial loss of electoral support in the 1957 national legislative elections precipitated a new crisis which reached a climax by spring 1960. Student protest and clashes between the students and the security forces instigated a military intervention in civilian politics for the first time in recent Turkish history on 27 May 1960. Another first was the suspension of the activities of the TGNA for one year.

The TGNA of the period from 1950 to 1960 was a legislative body of elites in dissent over the fundamental features and rules of the political regime. The turnover in deputies of the TGNA after the 1950 national elections, which amounted to 80 per cent of the seats, encouraged the DP elite to settle for nothing less than the full control of the legislative process (see Table 7.1). All intralegislative positions changed hands following the May 1950 national elections. Disciplined party voting seems to be the modal practice of the

Table 7.1 The results of the Turkish parliamentary elections and the distribution of seats in the TGNA, 1950–60*

		Democrat Party	Republican People's Party
1950	Votes	53.3	39.9
	Seats	83.8	14.2
1954	Votes	56.6	34.8
	Seats	91.6	5.6
1957	Votes	47.3	40.6
	Seats	69.6	28.7

*   Only major political parties of the period are included.

Source: State Institute of Statistics publications of National Elections Results, (1966) Publication No. 513, Ankara.

1950s. During that period the TGNA evolved from what Weinbaum called a 'subordinate' to a 'submissive' legislature (1975: 35–41).

The 1961–80 parliamentarianism

The Constitution of 1961 was designed to prevent the political problems of the fifties from re-emerging. The designers aimed at providing numerous checks and balances to control arbitrary rule of party elites who control the majority of the seats in the TGNA. They also devised measures to encourage mass participation in politics. However, the basic problem of dissipating discord over the substance of legitimate political rule was ignored. With the return of multi-party politics the issue of political legitimacy was asserted in the Turkish polity. The coup of 1960 was undertaken to oust the DP from power. After the coup all high-level DP officials, deputies of the TGNA and the members of the DP cabinet of ministers were prosecuted, and the party was disbanded once and for all. Apparently, the DP elite and its sympathizers could not take part in the constitution-making efforts of 1960–1. Consequently, the founders of a new political party which adopted the ideas and the symbols of the DP, the Justice Party (JP), having secured the majority of the national vote in the 1965 national elections (see Table 7.2), declared that the 1961 Constitution was unfit for the country. JP leaders further asserted that the various positions, practices and duties that the new Constitution established and allocated to various persons and institutions were illegitimate. The RPP, which survived the 1961 military intervention, initially as a coalition partner with the JP until 1965, and later on as the major opposition party of the country, started to defend the 1961 Constitution against the criticisms of the JP.

The number of citizens participating in the political process, the frequency of acts of political participation and their variety started to increase in the late 1960s. Student demonstrations in 1968–9 and official reactions to these further destabilized the system and precipitated another intervention by the military in civilian politics in 1971. The 1971 quasi-military regime refrained

Table 7.2   The results of the Turkish parliamentary elections and the distribution of seats in the TGNA, 1961–80* (%)

		Justice party	Republican People's party	National Action party	National Salvation party
1961	Votes	34.8	36.7	–	–
	Seats	35.1	38.4	–	–
1965	Votes	52.9	28.7	–	–
	Seats	53.3	29.8	–	–
1969	Votes	46.5	27.4	3.0	–
	Seats	56.9	31.8	0.2	–
1973	Votes	29.8	33.3	3.4	11.8
	Seats	33.1	41.1	0.6	10.6
1977	Votes	38.3	42.4	6.8	8.4
	Seats	42.0	47.3	3.5	5.3

*   Only major political parties of the multi-party era are included. The DP was abolished in 1960, and the RPP, JP, NAP, and the NSP were disbanded in 1982. New political parties were established to mobilize their supporters. The JP was one of those parties that was founded to attract voters who were strongly affiliated with the DP of the fifties; the NAP and NSP emerged as major political organizations in the seventies.

Source: State Institute of Statistics (1977), Publication no: 817, Ankara.

from designing a new constitution; and mainly amended the Constitution through acts by the elected members of the 1969 TGNA.

However, the 1973 national legislative elections brought about a major change in the distribution of votes. The re-alignment of voters paved the way for unstable coalition governments (Erguder, 1981: 50–61; Ozbudun, 1981: 230–4). The crisis over the legitimate bases of political rule was left unresolved. Protest and unconventional and especially violent expressions of political participation could neither be overcome nor constrained by the institutionalized patterns of transactions. Oil crises and other politico-economic crises further drove the polity into greater instability. By 1980 Turkey moved very near civil war. The 1980–3 praetorian regime was established to re-establish political stability and multi-party politics.

The major trends of the polity were readily reflected in the TGNA. Hence, the TGNA of the 1961–80 period was originally an arena of settled discord between the major elite groups in the country. Social and demographic changes, industrialization, urbanization, and revitalization of religious movements, national and leftist radicalization during the late sixties and all of the seventies were reflected in the TGNA. It started to host political parties of almost every tendency from the far left to the far right, in both the lower chamber and the senate. The RPP declared itself to be on the left of centre, and the JP emerged as the leading conservative right of centre party of the country. The National Salvation Party (NSP) represented the religious right wing, while the National Action Party (NAP) stood for the ultranationalist anti-communists. These four political parties controlled almost all of the seats in the

TGNA (see Table 7.2). Except for a brief period in 1978–9, Turkey was governed by unstable coalition governments during the seventies. The TGNA of the 1970s witnessed almost unceasing legislative battles, which from time to time evolved into unruly forms of legislative behavior (Kalaycioğlu, 1988: 51–8). However, effective legislative opposition was hardly absent from the TGNA of the 1961–80 period. The parliamentary timetable and the legislative agendas were considerably influenced by the opposition parties in the TGNA. Questions and motions of interpellations were effectively used to combat the legislative majority, to terminate the process of legislation and even to call for votes of confidence and oust governing coalitions, as was the case in 1987. Nevertheless, the tenseness of the political interactions in the TGNA not only nurtured unruly legislative behavior, but also led to clogging of legislation and even to complete paralysis of the legislative process in the TGNA, in 1980. The TGNA had lost its resilience in coping with the challenges of its environment just before its activities were suspended by the National Security Council in 1980.

Since 1980, the Turkish political system has been going through another experiment with multi-party politics. The 1982 Constitution and the political laws stemming from it constitute a political regime which it is hoped will possess the optimum combination of democracy and effective government for Turkey. The TGNA has once more been established with a modified structure. If it managed to develop viability it might well contribute to regulating and containing political conflict. A closer scrutiny of the TGNA will enable us to assess the institutional conditions and political factors which are likely to enhance consolidation of democracy, and therefore to understand better the role that parliaments play in that process in Turkey.

Consequently, the first part of this chapter is allocated to the origination of the legislative system of the late eighties. The second section is concerned with the transition of the Turkish political system to the democracy and the re-establishment of the TGNA in the 1980s, and the *de jure* and *de facto* function of the legislative system in the new political regime of the country. The third section is on the internal structuring of the TGNA in 1961–80, and the 1983 and 1987 Parliaments. The relationships between the parliamentary party groups with reference to the floor, the commission interactions of the government and opposition parties are analysed in that section. The fourth section comprises an examination of executive–legislative relations in the pre- and post-1980 TGNAs in terms of their interactions during the process of legislation. The final section is on the relationships between the legislative system and the electorate, where I shall examine the mode of representation in Turkey.

Setting up the legislative system of the 1980s

The 1982 Constitution of Turkey and the new political laws are principally designed to guarantee that the pre-1980 politicians and political traditions do not exert their 'ominous' influences on the 'new era' of democratic politics. After the 6 November 1983 national elections the TGNA re-started its activities in a new political context. Three major concerns have been instrumental in characterizing the current post-1983 regime of the Turkish political system. Firstly, there was and still is a public demand for 'law and order' over most other goals of the system.[2] Second, the current political regime was designed to avoid what its engineers diagnosed to be the ailments of the Turkish democracy in the pre-1980 period. Third, the propensity of political elites and of the masses to resurrect multi-party politics.[3] Consequently, the executive branch of government is bolstered with various legal provisions to enable it to work more efficiently and effectively. Finally, the 1983 Parliament was embedded in an environment of executive supremacy; new, amateur politicians and masses more keen on preserving 'law and order' than on risking political destabilization through political activism (Kalaycıoğlu, 1988: 47–51).

The legal status of the TGNA in the post-1983 regime was determined by the new Turkish Constitution of 1982, and also by the internal rules of procedure. The 1982 Constitution elaborated the major features of the current parliamentary structure, its legal status and structural picture, and determined the rules of the 'parliamentary game'. The parliamentary Rules of Procedure (RP) also affect the establishment and implementation of those rules. In the following we will focus on the legal aspects shaping the intra-legislative structure of the post-1983 TGNA.

Constitutional provisions concerning the legislative branch of government

The parliamentary procedures of debate, and decision-making through accommodation and/or compromise over the fundamental rules by the major political actors (such as political parties, interest groups or political leaders) to a great extend failed to take place during the writing of the new constitutional provisions of the legislative branch of government. The 1982 Constitution is not a document of consensus, but the projection of a view of Turkish polity as adopted by the National Security Council and approved by popular referendum without detailed deliberation by the political elites and the masses. The input of the prospective legislators in designing the rules through their influence on the constitutional provisions was so minimal that they may safely be disregarded.[4] The major actors determining the basic features of the Constitution were the praetorian rulers of Turkey. The influence of organized interests on the framers of the Constitution is a matter of some speculation, but no hard evidence has yet been unearthed.[5]

The final document had the support of the 90 per cent of the electorate who participated in the referendum, and the participation rate was also 90 per cent. There is no question that the 1982 Constitution has popular approval, but it is also the case that the current political actors disagree on the fundamental rules, including the election laws.[6]

The TGNA has been somewhat modified in structure by the 1982 Constitution. The senate has been abolished. The number of seats in the lower and now sole chamber of the TGNA was lowered initially to 400 from 450. However, in the elections of 29 November 1987 the number of parliamentary seats was raised back to 450. The period of tenure for deputies was extended from four to five years. Hence, under normal conditions, from 1983 on national legislative elections were to be held every five years. Actually, Turkey held its second national legislative elections in 1987, and it is highly likely that the next elections will be held considerably before 1992.

Some new requirements have been introduced concerning the eligibility of legislators. Literacy must now be demonstrated by means of a primary school diploma. Anyone who has been convicted of smuggling, conspiracy in official bidding or purchases, of offences relating to disclosure of state secrets, of involvement in ideological and anarchistic activities, and/or incitement to and encouragement of such activities may not be elected deputies (article 76). All of these restrictions are new additions to those embodied in the 1961 Constitution and its amended form in 1971.

Finally, the composition of the TGNA is determined by a new electoral system of reinforced majoritarianism, with a high national threshold of 10 per cent of the valid national vote. The electoral law for the 1983 national elections was designed to cure one of the ailments of the pre-1980 multi-party politics—the crises over coalition formation,[7] and to create majorities in the TGNA. Any political parties which were unable to obtain ten per cent of the national vote were denied representation in the TGNA in 1983. The same ten per cent national threshold is still preserved in the electoral law. Furthermore, the party that receives a small plurality of the national vote is now able to control the majority of the seats. Thus, the Motherland Party (MP) was able to obtain 64 per cent of the parliamentary seats with 36 per cent of the national vote (see Table 7.3).

The MP was able to procure the above-mentioned proportion of the national seats by erecting an electoral district-level threshold.[8] The objections of the opposition parties to the 1987 electoral law have precipitated a new and continuing controversy over the legitimacy of the 1987 Parliament. The 1989 local elections indicated that popular support of the ruling MP has eroded since the 1987 elections. Hence, the opposition parties have become more vocal on the issue of the mismatch between the distribution of the national votes and the

Table 7.3 The results of the Turkish parliamentary elections and the distribution of seats in the TGNA, 1983–7* (%)

		Motherland Party	Populist Party	Social Democratic Populist Party	National Democracy Party	True Path Party
1983	Votes	45.1	30.5	–	23.3	–
	Seats	52.8	29.2	–	17.7	–
1987	Votes	36.3	–	24.4	–	19.9
	Seats	64.9	–	22.0	–	13.1

* Only major political parties of the period are included in the Table

Source: State Institute of Statistics Publications of National Elections Results Ankara, (1985), and Erguder (1987 : 23).

seats in the TGNA. They have started to question the legitimacy of the MP rule and to call for early national elections. The 1982 Constitution and the political laws emanating from it seem to have created no fewer problems than the purported to solve.

In fact, the provisions of the 1982 Constitution were drawn up to deal with the problems of the 1960s and 1970s. For example, provisions concerning the loss of membership have also been re-structured to inhibit deputies from changing political parties. The coalition governments of the 1970s were forced to make concessions to some deputies of the TGNA that they might otherwise have not made if such deputies had been unable to switch their allegiance from one political party to another. Against the background of such practices, the 1982 Constitution stipulates that the unseating of deputies shall be decided by an absolute majority of the total number of the General Assembly in respect of deputies who are convicted of offences precluding their election to the TGNA, who are deprived of their legal capacity, who resign from their party in order to join another party or to take up a ministerial position in the cabinet during the election period (article 84). The 1982 Constitution further restricts deputies who resign from their political parties from being nominated as a candidate by the central organs of any party existing at the time of their resignation (article 84). However, in the period from 1983 to 1987 more deputies switched parties than ever before in Turkish history.

The picture one gets from reading the 1982 Constitution is that it determines the main functions[9] as well as the rules of parliamentary procedure[10] to a considerable extent. The legislative system is left with the minor role of filling the gaps in the rules of parliamentary procedure left untreated by the Constitution. However, one interesting point to note is that the great majority of the parliamentary elite of Turkey, especially the more influential pre-1980 deputies of the TGNA, had not been consulted while the 1982 Constitution was being drawn up (Ozbudun, 1986: 35–40)

Most of the provisions concerning the TGNA added to the 1982 Constitution were introduced with the hope of improving the efficiency of the legislative system. The adoption of the new provisions came through a decision-making process which seems to have followed a four-stage approach. In the initial diagnostic stage a problem with a certain parliamentary procedure was identified. In the second stage, deductive-rational arguments were preferred as scenarios to cope with this problem. They were either discussed in the Consultative Assembly[11] or by the commission of the Consultative Assembly which drew up the initial version of the Constitution. In the third stage, one of the proposed solutions to the 'problem' was selected by the Consultative Assembly. Finally, the NSC would either adopt that solution or provide a completely different solution. The final document consisted of the decision of the NSC. Consequently, the 1982 Constitution is not a political document that reflects the consensus of the political elite in Turkey. Such a consensus may now emerge following an amendment to the Constitution and/or initially by reaching agreement over the new rules of procedure, stipulated by the Constitution as a matter to be decided upon by the current TGNA.

Parliamentary rules of procedure

Every new constitution since 1961 required that the TGNA draw up its own rules of procedure. It usually takes three assemblies for the TGNA to establish new rules of procedure (RP). In the meanwhile, the TGNA functions according to the amended version of the pre-coup RP. Furthermore, previously the RP were always drawn up by the parliamentary majorities, which were controlled by a single and disciplined political party, but the TGNA was continuously confronted with the endemic and cyclically rising unruly behaviour of the deputies in the multi-party period since 1946. This was especially high from 1973 to 1980.

In a recent paper I have examined how effective the RP were in the past (Kalaycioğlu, 1988: 47–62). According to this study there has been a distinct rise in the unruly (at times violent) floor behaviour of the TGNA deputies since the advent of multi-party politics. Acts in violation of articles 66 to 70 of the RP increased markedly in scope and intensity during the 1953–60, 1965–71, and 1975–9 sessions of the TGNA.

Nevertheless, from 1946 to 1980 unruly legislative behaviour tended to increase over the years (see Table 7.4). The data illustrate that the RP had not enjoyed the unqualified endorsement of Turkey's major political parties. Between 1950 and 1980 the above-mentioned articles of the RP were virtually routinely violated.

The adoption of the 1973 RP by the TGNA was a controversial process. At the time of their formulation by a government-dominated commission, systematic objections to about 10 per cent of the rules were registered by the opposition party spokesman (*The Minutes of Assembly Debates*). However, as the final draft of the RP adopted by the TGNA makes clear, these objections were ignored. Hence, the RP had not commanded universal assent during their

Table 7.4   Trends of unruly floor behaviour by deputies in the TGNA, 1946–80

		The Number of Occurrences	Yearly Average
1946–80	Y = 9.33 + 0.21 ×	425	12.5
1946–60	Y = 5.24 + 0.97 ×	194	14
1961–71	Y = 6.0 + 0.62 ×	107	10.7
1973–80	Y = 16.87 + 0.61 ×	124	18
1983–7	(too few cases)	5*	1.2

Y = the number of unruly legislative acts occurring in the TGNA (per annum).
X = time (years).
Note: All violations of the rules of procedure concerning articles 65–9 are taken into consideration. These range from loud protests leading to a recess to physical fights (for more information see Kalaycioğlu, 1988: 51–3).

* One example of unruly legislative behaviour occurred in 1985, four such incidents took place in 1986–7, and four in 1988.

Sources: Vatan (1946–60), *Cumhuriyet* (1946–88), and *Milliyet* (1960–88) (daily newspapers); the *Minutes of the Floor Debates of the TGNA* for 1946 to 1988.

original formulation. The document is not a product of compromise. It had been legislated like all other bills by votes cast along strict party lines. This being the case, the contents of the document were not always accepted as binding by the deputies. In periods of mounting tension, within and outside Parliament, articles 66 to 70 were routinely violated by both the opposition and the government party deputies.

The 1983 Assembly started out by adopting the RP from 1973 with only minor modifications. Simultaneously, the process of drawing up the new RP for the TGNA was initiated in the post-1983 TGNA. It is still continuing, and it looks as if it will take another few years to complete. The commission in charge of the revision is dominated by the government party, and the ongoing process seems to be a replica of past experiences.

Procedural rules concerning the house activities of the legislators

The RP contain detailed guidelines governing the proceedings of the General Assembly as well as the commission activities. Accordingly, the RP give precedence to matters of procedure over others in floor debates. It is also stipulated that an agenda is to be prepared prior to each session. No deputy may speak on the floor without obtaining the speaker's permission. Within some explicitly defined limits, the speaker may determine who takes the floor (RP, article 62). The speaker is without a vote and unless called upon to do so may not participate in the debate (RP, art. 65). Only the implementation of article 62 has caused some problems. Deputies objected to the limitation imposed on their 'right to defend their views' by the speaker. Some objections precipitated unruly behaviour as reported in Table 7.4.

The RP also contain five articles which set forth guidelines to be followed in addressing the General Assembly. These govern the general order of debates, and specify measures to be taken in the event of unruly legislative behaviour which disrupts due process (rp, art. 66–70). The speaker may call for a recess of up to one hour in case of such behaviour (RP, art. 69).

It is noteworthy to mention that the deputies concerned have even been rewarded for their unruly behaviour on the floor. In the past a deputy's unruly legislative conduct appears to have boosted his popularity rather than failing to decrease his chances of re-election.[12] It seems as if unruly legislative behaviour has been rationalized by the deputies and their constituents alike as symptomatic of uncompromising devotion to the interests and ideals of the latter. A deputy's chances for re-election have been further enhanced to the extent that he has been able to combine unruly behaviour with success in securing some needed service for his constituency on the one hand, and proximal ties with his party leaders, on the other. Under such circumstances it is hardly surprising to discover that the RP have not been 'binding' for all deputies (Kalaycioğlu, 1988: 49–51). In short, re-election concerns and party affiliation have been more determinative of the legislative behaviour of the TGNA deputies than have the rules, norms and legal provisions that make up the rules of parliamentary procedure.

Post-1983 rules of procedure and rule-abiding legislative behaviour:
some explanations

With the exception of a group of about 40 deputies who had served in the pre-1980 TGNA, the 1983 Assembly was composed of deputies with almost no experience in national politics (Kalaycioğlu, 1986a: 332). The 1987 national legislative elections remedied that situation to a certain extent. However, the majority of the deputies in the 1987 Assembly have served in the TGNA for no more than a single term (*The Album of the 18th Assembly*, 1988: 16, 23ff). Thus, it is impossible to expect the existence of a learning process through which a large group of elder statesmen instruct the incoming freshmen deputies about 'proper legislative conduct'.

Nevertheless, the current TGNA carries on with the task of re-designing its RP. In September 1985 the chairman of the constitution commission announced that the new RP had been drawn up by his commission and submitted to the Speaker's Office. Unfortunately, these proposed RP have neither been fully made public, nor successfully sailed through floor debate in the TGNA. However, the chairman of the above-mentioned commission has written an article outlining some of the basic features of the proposed RP (Coskunoğlu, 1985: 35–7). It appears from that article that basic modifications were proposed on matters pertaining to the roles of political parties and commissions.

The main goal of the commission seems to be the institution of what its chairman refers to as an 'efficient legislation process'. This could be taken as an indication of the fact that the majority party will have even more leeway in moving its legislation through the TGNA. Incidentally, the seats of the commission in question are distributed among the parliamentary parties according to the proportion of seats they control in the TGNA. Thus, it is hardly surprising that the commission chairman, who also is a member of the MP pays so much attention to speedy and efficient legislation. The interviews I conducted[13] seem to indicate that the commission chairmen, all of whom are government party deputies, tend to consider the current legislative process as cumbersome and lengthy. Nevertheless, a major change in the structure and function of the commissions and parliamentary groups seems unlikely to occur. A basic desire to avoid coalition governments and to consolidate party government in a parliamentary regime seems to be the salient concern of most commission chairmen and deputies of the ruling MP.

The result is an exclusionary model of parliamentary politics which aims at keeping minor parties out of parliamentary (yet not necessarily out of local) politics. Minor parties which are not able to obtain more than 10 per cent of the national vote are not allotted regular propaganda time on the two national TV channels and the state-run radio. The restrictions imposed on the minor parties in parliamentary politics not only reinforce their minor status, but also make them more anti-establishment and radical in their relations with Parliament and the political regime. Nor does the increased representation of the government party in the TGNA seem to nurture a milieu of accommodation between that party and the opposition. It is currently very clear that the new RP are not likely to result in a document of accord, but more a declaration of rules and norms necessary for 'efficient legislation' of government policies.

The 1983 and 1987 assemblies faced the task of establishing binding rules and norms of legislative conduct. A number of factors made this task especially difficult. In the 1983 assembly only one political party, the ruling MP, was able to survive until the 1987 national elections. Lack of structure in political parties and their parliamentary groups and the high number of deputies who switched parties enfeebled the TGNA in coping with the challenge of drawing up its RP. The extreme disproportionality between the distribution of the national vote and the seats in the TGNA among the parties and the ensuing debate on the legitimacy of the 1987 assembly further disabled it from working on its parliamentary RP.[14]

The skewed distribution of seats among the MP, the Social Democrat Populist party (SDPP) and the True Path party (TPP) has had three consequences. First of all, it has encouraged the executive to be lax in its enforcements of the legislative rituals and processes. Second, it has exacerbated tension between the governing and opposition parties which in turn tends to generate unruly legislative behaviour. Such behaviour has become more evident in the TGNA proceedings since June 1985. Third, an intense debate over the legitimacy of the current MP government has been occupying the agenda of Turkish politics ever since the national elections of 29 November 1987, and even more so after the heavy loss the MP suffered in the local elections held on 26 March 1989.

In conclusion, I would like to assert that although the 1983 Parliament has developed more stable patterns of rule-abiding legislative behaviour, it does not possess agreed rules of legislative conduct. The newly elected deputies lacked experience in national and/or parliamentarian politics (Kalaycioğlu, 1986a: 332ff). These deputies have struggled to adapt themselves to their new environment. Meanwhile, the TGNA has been under almost total control of the MP. The opposition was in disarray until the 1987 national elections. It did not have the 'numbers' to oppose the ruling party's legislative programme with much effectiveness. This does not mean that all has been plain sailing for the MP leadership. There have been rebellions by the MP backbenchers, who have succeeded in altering or halting proposed legislation. It appears, moreover, that MP leaders feel insecure, despite the fact that they hold an overwhelming majority of seats. They have been haunted by the thought that they might lose a large group of their deputies to the other major right-wing party, the True Path party (TPP). A closer scrutiny of the relationships between parliamentary parties will contribute to our understanding of the evolution of the TGNA.

The structure of parliamentary party group relations

The pre-1980 TGNA has often been noted for its disciplined political parties (Ozbudun, 1968:). Strict voting along party lines has been asserted to be the rule. However, there have been exceptions to this rule in the past, and no doubt there will be in the future. Nevertheless, most students of Turkish politics have insisted that the Turkish political culture nurtures overwhelming identification of the individual deputies with their political parties. In the past, this identification has driven party members to view the world in terms of friend versus foe (Frey, 1975: 65ff). Such a polarizing world view has been considered as one of the major causes of tension and instability in Turkish politics.

The re-organization of parties and the parliamentary groups after 1983

Turkish political parties have always had strong leaders. These leaders have ruled their parties through central committees consisting of close friends and associates. Personal, informal and close relations with these leaders have often played a critical role in determining an ambitious party member's chances of upward political mobility. However, it is also true that previous political parties (the RPP and the JP) did develop national organizations and somewhat institutionalized recruitment patterns for political office (Tunaya, 1975; Ozbudun, 1968). Some local party branches were forces to be reckoned with by the central committee. The leaders of these parties had to take powerful party factions and branches into consideration in their management of the internal affairs of their parties.

Post-1983 political parties differ from their predecessors. They operate in the absence of agreed-upon rules and traditions which regulate party affairs. The selection of candidates for political office, the resolution of conflicts among party functionaries and the management of parliamentary party groups are controlled exclusively by the central committees and/or by the leaders of most political parties. In the absence of strong and viable party organizations, a premium is placed on the personalities of leaders, and their autocratic handling of all matters concerning their political parties has become the norm (*Milliyet*, 1 June 1988: 8).

Not since 1950 have deputies' election chances been so dependent on favourable evaluations of their performance by party leaders. And not since 1950 has the power to establish party discipline in Parliament been so concentrated in the hands of party leaders. Having said this, however, not all deputies have sought re-election,[15] and of those who did, some could well win any electoral contest irrespective of their party connection.[16]

In the interim period from 1980 to 1983, the praetorian regime legally terminated and annulled all of the well-established parties including the conservative JP, and left-of-centre RPP, the religious National Salvation Party (NSP) and the ultra-nationalist and anti-communist National Action Party (NAP). The only new political parties allowed were those with 'no apparent' links with the above-mentioned old parties. The Political Parties Act (PPA) stipulates that the post-1983 political parties shall not adopt the signs, symbols and the slogans of the parties of the pre-1980 period (PPA, art. 96). Party programmes and platforms may have no reference to the actions of past political parties which might suggest that a newly founded party is the continuation of one of the parties of the old regime (PPA, art. 96). Finally, the leaders and members of the central committees of the pre-1980 parties and their members who had served in the 1977 Parliament were not permitted to run for office in the 1983 general elections (PPA, temporary art. 1). The leaders of the parties of the old regime have been banned from political activity. With these restrictions in force, only three newly founded political parties ere permitted to enter the general election of November 1983 (see Table 7.3.). All the deputies of the 1983 Parliament came from these three political parties until 1985. With the dissolution of two of the three original parties, the founding of other new parties and the by-elections of 1986, the composition of the deputies of the TGNA began to diversify. The 1987 elections led to the rearrangement of the parliamentary party groups of the TGNA. At present, three major political parties, the ruling MP, the TPP and the SDPP are represented in the TGNA (see Table 7.3).

To establish a parliamentary group means to achieve the status of a major political party. This status helps the party in question to air its views on the Turkish radio and television (TRT) regularly, to be in closer contact with the press and with the president's office. In short, any party that controls more than 20 seats in the TGNA enhances it chances for the propagation of its ideology through a variety of mass media.

The Turkish political parties are still at low levels of institutionalization. They are still in the process of getting organized nationally and establishing stable links with the electorate. The party system is still fraught with uncertainty (Erguder, 1987: Kalaycıoğlu, 1986b). This is reflected in the recent local elections, and previously in the intra-parliamentary performance of political parties, as witnessed by the heavy flow of TGNA deputies across party lines in the Spring of 1986. This flow was heavy in spite of the fact of the above-mentioned constitutional provisions against it (see above). The question arises as to whether or not, under these circumstances, the present parliamentary party groups can achieve the level of membership discipline characteristic of their performance in the pre-1980 period.

Party control and loyalty in the TGNA

The TGNA deputy is hardly a free agent. There is a considerable amount of party control over the deputy. Most important of all, his chances for re-election are closely correlated with his rank on the list of candidates that appear on the ballot. A candidate who fails to appear on the top ranks of the list of a major political party jeopardizes his chances or being elected (or re-elected). The central committees of the political parties, and in some parties particularly the leader of the party, have a great say in the placement of the names of candidates on the ballot. On some occasions the party leader personally determines who gets to head the ballot list in a certain district.

In the fall of 1984, I conducted structured interviews with 125 (out of 400) deputies of the TGNA, and again conducted a similar survey with 220 (out of 450) deputies in 1988. In addition to questions designed to probe the socio-economic backgrounds and political career patterns of the respondents, the questionnaires included questions designed to tap the political attitudes of respondents. Among the latter were a battery of questions about the attitudes of the deputies toward their respective political parties. Two unidimensional, additive scales of party loyalty of TGNA deputies were constructed on the basis of four questionnaire items,[17] one for 1984 and the other for the 1988 samples. The distribution of attitudes of party loyalty of TGNA deputies is illustrated in Figure 7.1.

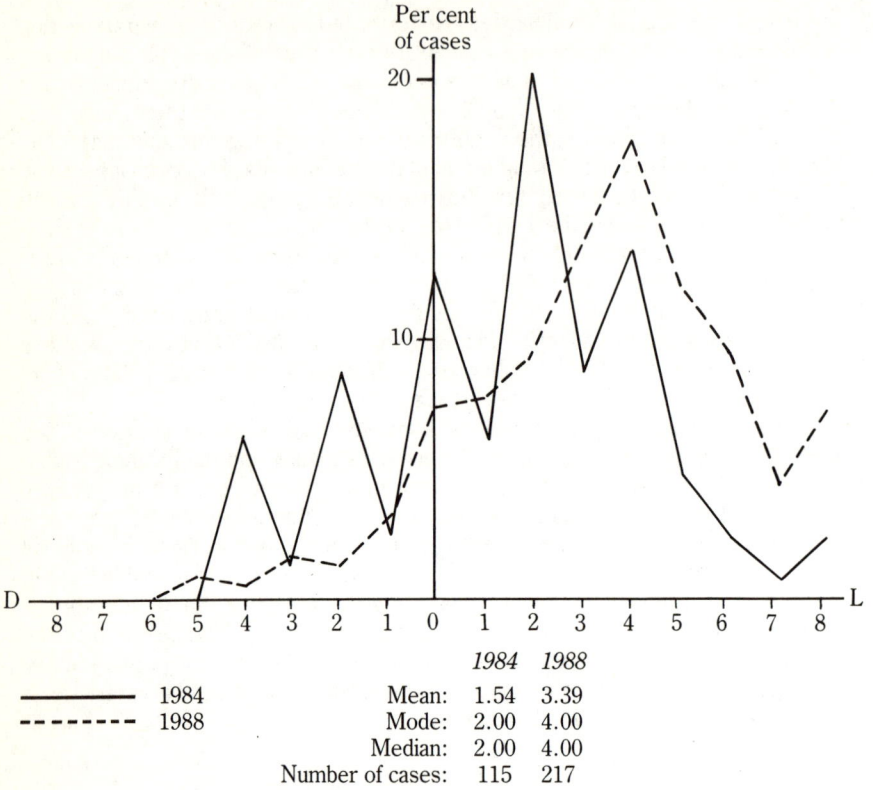

Figure 7.1 Party loyalty among the deputies of the TGNA

Note: 'D' refers to total disloyalty, and 'L' refers to total loyalty toward the party of the deputy in question. Zero refers to a point of indifference, indicating a balance of negative and positive attitudes toward the party organization, or a position of apathy toward the party.

Source: Survey data collected by the author during autumn 1984, and spring 1988

As may be observed in Figure 7.1 distributions are skewed to the left. Most deputies evince attitudes of loyalty to their political parties. However, their responses are not concentrated on the far right-hand side of the scale. This would have been the case, if they had fully identified themselves with their political parties. It is plausible to assert that as the deputies gain experience in national-level politics, and serve for longer periods in the TGNA, as well as in their party organizations, their identification with their political party (parliamentary group) increases. Their moderate party loyalty in 1984 seems to be giving way to a stronger sense of party loyalty in 1988. Further evidence for this assertion may be gleaned from the fact that, within a year of the date on which the 1984 questionnaire was collated, a number of respondents actually participated in the dissolution of their parties and joined other parties or organized new ones. It is important to note that deputies of the ruling MP

Table 7.5   Party affiliation and loyalty of the deputies, 1984 and 1988 survey results

			1984 Survey			1988 Survey		
			Political parties			Political parties		
			NDP	PP	MP	TPP	SDPP	MP
	Low	1	0.0	0.0	0.06	0.18	0.14	0.15
Party		2	0.25	0.39	0.32	0.43	0.29	0.32
loyalty		3	0.67	0.58	0.56	0.28	0.41	0.42
	High	4	0.08	0.03	0.06	0.11	0.16	0.11
			1.00	1.00	1.00	1.00	1.00	1.00
Number of Observations =			75			210		

Note: Only column percentages are reported. The party loyalty scores of the deputies presented in Figure 7.1 are converted into a four-point scale.

Source: Survey data collected by the author during autumn 1984 and spring 1988

exhibited attitudes toward their political party very similar to those evinced by deputies of the opposition parties of the time: NDP and PP in 1984 and SDPP and TPP in 1988 (see Table 7.5). Strong affiliations with their party does not appear to be characteristic of the deputies of the TGNA. This is in contrast to the feelings of party loyalty observed by Frederick W. Frey and others among the deputies who had served in the previous parliaments (Frey, 1975: 65ff; and Mardin, 1965: 384). This contrast should also be considered as another indication of the low level of institutionalization characteristic of current parliamentary parties. Nevertheless, in 1988 they are more concentrated on the right-hand side of the scale than was the case in 1984 (see Figure 7.1). This observation may be an indication of the fact that intense feelings of party loyalty and group identification are in the process of being developed by the new deputies of the TGNA. However, we can only be sure by making further surveys of the deputies in future Assemblies.

Internal conflict among the opposition parties

The lack of institutionalization is most problematic for opposition political parties. The SDPP, for example, has neither fully solved its internal problems nor was it able to establish or fully activate its local branches throughout the country until the 1987 national elections.[18] The current leader of the SDPP was only elected to serve in the TGNA during the 1986 by-elections. Meanwhile, the SDPP appears to be going through a phase of organizational consolidation. This phase will continue until the next generation of leaders takes over. The current leader of the party still resembles a caretaker figure, rather than an ambitious politician. However, the SDPP appears to be the heir to the RPP legacy, both in terms of party platform and electoral support. It is also evolving into a vocal opposition. The recent performances of that party in the last national and local elections seem to indicate that it has enough political clout to be considered as a major contender for political power in the next general elections. Nevertheless, its general convention of June 1988 demonstrated that it is ridden by different factions. The major factions fail to agree upon the basic features of party organization, management, and ideology.[19] It looks as if the SDPP will have to go through a long process of internal debate, conflict and struggle before it manages to develop a viable organization and a coherent political platform.

The True Path Party (TPP) also formed a parliamentary group in the TGNA in May of 1986. The relatively high level of organizational capability of this party is due to the fact that it inherited some of the local branches of the former JP organization. In fact, Mr Suleyman Demirel, who was leader of the JP of the 1970s, which became completely dissolved by the praetorian regime of the 1980s, has now been elected leader of the TPP in the TGNA as well. That party performed worse than public opinion polls had predicted in the national legislative elections of 29 November 1987. The TPP constitutes the third largest party group in the TGNA. It also suffers from problems of internal organization. Recent disputes between Mr Cindoruk, the ex-leader of the TPP, and Mr Demirel, its current leader, at the party convention seem to indicate that there are problems within the party organization. The ruling older generation of leaders of the TPP and the upwardly mobile younger members seem to be at odds with each other. The executive committee of the party is still dominated by the 'old guard,' who stood by Mr Demirel's side during the JP years. The younger members seem to be bent on ousting them from office, and on changing their traditional style of management. The internal conflict within the TPP between the old guard and the younger politicians is likely to continue into the near future.

In the post-1983 period the only other parliamentary group in the TGNA was the Democratic Left Party (DLP), which failed to win any parliamentary seats in the 1987 parliamentary elections. This party was established by former Prime Minister Bulent Ecevit's wife, Rahsan Ecevit, who resigned the seat of the leader of the party when her husband's political rights were re-established with the referendum of 6 September 1987. Mr Ecevit has been leading that party during election periods ever since that date. The DLP and its leader have been unable to win more than 10 per cent of the national vote to earn representation in the TGNA since the 29 November 1987 national elections.

All of these internal conflicts started in the autumn of 1986, some three years after the re-initiation of multi-party politics in 1983. Thus, it is possible to contend that the parliamentary party groups in the 1987 Parliament are still going through a transitional process of establishment and organization. However, the overall propensity toward 'law and order' among the masses, and their dislike of politicians who favour destabilization seem to hamper the development of a polarized party system within the TGNA. It is interesting to note that, in spite of the recent qualms about the legitimacy of the government aired by the opposition party leaders, the polarization of the party system has not yet materialized.

Party groups and the executive–legislative subsystem in the legislative process

Turning now to the role of the parliamentary party groups in the legislative process, one cannot help but notice the substantial control exercised by party groups over the activities of the post-1983 parliament. According to Mr Coskunoğlu, chairman of the Parliamentary Commission drafting the new rules of procedure of the TGNA, the new legislative provisions defined by the 1982 Constitution are being incorporated into the old RP, and some new procedures and practices are being codified as well. The modifications seem to be designed to speed up the legislative process which in effect only means augmenting the government party's influence on the commission proceedings and the floor debates (Coskunoğlu, 1985: 36–7). The relative importance of parliamentary party groups and of government will probably peak with the adoption of the new RP by the TGNA.[20]

Legislative activities concerning bills, questions, parliamentary inquiries, interpellations and commission assignments are determined by the relative sizes of the party groups and their relationship to government in the TGNA. The overall amount of legislative activities engaged in by deputies has diminished in the 1983–7 period as compared with past assemblies (see Table 7.6).

Table 7.6 Legislative activities in the Turkish Grand National Assembly, 1961–87

	1961–5	1965–9	1969–73	1973–7	1977–80	1983–7*
Government-sponsored bills	886	694	870	546	600	306
Other bills	884	898	922	820	951	455
Oral questions	1,087	827	245	424	375	876
Written questions	800	1,232	1,771	1,745	901	2,172
General debates on specific issues by the General Assembly	15	43	68	12	25	22
Legislative investigations	50	12	21	176	98	7
Legislative inquiries	23	53	125	173	89	63
Interpellations	5	84	23	6	60	3

Note: About 80 per cent of the government-sponsored bills are adopted by the TGNA. Actually, of the 306 government-sponsored bills 255 (83 per cent) have already been adopted by the current TGNA. Moreover, about 36 per cent of these were proposed by the deputies of the majority party. The same percentage is 21.8 for the non-government-sponsored bills, in the 1983 Parliament.

*   The figures for this column are my calculation on the basis of information provided by the TGNA Office of Legal Acts and Resolutions, and *Minutes of the 17th Assembly*, v. 26–43. The data on bills are missing for 1987. I would like to thank Mr Omer Faruk Gençkaya, a graduate assistant at Boğaziçi University, Department of Political Science, who compiled the above data and who was kind enough to permit me to use them.

Source: Ezherli, Ihsan (1986). *Turkiye Buyuk Millet Meclisi (Turkish Grand National Assembly): 1920–1986*, Ankara, TGNA Publications, No: 10, 114–16

Legislative bills

According to the 1982 Constitution and the RP a deputy may draft and propose the adoption of a bill by the General Assembly of the TGNA on his own initiative. However, it appears that no bill of major consequence to government has so far been drafted and/or proposed to the General Assembly in this manner. It is also true that the opposition has not proposed any bills of consequence that have been adopted by the General Assembly. In fact, with the exception of bills supported by powerful cliques within the ruling MP, (i.e. the Alcoholic Beverages Act of 1984, which prohibits advertisements by the media of alcoholic beverages, including beer), bills not initiated by and/or in support of government have rarely been adopted. There have been cases of multi-partisan support for bills pertaining to public services and goods, but such support is exceptional.[21] The great majority of the bills so far adopted by the General Assembly are sponsored by the government. Furthermore, the number of draft bills proposed by the government or individual deputies is at its lowest ebb since the inception of the multi-party era in 1946. In the period between November 1983 and March 1986, a total of 532 prospective bills were tabled in the TGNA. The same figure is 551 for June 1977 to 12 September 1980, which is often alluded to as a period of parliamentary paralysis in Turkey. Between 1961 and 1980, the number of bills tabled in each four-year session of the TGNA never dropped below 1,500 (Ezherli, 1986: 114–16). We have thus a clear indication that the MP government is not inclined to use the facilities of the TGNA in the law-making process.

Finally, the findings of my 1984 study suggest that most deputies are concerned with the highly diffuse political issues such as inflation or unemployment. Very few of the deputies interviewed had specific solutions to those problems that they perceived as the most important for their constituents (see Table 7.7). It is significant in this regard that seniority and/or lengthy exposure to constituency feedback are characteristic of those deputies who have proposed bills in the 1983 parliament.

Table 7.7   Actions undertaken by deputies to solve the most urgent constituency problems, 1984 (%)

Type of action	Participating deputies
Initiated no action	23.0
Has been pondering a suitable course of action	50.4
Drafted bills (not submitted)	3.5
Drafted bills (already submitted)	0.9
Contacted central bureaucracy	5.3
Contacted local government	2.7
Contacted local party organization	0.9
Contacted ministers	6.2
Other	7.1
Total	100.0

Source: Survey data collected by the author during autumn 1984

Measures of legislative control

While not all deputies are capable of drafting bills, an activity which requires technical knowledge which they may neither possess nor have access to, all deputies can address questions to ministers and/or the prime minister. Of all their duties this is the easiest to fulfil. Unlike drafting bills, framing questions requires a minimum of technical and/or legal knowledge. Hence, there is a tendency for deputies to point to the questions they have asked and the answers of ministers to these questions, especially if these appear in daily newspapers, as evidence of their concern for the problems and issues of their constituents. However, oral and written questions are almost exclusively posed by the opposition party deputies on the floor. Government party deputies conduct similar acts in the party group meetings, where opposition deputies are not present. Traditionally, it is accepted that posing questions to cabinet ministers by government party members during the floor debates undermines party solidarity and discipline.[22]

In the 1970s, the signatures of 10 deputies were sufficient to bring a motion of interpellation to the floor of the TGNA. Past opposition parties systematically harassed governments by tabling one motion of interpellation after another. It appears that the framers of the present Constitution took pains to insure that making such motions should be as difficult as possible. As a consequence of the new legal restrictions, the power to move interpellation has been effectively removed from individual deputies and placed in the hands of parliamentary party groups. Since the current Constitution does not permit an individual deputy to move interpellation or initiate parliamentary investigations. It stipulates that 'a motion for interpellation may be tabled either on behalf of a political party group, or by the signatures of at least twenty deputies' (art. 99). A consequence of these provisions is that it is now easier for the government to blame the opposition for legislative impasse in the event that they again resort to such methods of harassment as mentioned above.

In the 1961–80 period a single deputy could introduce a motion for a parliamentary investigation of any member of the cabinet. Now, the required number of signatories for such a motion is one-tenth of the total number of deputies. In the pre-1980 period, motions for parliamentary investigation were frequently made to forestall legislation proposed by government. To root out this practice, the 1982 Constitution has made it more difficult for individual deputies to table motions for parliamentary investigation. However, this is not a domain completely dominated by the opposition deputies. One cabinet minister was ousted from office after a parliamentary investigation supported by the majority of party deputies, including even the prime minister.

A motion for general debate may be tabled by a parliamentary group or by at least 10 deputies. Such a motion is immediately entered on the list of incoming applications to the speaker's office and circulated. The promptness in the handling of such motions has made them more appealing to opposition deputies of the post-1983 Parliaments.

Executive supremacy

The leadership of the parliamentary party group of the TGNA cannot be sharply distinguished either from the leadership of the extra-parliamentary party organization or from the top executive, (except for the civil servants), if the party group in question is in government. Consequently, the government (through its majority backing in the TGNA, and the overlap of party leadership across the two branches of government) has a considerable amount of control over the legislative process in the post-1983 Parliament.

In fact, the MP governments have so much control over the legislative process that they have managed to thwart efforts to debate their economic and other policy steps on the floor of the TGNA. They have also managed the legislative process by appealing to Article 91 of the 1982 Constitution which enables the government to request authorization to issue decrees having the force of law. The purposes, scope, principles and the operative period of such decrees having the force of law need to be specified by the TGNA, though once published in the *Official Gazette* they must be referred to the TGNA for approval. In spite of its majority, the MP governments have had considerable difficulty in procuring the support of the TGNA commissions (see Table 7.8). As a matter of fact, only 32 per cent of the decrees having force of law that were referred to the TGNA commissions were adopted by them. The rest were still being considered in 1987 at the end of the term of the 17th Assembly. Thus, it seems as if the government circumvents the legislative process, even though it is relatively easy for it to push its proposed bills through the parliamentary process (see Table 7.8). In effect, this has meant that the government has been able to avoid the necessity of working through commissions and subjecting every feature of its bills to debate on the floor of the TGNA, presenting Parliament instead with a *fait accompli*. What this amounts to is the government's safe bet on the partisan support of its majority in the TGNA on the one hand, and on the considerable amount of autonomy from legislative control on the other. Hence, executive action gains precedence over the legislative in making major socio-political adjustments. By means of governmental decrees issued systematically over the last five years, the MP governments have made some drastic changes in the Turkish economy.

Autonomous contributions of the TGNA to the political process were neither intended nor envisaged by the framers of the 1982 Constitution. The Constitution and the RP of the TGNA inhibited autonomous action by the legislators, while encouraging autonomous executive action. This is not by accident. The framers of the current Constitution believed that necessary executive actions had been unduly frustrated by the provisions of the 1961 Constitution (Heper, 1986; Kalaycioğlu, 1988: 59–61).

Finally, the disarray of opposition parties further enabled the MP governments to ignore their presence in the TGNA, until the March 1989 local elections in which the MP suffered a heavy loss, and where there was no single winner. In conclusion, it appears that the institutionalization process which the new political parties of the post-1983 period are going through has reached a new stage. However, it is too early to make any predictions about how the

Table 7.8 Governmental decrees having force of law, government-sponsored and other bills in the TGNA, 1983–7

Sessions	Governmental decrees having force of law			Government-sponsored bills			Non-government sponsored bills		
	Submitted	Adopted	% adopted	Submitted	Adopted	% adopted	Submitted	Adopted	% adopted
1983–4	163	51	0.31	66	62	0.94	137	37	0.27
1984–5	8	4	0.50	105	91	0.87	118	26	0.22
1985–6	8	6	0.75	70	57	0.81	82	28	0.34
1986–7	23	4	0.17	66	46	0.70	118	31	0.26
Total (1983–7)	202	65	0.32	306	255	0.83	455	122	0.27

Notes: The first colum of the table indicates the total number of bills submitted to the office of the speaker during the corresponding session. The second column indicates the number of bills completely processed and adopted by the TGNA as law. The third column refers to the percentage of the adopted bills to the submitted.

Source: *Bulletins of the TGNA Commissions*, (I–VIII), (Official Publication of the TGNA). Mr Omer Faruk Gençkaya, a graduate assistant at Boğaziçi University, Department of Political Science, compiled the above data and was kind enough to permit me to use them.

executive supremacy over the legislature will be affected from the recent developments in electoral behaviour and party structuring.

The commission structure and activity in the TGNA

If legislatures are to be classified as either plenary bodies or committee-orientated institutions (Rockman, 1984: 409), (the British and French Parliaments exemplifying the former and the West German Bundestag the latter), the TGNA falls within the former category.

The composition and activities of the commissions of the TGNA reinforce executive supremacy over the legislature. Almost every ministry has a matching standing commission in the TGNA. As the number and functions of ministries have changed, so have the number and scope of commission activities. However, the structure of the TGNA has also determined the number of commissions (Karamustafaoğlu, 1965: 189; Ozbudun, 1986: 255). The bicameral structure of the pre-1980 TGNA hosted a total of eleven commissions in the National Assembly (the lower house), and twelve similar commissions in the senate, and three joint commissions during most of the 1961–80 period. In contrast, the current unicameral TGNA has fourteen commissions.

There are a few commissions which have been organized to investigate and/or oversee the activities of more than one ministry (the public works, reconstruction, transportation and tourism commission is one example of this type). However, most commissions have less diffuse policy areas, (such as defence; foreign policy; or health and social welfare etc.). Finally, there is a commission which has been established to investigate and control the accounts of the TGNA. Other, non-financial affairs of the TGNA are managed by the speaker and his advisory council (RP, arts. 20,36).

Members are elected to their respective commissions by the TGNA for a period of two years. The number of members assigned to each commission is determined by the speaker in accordance with the relative strength of each party group. Each party group selects its own list of candidates for each commission and submits this list to the speaker. The candidates are then elected by the General Assembly. No political party may submit more candidates than its quota allows. The rule is that the government party (or coalition) occupies the majority of the seats in each commission. The General Assembly has traditionally followed plebiscitary means of adopting the submitted lists of candidates. During its first meeting each commission elects its chairperson, vice-chairperson, reporter and a secretary by a simple majority vote. Consequently, it is not surprising to discover that all the positions in all the commissions are occupied by members of the ruling MP (RP, arts. 21–36).

Upon close observation it becomes clear that the assignment of deputies to commissions is not based on considerations of seniority. The commission members have generally not been selected on the basis of their previous experience in Parliament (see Table 7.9), nor has previous service in the same commission been a criterion of selection (see Tables 7.10, 7.11). However,

Table 7.9   Expertise and seniority of commission members in the TGNA, 1983–8 (%)

Commission	Members with relevant occupations			Members with previous legislative experience		
	1983	1986	1988	1983	1986	1988
Justice	95.2	95.2	91.3	0.0	0.0	34.7
Constitution	100.0	90.5	86.9	14.3	19.0	56.5
Public works, construction, transportation and tourism	90.4	95.2	91.3	0.0	4.8	13.4
Foreign affairs	47.6	66.6	34.7	14.3	14.3	60.8
Interior affairs	57.1	42.9	69.6	4.8	0.0	17.4
State economic enterprises	74.3	68.6	77.1	2.9	2.9	48.5
National education	85.7	80.9	52.1	4.8	4.8	17.4
National defence	80.9	76.2	30.4	4.8	9.5	52.2
The Economic Plan and the budget	87.5	85.0	87.5	2.5	7.5	50.0
Health and social services	80.9	80.9	86.9	0.0	0.0	26.1
Industry, technology and commerce	90.5	90.5	82.6	14.3	4.8	21.7
Auditing of the governmental expenditures	53.3	80.0	–	6.6	0.0	–
Agriculture, forestry, and village affairs	76.2	80.9	69.6	4.8	0.0	26.1
Petitions	*	*	*	–	–	25.0
Accounts of the TGNA	72.7	63.6	90.9	9.1	9.1	90.9

Note: The relevant occupations of the commission members were determined according to their pre-legislative vocations. For example, for the Justice Commission lawyers were considered as those members with relevant occupations.

– = Missing data

* = Relevant occupation does not make sense for this commission

Source: Calculated by the author using data provided in the *TGNA Documents on Commission Assignments* (1983, 1986, 1988)

occupational expertise plays a major role in recruitment for such positions (see Tables 7.9 and 7.11). This does not mean, however, that most commission members are specialists. In fact, the proportion of 'non-experts' in some commissions is high, (for example, the foreign affairs and the internal affairs commissions). The majority party group seems to evince a preference for assigning non-experts to some commissions. There appear to be commissions which the government expects to make rapid decisions on drafts it has proposed. The rationale seems to be that non-experts are less likely to debate details and attempt to modify the content of drafts. This understanding is predicated on the assumption that commission members will cast their votes along party lines. That votes are cast like this in the great majority of cases cannot be doubted. However, we do not yet possess hard evidence as to the frequency of exceptions to this rule.[23]

Commissions organized to investigate and control specific policy matters are usually in close contact with their corresponding ministries and executive agencies (Karamustafaoğlu, 1965: 151–2). The prime minister and other

Table 7.10 The turnover rates in the commissions of the TGNA, 1964–87 (%)*

Commission on	1986–7	1983–7	1983–6	1975–83	1971–5	1967–71	1964–7
Justice	74	83	52	100	96	86	84
Constitution	83	78	43	95	96	86	88
Public works, construction, transportation, and tourism	91	91	52	100	100	100	95
Foreign affairs	74	78	52	95	93	100	84
Interior affairs	91	87	52	100	100	95	88
State economic enterprises	83	83	57	–	–	–	–
National education	100	100	38	100	96	81	84
National defence	87	91	43	100	96	85	80
Economic Plan and budget	78	85	55	98	91	94	89
Health and social services	78	78	43	100	96	86	80
Industry, technology and commerce	91	91	52	100	96	100	86
Auditing of the governmental expenditures	–	–	93	–	–	95	90
Agriculture, forestry and village affairs	87	87	62	100	43	86	84
Petitions	100	94	–	–	–	–	–
Accounts of the TGNA	91	–	–	–	–	–	–

* Percentages of those who lost their seats are reported
– Incomplete information

Source: Calculated by the author using data provided in the *TGNA Documents on Commission Assignments* (1967, 1971, 1975, 1983, 1986, 1988)

Table 7.11 Turnover rates of the administrative positions in the commissions of the TGNA, 1964–87 (%)

Changes among commission	Proportion of change						
	1986–7	1983–7	1983–6	1975–83	1971–5	1967–71	1964–7
1. Chairpersons	71	71	20	100	100	86	94
2. Vice-chairpersons	79	79	53	100	100	95	94
3. Reporters	86	93	60	100	100	95	100
4. Secretaries	86	86	47	100	100	100	94

Note: Every newly elected National Assembly selects standing commissions for a period of three years. At the end of the third year (session), (in the pre-1980 Parliaments at the end of every second year), new commission elections are held, and the commission assignments of the members are either renewed or cancelled. After the second round of elections the standing commissions serve for a period of two years, or until the next national parliamentary elections.

Source: Calculated by the author using data provided in the *TGNA Documents on Commission Assignments* (1967, 1971, 1975, 1983, 1986, 1988)

ministers of his cabinet are permitted to participate in the commission meetings. Commission chairmen are authorized to demand information from the related executive agency(ies) and executive agency representatives may be invited to testify before their commissions. There is no clarity in the RP about the sanctions that the commission may impose on non-cooperative executive agency heads.[24] Non-member deputies of the TGNA are allowed to sit in on the 'public' sessions of commissions, but the commission may elect to hold closed sessions whenever deemed appropriate. Only Cabinet Ministers may participate in closed sessions; other 'outsiders'. deputies of the TGNA or not, are excluded (RP, art. 32).

Commissions are charged not only with investigation but also with legislation. Drafts of bills are referred to the appropriate commissions. The commissions decide on the substance of drafts and must present their resolutions and reports to the General Assembly within 45 days. A commission member may elect to abstain from a decision rendered by the commission in its report, in which case the member in question is permitted to state his objections during the floor debates. However, an abstaining member may not raise any objections to the report other than those he has filed in advance of the floor debates.

Multi-party support for legislation is rare. It occurs either in respect of matters perceived as truly national by all political parties concerned (for example the declaration of war or martial law in times of severe political instability), or in respect of issues perceived to be devoid of electoral consequences (a bill that changed the name of a Faculty of Istanbul University attracted multi-party support in 1986, and a recent resolution of the TGNA to conduct an inquiry into the ecological problems of Turkey was made possible by the non-partisan support of both the majority and minority party groups in 1988).

It is again worth emphasizing that all commissions are dominated by ruling party deputies. It is hardly surprising then that the substance of commission reports usually reflects the policy stands of the majority party group which in turn coincides with the policy preferences of the government. Should commission reports contradict the policy preferences of the majority party group, the General Assembly may refer them back to the commission. Nevertheless, in practice commission reports are usually adopted by the General Assembly. In only minor cases are they withdrawn by the commission chairperson, who is always a member of the majority party, or revised by the General Assembly. Systematic and routine conflict between a commission and the General Assembly has not occurred in the post-1946 era.

The autonomy of the commissions is considerably circumscribed by the parliamentary party groups. However, the smaller sizes of the commissions in comparison to the General Assembly, and the frequent interactions of its members enable individual members of party groups to make a greater contribution to the legislative process than would otherwise be possible. Political party groups seem to be more open to negotiation, and perhaps even to some compromise during commission proceedings. Commission meetings are not disrupted by unruly behaviour of members. This may be partly because commission proceedings are rarely reported by the media. The legislative behaviour exhibited in the privacy of commission debates on matters of expertise differs from that manifested in the more public debates of the General Assembly.

The commission chairpersons, are usually ministerial hopefuls. They do not refrain from contradicting the cabinet ministers, who are their rivals. However, unless they have strong ideological or other reasons, they seem to try to avoid getting into conflict with the whole cabinet and/or the prime minister. On matters concerning higher education and economic corruption, such as 'fictitious exporting',[25] the commission chairpersons did not shun public announcements that ran counter to preferences of the cabinet ministers involved in the issues, in the 1987 Parliament.

Two conclusions may be drawn from our examination of the TGNA commissions. One is that TGNA commissions exhibit a concern for expertise, but there is no hard evidence that this raises them above partisan relations in the TGNA. Second, in the TGNA neither commissions nor their members are accorded that special status which their counterparts in the United States Congress or the German Bundestag enjoy. I would like to add that I do not believe that the present or any future Turkish government will favour efforts to transform the TGNA into a 'committee-orientated legislature'. Such a change could lead to a reduction in executive control over the legislative process. It is not only the case that the ruling elites are for 'strong government' in the 1980s, but it should not be forgotten that the authors of the 1982 Constitution did their best to minimize constraints on the executive.

The legislative–executive subsystem in Turkey

Current executive–legislative relations seem to indicate a proclivity toward executive initiative and autonomy. Both the floor activities and commission work are dominated by the majority party group, which in turn is under almost full control of the party leader and his close associates. The latter are both deputies of the TGNA and members of the central committee of the party. Consequently, the decision-making locus has shifted to the executive, which exerts its influence over the legislative process as long as the group discipline of the majority group is maintained. The high approval rates of the government-sponsored bills, and very low levels of deputy input in the legislative process are indicative of the fact that the TGNA after 1983 has veered towards what Weinbaum called a 'subordinate' type of legislature (1975: 37–9). Nevertheless, it is still not very clear that the TGNA will evolve into a typical example of a subordinate assembly. A few cases of back-bench uprisings and even rarer cases of across-party agreements over issues like ecology and corruption have enabled the TGNA to delay, abort or terminate legislation. The *ad hoc* TGNA commission set up to investigate ecological problems hosts both government and opposition deputies. In April 1989, the TGNA decided to adopt a resolution tabled by opposition party deputies to inquire into the assertions of corruption in tax rebates paid to private companies who failed to provide proof of the economic activities that qualified them for tax breaks. Hence, it is yet uncertain whether in the 1990s the TGNA will evolve toward what Weinbaum called the 'coordinate' or continue being a 'subordinate' type of Assembly (1975: 35–9).

Government stability and the increasing need to accommodate the differences between the parliamentary party groups may pave the way for a coordinate assembly, which holds the cabinet responsible not only in form but also in substance to its partisan majority (ibid: 36). The lengthening of legislative tenure and a concomitant drop in the turnover rate of the seats of the TGNA are likely to enhance the role that deputies play in the legislative process, especially in such positions as the commission chairpersons. Chairpersons with occupational expertise and parliamentary experience seem to be developing a practice of increasing their input in the legislative process. In short, the current legislative–executive relations in Turkey are still in flux, and it is still uncertain into what type of a legislative system the TGNA will grow. The two likely candidates are the subordinate and the coordinate types of legislatures.

Linkages with the constituents: trends involving other environmental relations

If legislative–executive relationships constitute one major linkage between the legislative system and its environments, the interactions between the individual legislators and their constituents comprise the other. Simply labelled as 'representation', the relationship between a legislator (representative) and his constituents (represented) is a major concern of the 'theory of democracy' on the one hand, and systematic analyses of pluralist political systems on the other (Pitkin, 1967: 3–19; Wahlke, 1971: 142). Below, a brief analysis of the inter-actions between the TGNA deputies and their constituents will be attempted.

The relationship between the TGNA deputies and their constituents may be examined through an empirical analysis of the dimensions of the representational

linkage. Such an endeavour would require a scrutiny of the policy responsiveness, service and distributive responsiveness of the representatives and the
legislative system, and those outputs of the legislative system that engender
public support for it (Wahlke, 1971: 142ff; Eulau and Karps, 1977: 233–8;
Patterson *et al* 1975; Kuklinski, 1979: 121–40; Jewell, 1983: 303–37). The
limits of this chapter do not permit me to analyse fully the representative
linkage between the TGNA deputies and their constituents. Furthermore, the
support-engendering activities of the deputies of the current TGNA are very
hard to observe in the absence of any systematically collected empirical data.
Hence, I wish to focus on the role that the deputies of the TGNA play *vis-à-vis*
their constituents, interest groups and political parties.[26]

The 1983 assembly gave the impression that the relationship between the
constituents and their legislators is devoid of organized channels or intermediary
structures that regularly process demands that are conveyed to the deputies.
The relationship between the TGNA deputies and their constituents is best
characterized as personal and proximal. About three-quarters of the deputies
contend that they personally meet more than 25 constituents per working day,
while the TGNA is in session in Ankara, and many more when they go and visit
their constituencies. About 70 per cent of the deputies who participated in both
the 1984 and 1988 studies indicated that they spend more than half their time
dealing with the personal problems of their constituents. Most of these
contacts seem to involve face-to-face meetings. Some constituents spend
several days trying to contact their deputies personally. Only a small percentage
of the constituents seem to go to the trouble of making an appointment with the
deputies. Constituents use such media as telephones or letters just to check on
ow their deputies are handling their previously made personal demands or
complaints with the public bureaucracy.

Constituents tend to choose to establish contacts with those deputies whom
they think are somehow acquainted with them. The substance of such
acquaintance is usually a blood tie, or living in the same provincial or
subprovincial district where the deputy was born and raised and/or the deputy's
family actually comes from. The latter is called *hemsehrilik* in Turkish, and it
provides a tie between individuals only less than a blood tie (Dubetsky, 1976:
433–51; Heper, 1983: 65–7). Often people with proximal ties, (such as close
relatives or friends) are employed to establish the first contact between the
constituent and the deputy. The intermediary usually does this service out of
hemsehrilik, (or a sense of belonging to the same locale), or some other close
tie, such as a blood tie or peer group solidarity. The intermediary's main
function is to introduce the individual constituent as a respectful member of the
community, a good citizen residing in the deputy's district. His lineage
relationships, the extended family he belongs to and his previous political
activities (if he has any) are often referred to in the introductory remarks.
From then on, the constituent is usually on his own. He usually continues his
contacts with the deputy until he is satisfied with the way his 'case' has been
handled by the deputy in question.

The substance of the demands conveyed to the TGNA deputies are usually
particular, personal problems of the individual citizen. These range from help
with job applications, transfers and promotions in the public or local bureaucracy

to hospitalization of a rural constituent in Ankara. The most frequent constituency demand is for a job. The deputy is often contacted to solve a problem associated with a certain member of the public bureaucracy back home. He occasionally receives complaints about local or public bureaucrats. More frequently, a deputy is asked to facilitate the bureaucratic procedures concerning a particular appeal or petition of his constituents. Finally, deputies are also pressed to help their districts to procure some infrastructural investments, such as electrification of some villages, irrigation projects, metalled roads etc.

It seems as if the deputy is perceived as a barrister who defends the rights of his constituents against the state bureaucracy, and also solves the special personal problems of the individual members of his constituency. No serious attempts have so far been made to facilitate contacts between the legislators and their constituents in Turkey. No intermediary mechanisms, such as local party offices, or interest associations seem to be established to process constituency demands systematically.

Nevertheless, the local party bosses are a major source of political demands. Their efforts in conveying demands and playing the role of intermediaries between the voters and the deputies increase in magnitude and variety in rural districts. The local party leaders of the larger cities and the metropolitan areas do not frequent the offices of the TGNA deputies. They tend to establish contacts directly with either the cabinet ministers or with the top-level civil servants, without the intermediation of the TGNA deputies.

Interest associations tend to contact the public bureaucracy or the members of the cabinet directly, usually circumventing the TGNA deputies. Relationships between the interest associations and the TGNA deputies are sparce. Commission chairpersons and vice-chairpersons, as well as the prominent members of the commissions, contend that they are lobbied by such organized groups as the Turkish Bar Association, the Turkish Chamber of Medicine, trade unions etc. Similar contacts also tend to occur between the interest group representatives and the speaker of the TGNA. However, they all are quite infrequent and irregular, suggesting that the interest associations do not perceive the TGNA to be an indispensable locus of political decision-making. They only contact legislators when bills they consider to be very 'critical' for their members or associations are taken up by the TGNA. I was unable to find any evidence which indicated that the interest groups pressure the TGNA deputies for new legislation. They tend to pressure the government or the public bureaucracy, which in turn pushes the necessary legislation through the regular legislative channels, or promulgates governmental decrees having force of law. TGNA deputies are not considered to be powerful enough to exert any major influence independent of government. This is hardly surprising when one recalls the executive–legislative relationship I have tried to describe in the previous section of this chapter.

Due to the ostentatious control of the political party leadership over them, TGNA deputies have to play the role of 'partymen'. Constituency service activities and party orientated actions of the deputies occur at two different levels, and they almost never come into conflict. When and if such a conflict arises, most of the deputies who were interviewed contended that they would rather act according to the dictum of the party than bow to the pressure of the constituents.

Consequently, the linkage between constituents and representatives seems to be devoid of substance that may enable the TGNA deputies to contribute to policy formation. Policies are made under the supervision or predominance of the governing party elite, who share political power with the high-level bureaucrats of the Turkish public bureaucracy. The TGNA and individual deputies make a relatively greater contribution to policy evaluation (or control of government), rather than to policy formulation. Pork barrel policies of the TGNA deputies may have an impact on government policy only in the long run, with the cumulation of specific decisions to allocate resources in favour of some districts. However, such activities are neither systematically designed nor checked by the governments or the government party elites.

We have no recent data about the impact of the TGNA and of its deputies on public support for the current Turkish legislative system. There are indications that suggest that there was a great deal of support for it in the past (Kalaycioğlu, 1980: 125ff). Therefore, it is quite hard to reach a sophisticated conclusion about the representational linkages of the TGNA with its environment. Nevertheless, it seems as if the constituents value their access to the TGNA, and they would not welcome the severance of this link, through which they push their demands and defend their interests. Consequently, it is quite tenable to assert that the TGNA's chances for survival are further enhanced by these public expectations (Kalaycioğlu, 1980: 123–39).

Conclusion: submissive assembly and nascent institutionalization

TGNA entered a new phase of its entrenchment in 1983. This new phase was entered upon against the background of the deep discord, the unruly legislative behaviour and the periodic suspensions of legislative activities. After the introduction of multi-party politics in 1946, elite consensus concerning the image of the 'Good Society and Polity', the rules of the political game and the role of the TGNA in the political regime broke down. Since 1950, the TGNA has been embroiled in political dissent over all these basic rules, norms and goals. The high rate of turnover in parliamentary seats has handicapped past political leaders in their efforts to fashion a binding set of rules for legislative conduct. Until 1980, the absence of binding rules has been the occasion for waves of unruly legislative behaviour in the TGNA which have accompanied periodically mounting political tension and environmental stress.

Since 1950, the TGNA has been more or less an appendage of the parliamentary party groups. Political leaders from the majority parties have both headed their parties and occupied top executive positions in the government. Meanwhile, government parties have been disciplined organizations which, under the strict control of these leaders and central committees, have controlled both the legislative and executive branches of government. Operating in the absence of internalized rules regulating executive–legislative relationships, there has been little chance for the legislature to achieve a significant measure of autonomy *vis-à-vis* the political parties. Under present circumstances of a highly majoritarian electoral system favouring the biggest party, the legislature is likely to remain subordinate to the influence of the governing party or coalition.

The rupture which the 'Political Parties Act' introduced into the Turkish party system in 1983 has diminished the influence of the older generation of political party elite in the 1983 Parliament. Furthermore, the distinct distaste of the voters for increased tension and polarization in politics is so perceptible that the older generation of politicians had to refashion their style of exacerbated, polarized conflict and look and sound much more moderate than they used to. A new, younger and more pragmatic and less ideologized generation of politicians has moved into Turkish politics. However, the old guard, such as ex-Prime Ministers Demirel and Ecevit are still around and challenging the younger generation of politicians. Nevertheless, the younger and pragmatic politicians who have started to control two out of the three major parties in the TGNA may prove to be more successful in consolidating Turkish democracy.

Commission activities in the post-1983 TGNA continue to be dominated by the parliamentary party groups, and especially the majority party. Not surprisingly, there is hardly any evidence to indicate that commission decisions will become more independent from the policies of the government and of the majority party group in the Parliament. Only growing expertise and specialization of the TGNA deputies, perhaps accompanied by a rising importance of functional representational linkages instead of regional/territorial ones may contribute to the political importance of the standing commissions of the TGNA, especially in the process of legislation.

The Turkish experience with democratic consolidation and parliamentary institutionalization has so far followed a cyclical pattern. In fact, the TGNA pre-dates the Turkish era of multi-party politics. Throughout the one-party epoch of 1923–46 the TGNA started to demonstrate signs of institutional rigour and viability. However, the multi-party era especially after 1950 has, in fact, hindered rather than encouraged its institutionalization. Two military coups and one intervention in civilian politics in-between brought along disruptions in the establishment of stable patterns of interactions among the major actors in the TGNA. The post-1983 Parliament is an end-product of quite a popular praetorian regime that did away with a paralysed Parliament in 1980 and established a new Constitution, with the clear intention of redesigning the political regime of the country. An elaborate screening procedure was followed to enable a tremendous turnover of TGNA deputies during the 1983 national elections. Hence, it is quite appropriate to argue that the 1983 Parliament has restarted the institutionalization process of the TGNA almost from scratch.

The scarcity of senior deputies, the overwhelming control by the party leaders and executive committees of the procedures of the TGNA, the lack of knowledge about even the established practices of the previous Turkish parliaments among the TGNA deputies of especially the 1983 Parliament, the lack of legislative autonomy of executive control and the absence of principles and norms that constrain the executive in its interactions with the legislative branch of government are all indicators of the nascent institutionalization and the submissive nature of the post-1983 TGNA.

I have tried to draw as clear a picture of the initial stages of the institutionalization process of the post-1983 TGNA as possible. Being a very slow process, the institutionalization of the TGNA may take many more decades to develop into a stable pattern of its own. Nevertheless, I wish to conclude that the institution of the TGNA will not gain value and stability and hence the consolidation of democracy will not be achieved until the Turkish political elites agree upon the norms that guide legislative conduct and the interactions between the legislative and the executive branches of government in both the Turkish political system on the one hand, and the fundamental aspects of a democratic regime, such as electoral laws or a system of interest representation, on the other.

Notes

1. The term 'state elites' is used by Metin Heper to refer especially to the military commanders and civilian bureaucrats who perceive their mission in life as guarding the welfare of the Turkish State (Heper, 1985).
2. In the late sixties and throughout the seventies more people started to take part in a variety of activities that enabled them to influence political decisions. The number of voluntary associations soared, as did their memberships (Yucekok, 1972; Bianchi, 1984: 155–66). Not only conventional channels of political participation such as voting, electoral campaign activity, contacting bureaucrats (Kalaycioğlu, 1983: 85–442). but protest participation began to be practiced by more people, more regularly and throughout the country (Ergil, 1980: 104–67). Such pathological forms of protest participation as assassinations, bombings, political kidnappings etc. also emerged and constituted a stable pattern by late seventies, leading to about 25 murders per day by 1980.
   A high death toll due to acts of political violence, estimated to be around 5,500 for the 1970–80 period, has engendered a search for 'law and order' among Turkish citizens. They were ready to accept any multi-party regime that did not incorporate a slant toward the 'bloody seventies'. (*ANAP Seçmen Araştirmasi Raporu* (MP Report on Electoral Behaviour (1987): 5).
3. Election and participation studies of the Turkish electorate clearly indicate that they prefer a multi-party regime to a partyless or one-party regime. The memories of the pre-1946 years of one-party rule are still fresh, and praetorian regimes are considered as temporary solutions for seemingly insoluble political problems (Erguder, 1987: 22; Sunar and Sayari, 1986: 177–86).
4. The final version of the 1982 Constitution was voted on by the five-member praetorian National Security Council (NSC), incumbents of which were the chief of military staff and the commanders of the army, navy, air force and the gendarmerie. A Consultative Assembly was set up by the NSC to 'advise this body' on the drawing up of the Constitution. Hence, the latter was not a Constitutional Assembly, neither did it possess any legislative power. The Constitution was initially drawn up by the Consultative Assembly, whose members were not popularly elected but appointed by the NSC. The draft of the Constitution was submitted to the NSC, which deliberated and adopted it, with some modifications, in 1982 (For a more detailed description of the process see Ozbudun, 1986: 31–5). Finally, the last version of the Constitution was popularly agreed through a referendum held in the autumn of 1982. About 90 per cent of the electorate participated in the referendum and about 92 per cent of them approved the 1982

Constitution. Consequently, there was very little impact on the 1982 Constitution by the politicians of the post-1983 multi-party era who were excluded from the Constitution-making process by the NSC (Sunar and Sayari, 1986: 184–6).

5. Various views on what to change in the 1961 Constitution had been aired prior to the praetorian intermission in the multi-party era. However, none of those who proposed drastic changes in the amended form of the 1961 Constitution were clearly identified with an interest group. Those who favoured changing the executive branch of government were more conservative members of the Turkish academia, and some bureaucrats with connections with the praetorian elite. Leading figures of the RPP and academicians with left-of-centre views defended the status quo, namely the 1961 Constitution. The constitution-writing process is somewhat vague (Balcigil, 1982).

6. It is interesting to note that Turkey had a new electoral procedure before every major election in the last five years. The governing Motherland Party revised the electoral laws before every election. This development has caused an uproar from the opposition parties, and the row is still continuing. One thing is certain, the governing party and the opposition parties have different ideas about the 'proper' electoral laws of the country.

7. The 1970s constitute a period of coalition politics which was rife with governmental instability and political violence. The lack of ability of coalition governments to cope with the challenges of the economy and society has given coalition a bad reputation in Turkey.

8. The current electoral law is designed to create majorities in the TGNA from the votes of the political party that receives a small plurality of the vote. The MP was able to obtain 64 per cent of the seats in the TGNA, as opposed to the 36 per cent of the national vote it was able to procure. First of all, a national threshold is established. Any party that fails to obtain ten per cent of the eligible national vote is not represented in the TGNA. Second, every electoral district has a district-level threshold, which is computed by dividing the number seats of that district with the eligible votes cast in that district. For example, if a district has a contest for three seats, a candidate must obtain 33.3 per cent of the eligible vote to win. Furthermore, if only one party gets over 33.3 per cent of the eligible vote there, its candidates win all of the three seats, even if one of the other contestants gets 33.2 per cent of the vote. Consequently, a party that hardly obtains the plurality of the national vote ends up with a more than safe majority of over 60 per cent of the seats in the TGNA. This situation has been criticized as being unjust by the opposition parties ever since the 1987 national elections, and remains a major area of conflict. As a matter of fact, coalition-making is considered as highly dysfunctional by the elites as well as the Turkish masses. The MP justifies its election law on the grounds of establishing governability, and avoidance of the coalition politics of the seventies. The latter is often suggested as a major cause of the political instability of that period.

9. The main functions of the TGNA are defined by the 1982 Constitution as 'enactment, amendment, and repeal of laws; the supervision of the Council of Ministers and the Ministers; the authorization of the Council of Ministers to issue governmental decrees having force of law . . . the debate and approval of the budget draft and the draft law of final accounts; the making of decisions regarding the printing of currency and the declaration of war; the ratification of international treaties, deciding on the proclamation of amnesties and pardons . . . the confirmation of death sentences passed by the courts . . .' (art. 87). Various legal provisions are designed to enable the TGNA to perform these functions.

10. The 1982 Constitution goes into the design of the activities and internal procedures of the TGNA in considerable detail. Article 93 stipulates that the TGNA meets

every year on the first day of September. The TGNA may not have a recess exceeding three months per annum. The same article also enables one-fifth of the deputies to call the TGNA into session by means of a written petition that they submit to the speaker. Articles 94 elaborately defines the composition, election and the time of election of the speaker's council. The same article further stipulates that the speaker may not participate in the floor debates and cast a ballot while he presides over a session. Article 95 requires that the RP are to take into account the relative strength of each party group in the TGNA. The same article alludes to the size of a party group in Parliament.

Articles 96 stipulates the lowest number of deputies who constitute a quorum in each session. Article 97 indicates that legislative activities are public, unless the Assembly decides otherwise. Articles 98–100 give detailed descriptions of the possible mechanism of control that the TGNA may employ to gather information and to oversee the activities of the agencies of the executive branch.

11. For more information on the Consultative Assembly of 1981–2 see note 2.
12. A count of those deputies who regularly engage in unruly floor behaviour seems to indicate that they tend to get re-elected. There does not seem to be any mechanism or norm that imposes severe sanctions on those who violate rules of floor debate.
13. The author has conducted unstructured interviews with five chairpersons of the TGNA commissions of the 1983 and 1987 Parliaments. The reference here is to these interviews.
14. The establishment of a party to the right of centre and another to its left, with leaders and cadres acceptable to the military rulers of the country in 1983 resulted in the emergence of the National Democracy Party and the Populist Party. However, as soon as the other political parties were permitted to establish their organizations, the NDP and the PP started to lose their electoral support. In a matter of two years they had to shut down their operations, owing to lack of electoral support. The True Path Party and the Social Democratic Party emerged in their place to oppose the ruling MP. The TPP and MP took over some of the cadres and deputies of the NDP, and in the meanwhile, Social Democrats merged with the PP and changing their names to the Social Democrat Populist Party (SDPP). Since the 1987 national legislative elections the MP, the SDPP, and the TPP emerged as the three parliamentary parties of the country, gathering 75 per cent of the vote. The Democratic Left Party of former prime minister Bulent Ecevit, which is another left-of-centre party that depends upon his charisma and the Prosperity Party, which is an extension of the old religious (Islamist) National Salvation Party of the 1970s emerged as the potential contestants for power, with each controlling about 8–9 per cent of the national vote.
15. In fact, about 10 per cent of the deputies stated that they did not intend to seek re-election. About half the participants in the 1984 study believe that they would not suffer significantly if they lose in political contests. Loss was defined in terms of financial resources, and loss of respect in the eyes of family, peers and neighbours.
16. Some deputies have enjoyed such elevated social status in their electoral districts that they have been elected whenever they ran for public office, irrespective of party ticket. However, such deputies do not normally comprise more than about 15 per cent of the candidates who participate in any national legislative election.
17. The questionnaire items included the following statements with which respondents were requested to agree or disagree:
    — 'Political party membership is a supreme duty beyond and above every personal need or desire.'
    — 'In order for the state to be governed and for his party to come to power, a party member ought to devote his life to his party.'

— 'It is incumbent upon a party member to be loyal to the decisions of the party, even if it contradicts his own thought and convictions.'

— 'In order to prove that his party's orientation and views are the best, a party member should consider making any possible type of sacrifice one can think of.'

18. The SDPP still tries to cope with forming its organizational principles. Its internal turmoil does not seem to approach a point of termination. Some of its local branches still suffer from serious infighting. It also has failed to enter a group of local election contests in small municipalities, in spite of the fact that it emerged as the party with the highest popular support after the 1989 local elections. The MP also seems to experience internal organizational strains among its liberal/modern versus conservative/religious factions, more so after the 1989 local election defeats. The consolidation and institutionalization of the political party organizations are still distant goals. Personalities and the leaders of the political parties, such as former Prime Ministers Suleyman Demirel of TPP and Bulent Ecevit of DLP, and current Prime Minister Turgut Ozal of the MP seem to carry more weight as symbols than their political party banners and flags.

19. See the Turkish daily *Milliyet*, 25 June 1987, pp. 1 and 6.

20. The adoption of the 1973 rules of procedure of the TGNA, (still in force) was the result of twelve long years of negotiation between various ruling and opposition parties. The post-1983 TGNA was unable to strike such an accord until the summer recess of 1988.

21. One should not be deceived by the number of 'joint' proposals of bills in the current TGNA. All of them have been merged with proposals made by the deputies of the ruling MP, a process in the course of which proposals are reshaped. Furthermore, these proposals are submitted to MP-dominated parliamentary committees which modify drafts as directed by the MP leadership. The 'real' input of the opposition is better gauged by the number of 'autonomous' (not connected to any party group) proposals made by the deputies of opposition parties which are processed without amendment by commissions on the floor of the TGNA. I was able to discover only six such bills in the period between 11 November, 1983 and 30 June, 1987, out of 122 non-government-sponsored bills that were adopted by the TGNA in the same period.

22. Some majority party deputies resent the fact that they cannot criticize their cabinet ministers in public. Their constituents seem to demand that these deputies convey their demands to the government. Party group meetings do not get fully reported in the national press. Nevertheless, one rule seems to be well established: the government party deputies criticize the cabinet ministers in the party group meetings, and the opposition party deputies criticize the cabinet ministers and the government during the floor debates.

23. With the exception of the budget and planning commission, minutes and voting records of the commissions of the TGNA are not systematically kept. Very occasionally the minutes of a commission's proceedings are preserved for future reference. Such occasions have been warranted by critical bills, as for example the State Employees Act of 1970. I have been unable to find hard evidence with regard to commission voting patterns. However, I conducted unstructured interviews with five commission chairpersons, and three ex-commission chairpersons on this issue. It is my understanding from these interviews that votes are cast along party lines in the commissions, except where there is a 'legal–technical' question which impels cross-party compromise. It is not unusual for a commission chairperson to request the opinion of the prime minister and/or minister informally before calling for a vote on a resolution. After such communication the chairperson may suggest further modifications to bring the resolution into line with the minister's point of view, if he so desires.

24. The commission chairpersons argue that they are not without means of punishment

which they may employ to sanction non-cooperative ministers and agency heads. One such measure is to delay legislation so long as lack of cooperation persists. The chairpersons indicate that they, although very occasionally, use this threat, which often prompts anticipated repercussions.

25. The issue concerning export of goods to companies which do not exist, or exports with prices marked much above their world market prices, or exports of materials with no value, such as worn and torn leather, with the object of collecting tax rebate and export subsidy from government started to attract increasing attention from the mass media. The police interrogation of some companies and the proof of payments of large sums of money to some companies without proper documents followed by court cases have elevated the export policies of the government to a major political issue. After the defeat of the ruling MP in the local elections, a proposal by the opposition parties for parliamentary investigation was adopted by the General Assembly. It constitutes a very rare example of political agreement over the multi-party investigation of a major political issue by the government and opposition party groups in the TGNA.

26. I use the same data as the 1984 and 1988 studies for the analysis below. I also conducted unstructured interviews with nine commission chairpersons in 1984, and with six in 1988. I will also use the relevant parts of these interviews below.

References

Agor, Weston H. (1971). (Senate: Integrative Role in Chile's Political Development) in Herbert Hirsch and M. Donald Hancock (eds), *Comparative Legislative Systems: A Reader in Theory and Research*, New York, The Free Press, 245–60.

Balcigil, Osman (1982). *Iki Seminer ve Bir Reform Onerisinde Tartişilan Anayasa*, Istanbul, Birikim Yayinlari.

Bianchi, Robert (1984). *Interest Groups and Political Development in Turkey*, Princeton, Princeton University Press.

Coskunoğlu, Kamil T. (1985). 'Yeni Içtuzuğun Getirdikleri: Hizli ve Verimli Calişma', *TBMM Dergisi*, No. 1, 35–7.

Dodd, C. H. (1979). *Democracy and Development in Turkey*, University of Hull, The Eothen Press.

Dubetsky, Alan (1976). 'Kinship, Primordial Ties and Factory Organizations in Turkey', *International Journal of Middle East Studies*, **7**, 433–51.

Ergil, Doğu (1980). *Turkiye'de Teror ve Siddet: Yapisal ve Kulturel Kaynaklari*, Ankara, Turhan Kitabevi.

Erguder, Uston (1981). 'Changing Patterns of Electoral Behavior in Turkey', *Boğazici University Journal (Administrative Sciences)*, 8–9, 45–69.

—(1987). '1987 Erken Seçimlerinin Analizi', unpublished manuscript, Boğaziçi University, Istanbul.

Eulau, Heinz and Paul D. Karps, (1977). 'The Puzzle of Representation: Specifying Components of Responsiveness', *Legislative Studies Quarterly*, **2**, 3, 233–54.

Ezherli, Ihsan (1986). *Turkiye Buyuk Millet Meclisi (1920–1986)*, Ankara, TBMM Kultur, Sanat ve Yayin Kurulu, No. 10.

Fenno Jr, Richard F. (1966). *The Power of the Purse: Appropriations Politics in Congress*, Boston, Little, Brown and Co.

Firy, Frederick W. (1975), 'Patterns of Elite Politics in Turkey' George Lenczowski (ed.), *Political Elites in the Middle East*, Washington D.C., American Enterprise Institute for Public Policy Research, 41–82.

Harris, George (1970). 'The Cause of the 1960 Revolution in Turkey', *Middle East Journal*, **24**, 3, 436–42.
Heper, Metin (1983). *Turkiye'de Kent Goçmeni ve Burokratik Orgutler*, Istanbul, Uçdal.
—(1985). *The State Tradition in Turkey*, Walkington, Eothen Press.
—(1986). 'Ataturk te 'Devlet Duşuncesi' in Ersin Kalaycioğlu and Ali Yaşar Saribay (eds) *Turk Siyasal Hayatinin Gelişimi*, Istanbul, Beta, 233–52.
Huntington, Samuel P. (1968). *Political Order of Changing Societies*, New Haven, Yale University Press.
Ipekçi, Abdi with Omer Sami Coşar (1965). *Ihtilalin Içyuzu*, Istanbul, Toker Matbaasi.
Jewell, Malcolm E, (1983). 'Legislator–Constituency Relations and the Representative Process', *Legislative Studies Quarterly*, **8**, 3, 303–37.
Kalaycioğlu, Ersin (1980). 'Why Legislatures Persist in Developing Countries: The Case of Turkey', *Legislative Studies Quarterly*, **5**, 1, 123–39.
—(1983). *Karşilaştirmali Siyasal Katilma: Siyasal Eylemin Kokenleri Uzerine bir Inceleme*, Istanbul, Siyasal Bilimler Fakultesi.
—(1986b). 'Turk Yasama Sistemi ve Siyasal Temsil' in Ersin Kalaycioğlu and Ali Yasar Saribay, (eds), op. cit., 313–32.
—(1986b). 'The By-Elections of 1986', Current Turkish Thought, 60, Fall 1986, 7–11.
—(forthcoming). The 1983 Parliament: Changes or Continuities in Metin Heper, Ahmet Evin and Udo Steinbach (eds), *State and Society in Turkey: The Transition to Democracy in the 1980s*, Berlin and New York, de Gruyter Press.
Karmustafaoğlu, Tuncer, (1965), *Yasama Meclisinde Komisyonlar*, Ankara, A. U. Hukuk Fakultesi Yayinlari.
Karpat, Kemal (1959). *Turkey's Politics: The Transition to a Multi-Party System*, Princeton, Princeton University Press.
Kuklinski, James H. (1979) 'Representative–Constituency Linkages: A Review Article, *Legislative Studies Quarterly*, **4**, 121–40.
Lenski, Gerhard and Jean Lenski (1974). *Human Societies*, 2nd ed., New York, McGraw Hill.
Loewenberg, Gerhard (1971). 'The Role of Parliament in Modern Political Systems in Gerhard Loewenberg (ed.), *Modern Parliaments: Change or Decline?*, Chicago, Aldine Atherton.
Ozbudun, Ergun (1968), *Bati Demokrasilerinde ve Turkiye'de Parti Disiplini*, Ankara, A. U. Hukuk Fakultesi Yayinlari.
—(1981). 'Turkish Party System: Institutionalization, Polarization and Fragmentation', *Middle Eastern Studies*, **17**, 2, 228–40.
—(1986), *Turk Anayasa Hukuku*, Ankara, Yetkin Yayinlari.
Patterson, Samuel C., Ronald D. Hedlund, G. R. Boynton (1975), *Representatives and Represented: Bases of Public Support for the American Legislatures*, New York, John Wiley.
Pitkin, H.F. (1967): *The Concept of Representation*, University of California Press, Berkeley.
Polsby, Nelson (1971). 'The Institutionalization of the U.S. House of Representatives', in Herbert Hirsch and John D. Hancock (eds), op. cit., 188–221.
Prewitt, Kenneth, Heinz Eulau, and Betty Zisk (1966), 'Political Socialization and Political Roles', *Public Opinion Quarterly*, 569–81.
Rockman, Bert A. (1984). 'Legislative–Executive Relations and Legislative Oversight', *Legislative Studies Quarterly*, **9**, 3, 387–440.
Sayari, Sabri (1978). 'The Turkish Political System in Transition', *Government and Opposition*, **13**, 39–57.
Sunar, Ilkay and Sabri Sayari (1986), 'Democracy in Turkey: Problems and Prospects', in Guillermo O'Donnell. Philippe C. Schmitter and Lawrence Whitehead (eds),

Transitions from Authoritarian Rule: Southern Europe, Baltimore, London, The Johns Hopkins University Press.

Sisson, Richard (1973). 'Comparative Legislative Institutionalization: A Theoretical Exploration,' in Allen Kornberg (ed.), *Legislatures in Comparative Perspective*, New York, David McKay.

Tunaya, Tarik Zafer (1975). *Siyasi Muesseseler ve Anayasa Hukuku*, Istanbul, Sulhi Garan Matbaasi.

Wahlke, John C. (1971), 'Policy Demands and System Support: The Role of the Represented' in Gerhard Loewenberg (ed.), *Modern Parliaments: Change or Decline?*, Chicago, Aldine, Atherton, Chap. 8.

Weinbaum, M.G. (1975): 'Classification and Change in Legislative Systems, with Particular Application to Iran, Turkey and Afghanistan', in Boynton and Kim (eds.), *Legislative Systems in Developing Countries*, Duke University Press, Durham (N.C).

Yucekok, Ahmet N. (1972), *Turkiye'de Dernek Gelişimleri*, Ankara, Siyasal Bilgiler Fakultesi Yayinlari.

—(1983), *Siyaset Sosyolojisi Açisindan Turkiye'de Parlamentonun Evrimi*, Ankara, A.U. Siyasal Bilgiler Fakultesi.

Official Documents

Album of the Turkish Grand National Assembly, (1984) Ankara.

Election Results (1966, 1977, 1985) *State Institute of Statistics Publications*, No. 51; No. 817; No. 1071, Ankara.

The TGNA Commission Bulletins (1983–7) (Sessions I–VIII), Official Publications of the TGNA.

The Constitution of the Turkish Republic and Rules of Procedure of the Turkish Grand National Assembly, Official Publication of the TGNA.

The Minutes of the TGNA, Official Publication of the TGNA.

'Anavatan Partisi Seçmen Araştirmasi Raporu', (July 1987), conducted by Sosyal ve Iktisadi Araştirmalar Vakfi, (mimeo.).

Newspapers

Milliyet (daily), Published in Istanbul.
Cumhuriyet (daily), Published in Istanbul.
Vatan (daily), no longer published.

Part III   Comparative perspectives

8 Political parties, parliaments and democratic consolidation in southern Europe: empirical and theoretical perspectives

Geoffrey Pridham

Introduction: parliaments, parties and democratic transition

To state that there are different kinds of liberal democracies involves a truism, but it serves to point out the significant element of political choice within this broad category of political system. While there are certain key requirements of liberal democracies (such as balanced institutional structures and political pluralism), they may also vary cross-nationally in structural, political and also cultural respects. Thus, structurally, they have often been sub-divided according to whether they are 'presidential' or 'semi-presidential', 'prime-ministerial' (executive-in-parliament orientated) or 'assembly' types of government. Clearly, such structural differences provide varying opportunities for the role of political parties in the functioning of such systems; although, equally, one should not forget how much parties themselves can determine these structural arrangements or 'rules of the game' in the outcome of constitutional settlements. It is with the last two of the above-mentioned types of liberal democracy that the concept of 'party government' is usually associated. Hence, linked to this, is the overall question of parliamentary institutions as central or not in the decision-making process which therefore may be seen as an important test of the kind of liberal democracy in question.

Even though there is some risk of tautology in this line of reasoning, it is already obvious that political parties may play a crucial role in the definition of types of liberal democracy. One may in fact speak of a two-way relationship: in the inauguration of such systems, parties perform a major if not the principal part in deciding on the relative weight of the various institutional structures (the constituent process); and these structures, if viably established, may subsequently condition the behaviour and even the strategies of the parties. Of course, this relationship may well not be so clear-cut sequentially, for there is invariably in practice some ongoing process of 'interpreting' a new constitutional settlement in moving from transition towards consolidation (that is, creating the 'material constitution') and more explicitly, in certain cases, of an element of constitutional revision. Indeed, the link between the institutionalization of parliaments and the role of parties is underlined further when considering political and cultural variation between types of liberal democracy, for example political traditions and situational trends, the constellation of political forces and degree of wider consensus around parliamentary institutionalization, not to mention 'cultural' adaptation favouring this in the course of democratic transition. Whatever the particular scenario of forming a new liberal democracy, political parties are undeniably essential agents in this process.

The forgoing argument leads one to hypothesize that the role of parties is therefore probably decisive in the connection between the 'theory' and 'practice' of parliamentary institutions. In doing so, it is possible to distinguish between three hypothetical levels of political choice so far as the 'theory' (constitutional basis of parliaments) is concerned:

(a) *macro-choice*: in effect, the choice of political system or model, where liberal democracy is not the exclusive one, that is parliaments may exist in other categories of system though not expressive of political pluralism;
(b) *meso-choice*: within the option of liberal democracy there is scope for structural variation, e.g. 'presidential' or 'assembly'; also, centralist or federal with different consequences for the role of parliamentary institutions; and electoral laws which have a formative influence on party systems and therefore on the political composition of parliaments;
(c) *micro-choice*: defining the 'rules of the game' involving the institutional structures agreed on, including specific functions and procedural arrangements (constitutions tend to vary considerably as to how far these 'rules' are detailed, although supplementary documents—rules of procedure for parliaments and executives—may also elaborate these).

These three levels are obviously closely interconnected and not always clear-cut in their temporal sequence, although it is logical to expect them to lead from one to the other in the order presented. In situations of high instability it is possible, however, that such a sequence is not straightforward or indeed it may be reversed. But the end of transition to democracy must in any case be identified with the 'closing of options' on at least (a) and (b). In this process, political parties play an important and visible role as in constituent assemblies (pre-parliaments), although in some cases this is alongside other actors like political figures somewhat independent of their parties (Karamanlis's influence on the 1975 Greek Constitution), traditional agents of power notably the military (the MFA in the Portuguese constituent process of 1974–6) or even foreign governments (the obvious example is West Germany).

In looking at the 'practice' of parliaments, the overriding theme is one of their continuing institutionalization leading from transition well into consolidation and beyond. The most simple version is when attention concentrates on implementing and institutionalizing (c), with a growing consensus on rule-abiding behaviour although some parties might continue to disagree over specific items of the constitutional settlement or press for changes in them, for example advocate greater procedural opportunities for parliamentary oppositions. However, the experience of transition may be such that some problems are referred back to (b)—for example constitutional revision in Portugal in the early 1980s, the Greek constitutional revision of 1985—and in exceptional situations even to (a), with counter-revolutionary attempts, for example Spain in February 1981. Eventually, however, parliamentary institutionalization emerges whatever meso-level choice is confirmed, with parties playing the major part and sometimes a greater part than in the original constitutional settlement, as in Portugal. Ultimately, this cannot avoid broader interpretative problems like the theme of the decline of parliaments, a phenomenon evident in Western Europe before most of the southern European countries embarked on transition. In moving from authoritarianism to liberal democracy, their parliaments naturally acquired a more significant role than before in the policy process. But the concern here is not so much diachronic as comparative: what *types* of liberal democracy have consolidated themselves; and, in particular, what is the role in them of parliamentary institutions? Furthermore, how much is any such variation due to political parties and their part in democratic consolidation?

The party-political context of parliamentary institutionalization: modes of transition and political choice

Taking empirical perspectives first of all, the preceding introductory points already reveal differences between the various southern European countries, at least in the sequence of transition stages if not in the outcome of that process. That is, it is quite possible for democratic transitions—including those which are simultaneous and occurring in the same regional environment—to lead to different forms of liberal democracy, as suggested at the start of this chapter. National-specific conditions and determinants usually count for much, and these must include the constellation of political forces in each country: which ideologies they represent, their relative political weight and their particular strategies for transition and consolidation. This differentiating approach is altogether more useful than assumptive judgements in some of the literature on these new democracies that they have at last caught up with political development elsewhere in Western Europe.

Pursuing more fully the three levels of political choice in democratic transition, differences of sequence become highlighted. This is useful to note when assessing the scope for and pace of parliamentary institutionalization.

'Parliamentary institutionalization' involves the acquisition of a certain legislative effectiveness, organizational articulation and rule-abiding patterns and—more broadly—political viability and autonomy. It must be seen as an important component of democratic consolidation. In the case of Spain,there was a gradual move from (a) to (b) in the mid-1970s with the dismantling of the Franco regime and its replacement by a constitutional monarchy. The years 1981–2 were, however, crucial in the confirmation of this settlement because, first, there was a military challenge, which although overcome, seems initially in its aftermath to stall the consolidation process, for example the government took heed and checked regional devolution which had provoked the military with its traditions of centralism. However, eventually, retrospective judgements of the attempted coup served to strengthen attachment to the new democracy—involving a reversal of the mood of *desencanto* at the mass level in the late 1970s—and this new trend was underlined by the relatively painless alternation in power in the autumn of 1982. Thereafter, attention was free to concentrate on micro-level matters of political choice, especially once the question of the military's role was gradually settled. With Portugal, the sequence in this neighbouring state is obviously different because it started with a revolutionary upheaval: attention in 1974–6 was very much on the macro-level of choice; and since the 1976 Constitution involved something of a political truce questions relating to (b) reappeared in the constitutional revision in 1979–82. Thus, in Portugal, transition took virtually a full decade. By contrast, Greece moved swiftly from (a) to (b) not least because the colonels' regime had been short-lived and had really failed to institutionalize itself seriously (Diamandouros, 1986:145). Furthermore, the discredit it earned over the debacle in Cyprus allowed Karamanlis a welcome freedom to act with decision. However, the settlement on (b) remained somewhat uncertain because of the high degree of party-political polarization in Greek politics, notably between the ruling New Democracy party and PASOK, which came to power in 1981. This problem remained beneath the surface until the abrupt crisis over presidential power in spring 1985, shortly before the parliamentary election of that year. Since then, attention has turned more to matters of micro-choice than to parliamentary procedure and organization and the rights of the opposition (Alivizatos, chapter 5 in this book).

The two other countries are more difficult to assess along these lines, but for rather different reasons. In the case of Italy, we have the longest-standing of the five democracies by as much as a generation. But it is one in which there has not been an easy progression from (a) through (b) to (c). First, the choice (a) was conditioned by foreign (notably American) constraints but it was nevertheless based on broad cross-party agreement over the 1948 Constitution. All the same, a persistent element of doubt remained long afterwards because of the 'Communist question' (*fattore K*) and some ambiguity in the PCI's position in the earlier postwar period on what form of system it preferred. This problem has gradually diminished, particularly in the light of the party's evolution in the 1970s, although the PCI has long shown increasing signs of 'socialization' through parliamentary democracy. Notwithstanding, this persistent problem raises the question as to when post-Fascist democracy in Italy became consolidated. Second, there was in Italy the unusual situation of the belated implementation of aspects relating to meso-level choice, notably in the introduction in 1970 of the 'ordinary' regions provided for in the 1948 Constitution—a clear example of where party politics was determinant. Third, there have been fairly recent phases of constitutional or institutional reform which make it difficult to judge the Italian case in this respect. The 1971 reforms of parliamentary procedure involved a modest shift from dominance of the executive toward 'assembly' government, where again party-political determinants—as the growth of legislative concurrence between parties in government and the PCI opposition—were uppermost (Hine, 1981: 68–9). Since the 1970s, the new issue of institutional reform has among other things aimed at chances that point to meso—as well as micro-level choice, including a strengthening of the executive and of the prime minister and electoral reform of a kind that could re-structure the party system (Bartolini, 1982). This does not necessarily have to mean that constitutional reform negates the achievement of consolidation (it was, for instance, an issue in the United Kingdom in the 1970s). It is merely to show that Italy has a system that rather defies conventional categorization: while obviously not 'presidential' or 'semi-presidential', it is also not a definite case of 'prime-ministerial' or 'assembly' government. *Paritocrazia* or 'government by parties' is the most realistic label, although it leaves open the question of how much political parties have— at least in Italy—determined the course and nature of parliamentary institutionalization.

Turkey is different from Italy by virtue of being at the other end of historical sequence when comparing the five countries under examination. This complicates our analysis if only because the transition which started in Turkey in 1983 has not yet led to a process of consolidation. In fact, it is evident that transition is still in progress, with some basic problems—notably, the full acceptance of political pluralism—still not fully resolved. According to the 1982 Constitution, Turkey has a 'semi-presidential' system but the political role of the military remains, whereas the completion of transition requires that this cease—in this respect, its role is not comparable with that of the Portuguese MFA. Turkey therefore appears at present in limbo between (a) and (b) levels of choice, continuing to resemble somewhat a 'guided democracy'—the Constitution was drawn up with the approval of the National Security Council, which has maintained surveillance over political parties. Viewed more broadly over time, Turkey has moved back and forth between parliamentary and military regimes since World II War. This has meant, even when the latter have been so-called military 'interruptions'; that the macro-level of choice has remained as it were a leitmotiv of Turkish politics. Despite this, the link between the role of parties and the problem of parliamentary institutionalization —or the lack of it—is apparent. The state of party-political fragmentation, the very absence of party institutionalization, indeed the inability of Turkey to accommodate competitive or multi-party politics—all these unresolved difficulties have served to undermine the institution of parliament (Sunar and Sayari, 1986: 183).

From the foregoing examination of the five cases, it is possible to establish various empirically verifiable perspectives on our theme. For instance, there has been a trend of late towards parliament-based government and away from 'semi-presidential' forms, referring again to the Portuguese and Greek constitutional revisions of 1982 and 1985 respectively. That is evident to any observer of these countries' politics, although it is necessary to point out that this change in government form does not automatically promote parliamentary institutionalization. Namely, the shift in power has really occurred between presidency and prime minister/cabinet, while in the Greek case it has more blatantly enhanced the role of prime minister described by one study as a 'parliamentary autocrat' (Katsoudas, 1987: 28–30). Nevertheless, this shift in institutional power away from presidential forms is likely to create more potential for parliamentary institutionalization. Even in the case of Greece it has produced a new interest in the role of the parliament both in its internal organization and its external role of communication (Alivizatos, chapter 5 in this book). In Spain, there has been a significant element of 'prime-ministerial' government as in the German-style constructive vote of no confidence and the right to dissolve the Cortes (Kohler, 1982:26). Alternation in power in 1982 has been seen by some as favourable to parliamentary politics,inducing a state of government/opposition relations comparable with the rest of Western Europe (Pollack and Grugel, 1987: 246). However, the phenomenon of 'lonely' decision-making by the prime minister—a point of criticism in the last year or two of Suárez—has reappeared with Gonzalez, as over his rare addresses to the parliament. Clearly, too, the practice so far of one-party cabinets has facilitated the dominance of the executive,unlike in Portugal where incohesive coalitions have inhibited prime-ministerial performance. The election there in 1987, leading to the formation of a PSD government with an absolute majority, may well modify that situation.

Hence, taking the three democracies that commenced transition in the mid-1970s, there has been some common trend—one which may in principle favour parliamentary institutionalization—although national-specific differences are such as to call into question in one or other case how far this will happen. It is at this point that the presumed brevity so far of the consolidation process in these countries makes it difficult to draw conclusions. The most developed form of parliamentary institutionalization is not surprisingly found in Italy. This is partly owing to the seniority of post-Fascist democracy there, although not entirely so for the 1948 Constitution in any case hardly provided for 'prime-ministerial' government. Its spirit favoured a strong parliament if only because of a concern to prevent a dominant executive (Di Palma, 1982: 123–5). But, as noted before the Italian version of executive/legislative relations has itself been modified over time. The present Turkish situation remains in this context in abeyance, with little immediate prospect for parliamentary institutionalization.

A further perspective must be, reverting in time, the original attention given by parties to the parliamentary institution during the constituent process. One would expect this to reveal their conceptions of its role and perhaps too their willingness to countenance or promote parliamentary institutionalization. However, this is not always clear because of rival issues that may absorb the parties and the compromises which are intrinsic to formulating a constitution. The case of the Italian Constituent Assembly, where the Parliament was not an object of great debate, suggests that the degree of attention is no fair clue as to the priority accorded that institution. Although the Assembly met for a long period and witnessed some debate over alternative institutional models, the main issue concerning the Parliament was over the choice between one or two chambers. Somewhat by contrast, the Portuguese Constitution of 1976 provided for a relatively weak Parliament which was perhaps no real surprise given the determining role of the MFA though its 'pacts' with the political parties, stipulating conditions for the return to civilian rule (Opello, 1985: 148). Accordingly, the Council of the Revolution was to judge the constitutionality of parliamentary laws, just as parliamentary controls on the government were restricted (Braga de Cruz and Tobo Antunes, chapter 6 in this book). This was despite signs among the parties of a wish for parliamentary supremacy (Opello, 1985: 148). In the case of Spain, the organization of Parliament featured in debates on the Constitution, such as over the relative functions of the two chambers, although it was not an intense issue. Notwithstanding the common concern for stabilizing the executive, the latter was subject to some important controls as in the budgetary process and the role of committees (Bonime, 1985: 22–3). The provision for a strong executive was in the Greek Constitution paramount to the extent that the mechanism for parliamentary control, whether in plenary or committee, was severely curtailed. This reflected the long-held view of Karamanlis that the parliamentary institution had not functioned adequately in modern Greek politics (Katsoudas, 1987: 22).

It goes without saying that whatever conceptions parties or leaders may have held of this institution these were inevitably affected by their own particular interests. These are most visible in debates and negotiations over the form of electoral system. In Spain,the consensual nature of proceedings produced a compromise mixture of majoritarian elements (favoured by parties of the right) and proportional representation (PR) (favoured by the left and regional interests) (Bonime, 1985: 21–2). In Greece, on the other hand, where constitution-making was distinctly less consensual,the choice of a weighted PR system not only expressed a concern for one-party majorities to strengthen government but also political calculation. A plurality system was seen as likely to lead eventually to a Popular Front majority, while pure PR would have increased the parliamentary strength of the extremes (Mavrogordatos, 1983: 85–6). Such considerations as embodied in electoral laws have a direct impact on the constellation of political forces in national parliaments and, thus, in a variety of ways may affect their functioning.

One cannot complete discussion of the constituent process without some reference to the influence of historical determinants; that is how much political parties and their leaders draw lessons from past experience. As just mentioned, Karamanlis was among other things motivated by adverse memories of parliamentary practice in the 1960s. Naturally,this touches on historical interpretation, for Karamanlis's logic was that parliamentary breakdown had ushered in the colonels' coup, and so the former should be prevented through enhancing executive power (Psomiades, 1982: 266). By contrast, institutional priorities in the Italian constitution-making sought to prevent any reappearance of 'Caesarism'—hence the rejection of presidentialism and a majoritarian electoral system (Di Palma, 1982). Similarly, the Portuguese Constitution of 1976 was according to Opello largely 'a reaction to things past', in this case a distaste for both Salazar's *Estado Novo* but also instability of the First

Republic—hence, the hybrid system comprising both parliamentary and presidential components (Opello, 1985: 147–8). With Turkey,the overriding pattern has been of endemic parliamentary instability, which together with party system fragmentation and social disruption has led in the past to democratic breakdown. Diverse lessons may therefore be drawn from historical experience, but these usually involve some interplay with current situations including parties' assessments of their own prospects in the light of the emerging balance of political forces in early transition. Political parties utilize history as much as they are free to interpret it. Conceivably too, different ideologies are likely to find some form of expression over institutional arrangements, as reflecting on the type of system or form of liberal democracy they tend to prefer.

The aforementioned points highlight national-specific conditions, but there is one theme common to these various cases, namely that of legitimizing political authority following the end of authoritarianism. That must include creating anew a parliamentary tradition, which has been interrupted and in all likelihood, prior to authoritarianism, had suffered from a negative reputation. That basic task, one not achieved automatically by constitutions nor short-term, is a major requirement of democratic consolidation, pointing to the role of political parties both individually and collectively. The part they have played during regime transition helps to determine the outcome, if only by their decisions on the 'rules of the game'; and they may also begin then to develop patterns of behaviour which carry over into the consolidation phase. In this sense, they usually have a major formative influence on new liberal democracies, but outcomes in consolidation as affecting the importance of parliaments in the new systems are not totally pre-determined by decisions during transition. It is necessary now to explore the importance of parties in the process towards parliamentary institutionalization as principal component of democratic consolidation.

Political parties, parliaments and democratic consolidation: exploring a framework for analysis

At this stage of the discussion, emphasis has to turn to theoretical perspectives, since the problem of parties and parliamentary institutionalization forms an element of the wider problems of democratic consolidation which is a rather less tangible (and indeed often longer) process than democratic transition. Moreover, it ultimately involves looking at such conceptually demanding questions as the relationship between political behaviour and political structures. While the process of parliamentary institutionalization itself is not difficult to define, it is nevertheless multi-dimensional and not always easy to measure. Clearly, too, one has to judge parliamentary institutionalization against the type of liberal democracy agreed on in transition. That is, its achievement is not as such dependent on a system of parliamentary dominance, although obviously an 'executive-in-parliament' model is more favourable than a 'presidential' one.

Before formulating an approach to parties and parliamentary institutionalization, it is therefore necessary to put this question in context by taking note of theoretical work on the role of parties in democratic consolidation. Thus, Di Palma has argued parties have a special position in consolidation, since they formally monopolize parliament and are the key to reconciling functional interests to parliamentary politics. In his view, 'since consolidation is an ongoing process of structuration, increasingly constitutionalized political actors and their coalition strategies remain central in explaining outcomes' (Di Palma, 1985). That is, parties perform an important legitimizing function in the crucial transfer of loyalties to the new regime, in exercising decisional authority and in expressing social diversity and dissent. According to Schmitter, a competitive party system is crucial to system legitimation in both producing effective government and in ensuring that 'losers' in the game remain voluntarily in the system (Schmitter, 1985), with the implication that working the system should have a 'socializing' effect on party elites. Morlino has drawn attention to wider considerations in the determining role of parties: 'consolidation by means of parties is characterized above all else by the progressive organization and expansion of party structures and of the party system as a whole, which is in a position to control and if necessary to moderate and integrate all forms of participation' (Morlino, 1986: 231). He sees a coincidence between the self-reinforcement of pro-system parties and democratic consolidation, in guaranteeing the decisional process and organizing and controlling mass participation. Similarly, Di Palma has viewed the existence of viable anti-system parties as qualifying the nature of the 'democratic compromise' and the prospects for consolidation (Di Palma, 1986: 185–7). although in earlier work on 'founding coalitions' in new democracies he identified a mutual 'backward/forward' legitimation process whereby elites from the previous authoritarian regime—'once the democratic card has proved its winning potential'—may perform a 'backward' legitimation of an incipient democracy as well as legitimizing themselves 'forward' (Di Palma, 1980: 170).

So far as the theme of parliamentary institutionalization is concerned, these various working hypotheses indicate that the role of parties may well be indirect as well as direct. Namely, their strategies for consolidation—if that is not too grand a term for political motivation in this phase—and their performance in this respect cannot be assessed merely in intra-parliamentary terms. To take one important and obvious example, if we are considering parliaments as representative organs, then the role of parties as channels of sectoral or cross-sectoral interests and demands must be a primary factor. Or, on the question of anti-system parties, it is not politically impossible these might work 'correctly' in the legislative process but at the same time indulge outside parliament in activities aimed at destabilization. The PCP, as perhaps the most obvious candidate for this category, has since 1975—when it was strongly suspected of promoting the totalitarian alternative to liberal democracy in the upheavals of that year—followed a two-pronged strategy: according to Opello, 'the party, on the one hand, vigorously engages in political activities within the framework of elections and parliament and, on the other, confronts various governments with strikes and street demonstrations through its control of Portugal's major labour organisation' (Opello, 1985: 104). One may speculate as to whether the latter activity is deliberately 'anti-system' or whether, more recently, the PCP is becoming 'socialized' through its participation in the political structure (including in local government). But whatever the explanation,such problems relating to extra-parliamentary roles may well have implications for parliamentary institutionalization. The legitimation of political structures is hardly an exclusively institutional matter.

These and other relevant problems may be explored further by referring to comparative literature on the question of political parties and parliaments. Thus in his chapter on 'parties and the structure of government', Duverger develops a numbers of points on the theme of the functioning of political institutions and the relationship with party systems and their structure (Duverger, 1964: 392–421). While acknowledging that this also depends on whether a system is parliamentary or presidential, he argues that a real separation of powers is a combination of both the party system and the constitutional setting with differences between these types of liberal democracy becoming blurred if the same party is in control of both parliament and the presidency. His main distinction is between two-party systems as favouring a concentration of powers, possibly to the detriment of parliament's role, as against multi-party systems which allow 'free play to constitutional separation' so that the 'parliamentary game' flourishes. In his view,therefore, 'multi-partism tends on occasion to superimpose a second separation of powers upon that resulting from the constitution or the nature of the institutions' (ibid: 401). On the other hand, 'in a presidential regime multi-partism tends rather to increase the authority of government and to decrease that of parliament' (ibid: 411), tending in turn to increase the personal character of the presidency; whereas, in the case of a two-party system, 'the parties are big enough to dwarf the president who appears to be more the leader of one of them than an independent personality' (ibid: 412). Duverger also draws attention to the differences that party-system structures hold for development of the opposition role—clearly a major concern in the achievement of parliamentary institutional-ization—in that two-party systems are said to make this into a real 'institution' (ibid: 414). Some of Duverger's hypotheses have less bearing on the southern European democracies, although the very absence of 'presidential' government —at least, the disappearance of 'semi-presidential' forms (to employ Duverger's own term)—creates favourable prospects for parliamentary institutionalization and also for the 'parliamentarianization' of parties. Linz has similarly argued that presidentialism jeopardizes democratic consolidation as it narrows available options, establishes individuals in prominent office surrounded by excessive expectations, discourages the development of party organization and discipline and risks parliamentary stalemate in the event of the opposition party gaining control of the legislature (O'Donnell et al 1986: Pt. IV, 60–1). In other words, our various national cases (with the likely exception of Turkey) present no structural obstacles to parliamentary institutionalization, even if democratic consolidation is regarded as incomplete.

It is not necessary here to enter into the debate about the decline of parliaments,for as Smith and others have pointed out it is more useful to distinguish between the various functions of the parliaments and examine these separately over time: elective, personnel (recruitment to government), rule-making (legislation) and communication or parliament as a 'forum' in providing political information and also legitimating (Smith, 1983). This same kind of approach is adopted by Baldassarre in a recent essay on the Italian Parliament and the effects on it of the 1971 reforms (a plausible attempt at its institutionalization, at least at an improvement in it), although he uses slightly different categories: representation, decision, control, electoral and legitimation (Baldassarre, 1985). In short, Baldassarre finds it necessary to look at parliament's role as a whole, in its different forms, in order to assess an institutional change aimed strictly at the parliament's internal organization. While his main theme is that the parliament's role is complex, whereby firm generalizations are not possible,nevertheless his approach allows some identification of change. For example, the control function is seen generally as weak, although this may improve when the opposition is more important and when the government coalition is heterogeneous; similarly, the legitimation function may vary, as being more effective for instance during the 'National Solidarity' alliance in the later 1970s when the PCI opposition was brought temporarily into the 'area of government' (ibid: 327–8; 334–5). In answer to the debate in Italy in the 1970s about the 'centrality' of parliament, Baldassarre takes the view that this asks too much of the parliamentary role and that the preferred term is 'partnership' with the government (ibid: 342). As his analysis makes clear, it is the continuing dominance of the political parties in the functioning of the Italian Parliament that relativizes the 1971 reform and its effects. This recalls Smith's conclusion that the issue of parliamentary decline is related to the growth of party government and that 'comparisons with nineteenth-century ideal-pictures can be misleading' (Smith, 1983: 159). In doing so, he emphasizes that a parliament's different functions do not change in a uniform way. Thus,the function of communication has clearly increased and with it the role of parliaments as a legitimation site: 'another associated contribution which assemblies make to the political system is to give the seal of legitimacy to those groupings whose activities relate to the assembly-government and party' (ibid: 179). We are reminded, for instance, that the new southern European democracies had come—or are coming—of age when the mass media, especially television, had already become an established element in the political game, with some likely consequences for parliamentary institutionalization. This may of course raise public expectations of a parliament's role; but it also lends it (literally) a special visibility that must affect the attitudes of parties and their leaders, including those in government office. Admittedly, government control or influence over the media—something of a controversial point in these countries—may qualify this; however, such control cannot be absolute. To take an important example, the fortuitous televising of the attempted military coup in the Spanish Cortes in February 1981 had a significant impact on public reactions, and arguably contributed to the subsequent reinforcement of support for democratic norms.

It appears from the discussion so far that there is a two-way relationship between the role of parties and parliamentary institutionalization, which broadly parallels the interplay evident between political behaviour and political structures. This is further illustrated when turning to the question of party structures. Duverger has established a link between these and the functioning of parliaments: 'the internal structure of parties exercises a fundamental influence on the degree of separation or concentration of powers. He continues:

In a parliamentary regime cohesion and discipline in the majority party obviously increase concentration. If voting discipline is strict, if the internal fractions are reduced to impotence or obedience, parliament's function is reduced to rubber-stamping government decisions, which are in fact identical with party decisions. The act of rubber-stamping gives rise to very free discussions in which the minority party can express its opposition, but is no more than platonic. By contrast if voting discipline is less strict the government majority is less certain; the party in office must take account of rivalries between its own factions which may compromise its parliamentary position; the prestige of parliament is raised and separation of powers is to some extent restored. Here too a simple change of majority may modify the nature of the regime . . . [Duverger, 1964: 398]

While this latter scenario is somewhat familiar in the case of Italy, Duverger was generally too exclusively concerned with party structures as intra-parliamentary. Von Beyme, however, has noted that party discipline is linked to the dependence of parliamentary groups on their party organizations, increasingly so: 'the balance of power between the central party organizations and the parliamentary party has shifted to the disadvantage of the latter in almost all the Western democracies' (Von Beyme, 1985: 313, 320). This is, among various reasons, due to the increasing functions of parties, the greater sophistication of political planning, state aid to parties and greater democracy within them (ibid: 320). There is, nevertheless, substantial room for party variation on this matter. Stressing that the relationship between parliamentary parties and their extra-parliamentary structures is more complex than Duverger allows—that it 'is not an easy road'—Von Beyme has also pointed out:

the distribution of power within the different bodies of the parties and its impact on parliament and government is an intervening variable, dependent on the type of party (bourgeois or socialist), on the party system (degree of fragmentation), on institutional variables (such as the power of the head of state, parliamentary rules, party laws, incompatibility rules) and the relations between parties and pressure groups. [Von Beyme, 1983]

Featuring a parallel concern Leonardi and others (1978) developed on the Italian case a framework for measuring the dual process of the 'institutional-ization of parliament' and 'parliamentarization of parties' (again, this was prompted by trends of legislative concurrence between government and opposition in the 1970s culminating in the 'National Solidarity' alliance). Their intention was to re-examine the previous view that the Italian Parliament was not an important centre of power given the 'lack of consensus in Parliament on the reciprocal relationship between the majority and the minority' as undermining that institution's decisional effectiveness, a situation linked to the DC's political dominance (Leonardi et al., 1978 163–6). While observing that by 1977 there had occurred 'a substantial degree of parliamentary institutional-ization' deriving from the 1971 reform, their conclusion on the other side of the process was party-variant. Using a three-dimensional framework—party-centred, government-centred and parliament-centred—they saw the PCI as more party-centred than the DC, with the latter not clearly in one or other category (it had previously been mainly government-centred) (ibid: 182–3).

Does then the Italian example offer any lessons for the other southern European democracies? Leonardi's argument is that the two sides of this process are sequential, with parliamentary institutionalization as a prerequisite for party parliamentarianization, the assumption being that parties adapt to institutional change (ibid: 181). However, as he also shows, institutional change itself in Italy has been an outcome of changes in party behaviour, in this case depolarization in political competition. In this sense, the Italian Parliament has lacked 'institutional persuasion' or political autonomy, suggesting that the constraints of the parliamentary institution on the parties have been minimal. The Italian example does in fact raise a variety of comparative questions for other cases, such as whether some of the problems presented by Leonardi are national-specific. The role of the parties in the early Italian transition after Fascism was for instance particularly strong (Pasquino, 1986). This has generally been less so in the Iberian, Greek and Turkish cases, where the military or certain elite figures as well as the parties have been determinant. Indeed, the parties in these other transitions have often been themselves less structured, just to mention the extreme instance of the Spanish UCD which, contrary to some premature judgements, never turned into an equivalent of the German CDU or Italian DC but instead collapsed. Much also depends on how far democratic transition in the new Mediterranean democracies has been really formative as far as parliamentary institutions are concerned, for the Italian example has revealed some change over time in the pattern of executive/legislative relations—although always within the context of party-political change. it we take the question of political competition, then some of the new democracies have demonstrated both variation (polarization in Greece, consensualism in Spain) but also pattern change (consensualism in Spain was replaced by government/opposition competition, a new trend encouraged by alternation in power).

Whether it is too soon or not to announce the achievement of democratic consolidation in the new democracies, evidently this process is well under way. Given that transition commenced more than a decade ago in the three cases of Spain, Greece and Portugal, it seems opportune to measure how far consolidation has been promoted by political parties in the development of their parliamentary institutions. Drawing on the problems and hypotheses identified in this section on consolidation theory and party studies, the following framework focuses on three dimensions of the role of parties and the functioning of parliaments for assessing their two-way relationship: direct; indirect and contextual. The first two dimensions deal in turn with the intra- and extra-parliamentary behaviour of parties respectively, while the last considers wider systemic and longer-term factors, since ultimately this theme has systemic implications. In this way, the various functions of parliaments are covered.

Political parties, parliaments and democratic consolidation:
a framework for analysis

(a) *Direct dimension: intra-parliamentary variables*
   The balance of political forces as determined by the electoral system and election outcomes;

Attitudes of individual parties and their leaders to parliamentary institutions and the relationship between these and other political institutions as reflective of their systemic outlook (types of liberal democracy, even alternatives to that model);

Party dominance in the functioning of parliaments, use of plenaries and committee structures, existence and use of parliamentary facilities;

Behaviour of parties in working executive/legislative relations: coalitions or one-party government, ministerial recruitment, government/opposition relations, alternation in power and the degree of basic policy consensus

Party structures and 'parliamentarization': party group discipline and control over deputies, the attraction of party leadership to parliamentary careers and other forms of parliamentary 'socialization'.

(b) *Indirect dimension: extra-parliamentary variables*

Party strategies in general including importance here of their parliamentary roles—the relationship between these strategies and the practice of coalitions;

Party structures and the balance of power between parliamentary groups and national party organizations, party identity and the parliamentary role, the degree of personalism in party leadership, controlling links between deputies and their constituents;

Parties and extra-parliamentary communication—parties as electoral actors, parties as societal actors, links with interest groups.

(c) *Contextual dimension: systemic variables*

Party system development, especially the consolidation of new party systems and the consequences of this for institutional performance; stability in party systems, or a changing constellation of forces?

The relationship between political parties and traditional agencies of power, for example monarchy, military, church, political parties and ideological space—implications here for intra-institutional cooperation or conflict;

Political parties and social change and effects on parties' evolving policy positions, patterns in the nature of party support, relationship with socio-economic and political cleavages;

The legitimation function of political parties, promotion of democratic norms—how far parties in the phase of democratic consolidation are actively or passively system-supportive, anti-system or ambiguous on this basic matter.

**Political parties, parliaments and democratic consolidation:
a tentative assessment.**

The intention here is to identify relevant patterns characterizing the relationship between parties and parliaments, what kind of liberal democracy this involves and how far these patterns indicate consolidation. The preceding framework will be applied, and conclusions will be strictly comparative.

The direct dimension: intra-parliamentary party variables

Taking first the balance of political forces, we have in these different cases variations of multi-party politics, although Greece has from the elections of 1981 and 1985 acquired a system that would be best described as three party, a type not considered by Duverger and really intermediary between his 'two-party' and 'multi-party' categories. When considering 'balance' in terms of parliamentary strength, one immediately thinks of electoral systems and their effects in determining this. This is important for both majority-building and eventually alternation in power. Thus, the various forms of weighted PR in the new democracies have as a whole tended to assist both, at least more than the pure PR adopted after World War II in Italy. According to Bruneau and Macleod, on Portugal, 'the electoral system adopted in 1975 has directly affected the political parties; it has effectively reduced the number of parties represented in the Assembly; in addition, the parties have been obliged to adopt strategies that will maximize the benefits reaped by the larger parties from the d'Hondt system of proportional representation (Bruneau and Macleod, 1986: 30–1). The socialists in Spain were able to win successive absolute majorities with 48 per cent and 44 per cent of the vote; those in Greece with 48 per cent and 46 per cent of the vote—initially, in both cases, from the position of opposition. In Portugal, straightforward alternation has not occurred although a centre-right alliance of three parties was elected in 1979, and then in 1987 the PSD gained an absolute majority, following its previous term as a minority government. The contrast has been obviously with Italy, where an absolute majority has been won only once—in the rather exceptional election of 1948, when the DC won 48 per cent and alternation has not occurred. The practice has been of multi-party and often heterogeneous coalitions, intermittent minority governments, a pattern that Portugal repeated for much of its transition phase and beyond. Taking these criteria, therefore, the three new democracies have been more successful in creating the basis for effective government than the longer-standing democracy in Italy, but this judgement cannot pass without reference to ideological problems.

The constellation of forces in national parliaments must also take account of which ideologies are represented. Di Palma has argued for 'maximum inclusion' of parties as likely to overcome the resistance of 'extremist' parties to democracy, thus preferring pure PR and multi-party politics to 'precocious majoritarianism' or two-party rotation in power (Di Palma, 1986). That argument is made with democratic transition and early consolidation in mind, although it may not bode well for the conduct of government and legislative business as such. The interesting cross-national difference concerns the *political left*, which in Italy has been dominated by the communists and elsewhere by the socialists. This has had implications for basic policy consensus, the state of government/opposition relations and ultimately for possible alternation in power given the problem of communist parties' legitimacy.

The argument of Weiner and LaPalombara that 'the transference of power from one party to another, especially the first such transfer that occurs within a party system, is often the critical testing point for the legitimacy of the system (Weiner and LaPalombara, 1966: 412) is tempting, but one whose firm acceptance arouses charges of 'Anglo-Saxon' values, particularly by those working on Latin democracies. All the same, one could perhaps distinguish between the symbolism attached to alternation—for example in Spain, its painless acceptance in 1982 despite some dire predictions and yet another military plot shortly before the election of that year—and the practical consequences of alternation in terms of the stimulus it might give to legislative work (especially with a strong opposition, which has previously acquired governmental experience and with it policy expertise) and to party development. Again, the case of Spain has shown this may not necessarily occur, for the previous party of government (though not some of its leaders) disappeared from the political scene. In Greece, on the other hand, New Democracy has after an initially difficult period in opposition begun to regain political momentum with some prospects for a return to power at the next election.

Linked to such questions are party-political attitudes to the parliamentary institution, as in some way these are likely to affect behaviour within it. These may of course be modified in the course of early institutional experience for reasons of opportunism, conviction or some combination of both—one thinks of Rustow's hypothesis on the 'habituation phase' of a 'double process of Darwinian selectivity in favour of convinced democrats: one among parties in general elections and the other among politicians vying for leadership within these parties' (Rustow, 1970: 358). It is interesting, for instance, to note the degree to which deputies from parties of the right contain personnel from the predecessor regimes (Capo, 1986: 38), although this may be a matter more of sociological interpretation than attitudinal preference. Nevertheless, a high turnover in deputies as part of the transition phase—as, for example, happened with the rise of PASOK in the late 1970s (Lyrintzis, 1986)—is likely to promote attitudinal patterns favourable towards consolidation. This question is particularly relevant when considering parties whose ideological traditions might call into question their attachment to liberal democracy and which have not been discredited through association with the predecessor regime. The implication is that, with parties of the Right, such discredit might act, perversely or not, as an inducement to support for parliamentary politics.

Our interest therefore focuses on communist parties, where the PCI is a particularly important and revealing case. This is so as we know much more about its thinking during transition and early consolidation than that of communist parties in the new democracies. It is well known that the PCI came to place a special importance on the Parliament as from the 1950s, since its exclusion from government in 1947 meant this was the principal institution in which it could play a part, for the 'ordinary regions' which it had come round to advocating had not yet been established. As such, the PCI opposition came to attack the DC-led governments for their lack of respect for the Parliament and pressed for its greater control over the government, this tending to have a stabilizing effect on that institution (Galli and Prandi, 1970: 257–63). However, that followed a short period of uncertainty when in the elections of 1948 and 1953 the two major parties accused each other of exploiting if not undermining the Parliament (ibid: 257–9). In an analysis of Togliatti's speeches and writings, Sassoon sees a link between the PCI leader's conception of the 'centrality' of parliament and the liberal tradition in drawing a distinction between the principle of representation and the decision-making process (Sassoon, 1989). This was compatible with Togliatti having his own view of democracy as economic and social as well as political; it being possible to 'redefine' the parties of the working classes as 'pro-system' because of the ideological content of the 1948 Constitution (ibid). While critical of some aspects of the classical liberal tradition (some features of the doctrine of separation of powers, of bicameralism), Togliatti's conception nevertheless assumed that the Soviet model was non-repeatable in Italy (ibid).

Taking the opposition role as such, it is perhaps inevitable this may suffer in the early period after transition from problems of adapting to the practice of political pluralism. That is, in some basic way, the opposition role may be inhibited by a lag in political-cultural modernization, whereby attitudes to that role remain for a time conditioned by political socialization under the predecessor regime when opposition was illegal. This particularly affects those parties (that is of the political left, but also some centrist ones) which find it difficult to abandon the habits and mentalities of clandestine activity. Such adaptations to pluralist politics can be influenced by various changes during the formative stage: the nature of transition itself, notably how much it includes overt rejection of the authoritarian experience; the nature of parliamentary personnel, such as how much they represent new political elites and if so whether generational differences count; and, of course alternation in power and the consequences this might hold for perceptions of the opposition role. Available evidence on the Iberian democracies indeed suggests some difficulties in developing the opposition role. This has been marked by low esteem or profile (Braga de Cruz and Antunes, chapter 6 in this book), even though in the Spanish case the notion of 'loyal opposition' was linked to the consensual process in the transition (Pollack and Grugel, 1987: 244). In Greece, the opposition has, despite being more cohesive than in Spain, suffered from strong executive supremacy over the legislature, a feature also true of the latter. This leads one to take into account the rights of parliamentary oppositions as embodies in procedural arrangements for parliaments in new democracies. Here, the Italian Parliament has from the beginning been the most favourable to the opposition role, although that has also been facilitated by political conditions such as incohesion in governing majorities.

Finally, we may consider a variety of organizational variables affecting the functioning of parliaments. Party dominance in parliamentary work as in the management of plenaries, appointments to parliamentary offices and the operation of committees have generally tended to be strong, with even some signs of this in the newly elected Turkish parliament despite the weakness there of the opposition (Kalaycioğlu, *chapter 7 in this book*). This is certainly clear in the Portuguese Parliament (Bruneau and Macleod, 1986: 147–50), and it has been particularly marked in the Italian case. It is implicit too in attempts to improve procedural opportunities for political initiative in the Greek Parliament (Alivizatos, *chapter 5 in this book*). While as in Portugal, the rights of individual deputies may be written into parliamentary procedure, the usual story has been one of party control although Portugal suffered for a time from divisions between parties and their parliamentary groups (Braga de Cruz and Antunes, *chapter 6 in this book*). That apart, parliamentary group discipline has invariably established itself clearly, with the notable exception of Turkey where it has also been linked to limited loyalty on the part of deputies to their own parties (Kalaycioğlu, chapter 7 in this book). However, one point in the relationship between party groups and their parties has been the absence from the former of party leaders, in Turkey and Portugal (Bruneau and Macleod, 1986: 152–4) though not in the other countries. This would suggest some significant restrictions on the scope for parliamentary 'socialization' in political parties, although cross-national variation in this respect is another conclusion that must be mentioned.

Altogether, this examination of intra-parliamentary behaviour on a variety of questions highlights many deficiencies; especially in looking at the role of parliaments in controlling government (particularly weak in Greece and Portugal, not to mention Turkey). This is to some extent true, as just noted, of the personnel function in recruitment to national office, although as a whole this is not a major problem in southern European democracies. There is nevertheless scope for criticism when looking at the decision-making or legislative function of these parliaments. But there are different ways in which this may be assessed, for in some respects favourable patterns have begun to emerge. But there are two points that should qualify any final judgement: some recent trends indicate an improvement here, which may continue as consolidation progresses; and many of these criticisms may also be made about more established democracies in Western Europe.

The indirect dimension: extra-parliamentary party variables

The major difficulty here is one of sufficient evidence on relevant problems in the new democracies; although not for Italy, where for instance the question of party strategies has long been a matter of interest with some studies linking this with the problem of party structures. As for Spain, Greece and Portugal, these problems have to be deduced from more general works on their party systems even though they do not as a whole devote much attention to the direct relationship between parliamentary groups and national party organizations and therefore to the balance of power in party structures (Stock 1985; 1986). The two problems of party strategy and this power balance are of course related, for they reflect on the priority accorded to parliamentary activity, and so ultimately on the possibilities for parliamentary institutionalization.

Evidence from the Italian case is ample on these problems, just as Leonardi both identified patterns and underlined party variation. The latter is also likely to be true for the other democracies, with communist parties more party-orientated than those of the centre and the right. However, it is perhaps rather too soon to identify the general patterns of 'parliamentarization' in parties. As noted at the end of the previous section, there is a general picture of significant party-organizational control over parliamentary groups, hence limited scope so far for any such trend. This may also have implications for coalition politics, although that has not so far been a strong necessity in Greece and Spain with one-party majorities. In Portugal, on the other hand, it certainly is relevant, and it remains to be explored the extent to which incohesive coalitions there have been affected by extra-parliamentary control by party organizations. For example Soares resorted in 1983, while forming a coalition with the PSD, to an internal party vote before finalizing this. The matter at issue is that of counter-pressures between a certain flexibility intrinsic to parliamentary work, especially of the multi-party kind, and party-structural constraints when activists might 'stiffen' the positions of their leaders.

There is also a parallel question concerning the stabilization of party structures as a necessary feature of consolidation: strong or stable party structures, linking parliamentary and organizational levels, provide some guarantee for the continuity, viability and reliability of parties as parliamentary actors. The Spanish UCD, a prominent example of a 'founding' party in the new democracies, is virtually a classic case of a party which failed to stabilize and institutionalize itself, with detrimental consequences for effective opposition to the PSOE government. The UCD may be seen as an archetypal 'party of the government', rather than governing party, created by Suarẽz as an electoral vehicle for his premiership, but one which eventually fell victim to internal factions under pressure of declining government performance. It turned out to be very much a party for the transition, of the transition—but not for consolidation.

The performance of parties as electoral and societal actors is well documented, not least because of the numerous electoral events in the new democracies since transition began. In this dimension, we are concerned less with their patterns of support as with how far their activity in this respect contributes to the viability of the parliaments as representative institutions. That may not always be so obvious, as when the Portuguese PS campaigned in 1975 clearly as a bulwark against the anti-system tendencies of the PCP. It may of course be supposed that the repeated participation of different parties in successive elections may implicitly lend credibility to the parliament. But then this also touches on other matters such as party strategies and the reputation of a parliament as a by-effect of government or system performance as a whole. From another angle, the question of parties as societal actors must include mention of their special inks with socio-economic interests, as relevant to parties' legislative activity and part in the policy process. Here, the new democracies show a lack of institutionalized links, aside from those between the Iberian communist parties and their respective trade unions. So far, at least, there is nothing strictly comparable with the collateralism typical of the Italian party system.

Altogether, apart from the Italian case, it is difficult to draw firm conclusions about these parliaments in the light of the indirect dimension. On the elective function, the new democracies have proved surprisingly effective in the sense that elections produce a fairly orderly though not always durable succession of governments, including alternation in power. This record, even before the completion of consolidation, seems all the more impressive compared with Italy, which has continued to have non-durable governments (Craxi's 1983–6 government remains one exception) and has resulted in early elections five times in succession after 1972. On the representative function, Italy has again been open to criticism for an evident gap between legislative work and public issues (Baldassarre, 1985: 307–9); while in the other cases further research is necessary before an informed judgement can be made. This is likely to show national variation, with some negative conclusions but perhaps also positive ones (Bruneau and Macleod, 1986: 154). As to the communication function, in the case of the new democracies it is too soon to say, but that leads us to the third dimension.

The contextual dimension: systemic concerns and parliamentary institutionalization

The contextual dimension raises a variety of different, broader questions which, also being longer term require answer that are not always possible in the case of the new democracies. Thus, the Italian party system has long been consolidated; indeed, the party-political actors present during transition have been the same as those in consolidation and follow—a point that underlines the stabilizing effect of their organizational roots as well as the high level of electoral stability in postwar Italy, not to mention the historical identities of these parties. Undoubtedly, the very consolidation of the party system in Italy has been an important background factor when assessing the role of parliament in that country. With the new party systems, problems of party-system consolidation have apparently remained: in fact, in a case like Spain, where early predictions of such consolidation soon proved premature (they were based on consistency of party support between the 1977 and 1979 elections) the issue is still open (Bar, 1984). Moreover, these new democracies have evidenced a marked lack of electoral stability, similar to re-alignment effects in other established democracies, but clearly to do with the youth of these party systems.

In other respects, it is possible to draw clearer conclusions about this dimension. On the problem of traditional agencies of power, the settlement of the controversial monarchy issue early on in both Italy and Greece was a necessary institutional achievement—certainly in Greece it removed an historical obstacle to inter-party harmony. However, in Spain, while the monarchy itself overcame 'historical baggage', thus entering the area of cross-party consensus, the military remained a source of potential disquiet. Only with the reforms quietly introduced by the PSOE government in the 1980s has this problem begun to be resolved, and a rival power factor to the parties removed in the process. The same thing effectively happened in Portugal with the constitutional revision of 1982. On the question of ideological space, we have already noted the persistence of this problem in Italy, certainly well beyond the phase of transition. Except in Portugal with the PCP, there appears no comparable problem in the new democracies, if one regards party-political polarization in Greece as to some significant degree largely rhetorical. Of particular interest here is the divisive inheritance of the civil war experience and attempts, such as by Papandreou, to alleviate if not reduce this cleaveage. Whereas in Spain this experience, admittedly a decade earlier in time, has been handled tactfully by the political parties, although assisted too by modernizing trends at the mass level (Gunther, *et al.* 1986). Such modernization has been slower in Portugal and Greece, but then on the question of socio-economic cleavages we are entering an area of problems faced by all democracies, not simply those seeking consolidation.

Altogether, such problems take the discussion beyond the framework of institutional development, even if they present various implications of a more long-term nature. These tend to concern the basic question of system legitimation as a precondition among other things of parliamentary institutional-ization. Here, identifying the different parties in each country as pro- or anti-system, it not ambiguous, has some relevance. Broadly speaking, patterns have increasingly favoured system supportiveness, and the prospects for Rustow's process of 'Darwinian selectivity' seem reasonable.

Conclusion

System consolidation is a theme common to southern European democracies, and one that involves looking to the near future as well as the recent past. With the Iberian countries and Greece, which embarked on democracy in the mid-1970s, this process of consolidation is well under way; indeed, according to some views of system consolidation, they may have virtually achieved this. The other two examples of Italy and Turkey are different for reasons of time-scale, although the Italian case also shows that national-specific factors—specifically, problems relating to communist party legitimacy—may well occasion conflicting interpretations about when consolidation was completed. But whatever degree of national variation in the process and outcome of democratic consolidation, it is necessary to establish viable criteria for measuring this development. Examining the role of political parties in the institutionalization of parliaments—as a central component of the consolidation of democracies—is one important way of pursuing this problem.

Analysing the link between democratic transition and consolidation in this respect, it becomes evident that questions of macro-choice are now a matter of the past. This also seems true for those of meso-choice: it is not impossible, but unlikely, that recent shifts away from semi-presidential forms of govern-ment to those which are parliament-based will be reversed. If this shift occurred more or less by consensus among the principal party-political actors (as in Portugal), that conclusion may be a confident one; if, as in Greece, it was not consensual, there remains an element of uncertainty: future development depends on the approach of the opposition, although in this particular national case the signs are positive from the point of view of parliamentary institutional-ization. Cross-national differences are present, however, over the relationship between executive and legislature, but then that is not unusual when comparing parliamentary democracies in general. Some of these southern European systems might be considered deficient in certain respects, as in the controlling or legislative functions of their parliaments; but that does not have to disqualify them as liberal democracies. Such deficiencies may in the course of time be rectified, if the examples of postwar Italy and the Federal Republic of Germany are indicative, and here of course the role of political parties is crucial.

Therefore, the problem of parliamentary institutionalization verges on the micro-level of political choice: rules are formulated in constitutions and in parliamentary regulations, but their effectiveness depends on patterns of behaviour and political practice. The evidence so far on the three new democracies of Spain, Greece and Portugal is that such patterns have been emerging but essentially in the intra-parliamentary arena, while external or systemic questions of parliamentary institutionalization remain very open to further development. Lessons from the Italian experience since World War II only support that conclusion.

In other words, political parties are the central actors in the early evolution of the 'material constitution' as the overarching theme of parliamentary institutionalization. That should be obvious given the greater importance of political parties in these systems than in some more established European liberal democracies, even though the other southern European countries have as yet not reached the articulated pervasiveness of Italy's *partitocrazia*. In the course of time, the 'parliamentarization of parties' is possible, but that is a problem that looks beyond democratic consolidation. Meanwhile, summarizing the various criteria examined in this chapter, it is evident that consolidation in the form of parliamentary institutionalization has certainly progressed, but is not complete. This does not have to mean that micro-choice institutional options have to become strictly 'closed' on the contrary political institutions are also required to adapt when necessary.

These problems apart, there are two other concluding points. It is difficult to argue that there is some kind of southern European typology of parliamentary institutions. Their main similarity is that they lack an uninterrupted history, that by virtue of historical sequence they have faced certain comparable problems at the same time—though, here, Italy and Turkey stand apart. Second, it could be that these southern European democracies might differ from the 'Anglo-Saxon' ones in holding less grand expectations of their parliaments which, if true, might ironically be one of their distinguishing characteristics.

References

Baldassarre, A. (1985), 'Le "performances" de parlamento italiona nell'ultimo quindi-cennio' in G. Pasquino (ed.), *Il Sistema Politico Italiano*, Bari, Laterza.

Bar, A. (1984), 'The emerging Spanish party system: is there a model?' in *West European Politics*, October.

Bartolini, S. (1982) 'The politics of institutional reform in Italy' in *West European Politics*, July.

Bonime, A. (1985), 'The Spanish state structure: constitution making and the creation of the new state' in T. Lancaster and G. Prevost (eds), *Politics and Change in Spain*, New York, Praeger.

Bruneau, T. and A. Macleod (1986), *Politics in Contemporary Portugal*, Boulder, Lynne Rienner.

Capo, J. (1986), 'Party coalitions in the first democratic period in Spain' in G. Pridham (ed.), *Coalitional Behaviour in Theory and Practice*, Cambridge, Cambridge University Press.

Diamandouros, N. (1986): 'Regime change and prospects for democracy in Greece' in G. O'Donnell, P. Schmitter and L. Whitehead (eds), *Transitions from Authoritarian Rule: prospects for democracy*, Baltimore, Johns Hopkins University Press.

Di Palma, G. (1980), 'Founding coalitions in Southern Europe' in *Government and Opposition*, Spring.

—(1982), 'Italy: is there a legacy and is it Fascist?' in J. Herz (ed.), *From Dictatorship to Democracy*, Westport, Greenwood Press.

—(1985), 'Notes *ai margini* of the democratic consolidation project', paper for conference of European University Institute, Florence.

—(1986), 'Party government and democratic reproducibility: the dilemma of new democracies' in F. Castles and R. Wildenmann (eds), *Visions and Realities of Party Government*, Berlin: de Gruyter.

Duverger, M. (1964): *Political Parties*, London, Methuen.

Galli, G. and A. Prandi (1970), *Patterns of Political Participation in Italy*, New Haven, Yale University Press.

Gunther, R., G. Sani and G. Shabad (1986), *Spain after Franco: the making of a competitive party system*, Berkeley, University of California Press.

Hine, D. (1981), 'Thirty years of the Italian republic: governability and constitutional reform' in *Parliamentary Affairs*, Winter.

Katsoudas, D. (1987), 'The constitutional framework' in K. Featherstone and D. Katsoudas (eds), *Political Change in Greece*, London, Croom Helm.

Kohler, B. (1982), *Political Forces in Spain, Greece and Portugal*, London, Butterworth.

Leonardi, R., R. Nanetti and G. Pasquino (1978), 'Institutionalisation of parliament and parliamentarsation of parties in Italy' in *Legislative Studies Quarterly*, February.

Lyrintzis, C. (1986): 'The rise of PASOK and the emergence of new political personnel' in Z. Tzannatos (ed.), *Socialism in Greece*, Aldershot, Gower.

Mavrogordatos, G. (1983): 'The emerging party system' in R. Clogg (ed.), *Greece in the 1980s*, London, Macmillan.

Morlino, L. (1986), 'Consolidamento democratico: definizione e modelli' in *Rivista Italiana di Scienza Politica*, August.

O'Donnell, G., P. Schmitter, and L. Whitehead (eds) (1986), *Transitions from Authoritarian Rule: prospects for democracy*, Baltimore, Johns Hopkins University Press.

Opello, W. (1985), *Portugal's Political Development: a comparative approach*, Boulder, Westview Press.

Pasquino, G. (1986), 'The demise of the first Fascist regime and Italy's transition to democracy' in G. O'Donnell, *et al.*, op. cit.

Pollack, B. and Grugel, J. (1987), 'Opposition in contemporary Spain: tradition against modernity' in E. Kolinsky (ed.), *Opposition in Western Europe*, London, Croom Helm.

Psomiades, H. (1982), 'Greece: from the colonels' rule to democracy' in J. Hertz, (ed.), *From Dictatorship to Democracy*, Westport, Greenwood Press.

Rustow, D. (1970), 'Transitions to democracy: toward a dynamic model' in *Comparative Politics*, April.

Sassoon, D. (1989), 'The role of the Italian Communist Party in the consolidation of parliamentary democracy in Italy' in G. Pridham (ed), *Securing Democracy: political parties and regime consolidation in Southern Europe*, London, Croom Helm.

Schmitter, P. (1985): 'The consolidation of political democracy in Southern Europe', paper for conference of European University Institute, Florence.

Smith, G. (1983), *Politics in Western Europe*, London, Heinemann.

Stock, M.J. (1985), *Os Partidos em Congresso 1981*, Evore, Gabinete de Investigaçao.

—(1986): *Os Partidos do Poder dez Anos depois do "25 de Abril"*, Evora, Universidade de Evora.

Sunar, I. and S. Sayari (1986), 'Democracy in Turkey: problems and prospects' in G. O'Donnell *et al*, op. cit.

von Beyme, K. (1983), 'Governments, parliaments and the structure of power in political parties' in H. Daalder and P. Mair (eds), *Western European Party Systems: continuity and change*, London, Sage.

—*Political Parties in Western Democracies*, Aldershot, Gower.

Weiner, M. and J. LaPalombara (1966), 'The impact of parties in political development' in J. LaPalombara and M. Weiner (eds), *Political Parties and Political Development*, Princeton, Princeton University Press.

9 Parliaments in the consolidation of democracy – a comparative assessment of Southern European experiences

Ulrike Liebert

Since the beginning of the processes of democratization in Portugal, Greece, Spain and Turkey in the midst of the seventies there have been numerous important new developments in several other areas of the world which have extended the comparative universe of research on processes of democratization.

This applies, first, throughout the eighties to Latin and Central America where historical legacy, modes of transition, pacts and deals, the role of the military, the church and socio-political movements, the socio-economic and the international context of democratic consolidation have been and are presently studied in a number of collective and comparative efforts (O'Donnell/ Schmitter/Whitehead 1986; Diamond/Linz/Lipset 1989; Alberti/Whitehead 1990). Our understanding, in particular, of those institutional provisions and political conditions favouring the transition to and stabilization of new democratic regimes and of those factors which complicate them is actually tested and advanced in the debates on political reform and democratic consolidation in this area (Nohlen/Rial 1988; with regard to Argentina; Smulovitz 1987; Botana 1988; to Brazil: Lamounier 1988; to Chile: Fernandez Beeza 1987; to Uruguay: Peixoto 1987; Franco 1988).

The topic of parliamentary versus presidential government is crucial in this Latin American debate (Lindahl 1987: Fernandez Baeza 1988; Liliana De Riz 1988; Perez 1988). Although not only the military regimes, but also the varieties of traditional presidentialism have failed to achieve regime consolidation in Latin America, parliamentary regimes, which historically have been short-lived and which do not make part of the constitutional tradition in this area, are even more discredited: identified with 'assembly-government' in the French tradition and with the primacy of parliament in decision-making terms, and combined with the fragmented and polarized multi party systems which characterize the majority of Latin American countries, this form of government has frequently contributed to serious ministerial instability, ungovernability and military intervention (Cumplido Cereceda 1985).

Secondly, our scholarly wisdom on factors and forms of democratic consolidation at the end of the eighties is challenged by the revolutions going on in Eastern Europe. We are testimonies of how not only military or authoritarian bureaucratic regimes of rightist dictatorships may collapse and be transformed more or less gradually and from above into democratic regimes. Even monolithic communist single-party regimes are driven by waves of revolutionary upheavals towards liberalization and transit into pluralist and parliamentary politics. Following the Soviet Union, by the end of 1989 Poland, the GDR, Czechoslovakia and Bulgaria are caught in these strikingly accelerated and almost irreversible processes. Although their outcome remains still to a high degree uncertain, it is more certain that in the 'round table' debates on political reform in Eastern Europe, the topic of a complete restructuring of parliament-government relations favouring the reinforcement of parliament is also one of the key issues (in Poland: Ziemer 1989; UdSSr: APN. August 1989; 'Changes and Amendments to the Constitution', Supreme Soviet of the USSR 1988; Hungary: House rules of Parliament, passed on January 11, 1989). Although the transitions from communist rule and the consolidation of some — new? — type of pluralist 'popular democracies' still need much time, the question of which role parliamentary government is going to play in Eastern Europe constitutes already a major challenge to our imagination.

In this perspective, southern European experiments with parliamentary government and democratic consolidation during the last decade or two could be valuable for a future broader comparative assessment including also Latin America and Eastern Europe.

The preceding chapters have analyzed in detail the records and failures of recent parliamentary practice in southern Europe. They have given an account of their major manifest and some of their latent functions and they pointed to some of the problems which they did or did not resolve. These evaluations have in common that they do not measure the new southern European parliaments by their proximity or deviation from ideal types, be it the Westminster, continental European or American model. The authors did neither share an euphoric view, nor did they appear disillusioned with respect to the promises of the parliamentary doctrines. Rather they choose their points of reference in the specific problems characteristic of the processes of democratization in their countries:

- the threat of multipartyism and ungovernability, reinforced by cross-cutting multidimensional political cleavages during transition, and the decline of effective opposition vis-a-vis dominant party government since 1982 in Spain.
- ideological polarization and the exclusion of the major opposition party from

government during 40 years, and the problem of integrating it nevertheless into the political process in Italy.
- extreme government instability and the politization of the military in Portugal.
- ideological bi-polarization in Greece.
- accommodation of violent partisan conflict and the breaking-up of the cycle 'democratic transition—political crises—military intervention' in Turkey.

Hence, parliaments in southern Europe were not expected to resolve either problems of economic performance nor of social equality. The major concern of the authors is rather to evaluate in how far the experimentation with fundamentally different types of parliamentary organization and of institutional links with the other political institutions and actors have finally matched and contributed to resolve the problems of democratic consolidation. Our intent is to explore in the final section somewhat more the interaction between these three topics: types of parliament, patterns of democracy and problems of democratic consolidation.

Classification and change of parliaments in southern Europe

Our case studies corroborate for parliamentary institutions in particular what Arend Lijphart and others have found out for southern European democracies in general: That the parliamentary regimes of Italy, Spain, Portugal, and Greece are *not* sufficiently similar to each other and sufficiently different from other parliamentary systems to fit a distinctive model (cf. Lijphart, Bruneau, Diamandouros and Gunther 1988). This is true with regard to many structural characteristics of the new legislatures, including formal organization, executive-relations, dependence from political parties, level of institutionalization and the status which parliaments enjoy in mass perceptions. These structural features of parliamentary practice are an outcome of the interplay between formal institutional variables and of political factors. We will summarize them under six headings:

1. legislative party systems
2. partyness of parliaments
3. nature of parliamentary majorities
4. parliamentary influence in legislative production
5. specialization of permanent committees
6. institutionalization

in order to be able to classify SE parliaments.

1 The parliamentary party systems

Southern European legislatures differ with respect to the systems of political party groups represented in parliament although social heterogeneity, the multidimensional nature of political cleavages and partisan conflict, and the multiparty systems are characteristic of all five countries. This is a result mainly from the electoral systems chosen. Two of them (Italy and Portugal) have opted for a more proportional type of proportional representation systems, the others for less proportional ones. The parliamentary group systems which emerged differ accordingly. The less proportional systems of Spain, Turkey and Greece produced systems in which mainly two groups hold more than 85 per cent of the seats, and dominant single party majorities could emerge, whereas the more proportional systems account for the moderate or even strong multipartyism in Italy and Portugal.

The most extreme case of fragmented multi-party systems at the parliamentary level in Southern Europe is the Portuguese Assembly, the seats having been divided here during the first, fourth and fifth legislative term among four groups, during the other three terms among three groups or alliances (Braga da Cruz and Lobo Antunes, in this volume: 163/4). The index of proportionality of the PR electoral System chosen, however, with 93 is below the average of the other existing PR-systems (Rose 1984: 75, cited after Gunther 1989: 841; see table 9.1).

The Italian parliamentary party system with its more than ten groups represented in parliament was nevertheless never one of 'rampant multipartyism'. The three most important groups controlled always together more than 75 per cent of the seats, beginning in the Constituent Assembly up to the last legislature (Cotta, in this volume: 63). This concentration cannot be explained by the system of proportional representation with its comparatively highest index of proportionality of 95 (Ross 1984: 75).

The more than ten parliamentary groups represented in the five Spanish legislatures up to now build also a multi-party system, but with even stronger trends towards concentration than in Italy: only two of them held always more than 70 per cent of the seats (Capo Giol et al., in this volume: 289), and one group achieved twice a dominant position with absolute majority. This concentration goes without doubts back to the type of proportional electoral system chosen in Spain: the index of proportionality is indeed much lower than the Italian one, ranging from 81 (in the 1977 elections) to 87 (in the 1986 elections) (Gunther 1989: 841).

The Greek political party system is also a fundamentally bi-party system in which throughout the period always one or the other achieved a clear majority, except in the 1989 elections. Although the type of proportional representation system chosen for Greece is similar to the Spanish one with an index of proportionality of 88, the 'manufactured majorities' became increasingly weaker and, after the reform of the electoral system with its proportional reinforcement, in 1989 became completely problematic (Alivizatos, in this volume: 136).

The Turkish parliamentary groups represented in the two legislatures of 1983 and 1987 were fundamentally three, one of them maintaining the dominant position with its absolute majorities, which, given the moderate index of proportionality of the electoral system, was also a manufactured one.

Table 9.1   Electoral proportionality and parliamentary Group Systems

	I	*S*	*P*	*G*	*T*
(1) Index of proportionality (electoral system)	95	84	93	88	87.2
(2) Legislative party system	moderate multi- partyism	bi-party and dominant party-s	strong multi- partyism	bi-party system	dominant party- system

Sources:
(1) Rose (1984: 75) and Gunther (1989: 841), except for Turkey (own calculation). 'Index of proportionality' means: The sum of the absolute values of the differences between each party's share of seats and its share of votes, divided by two and subtracted from 100.

(2) see respective tables in the chapters of this book.

2 The partyness of parliaments

Southern European legislatures differ perhaps least with respect to the institutionalized links between parliamentary groups and political parties. This 'partyness' of parliament is regulated by the parliamentary standing orders, group statutes and becomes manifest in all aspects of parliamentary activity. According to the continuum of legislative independence proposed by Nelson Polsby, with at one end the 'transformative legislature' largely independent from extra-parliamentary forces, and at the other end the 'arena legislature' which serves as a 'formalized setting for the interplay of significant political forces in the life of a political system' (Polsby 1975: 277), all of them would have to be classified as either 'arena'—or, in the Italian case, at least as 'modified arena' legislatures. In Italy, Greece, Portugal and Spain political parties are not only free and authorized to establish the lists of candidates who run for parliamentary elections, but—moderated only in the Italian chambers—parliamentary groups and political parties are linked by iron institutionalized ties.

The parliamentary standing orders consider the elected deputies to be members of the group corresponding to the party in whose name they were elected. The option of joining another group is not even envisaged in Greece; and party leaders are given here a special status—they are allowed to act automatically as leaders of their respective parliamentary groups. In the case that they are not elected deputies—they may participate in the activities of the sections and committees (art. 37). The Portuguese code calls expressively for the loss of the parliamentary mandate for deputies who join a party other than the one for which they stood for election. And the Spanish parliamentary standing orders block the formation of parliamentary groups originating from scissions within a party by prohibiting the formation of separate groups which were not represented in the elections. Only in Italy a minimum of twenty deputies may form a group without any necessary links with the parties and the passage from one group to another is left completely free (Long 1987).

In all parliaments, parliamentary groups divide influence and positions in the various parliamentary bodies among them in proportion to their size. This applies to the designation of the members of standing committees and the offices of the committee-chairmen. The committee chairmen, however, are elected generally by the majority of each committee, hence the governing majority; only in the case of Portugal, the chairmen positions of the committees are also divided among the parliamentary groups in proportion to their size (ibd.).

Party group discipline varies across and within parliaments. It appears strongest in the case of the two major Greek party groups, where discipline is maintained in certain instances by 'draconian means' (Alivizatos, in this volume: 146) and in Spain in the case of the Socialist party where 'dissident' group members are obliged to resign as deputies, but where at the same time loyalty of the deputy towards his party is quite developed. In Turkey party control is, in the context of a low level of party institutionalization, exclusively in the hands of the party leaders, while party loyalty and identification of the individual MP's is still weak (Kalaycioglu, in this volume: 197ff.). In Italy, the christian democratic deputies enjoy a significant autonomy vis-a-vis the central party leadership and have 'introduced a strong degree of individualism within the ranks of the parliamentary majority, whereas the communist group commands a very centralized and hierarchic party prganization (Cotta, in this volume: 80). In Portugal individual MP behaviour is also decided by parliamentary group leaders who control even the deputies' speeches (Braga da Cruz and Lobo Antunes, in this volume: 164).

Table 9.2   The Partyness of Southern European Parliaments

	I	*S*	*P*	*G*	*T*
institutional links party-parl.groups	moderate	strong	strong	strong	weak
parl. group discipline	weak (DC) strong (PCI)	strong (PSOE)	strong	strong	strong

3 The nature of parliamentary majorities

The parliamentary majorities in our five cases show a considerable variation with respect to their structure and stability.

At one extreme we find the Greek legislative system which produced until 1989 stable and coherent single-party majorities which backed the respective cabinets: from 1974–81 commanded by New Democracy, since 1981 by PASOK.

At the other extreme the Portuguese case is situated. Parliamentary majorities here changed not only in each of the six parliamentary elections up to now and but also with regard to no less than 11 different cabinets which Portugal experienced during less than a decade and half. Extremely fluid legislative policy majorities prevailed for example during the first and the tenth minority one-party governments of PS and of PSD, or during the three cabinets without a party base in parliament in the second and part of the third legislature (1979/80). Fixed and stable majorities were produced during the periods of majority-coalition government: the second government of PS and CDS during the first legislative term; the sixth, seventh and eights cabinet run by the pre-electoral coalition AD during the third legislative term, and the ninth post-electoral coalition cabinet of PS and PSD during the fourth legislature enjoyed such more stable and fixed parliamentary support. Hence, on the whole, cohesive and stable parliamentary majorities have prevailed in Portugal since the beginning of the III. legislative term in 1980, whereas the first two legislatures showed more fluid and indeterminate patterns with constant attempts at readjustment.

In Spain, parliamentary majorities during the first legislature were fluid depending from constant negotiations. During the second, they became unforeseeable and indeterminate due to the combination of the only relative majority of UCD and the abandonment of the strategies of consensus-building among the parliamentary elites. Only with the beginning of the third legislature, the parliamentary majority became rigidly fixed and stable under the absolute majority of PSOE which lasted until at least the end of the fourth legislature in 1989.

In Italy, since the end of the christian democratic absolute majority in 1953, oversized coalitions prevailed as a parliamentary actor with a relatively low degree of cohesion and stability (Cotta, in this volume: 78).

4 Parliamentary influence in legislative production

For the comparison of parliamentary legislative activity we have chosen for the Italian, Spanish, Portuguese and Greek case a time period corresponding roughly to their respective second legislative terms, and for the Turkish GNA to its first legislature. The differences in the origin of legislative production reveal the differing strength of parliamentary opposition and private members vis-à-vis the executive and the parliamentary majority sustaining it.

The legislative initiatives of private members were most numerous in the case of the Italian chamber with an average share of 60 per cent of member's bills over the total of introduced bills. They were weakest in the Greek assembly where only 13 per cent of the introduced bills had their origin in MP-initiatives. The share of the successful ones among these member's bills which were approved was instead highest in Portugal with a success rate of 60 per cent, while the Greek private members and parliamentary opposition group were completely unsuccessful not having even one of their proposals approved throughout the period of 1978–82.

However, the Greek Assembly possesses at least some veto-power with

Table 9.3   Influence in Legislative Production

Legislative Term	I II. 1953–58	S II. 1982–86	P II. 1978–82	G II. 1978–82	T I. 1983–87
Members' bills					
– introduced	60	36	30	13	60
– passed	25	11	60	0	28
(% over total)					
Percentage of					
– member's bills					
passed	19	13	48	0	22
– of Government					
bills passed	85	91	13	77	80

Sources:
Italy: Cotta, in this volume, p. 81
Spain: Capo Giol et al., in this volume, p. 111
Portugal: Interparliamentary Union 1986, p. 917
Greece: ibd.
Turkey: Kalaycioglu, in this volume, S. 201

regard to the government sponsored bills, only 77 per cent of which were approved by parliament, the rest rejected or delayed. The Greek Assembly's veto-power is, hence, even stronger than that of the second Italian and Spanish legislatures. Only the Portuguese Assembly handled the bills sponsored by the five governments during 1978–82 more obstructively: it approved only 13 per cent of them, in large part rejecting in particular the proposals of the fourth, fifth and sixth governments which had been appointed by the President without possessing any parliamentary basis.

5 Permanent specialized committees

All of the Southern European Parliaments are to some degree committee-oriented 'working legislatures', and not pure plenary 'talking parliaments', although with differences in the strength and autonomy of the committee systems. Although specialized and permanent committees which correspond with ministerial departments exist in Greece and Portugal, in Italy, Spain as well as in Turkey (Interparliamentary Union 1986: 636ff., Kalaycioglu, in this volume: 206ff), their status and autonomy vis-à-vis government is very different. These differences depend, among other reasons, on:

● the distribution of the committee chairmen among parties;
● research tasks conducted by committee secretariats;
● the availability of expert advisers;
● the possibility to consult autonomously extra-parliamentary experts and

interest group representatives, inviting them formally to 'hearings', or to participate in informal 'auditions'.

Only the Italian Chambers and the Spanish Congress employ proper expert advisers as part of the secretarial staff of the standing committees, a fact which enables them to draft committee reports based on proper policy preferences which may be in contrast with governmental ones. But alone the Italian committees may invite external experts and interest group representatives by this establishing their own source of information, independent from government.

Giving to each committee system a score for its strength and independence, calculated on the basis of the proper resources which committees command and their feasibility for specialization and cross-party compromise, the Italian Chamber would certainly receive the highest score, followed by Spain, third by Portugal and Greece, whereas the TGNA appears to have developed the by far weakest committee system up to now.

Table 9.4 Resources of Permanent Committees

	I	*S*	*P*	*G*	*T*
number of permanent committees	14	14	19	19	14
Distribution of chairmen among parties	among coalition groups	elected by each cttee	proport. to their strength	all from govt. party	all govt. party
Research tasks	limited	limited	no	no	no
Expert advisers	own staff	own staff	rarely from outside	staff prov. by ministry	no
Extra-parl. consultation (hearings)	experts interest groups	rarely	no	only through govt.	no
Score for Cttee-strength	*3*	*2*	*1*	*1*	*0*

Sources:
Interparliamentary Union 1986: 662ff.

The weakness of the Turkish committee system depends not only from its only recent creation and makes its procedings highly dependent on the policy preferences of the government, and only making cross party compromise an exception. This particular weakness of the Turkish committee system is not alone due to the fact that they are dominated by ruling party deputies (the same is true for Spain after 1982 and Greece), but depends in particular from the lack of proper staff experts, of resources for doing research and the extremely high turnover rates of the leading personal and committee members: not only in the first 1985-elections between 95 and 100 per cent of committee-members were renewed, but also again in the second elections in 1987 between 78 and 100 per cent of the members of each committee were complete newcomers (Kalaycioglu, in this volume: 208). However, not even under these circumstances committee meetings were disrupted by unruly behaviour of members, as plenary sessions frequently are, and, political party groups at least in principle 'seem to be more open to negotiation and compromise during committee proceedings' (ibid.: 209).

Growth in the autonomy and importance of committees is also an indicator of 'institutional complexity', which—next to 'institutional autonomy' and 'universalism'—defines according to Nelson Polsby 'parliamentary institutionalization' (Polsby 1968). Hence, it is not surprising that Italian specialized standing committees are best developed, by now. The procedures of the 'indagine conoscitive' (hearings) have been introduced here into the parliamentary standing orders only by the 1971-reform, that means after more than twenty years of 'institutionalization'. In the fifties, the Italian Chamber was as 'closed' with respect to external expertise as their southern European sister-institutions have been during the first decade and half of their existence.

Table 9.5 Turnover rates in SE parliaments (during the first three legislative terms)

turnover rates in legislatures	I	P	G	T
I	56	52	38	53
II	37	46	41	86
III	36	40	13	
average rate	43	46	31	75

Sources:
Italy: table 3.2, p. 79; Portugal: p. 181, FN 9;
Greece: table 5.1, p. 139; Spain: missing
Turkey: table 7.10, p. 208 – refers however to turnover rates in permanent committees

6 The institutionalization of parliament

As Richard Sisson has pointed out, the concept of institutionalization makes part of the theories and intellectual responses to an age of rapid social transformation wrought by processes of social mobilization, structural differentiation, functional specialization of social roles, in which societies develop the ideas of choice, contract and universal norms, and, in particular the capacity to create civic order by creating and maintaining institutions (Sisson 1973). An indicator of institutionalization in this sense may be hence the levels of unruly behaviour of deputies, because the more organizational rules and procedures acquire value and stability, the more the deputies' will comply to them. The level of their rule-abiding behaviour will remain low as loing as the rates of deputy turnover and renewal remain high or are even increasing instead of declining.

A decreasing trend made turnover rates from the first to the third legislatures decline in Italy, Portugal and Greece, whereas only in the TGNA renewal rates increased in 1986 with respect to 1983, and in 1987 with respect to 1986, at least at the level of committee turnover.

* * *

These comparisons reveal a pattern of variation among Southern European parliaments which combines several dimensions: nature of parliamentary group systems, majorities, level of internal specialization, decisional influence and level of institutionalization. They allow us to classify SE legislatures according to a scheme which Marvin G. Weinbaum developed in his 'classification and change in legislative systems' (Weinbaum 1975) in order to match legislative change in three countries which do not at all belong to the classic core of parliamentarism: Afghanistan, Iran and Turkey. His types of legislative systems, hence, have the advantage to apply not exclusively to full-fledged, consolidated legislatures but also to those which are still in the process of structuring and development.

The *coordinate legislature* (type I.) is one which maintains with the executive a relationship of cooperation and interdependence in processes of mutual consultation, typically based on cabinet government, but normally not on cohesive, single party majorities, but on more flexible coalitional ones with party discipline due to loyalty and identification, but not to coercive measures. The legislative initiative is here mainly in the hands of the executive, but the share of approved member's bills over the total is considerable; committees are strong, and turnover is low. Close to this description comes for instance the Portuguese Assembly during its IV. legislative term with the governing post-electoral coalition of PS and PSD (1983–85), as well as the Italian chamber during some of the legislatures in which high shares of the legislative initiatives of the governing coalitions at the parliamentary level were approved, for instance during the second, third and fourth legislatures (1953–68), with nearly 80 per cent or more of the bills sponsored by government were ratified (see table 3.4, in this volume, p. 81). Another example is the first Spanish legislature (1977–79) in which the changing alliances between the governing minority party and the other parliamentary actors produced a high degree of cooperation and interdependence.

The II. type, the *subordinate legislature* requires government to be made up by a single cohesive majority party and supported by a disciplined parliamentary majority. This implies that legislative initiative lies mainly in the hands of the executive, that the share of approved members bills over total is extremely small and parliamentarians have little opportunites to defeat government sponsored bills. In SE, this description comes close to the situation in the first Italian legislature under the absolute majority of DC (1948–53); another near to ideal typical model are the Greek legislatures since

1975, although member bills are here unsuccessful to 100 per cent; and it applies also to the Spanish III. and IV. legislatures (1982–89) and possibly to the VI. Portuguese legislature since 1987 under the majority rule of the social democrats.

The III. *submissive parliament* differs from the II. in its inability to set limits on executive discretion which imposes restrictions on the access to nominations, manipulates balloting, monopolizes rewards or physically coerces deputies, making of parliament a 'rubber stamp' which meets only on occasion. This classification seems to apply to the first Turkish GNA-legislature from 1983–87 (Kalaycioglu in this volume: 214ff.), although parliamentary influence on legislation, be it with respect to the share of non-government sponsored initiatives, to the share of approved member's bills or to the amount of government sponsored bills which were rejected pulls it more in the direction of the 'subordinate' type II.

The IV. *indeterminate type of parliament* displays a pattern of interaction with the executive which is highly fragile and threatened by immobilization, due to a lack of structures and values necessary to stabilize executive-legislature retlations—typical for instance for systems in which the prime minister owes his appointment to a superior executive,f and not to parliament. This case came true throughout the Portuguese governments appointed by the president without parliamentary support in 1979/80. The 1982 constitutional revision with the reinforcement of parliament ended this indeterminate relationship between parliament and government.

The V. *competitive dominant parliament*, on the contrary, possesses a strong *esprit de corps*, frequent and highly routinized conflict, a system of highly specialized standing committees which make it a 'worthy competitor of government', and which make parliament-executive relations subject of constant readjustments. Parliamentary influence on legislation is strong, and government chances to make its proposals approved, relatively weak. We can find examples of this type in many of the Italian legislatures, for instance since 1976, during the seventh, eighth and ninth legislatures, during which no more than 57 per cent, or, in the latter, only 43 per cent of the government sponsored bills were approved (Cotta, in this volume: 81). Also in Portugal, this type prevailed during a number of the legislative terms.

Trying to classify Southern European legislatures according to Weinbaum's scheme, we find not only inter-system differences, but also an important intra-system variation: all of the parliamentary systems have changed their type since the early transition period, and in part considerably. These changes depended from and had a considerable impact on the processes of democratic consolidation:

- While the Portuguese Assembly until 1981 came close to the type of the 'indeterminate legislature', due to its strong non-party factionalism, rampant multipartyism, wide diffusion of power, fluid parliamentary majorities and frequent estrangement from the executive, the Portuguese legislatures of the eighties resemble more the 'coordinate' type with cooperative and interdependent relations to the executive.
- The Spanish Cortes in the critical period 1979–82 belonged to the category

of the 'competitive-dominant legislature' given their routinized internal conflict, and constant readjustments of their relations with the executive. Then, however, they mutated into a 'subordinate' parliament which frequently was accused of being 'submissive', although parliamentary legislative influence did not decline as much as it should be expected in this case, and parliamentary rules and norms as well as its proper resources became constantly better institutionalized.

- The Italian Chamber, at least after the end of DC-majority government in 1953, during the fifties and sixties showed a more coordinate structure, and then during the seventies mutated into a fully 'competitive-dominant legislature', with the 'weakest government in parliament' (Manzella), a system of rampant multipartyism and intra-party factionalism, parliament-executive relations having to be readjusted constantly.
- The Turkish GNA of the eighties moved between the 'subordinate' and 'submissive' type of legislature (Weinbaum), insofar as its dependence was determined not only by the capability of the MP-majority to maintain discipline within its ranges but rested also on frequent abuses of power.
- Only in Greece, the clear cut 'subordinate' type of legislature predominated during the whole period, a continuity which in large part may be accounted for by the 'time factor': the only short interplay of the military regime, which made democratic life being reestablished after only 7 years of break.

Table 9.6 Classification and change of SE parliaments

leg. term	I	S	P	G	T
I.	subordinate 1948–53	coordinate 1977–79	indeterm. 1974–79	subordinate 1974–77	submissive 1983–87
II.	coordinate 1953–58	competitive 1979–82	indeterm. 1979–80	subordinate 1977–81	
III.	coordinate 1958–63	subordinate 1982–86	indeterm. 1980–83	subordinate 1981–85	
IV.	coordinate 1963–68	subordinate 1986–89	coordinate 1983–85	subordinate 1985–89	
V.	mixed 1968–72		coordinate 1985–87		
VI.	mixed 1972–76		subordinate 1987–		
VII.	competitive 1976–79				
VIII.	competitive 1979–83				
IX.	competitive 1983–87				

This intra-system change is particularly revealing with respect to our question about the role of different types of parliaments in democratic consolidation.

The role of parliaments in the processes of democratic consolidation

Our final evaluation of the performance of different types of parliaments with respect to the consolidation of the new democratic regimes will develop three lines of argumentation and hypothesis with respect to

1. the relation between types of parliaments and patterns of democracy,
2. the importance of institutional and political variables in accounting for these variations of types of parliaments;
3. the impact of types of parliament on the processes of democratic consolidation.

Types of parliaments and patterns of democracy

The existence of a close interrelation between the type of parliament emerging and the type of democratic regime being shaped in the course of transition to and consolidation of a new regime appears obvious. However, the varieties of types of parliament play a relatively little role in the available political science typologies of democratic systems. This is also the case with respect to the most influential approaches, namely Arend Lijphart's classification of twenty-two democratic regimes according to their 'patterns of majoritarian and consensus government' (Lijphart 1984).

Lijphart's well-known majoritarian 'Westminster model of democracy' is based among others on a two-party system, fusion of power and cabinet-dominance vis-à-vis parliament and unicameralism, or at least asymmetric bicameralism (Lijphart 1984: 6/7). The 'consensus model of democracy' rests instead on executive power-sharing (grand coalitions), a more balanced and independent relationship between executive and legislature, and balanced bicameralism and minority representation (ibid.: 23ff.).

We could well differentiate now both ideal types further into (1) majoritarian types of democracy, based on (a) either subordinate legislatures, or (b) submissive parliaments, as well as (2) 'consensus democracies' characterized by (c) coordinate, (d) competitive, or (e) indeterminate types of parliaments. Hence, the type of parliament which emerges as a result not only of political variables but also of institutional choice defines which type of democracy is going to emerge.

We can observe these effects in the cases of Southern Europe. In more recent editions and revisions of the Lijphart-typology, also the new democratic regimes of Spain, Portugal and Greece have been included into this compara-tive setting (Lijphart et al. 1987; 1988). These three new cases together with the Italian one have been described according to the degree and way in which they share or concentrate political power—as four fairly different empirical types. Although this classification raises the principal question whether it is legitimate to calculate average scores over a time-period which is not only much shorter than that of the other longer-lived democratic systems, but is characterized by still a high degree of uncertainty, of institutional and political experimentation, we will take these types not so much as empirical, but as ideal-typical and make them points of departure for our problematization.

Italy is characterized as a 'fairly straightforward example of the consensus model', combined with elements of federalism, given its mainly oversized and shortlived cabinets, multidimensional multiparty system and its fairly proportional system of representation (Lijphart et al. 1988). This strong consensualism may be explained by the social heterogeneity and political pluralism of the Italian society and the large size of its population which contradicted a more majoritarian development. The multi-dimensional issue space and the high salience of socio-economic, religious, and the medium salience of regime-support and foreign policy conflict without doubt points into this consensual direction. However, the consensus model suffers from one major and permanent defect in the Italian case: the exclusion of the major opposition party from governing coalitions. It is this defect, as Maurizio Cotta shows in his chapter, which accounts for the peculiarity that the Italian model has changed considerably from initially majoritarian government with a subordinate parliament, to a more coordinate variety of consensualism and finally, since the middle of the seventies, to a more competitive-conflictive one. Parliamentary change—which enhanced the 'centrality' of the Italian chambers—was introduced by the 1971-reform of the parliamentary standing orders (see above: 10). The price for this 'integration through competitive executive-legislature relations' is the extreme weakness of government in parliament and the short duration of cabinets.

Spain is classified by Lijphart et al. as 'relatively majoritarian' on the executives-parties dimension, inspite of the initial period of consensualism, due to its single-party minority cabinets until 1982, and majority cabinets since then, the strongly majoritarian party and electoral systems with rather disproportional results, but as more federal than unitary on the federal-unitary dimension, given its two-chamber system with asymmetrical power and incongruent composition, the trend towards government decentralization and the protected and rigid constitution (Lijphart et al. 1988). This majoritarian variety clashes, however, in the Spanish case with the high level of hetero-geneity of the Spanish society and the multidimensional nature of political cleavages (high salience of socio-economic, religious, cultural-ethnic, and medium salience of foreign policy issues; cf. Lijphart et al. 1988). Parliament, until 1982, was able to help to articulate and to regulate these cleavages fairly well by its coordinate (1977–79) and then its more competitive-dominant nature (1978-87). Since they have changed into a subordinate and weak bicameral parliamentary system, many of these cleavages lead to extra-parliamentary protest (the general strike in December 1988, organized by the trade unions), and, more recently, new centrifugal revendications by Spains regional-nationalist communities.

Greece's position in the Lijphart-scheme is the most eccentric one: it is 'after New Zealand and the United Kingdom the closest approximation of the majoritarian model', be it with regard to the composition of its cabinets (minimal winning cabinets during the entire 1974–86 period), their durability, the two-party system, the high index of disproportionality of representation produced by the electoral law. On the federal-unitary dimension, Greece's position is a unitary one with its unicameral parliament and high level of centralization. This type of democracy may be explained mainly by the impact of the Greek political tradition (Wenturis 1987). However, regarding the multidimensional nature of present partisan conflict in Greece, which includes a high salience of socio-economic and foreign policy-issues, and a medium salience of post-materialist issues and questions related to regime support, the Greek majoritarian model of democracy with its manufactured majorities and the subordinate type of parliament appear less able to overcome the Greek people's traditional animadversion to the ruling class. In fact, the attempt of rendering the electoral system more proportional, was followed immediately by a collapse of absolute majorities.

Portugal, has been classified by Lijphart et al. as diagonally opposite from Spain—as a 'consensual-unitary' type of democratic regime, due to its multi-partism, its extremely low cabinet durability, its basically proportional system of representation, its unicameral legislature and high degree of government centralization. Only the high percentage of time under minimal winning cabinets indicates in the majoritarian direction. However, these cabinets until 1987 were mainly pre- or post electoral coalitions (Lijphart et al. 1988). The consensual setting in the Portuguese case appears in principle feasible with regard to the pluralist nature of the political landscape and the multi-dimensional issue space of Portguese politics, with its insense socio-economic, religious and foreign-policy conflict and the medium salience of regime-support issues (ibd.). This consensual model was not workable institutionally as long as the powers of the President in the 'semi-presidential' constitutional system which prevailed until 1982 allowed for presidentially designed cabinets without parliamentary base, and legislatures remained either 'indeterminate' obstructing or paralyzing governmental policies, or became 'competitive-dominant'.

These processes of structuration of the respective types of parliament and of democracy in Southern Europe were, hence, by no means linear, but have passed a number of decisive institutional and political 'watersheds': constitutional changes and amendments, as in Portugal and Greece, high electoral volatility producing decisive changes in the party system, as in 1982 in Spain, or 1976 in Italy; revisions of parliamentary standing orders, as 1971 in Italy.

This classificational scheme makes several 'anomalies' become evident.

Turkey deviates from the rule that sizable populations tend to have a bicameral parliament. Inspite of its sizable population (50 millions), the bicameral parliament of the seventies has been abolished in favour of the new unicameral 1983—'Grand National Assembly'.

Politics in southern Europe in the past and present was throughout the region similarly affected by deep socioeconomic divisions—among classes, between latifundist agricultors in the south and small farmers in the north in Italy, Spain and Portugal—as well as by religious cleavages (among clerical and anticlerical forces in Italy, Spain and Portugal; between christians and moslems

Table 9.7 Types of parliament and patterns of democracy

	patterns of democracy			
types of	*majoritarian*		*consensual*	
parliament	*unitary*	*federal*	*unitary*	*federal*
I. cooperative.			Italy 53–76 Spain 77–79 Portugal 82–00	
II. subordinate	Italy 48–53 Greece 74–89	Spain 82–89		
III. submissive	Turkey 83			
IV. indeterminate	Greece 89		Portugal 74–82	
V. competitive			Spain 79–82	Italy 76

in the case of Turkey) (cf. Lijphart et al. 1988). Thus, in all southern European new democracies, as well as in the case of the Italian 'protracted' process of democratic consolidation during the seventies and eighties, the persisting social and cultural cleavages gave rise to manyfold political polarization and made conflict-regulation and the achievement of democratic consolidation particularly difficult. However, only three of the five southern European new democracies then have introduced a variety of the consensus model for sharing instead of concentration political power—Spain only from 1977–79: Portugal and Italy. Hence, the majoritarian character of the Greek, post 1982-Spanish and Turkish democraciesmay be explained only by other factors than socio-political ones, for instance by 'cultural influence' or 'political heritage' (the statist tradition in Greece, the trauma of ungovernability during the second Spanish Republic).

Institutional and political variables in accounting for parliamentary variation

Institutional variables—although not sufficient in explaining the outcome of the process of structuration of parliament—are necessary in accounting for it. Among them are to be included;

- the choice between 'parliamentary or presidential government'.
- the constitutional design and organization of a particular type of parliament which will be 'workable' with respect to the pattern of democracy emerging, with regard to the size and heterogeneity of society, the level of pluralism, the multitude of dimensions of political conflict and the type of the emerging party system, and cultural influences in a given country ('parliamentary house rules', statutes of parliamentary groups, etc.). For instance parliamentary or semi-parliamentary systems of government and in situations of extreme and polarized multipartyism, and an electoral system with a high

index of proportionality will probably produce chronic executive instability, as historical experiences in Latin America as well as present developments in southern Europe teach us. The durability of cabinets has varied widely during the last decade and more. It was lowest in Italy (extreme and polarized multipartyism, high level of proportionality, parliamentary government), with a medium duration of one year and half (1948–80). But it was also very low in Portugal with its extreme multipartyism and high scores of proportional representation, combined with semipresidential government (on the average during the period 1976–86: 24 months). The reinforcement of parliament in the direction of parliamentary government and the dominant position achieved by the social democrats have improved the Portuguese record, however. In contrast, in Spain (1977–86) and Greece (1974–86) government stability and duration was highest (55 months and 70 months respectively), in both due to manufactured majorities within the systems of parliamentary government in Greece de facto since 1985 (Lijphart et al., 1988). However, the pronounced cabinet instability in Greece in 1989 will moderate these good scores somewhat.

Presidential forms of government in situations of polarized multipartyism, on the contrary easily may lead to stalemates and institutional conflict between parliament and the executive:

- in the case that the representative assembly is endowed with important prerogatives and autonomous resources which allow it an effective participation in decision-making (budgeting powers, autonomy in agenda setting, committee staff and expertise etc.), conflict with the executive may become permanent and relations competitive with high percentages of executive-initiatives being aborted or altered at the parliamentary stage (an example for this type of competitive-dominant parliament-executive relations which account for difficulties in economic policies, can be found for instance in Chile until 1973);
- in the case of 'rubber stamp' legislatures in the framework of presidential government—the type of 'indeterminate' parliaments with rampant multipartyism and factionalism, obstructionist opposition against government and no substantial policy-powers nor autonomous resources available to parliamentarians, government stability and governability may be safeguarded, but parliament is not capable to contribute to regime legitimation and the building of popular support, which in turn may endanger democratic consolidation in the case of uncertain majorities in presidential elections (an example could be the case of the Brazilian Congress);
- On the contrary, as southern European experiences show, parliamentary government may be workable in multipartysystems with multidimensional and partly polarized political conflict under certain conditions:
  (a) the parliamentary body is either of the 'subordinate' type, based on low proportionality of representation, a fixed single-party or coalition majority, high party-group discipline and a certain professionalization of parliamentarians with not too high a turnover (the case of Greece); or
  (b) parliament is of the coordinate type with fluid parliamentary majorities, moderate party discipline, consensual and cooperative legislative activity

and an important system of standing committees and autonomous parliamentary resources (the case of the Spanish first, of several Italian and Portuguese legislatures).

Political parties and parliamentary institutionalization

The 'deviant case' of Turkey indicates the importance of the Party-variable for parliamentary institutionalization. While many studies on party-legislature relations suggested the capacity of strong parties to reduce the autonomy of the legislature (Polsby 1968), empirical studies on Third World legislatures in the seventies have pointed out that parliaments are far more vulnerable to extraconstitutional attacks against their prerogatives in systems where political parties are weak. Stronger parties help the legislature to generate the support it needs from mass publics to withstand challenges from bureaucratic elites (Jewell 1973). They maintain parliament as a functioning entity, although within certain parameters generally defined by the governing party (Mezey 1985). If after the decay of dictatorship parties are not too weak, they may protagonize the transition process in which parliament necessarily will become more central for their political strategies.

To the degree to which strong party organizations already existed or developed more or less rapidly, they proved also in southern European new democracies favourable conditions for the institutionalization of parliament. The antifascist mass parties steered transition to democracy in Italy and were able to repeal the restoration of monarchy. In Spain, the emergence of mass parties of the Left and the regional nationalists—partly from the underground, from emigration or newly organized ones—imposed to the king and to Prime-Minister Suarez to include them into the transition process. In Portugal, the more gradually organizing parties, at the beginning of the 'revolutionary transition' still completely marginalized, became more and more important participants in the steering and revision of the process of regime institutionalization.

Types of parliament and processes of democratic consolidation

Different types of parliaments obviously perform functions which are crucial to democratic consolidation—as political integration, conflict resolution, building popular support etc.—in different ways and to different degrees. There are important variations among how citizens in SE perceive their new parliaments, and how powerful they believe this institution is compared with other political actors. This emerges from the data on public perceptions collected by the authors of the four-countries study on political parties and political culture in southern Europe (Santamaria et al. 1986) (cf. tables 9.2 and 9.3).

By far most Spaniards—nearly half of them—consider the government as the most powerful state institution in their country, whereas the parties and parliament are mentioned by only neglectable minorities (2.2 per cent and 1.6 per cent respectively). We may explain this not only by the subordinate character of the Spanish Cortes, but in particular by their character as

Table 9.8   Public perceptions of the most powerful political actors and arenas (1986)

Institution, group	Spain	Italy	Portugal	Greece
1. Government	45.7	28.5	39.2	37.3
2. President/King	9.1	3.7	14.9	7.4
3. Parties	2.2	9.8	4.3	2.3
4. *Parliament*	*1.6*	*2.6*	*4.8*	*3.5*
5. Military	2.8	0.4	3.5	2.7
6. church	2.9	11.8	4.2	11.9
7. Press	0.8	2.0	0.7	3.1
8. Big Business	5.9	6.8	1.4	7.0
9. Multinationals	5.4	4.8	1.7	4.8
10. Banks	5.4	3.0	—	1.5
11. Unions	1.5	7.9	0.9	4.7
12. Organized Crime	1.4	8.6	0.5	1.2
13. Foreign	3.8	3.5	4.1	9.7
Parliament perceived as one of the three most powerful political actors	13.9	11	30.2	16.8
Does not know	10.4	5.5	17.8	2.1
No answer	1.3	1.6	1.6	0.7
Number of cases = 100%	2498	2074	2000	1998

Source:
Data Banc of the Centro de Investigaciones Sociologicas: Survey on 'The Political Culture in Southern Europe' Madrid 1986

committee-centered working legislatures a large part of whose proceedings are not public.

The disproportion between the public status of government vis-à-vis parliament in the other cases is always present but somewhat less accentuated.

- in Italy not even a third of the interviewed consider government the most powerful organ, whereas nearly ten per cent perceive the parties as most powerful and only 2.6 per cent of the interviewed persons believe the Chambers to be the 'central' institution. Its competitive-dominant character, hence, in public eyes is largely attributed to party interests and competition;
- in Portugal and Greece the share of supporters of the government-centric view is lower than in Spain but higher than in Italy. Parliaments are considered here by a higher share of the citizens as the most powerful organ: 4.8 per cent of the Portuguese and 3.5 per cent of the Greek share this opinion.

Of course, the answers are more telling—and differ more widely—if we aggregate those who put parliament on either the first, second or third place in their ranking of the most powerful institutions and groups (see Table 9.3):

- Nearly a third of the Portuguese considered the—at times competitive, at times coordinate—Portuguese Assembly as one of the three most powerful institutions in the country;
- with respect to the Greece subordinate, and the Italian competitive-dominant chambers the same percentage is only about half as large;
- and referring to the Spanish subordinate Cortes, the lowest percentage of citizens (11 per cent) perceived it as one of the three most powerful political actors.

Parliament and constitution-building

The role which parliament plays in the process of constitution-building during transition to democracy may have an impact on which type of parliament is going to be institutionalized. And it might have an impact not only in general on the chances for democratic consolidation, but probably also with respect to the course and speed this process is going to take: if consolidation is going to be a rather time-consuming process of institutionalization and legitimization of a new regime which may be finished after approximately three legislatures (Schmitter); whether it will be already finished after peaceful alternance in government having taken place (Morlino), or if consolidation is identical with the process of 'crafting' the rules of the competitive game in a way to make reluctant players drop their break-down strategies (DiPalma). Maurizio Cotta has formulated in his chapter a number of hypotheses concerning the impact of parliamentary constitution-building on the prospects for democratic consolidation.

Constitution-building in Southern Europe was of three different types.

- It has been resolved in relatively long processes of negotiations and cross-party consensus-building at the parliamentary level in Italy (1946/7) and in Spain (1977/78);
- In Greece and Portugal the original constitutional drafts were elaborated outside parliament and approved in extremely short time periods (3 months in Greece), but were subsequently revised. Although parliament discussed and amended many important issues of the governmental draft on the basis of consensual solutions, the final text was approved only by the governing conservative party majority, whereas the socialist opposition introduced its revisions only after having come to governmental power ten years later (Alivizatos, in this volume: 133ff).
- The Turkish 1982 Constitution is neither a result of parliamentary consensus-building nor a majoritarian, subsequently revised one, but was drafted in a technical manner by the National Security Council and approved by popular referendum (Kalaycioglu, in this volume: 189).

The cases of Italy and Spain suggest indeed that 'the stronger the role of a parliamentary-like body in constitution-making and the weaker the role of a technical body and of the government . . . the greater will be the chances of a constitutional text with less internal consistency, and which leaves greater space to compromises between different legal and political outlooks' (Cotta, in this volume: 72). At the same time both cases corroborate that a collaborative parliament, and consensual parliamentary constitution-making may increase the 'chances that the Constitution will be accepted by all the relevant political forces' (ibd.).

In fact, Spain represents such a pattern of democratic consolidation through rapid and consensual rule-crafting in which most—but not all—of the essential players participated, thus making the exit of consolidation very probable. But—as political developments showed—this exit remained by no means certain. The terrorist spiral, centrifugal developments of the party system and the dynamics of territoral decentralization culminating in an attempted military coup in the midst of the parliamentary hemicycle in February, 1981, illustrated the institutional fragility as well as the continuing politization of the army. And it was not even through the victory of the monarch and the regime over the anti-democratic forces, or the electoral hegemony achieved by the Socialist Party in October 1982 and the effected alternance in government produced by this victory which by themselves were sufficient to assure democratic consolidation. What was lacking were the proofs for the Socialist's capability to stabilize 'party-government' and to govern the economic crises by policies capable to find the consensus of the societal power groups.

The Spanish case shows also that consensual parliamentary constitution-building does not necessarily imply that the constitution will become 'more parliament-orientated than government-oriented', and individual parliamentarians will be treated more favourably, as Cotta sustains, and as it happened in the case of Italy; in Spain all major parliamentary groups agreed in a majoritarian parliamentary model and privileged governability and party group discipline to individual deputies' prerogatives (Capo, in this volume: 100), if for example traumatic past experiences (like the failure of parliamentary government in the Spanish second Republic) are basis of a corresponding cross-party consent.

Italy presents another and even more exceptional case of this pattern of rapid, inclusive and successful crafting and establishment of a constitutional consensus among all political forces, which however was followed by only a 'weak' (Morlino) or at least 'protracted' (Cotta) process of democratic consolidation, given that the major party of the opposition was kept out from government during the whole period. In so far as this 'weakness' may be explained by the profound socio-economic and ideological cleavages and the extreme political polarization which emerged during the cold war at the end of the forties, the Italian way to democratic consolidation was accomplished only when the PCI at the end of the seventies underwent profound changes which—at the cost of electoral support—helped it to become considered as an—at least potential—government coalition ally or even as an alternative.

Constitution-building under conditions of a subordinate parliament and of majoritarian democracy will be mainly in the hands of the cabinet. The majoritarian character of the new constitution would then decrease the chances of finding acceptance by all important actors. The case of Greece, seems to corroborate this hypothesis: As opposed to this pattern of 'swift crafting and—more or less—protracted consolidation' which we observed in Italy and Spain, in Greece (as well as in Portugal) there exists a second pattern of 'protracted crafting and subsequent consolidation'. Here the new rules of the democratic regime initially were initially established in a nearly exclusive mode not receiving any broader consensus. Consolidation hence was delayed until the initial Constitutions had been revised more or less substantially nearly a decade later during the eighties.

In Portugal, until the revision of the constitution had happened, the process of institutionalization of some of the major new institutions—for example the new Portuguese Parliament—remained blocked. Only the changing balances of power (between the military and civilian forces in Portugal and rotation in government in Greece) allowed in both cases for substantial constitutional revisions which finally constituted the basis for some broader consensus on the rules of the game.

In our last case, Turkey, the swift process of crafting the new constitution which profoundly reorganized the system of government was not followed by regime consolidation, but rather by problems of institutionalization, in particular at the level of the 'Grand National Assembly'. This goes also back to the highly exclusive nature of constitution-building by a governmental body, without any participation of the Assembly, but has also essentially to do with the limitations imposed upon the party system and the corresponding lack of stabilization of parliamentary groups.

References

Alberti, G. and L. Whitehead: *Prospects and Dilemmas of Democratic Consolidation in Latin America*; Theme of the ecpr-workshop, April 1990 in Bochum

Botana, N. (1988): El debate de la reforma politica; el caso argentino; in: Nohlen/Solari

Cumplido Cereceda, F. (1985): El sistema democratico en America Latina: su eficacia. El regimen presidencialista y las posibilidades del regimen parlamentario; in *Contribuciones* 1, Buenos Aires

De Riz, L., 'Regimen de gobierno y gobernabilidad. Parlamentarismo en Argentina? in: Nohlen and Solari (eds.), S. 273–287

Diamond, L., Linz, J., Lipset, S.M. (1989): *Democracy in Developing Countries*, Vol. IV, Latin America; Lynne Rienner, Boulder, Colorado

Fernandez Baeza, M. (1987): Tres tesis sobre un sistema de gobierno para Chile; in *Cuadernos del claeh 43*, Uruguay

idem (1988): 'Sistema parlamentario en Chile. Entre la razon y la tradicion', in: Nohlen and Solari (eds.)

Franco, R. (1988): El debate de la reforma politica, el caso uruguayo; in Nohlen/Solari (eds.)

Gunther, R., (1989): 'Electoral Laws, Party Systems, and Elites: The Case of Spain', in *American Political Science Review*, Sept. 1989, p. 836–858

Inter-parliamentary Union (1986): *Parliaments of the World, Vol. I, II*, Gower, Aldershot

Lamounier, B. (1988): El debate de la reforma politica: el caso brasileno; in Nohlen/Solari

Lindahl, G.G. (1987): El presidencialismo en America Latina y Uruguay; in *cuadernos del claeh 43*, Uruguay

Lijphart, A. (1984): *Democracies. Patterns of Majoritarian and Consensus Government* in Twenty-One Countries, Yale University Press, New Haven, London

Lijphart, A., Bruneau, T.C., Diamandouros, N. and Gunther, R. (1987): *Les Democracias Contemporaneas: Un Analisis Comparativo*, Barcelona, Editorial Arel

idem (1988): A Mediterranean Model of Democracy? The Southern European Democracies in Comparative Perspective; in *West European Politics*, 1

Long, G.: Parliamentary Rules of Procedure in Southern Europe; paper presented at the Conference on Parliaments and Democratic Consolidation in southern Europe, James Bofill Foundation, Barcelona, 29–31 October

Nohlen, D., Rial, J. (1988): 'Reforma politica y consolidacion democratica, Perspectivas comparadas; in: Nohlan/Solari

Nohlen, D. and A. Solari (eds.), *Reforma Politica y Consolidacion Democratica, Europa y America Latina*, Ed. Nueva Sociedad, Caracas 1988

O'Donnell, G., Schmitter, P.C. and Whitehead, L. (1986): *Transitions from Authoritarian Rule. Prospects for Democracy*, The John Hopkins University Press, Baltimore and London

Peixoto, M. (1987): El debate politico en el Uruguay; in *Cuadernos del claeh 43*, Uruguay

Polsby, N. (1968): The Institutionalization of the U.S. House of Representa-tives, in *The American Political Science Review*, 62

idem (1975): Legislatures, in Greenstein/Polsby (eds.), *Handbook of Political Science*, vol. 5, Addison-Wesley, Reading (Mass.)

Ross, R. (1984): Electoral Systems: A Question of Degree or of Principle? in Lijphart/Grofman (eds.) *Choosing an Electoral System*, New York, Praeger

Sisson, R.: Comparative Legislative Institutionalization: A Theoretical Exploration; in Kornberg (ed), *Legislatures in Comparative Perspective*, New York 1973

Smulovitz, C. (1987): 'Reforma constitucional y consolidacion democratica en la Argentina'; in *Cuadernos del claeh*, 43/3, Uruguay

Weinbaum, M. (1975): Classification and Change in Legislative Systems: With Particular Application to Iran, Turkey, and Afghanistan; in Boynton/Kim (eds.), *Legislative Systems in Developing Countries*, Duke

Index